WILDLIFE FOR IDIOTS

ADRIAN RAESIDE

WILDLIFE FOR IDIOTS

AND OTHER ANIMAL CARTOONS

HELLO
LION

EBRA

HARBOUR
PUBLISHING

1 2 3 4 5 — 26 25 24 23 22

HARBOUR PUBLISHING CO. LTD.
P.O. Box 219, Madeira Park, BC, V0N 2H0
www.harbourpublishing.com

TEXT AND COVER DESIGN by Libris Simas Ferraz / Onça Publishing
PRINTED AND BOUND in South Korea

HARBOUR PUBLISHING acknowledges the support of the Canada Council for the Arts, the Government of Canada, and the Province of British Columbia through the BC Arts Council.

LIBRARY AND ARCHIVES CANADA CATALOGUING IN PUBLICATION

Title: Wildlife for idiots : and other animal cartoons / Adrian Raeside.
Other titles: Cartoons. Selections
Names: Raeside, Adrian, 1957- author, artist.
Identifiers: Canadiana (print) 20220246300 | Canadiana (ebook) 20220246327 | ISBN 9781550179323 (softcover) | ISBN 9781550179330 (EPUB)
Subjects: LCSH: Animals—Caricatures and cartoons. | LCSH: Canadian wit and humor, Pictorial. | LCGFT: Comics (Graphic works)
Classification: LCC NC1449.R34 A4 2022 | DDC 741.5/6971—dc23

Canada Council for the Arts | Conseil des arts du Canada
Canada
British Columbia Arts Council
British Columbia

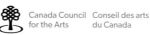

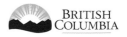

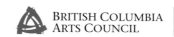

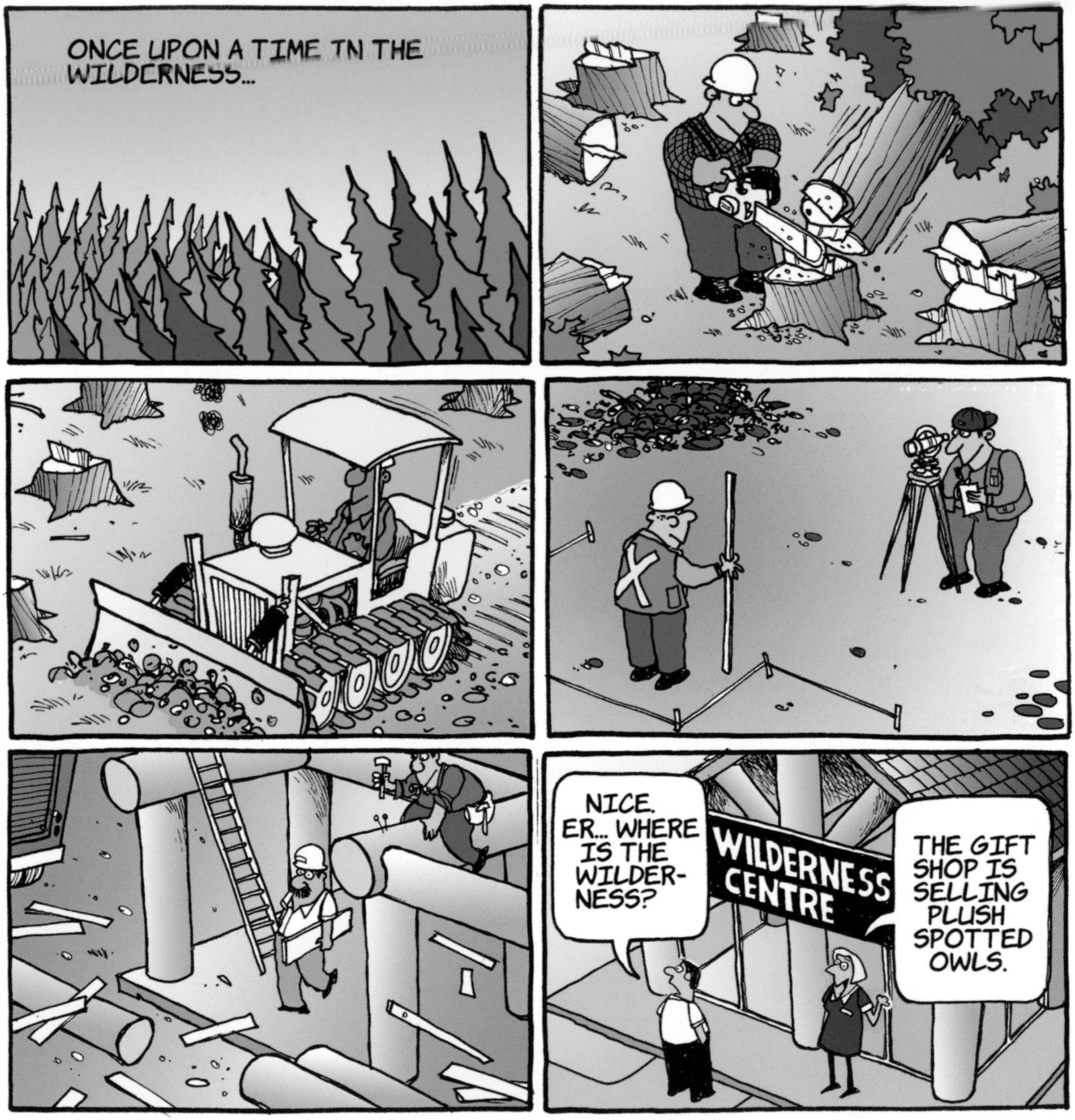
ONCE UPON A TIME IN THE WILDERNESS...
NICE. ER... WHERE IS THE WILDER- NESS?
WILDERNESS CENTRE
THE GIFT SHOP IS SELLING PLUSH SPOTTED OWLS.

INTRODUCTION

Humans and wild animals share a number of similarities. We all need food, water, shelter and the company of our own species, whether in the form of a herd, flock, pack or bridge club. We build homes, raise our young and care for each other, but we can also mess up and sometimes squabble.

As we don't understand the language of our fellow creatures—except for parrots, who just repeat what we say—it's hard to know what wild animals are thinking.

Does an elephant painting pictures ever step back and wonder, "Should that black splotch be more to the right of the round squiggle?" Is a lone wolf really alone, or just fed up with wolf pack gossip? Does the eagle who fails to snag a fish get the cold shoulder from his mate when he arrives back at the nest? Do sharks feel remorse if they bite a surfer instead of a seal? What would happen to the nest if birds got divorced? Would an alligator buy an alligator skin handbag if it was on sale?

Wildlife for Idiots answers these and many more questions from the animal kingdom.

- ADRIAN RAESIDE
(also an idiot)

IF WE SHAME DOGS FOR DOING WHAT COMES NATURALLY TO THEM, WHY NOT WILDLIFE?
ME AND THE PACK SNUCK UP ON A SHEEP AND ATE IT.
I ATE A COW. (THE WIFE KILLED IT, BUT I ATE IT.)
I TRAMPLED A CIRCUS TRAINER! AND IT FELT GOOD.
I BIT A SURFER I THOUGHT WAS A SEAL.

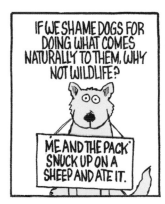

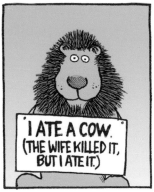

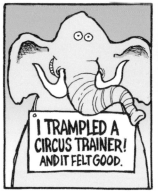

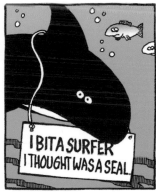

1 IN THE BEGINNING

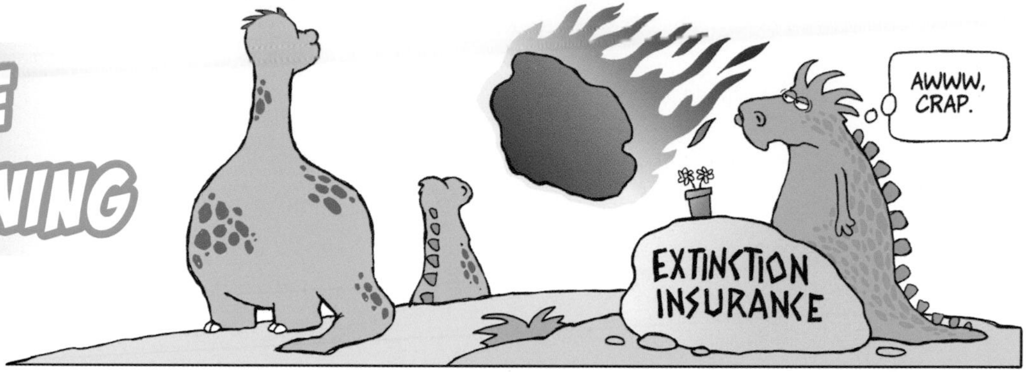

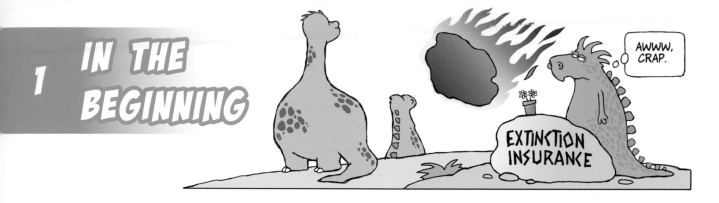

AWWW, CRAP.
EXTINCTION INSURANCE

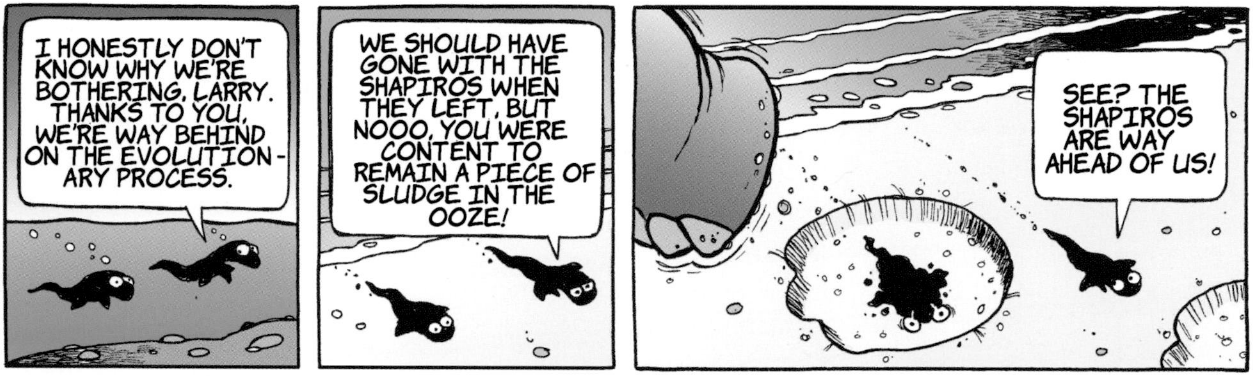

I HONESTLY DON'T KNOW WHY WE'RE BOTHERING, LARRY. THANKS TO YOU, WE'RE WAY BEHIND ON THE EVOLUTION-ARY PROCESS.
WE SHOULD HAVE GONE WITH THE SHAPIROS WHEN THEY LEFT, BUT NOOO, YOU WERE CONTENT TO REMAIN A PIECE OF SLUDGE IN THE OOZE!
SEE? THE SHAPIROS ARE WAY AHEAD OF US!

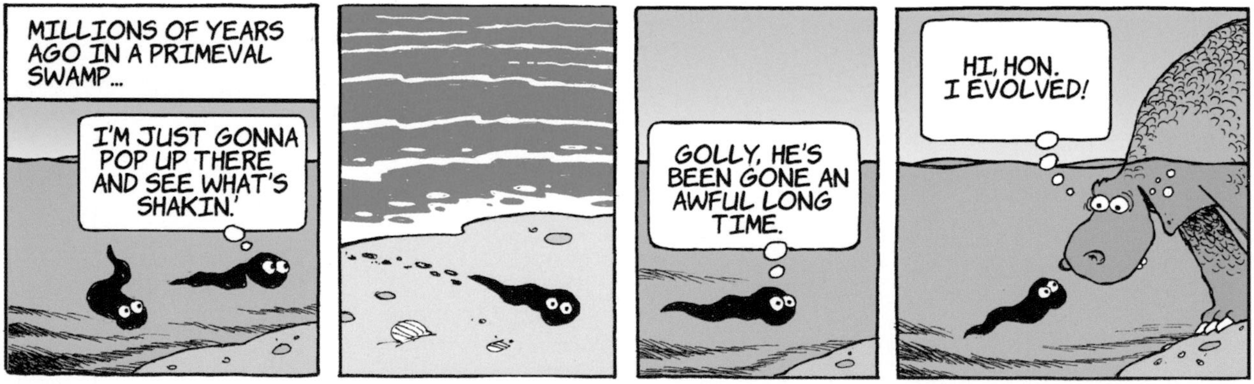

MILLIONS OF YEARS AGO IN A PRIMEVAL SWAMP...
I'M JUST GONNA POP UP THERE AND SEE WHAT'S SHAKIN.'
GOLLY, HE'S BEEN GONE AN AWFUL LONG TIME.
HI, HON. I EVOLVED!

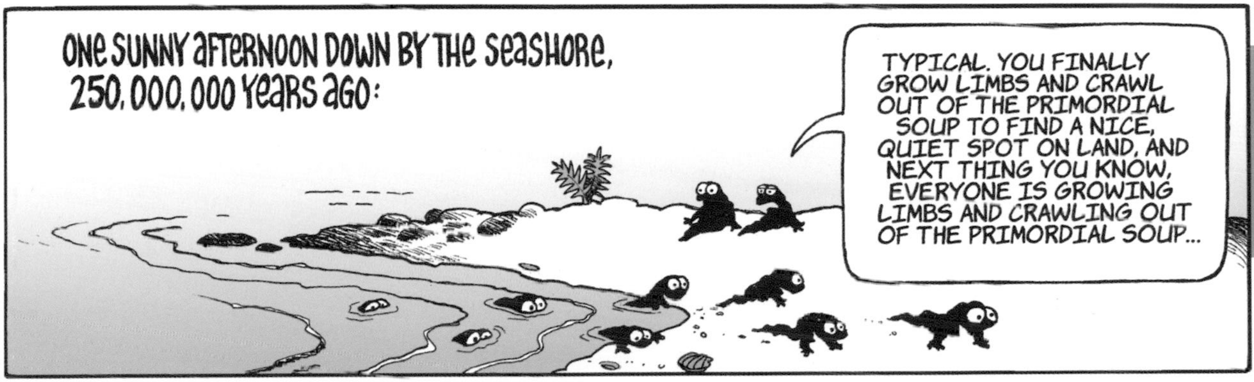
ONE SUNNY AFTERNOON DOWN BY THE SEASHORE, 250,000,000 YEARS AGO:
TYPICAL. YOU FINALLY GROW LIMBS AND CRAWL OUT OF THE PRIMORDIAL SOUP TO FIND A NICE, QUIET SPOT ON LAND, AND NEXT THING YOU KNOW, EVERYONE IS GROWING LIMBS AND CRAWLING OUT OF THE PRIMORDIAL SOUP...

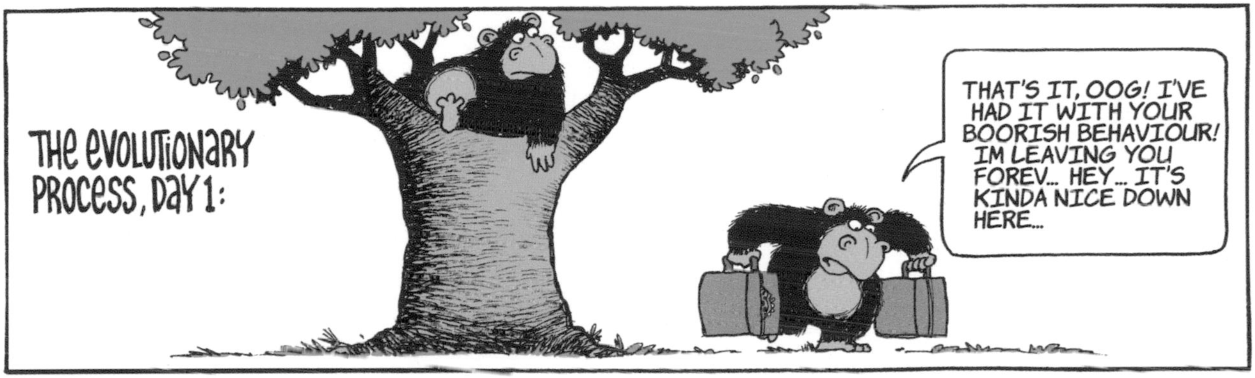
THE EVOLUTIONARY PROCESS, DAY 1:
THAT'S IT, OOG! I'VE HAD IT WITH YOUR BOORISH BEHAVIOUR! IM LEAVING YOU FOREV... HEY... IT'S KINDA NICE DOWN HERE...

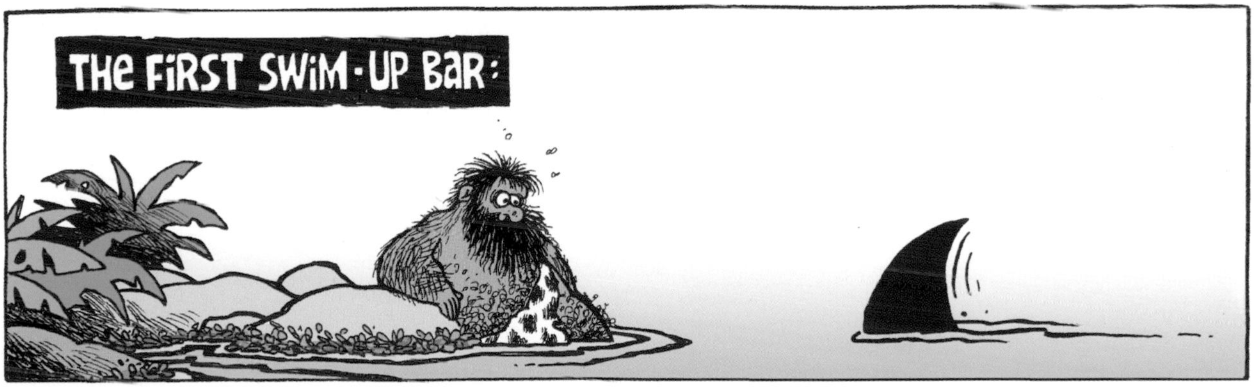
THE FIRST SWIM-UP BAR:

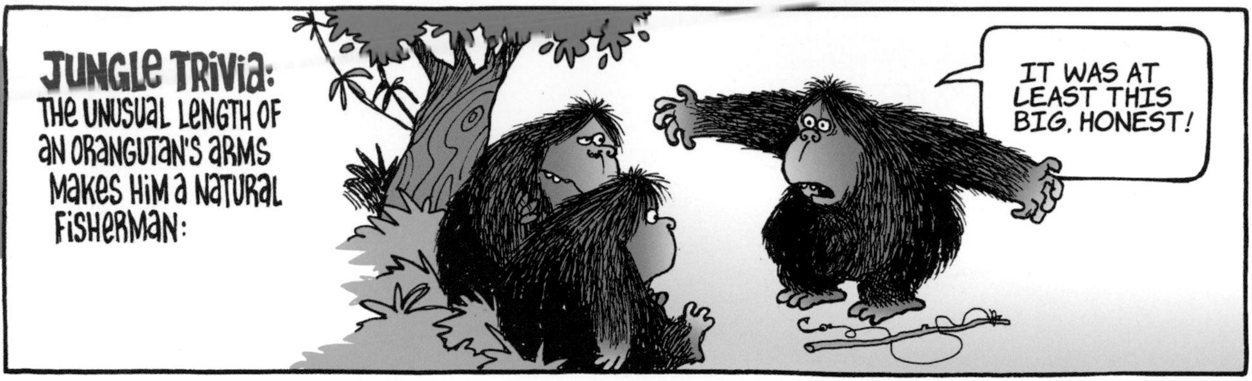
JUNGLE TRIVIA:
THE UNUSUAL LENGTH OF AN ORANGUTAN'S ARMS MAKES HIM A NATURAL FISHERMAN:
IT WAS AT LEAST THIS BIG, HONEST!

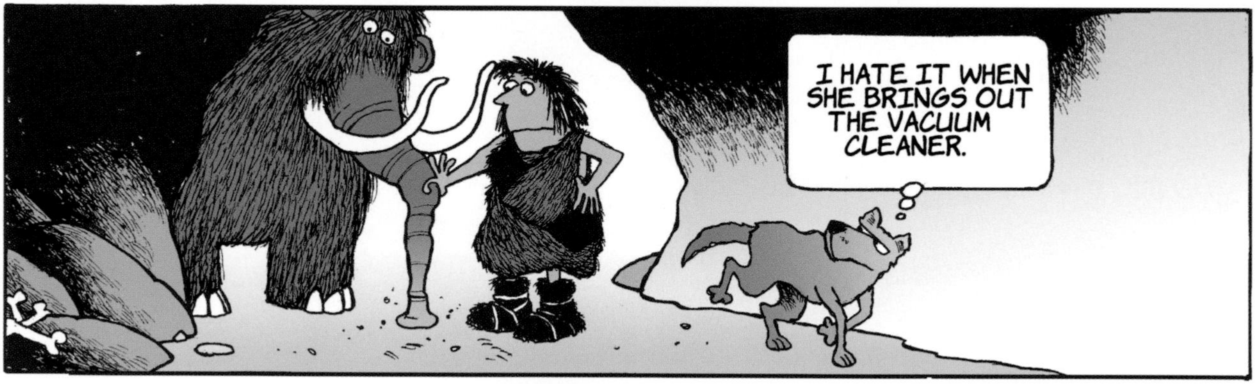
I HATE IT WHEN SHE BRINGS OUT THE VACUUM CLEANER.

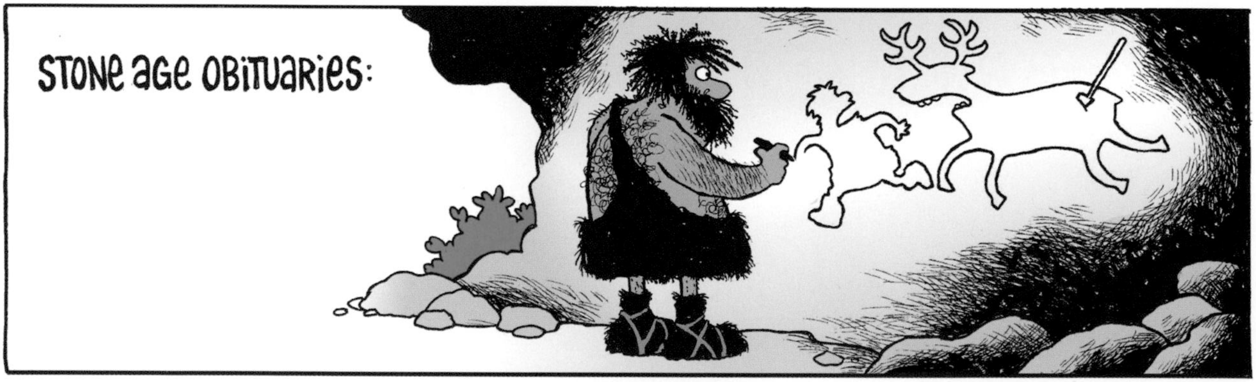
STONE AGE OBITUARIES:

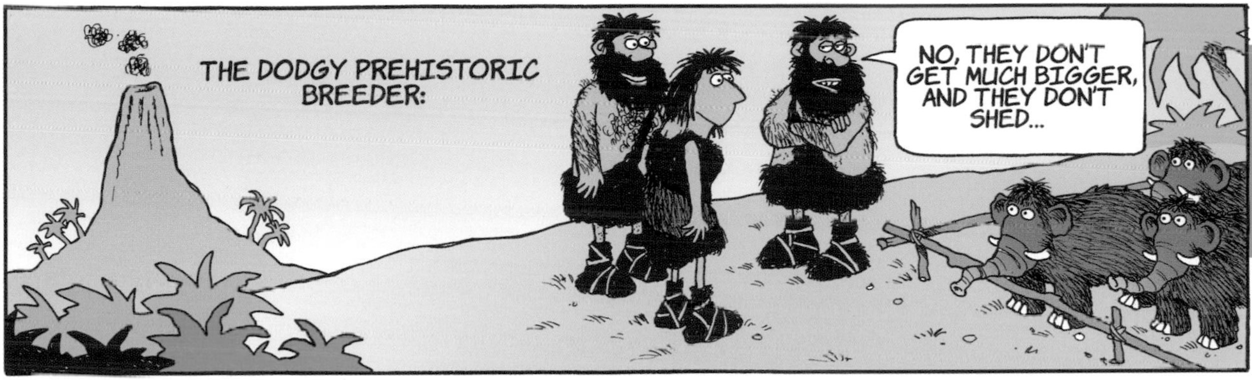
THE DODGY PREHISTORIC BREEDER:
NO, THEY DON'T GET MUCH BIGGER, AND THEY DON'T SHED...

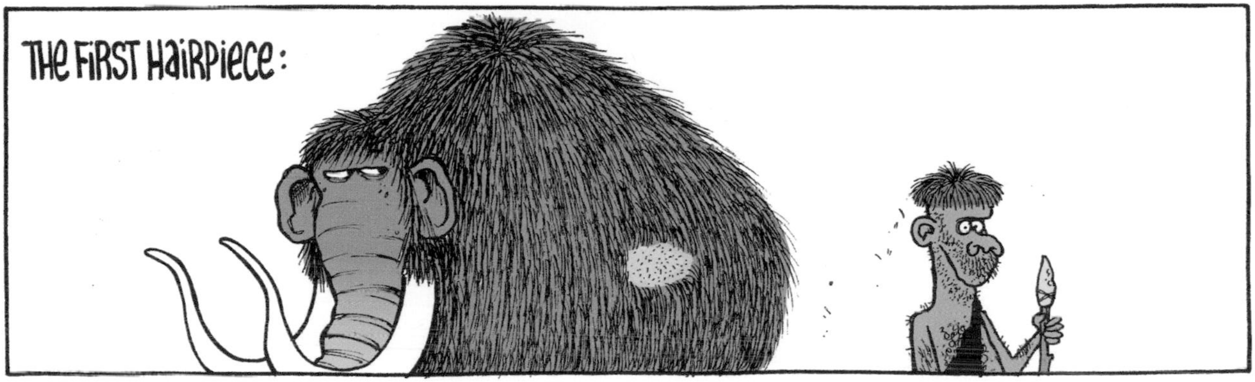
THE FIRST HAIRPIECE:

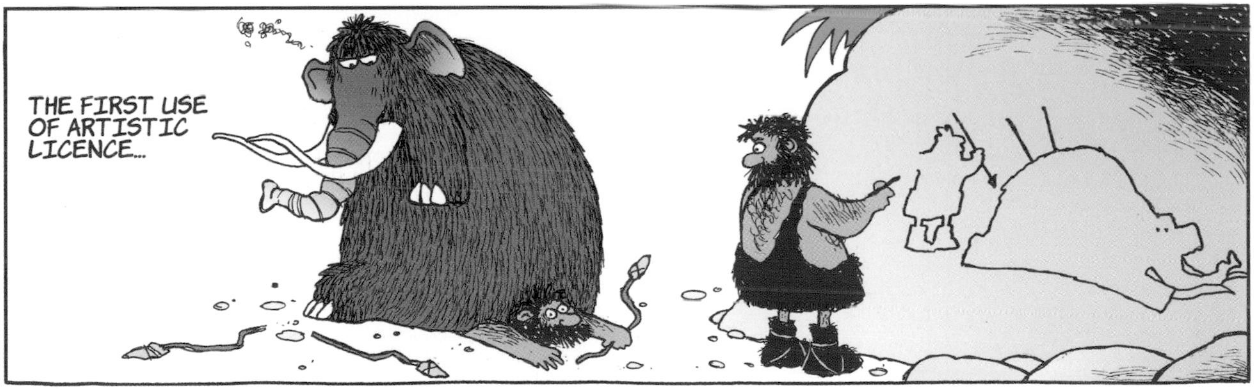
THE FIRST USE OF ARTISTIC LICENCE...

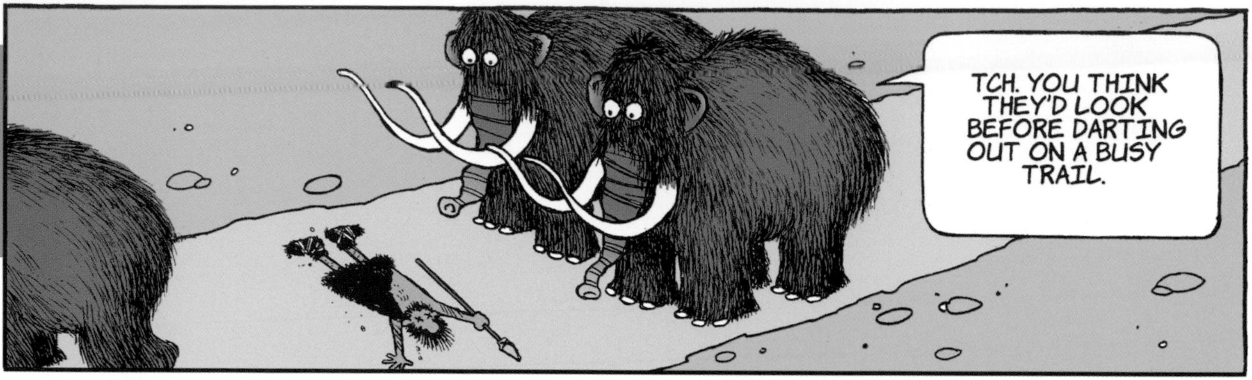
TCH. YOU THINK THEY'D LOOK BEFORE DARTING OUT ON A BUSY TRAIL.

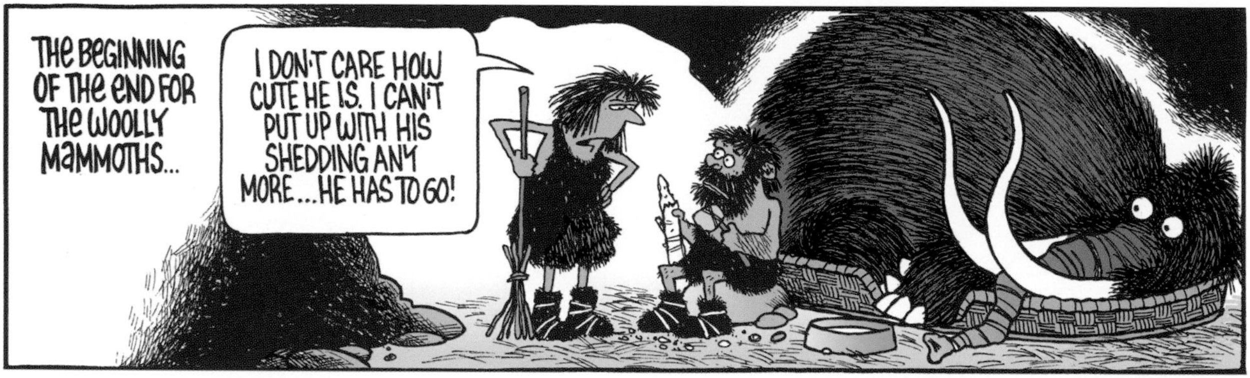
THE BEGINNING OF THE END FOR THE WOOLLY MAMMOTHS...
I DON'T CARE HOW CUTE HE IS. I CAN'T PUT UP WITH HIS SHEDDING ANY MORE...HE HAS TO GO!

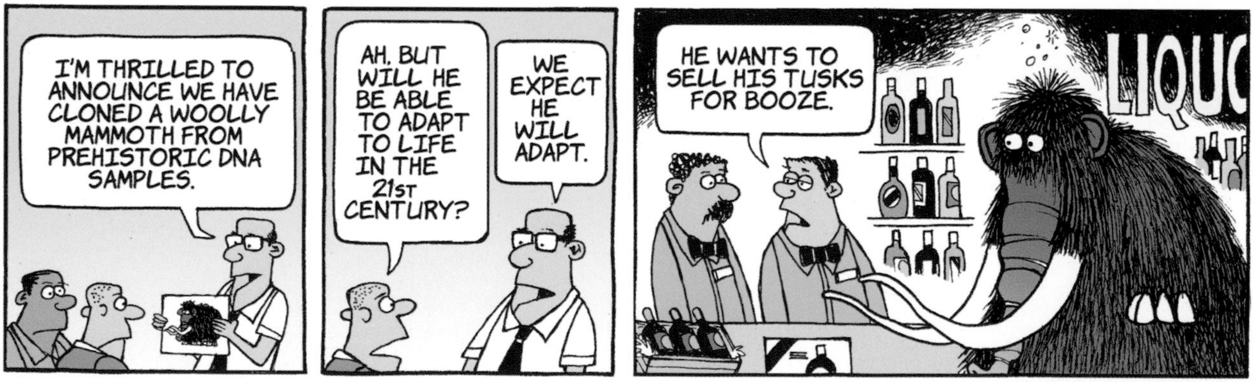
I'M THRILLED TO ANNOUNCE WE HAVE CLONED A WOOLLY MAMMOTH FROM PREHISTORIC DNA SAMPLES.
AH, BUT WILL HE BE ABLE TO ADAPT TO LIFE IN THE 21ST CENTURY?
WE EXPECT HE WILL ADAPT.
HE WANTS TO SELL HIS TUSKS FOR BOOZE.
LIQU

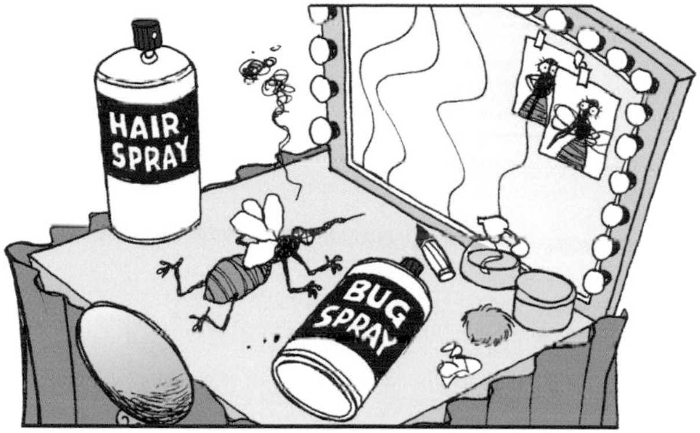
HAIR SPRAY
BUG SPRAY

ICONIC INVERTEBRATES 2

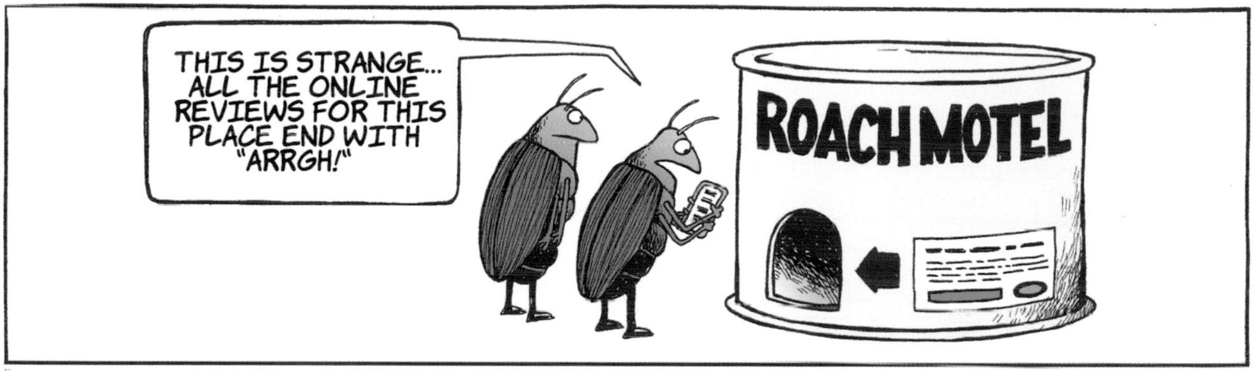
THIS IS STRANGE... ALL THE ONLINE REVIEWS FOR THIS PLACE END WITH "ARRGH!"
ROACH MOTEL

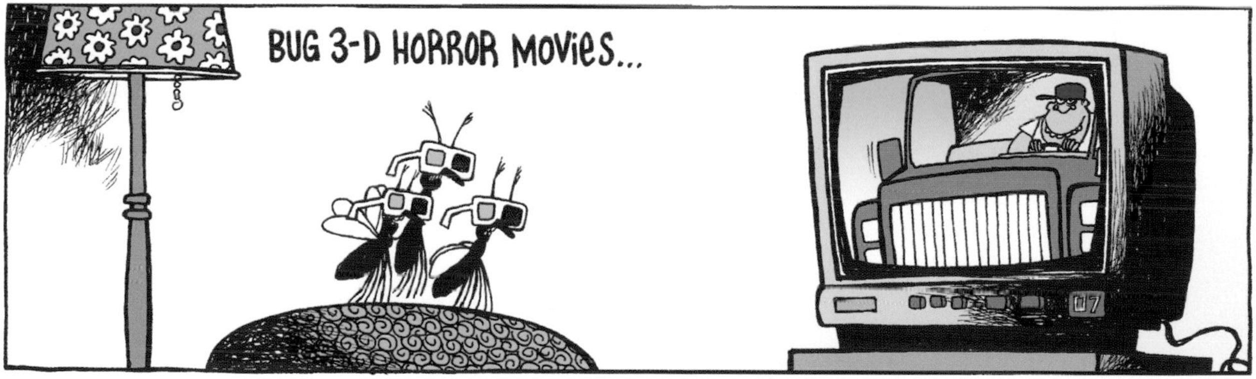
BUG 3-D HORROR MOVIES...

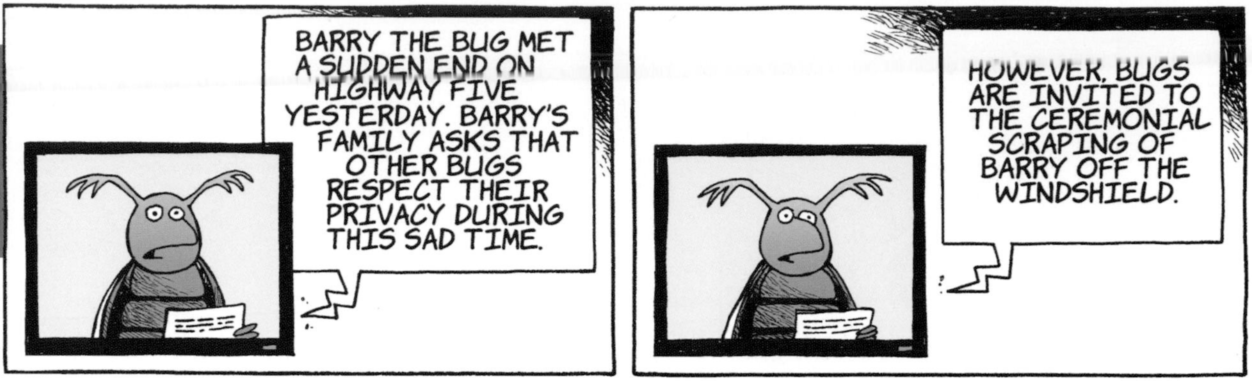

BARRY THE BUG MET A SUDDEN END ON HIGHWAY FIVE YESTERDAY. BARRY'S FAMILY ASKS THAT OTHER BUGS RESPECT THEIR PRIVACY DURING THIS SAD TIME.
HOWEVER, BUGS ARE INVITED TO THE CEREMONIAL SCRAPING OF BARRY OFF THE WINDSHIELD.

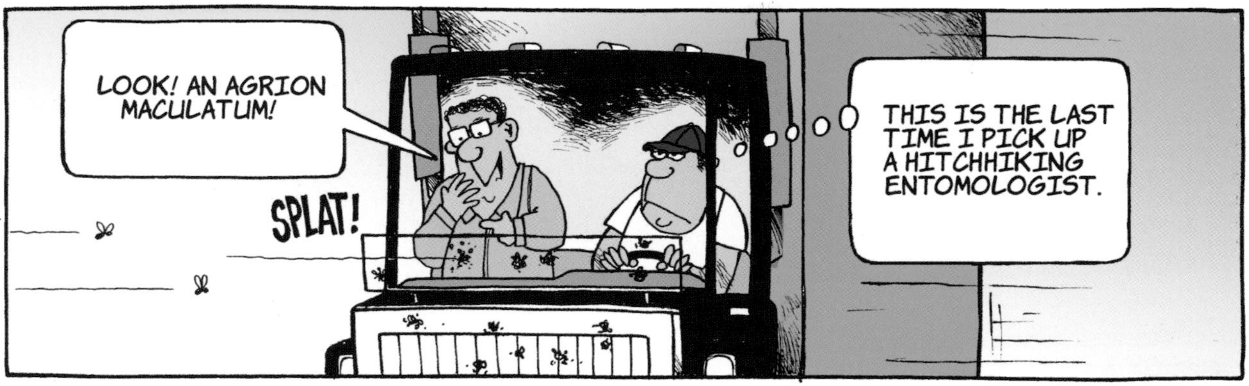

LOOK! AN AGRION MACULATUM!
SPLAT!
THIS IS THE LAST TIME I PICK UP A HITCHHIKING ENTOMOLOGIST.

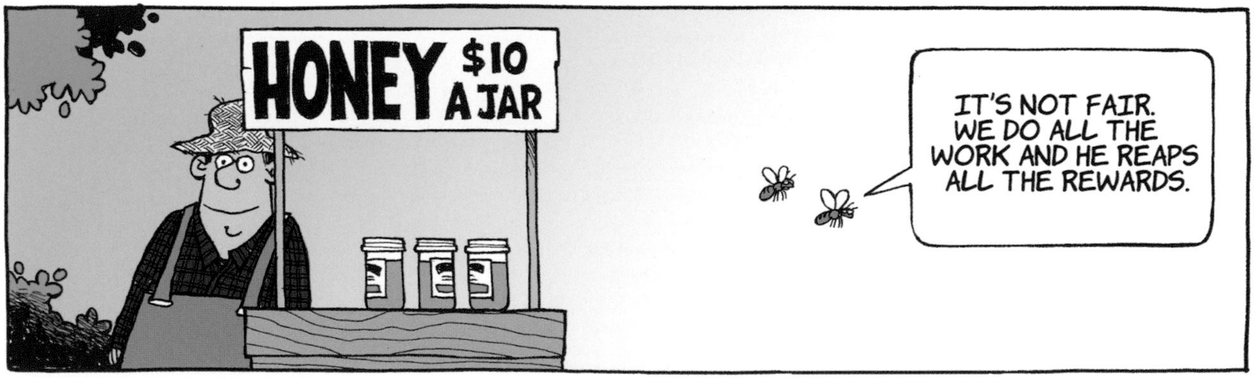

HONEY $10 A JAR
IT'S NOT FAIR. WE DO ALL THE WORK AND HE REAPS ALL THE REWARDS.

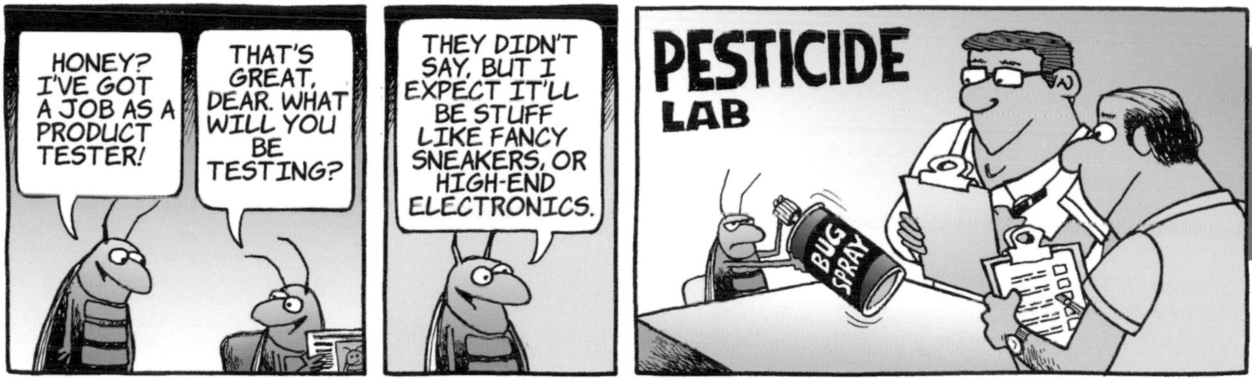
HONEY? I'VE GOT A JOB AS A PRODUCT TESTER!
THAT'S GREAT, DEAR. WHAT WILL YOU BE TESTING?
THEY DIDN'T SAY, BUT I EXPECT IT'LL BE STUFF LIKE FANCY SNEAKERS, OR HIGH-END ELECTRONICS.
PESTICIDE LAB
BUG SPRAY

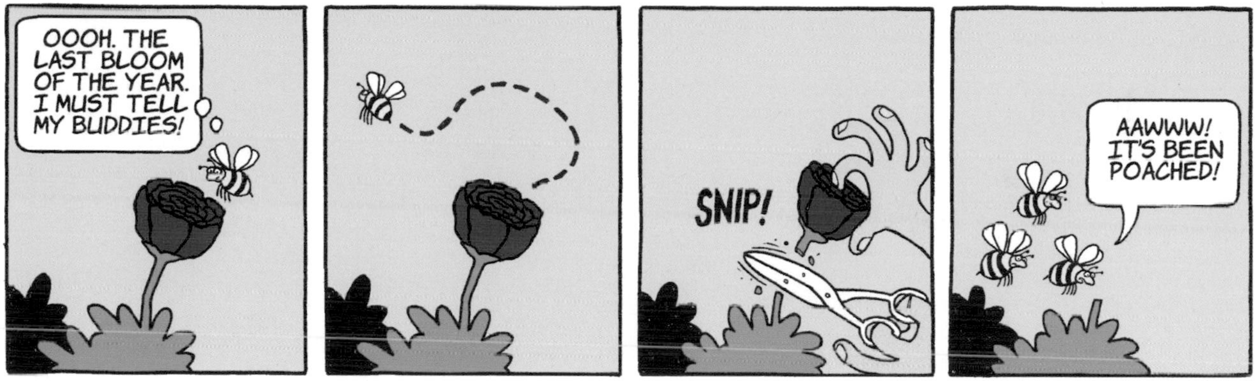
OOOH. THE LAST BLOOM OF THE YEAR. I MUST TELL MY BUDDIES!
SNIP!
AAWWW! IT'S BEEN POACHED!

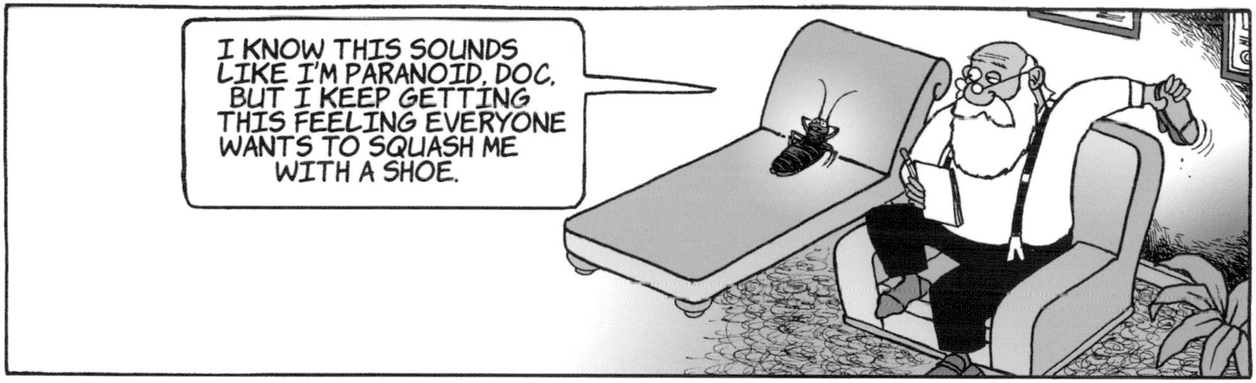
I KNOW THIS SOUNDS LIKE I'M PARANOID, DOC, BUT I KEEP GETTING THIS FEELING EVERYONE WANTS TO SQUASH ME WITH A SHOE.

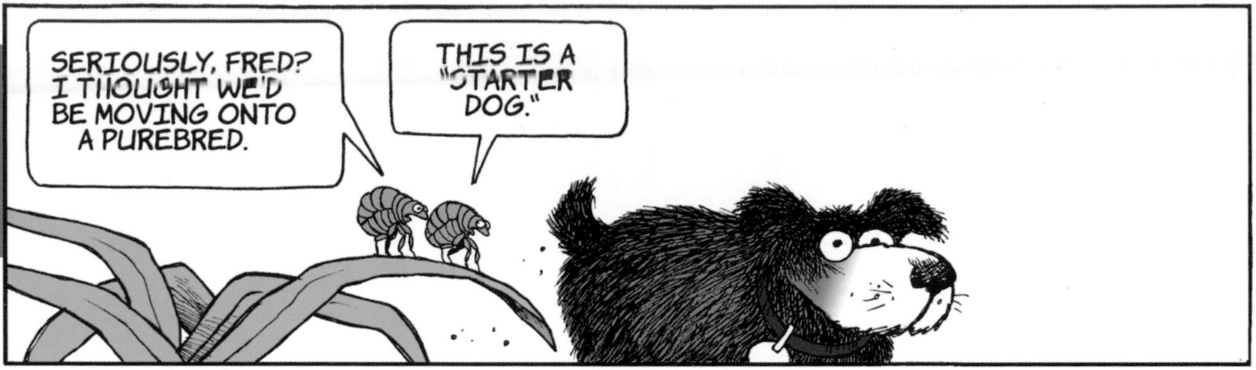
SERIOUSLY, FRED? I THOUGHT WE'D BE MOVING ONTO A PUREBRED.
THIS IS A "STARTER DOG."

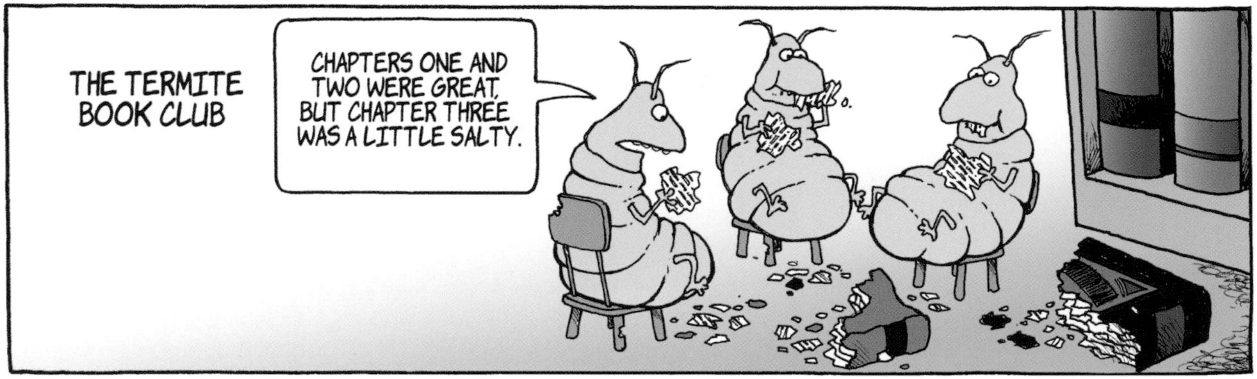
THE TERMITE BOOK CLUB
CHAPTERS ONE AND TWO WERE GREAT, BUT CHAPTER THREE WAS A LITTLE SALTY.

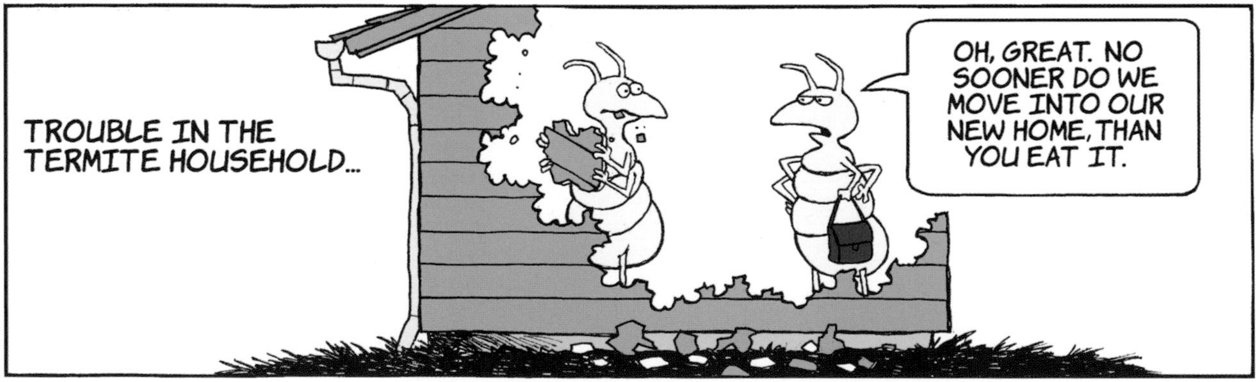
TROUBLE IN THE TERMITE HOUSEHOLD...
OH, GREAT. NO SOONER DO WE MOVE INTO OUR NEW HOME, THAN YOU EAT IT.

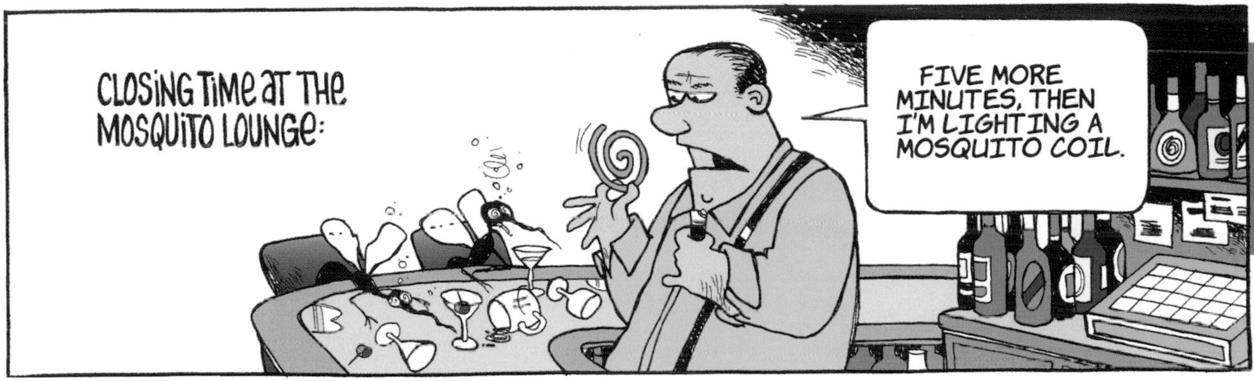
CLOSING TIME AT THE MOSQUITO LOUNGE:
FIVE MORE MINUTES, THEN I'M LIGHTING A MOSQUITO COIL.

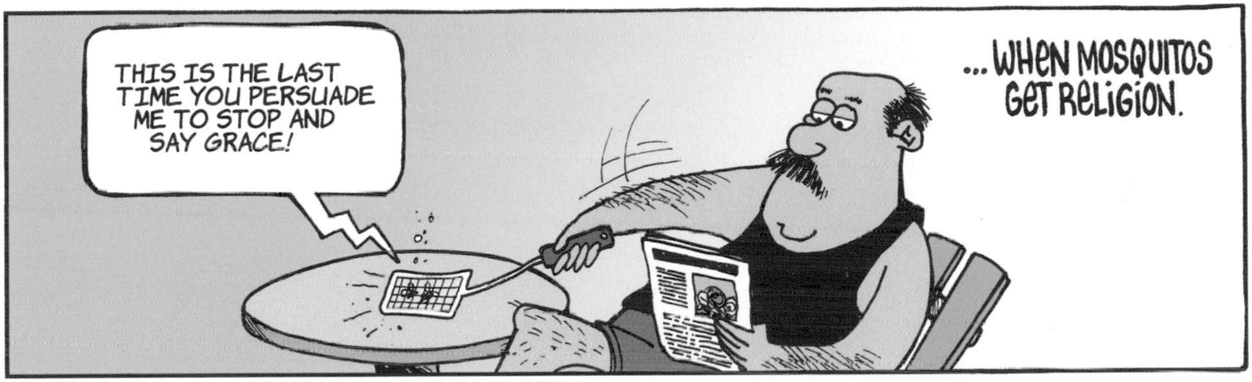
THIS IS THE LAST TIME YOU PERSUADE ME TO STOP AND SAY GRACE!
...WHEN MOSQUITOS GET RELIGION.

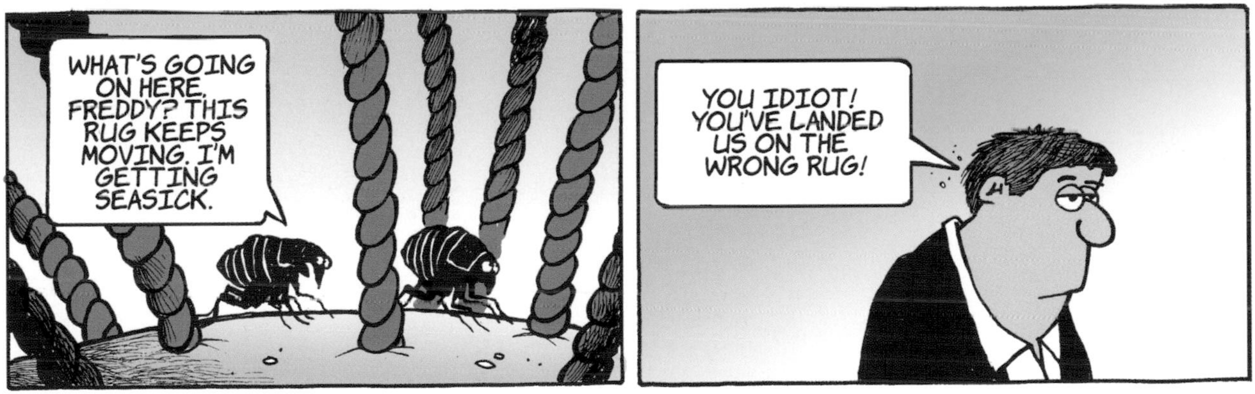
WHAT'S GOING ON HERE, FREDDY? THIS RUG KEEPS MOVING. I'M GETTING SEASICK.
YOU IDIOT! YOU'VE LANDED US ON THE WRONG RUG!

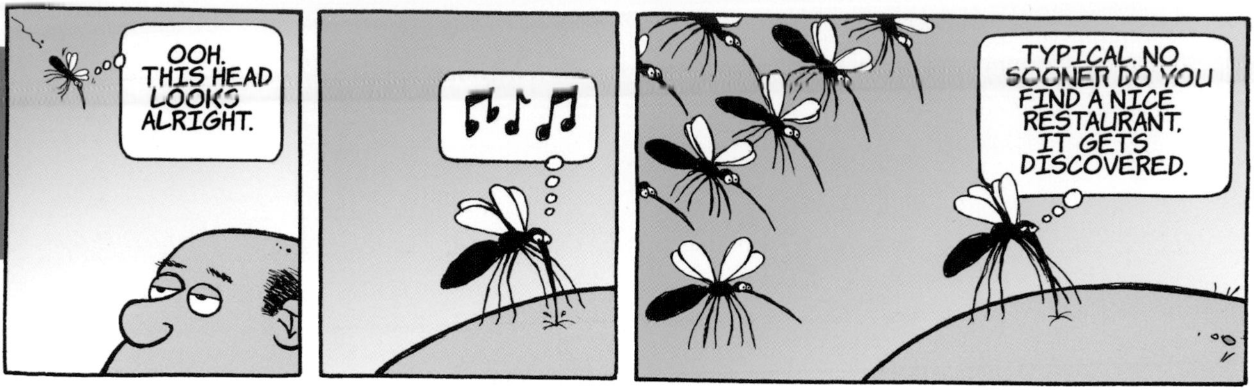
OOH. THIS HEAD LOOKS ALRIGHT.
TYPICAL. NO SOONER DO YOU FIND A NICE RESTAURANT, IT GETS DISCOVERED.

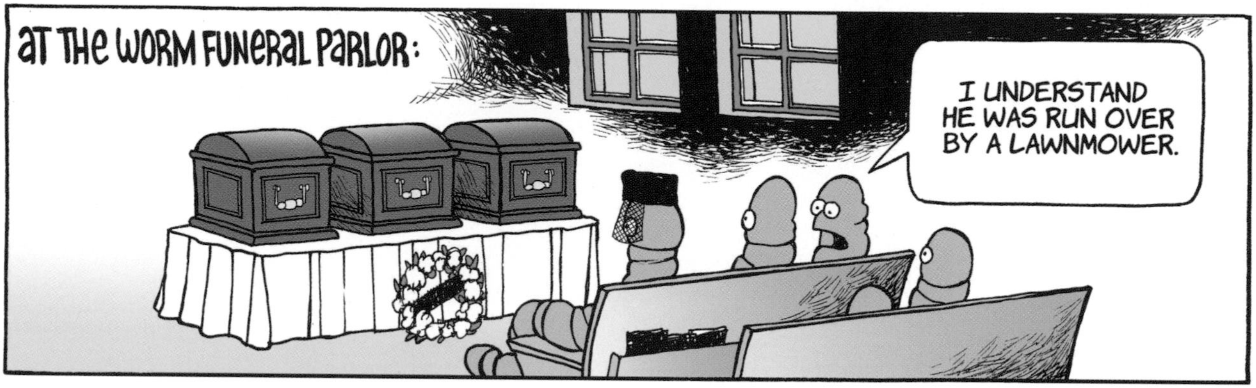
AT THE WORM FUNERAL PARLOR:
I UNDERSTAND HE WAS RUN OVER BY A LAWNMOWER.

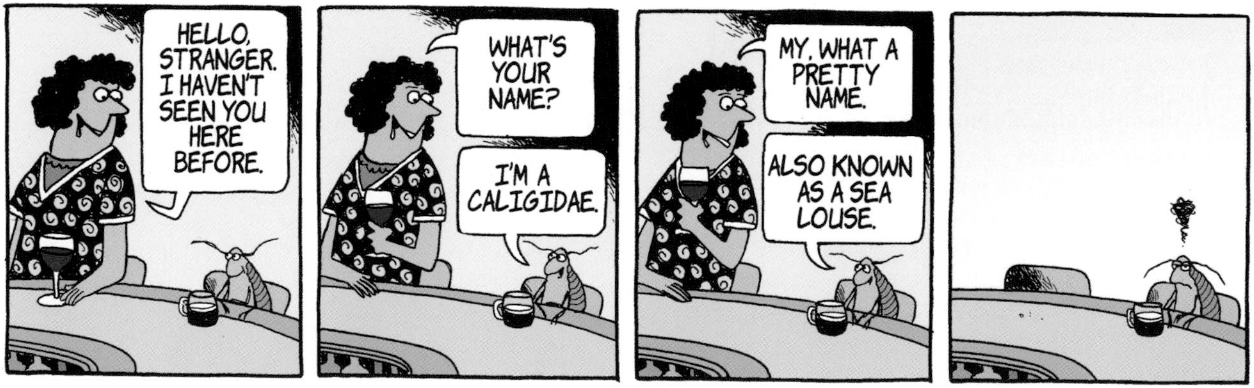
HELLO, STRANGER. I HAVEN'T SEEN YOU HERE BEFORE.
WHAT'S YOUR NAME?
I'M A CALIGIDAE.
MY, WHAT A PRETTY NAME.
ALSO KNOWN AS A SEA LOUSE.

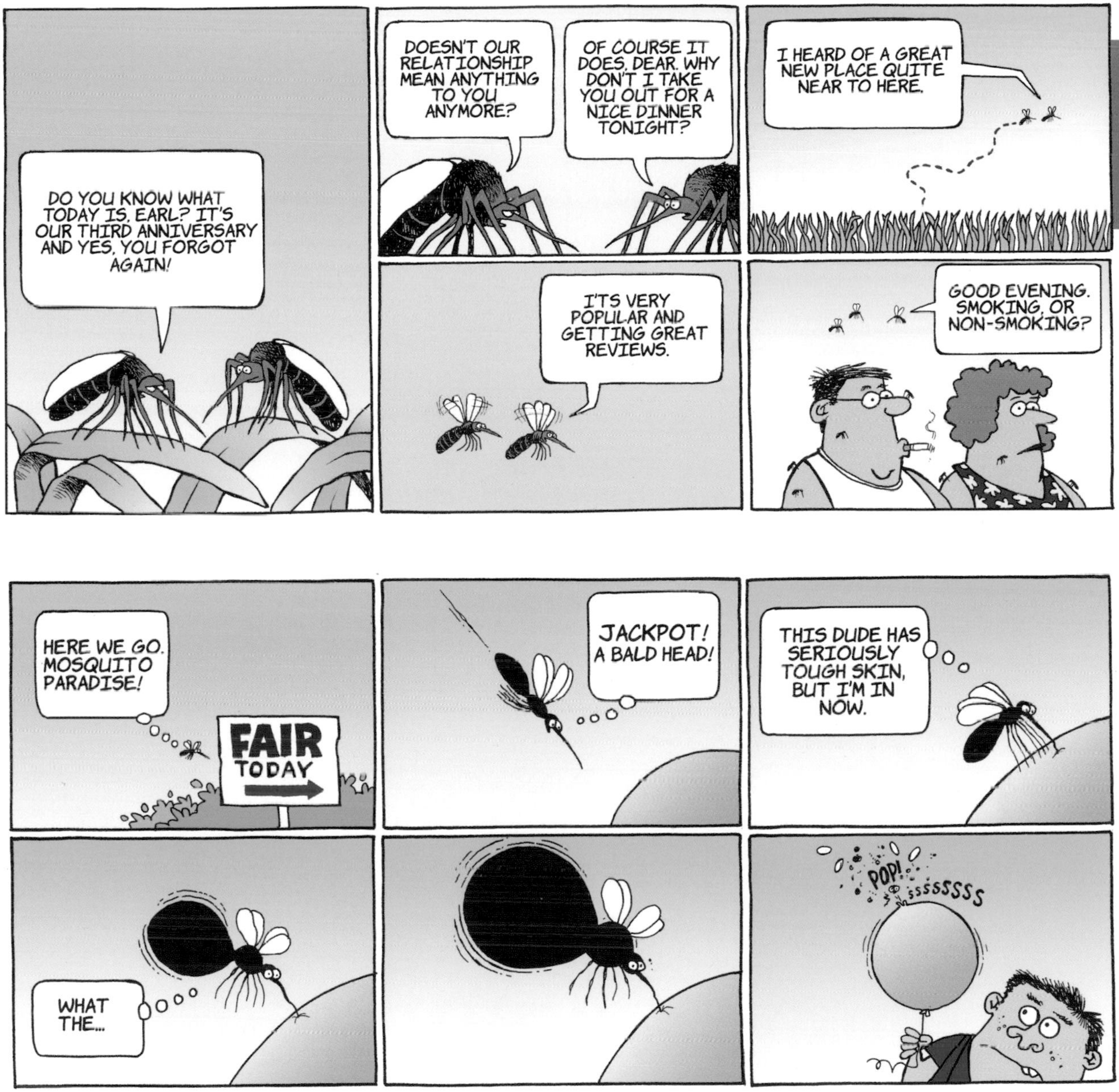
DO YOU KNOW WHAT TODAY IS, EARL? IT'S OUR THIRD ANNIVERSARY AND YES, YOU FORGOT AGAIN!
DOESN'T OUR RELATIONSHIP MEAN ANYTHING TO YOU ANYMORE?
OF COURSE IT DOES, DEAR. WHY DON'T I TAKE YOU OUT FOR A NICE DINNER TONIGHT?
I HEARD OF A GREAT NEW PLACE QUITE NEAR TO HERE.
IT'S VERY POPULAR AND GETTING GREAT REVIEWS.
GOOD EVENING. SMOKING, OR NON-SMOKING?
HERE WE GO. MOSQUITO PARADISE!
FAIR TODAY
JACKPOT! A BALD HEAD!
THIS DUDE HAS SERIOUSLY TOUGH SKIN, BUT I'M IN NOW.
WHAT THE...
POP!
SSSSSSSSS

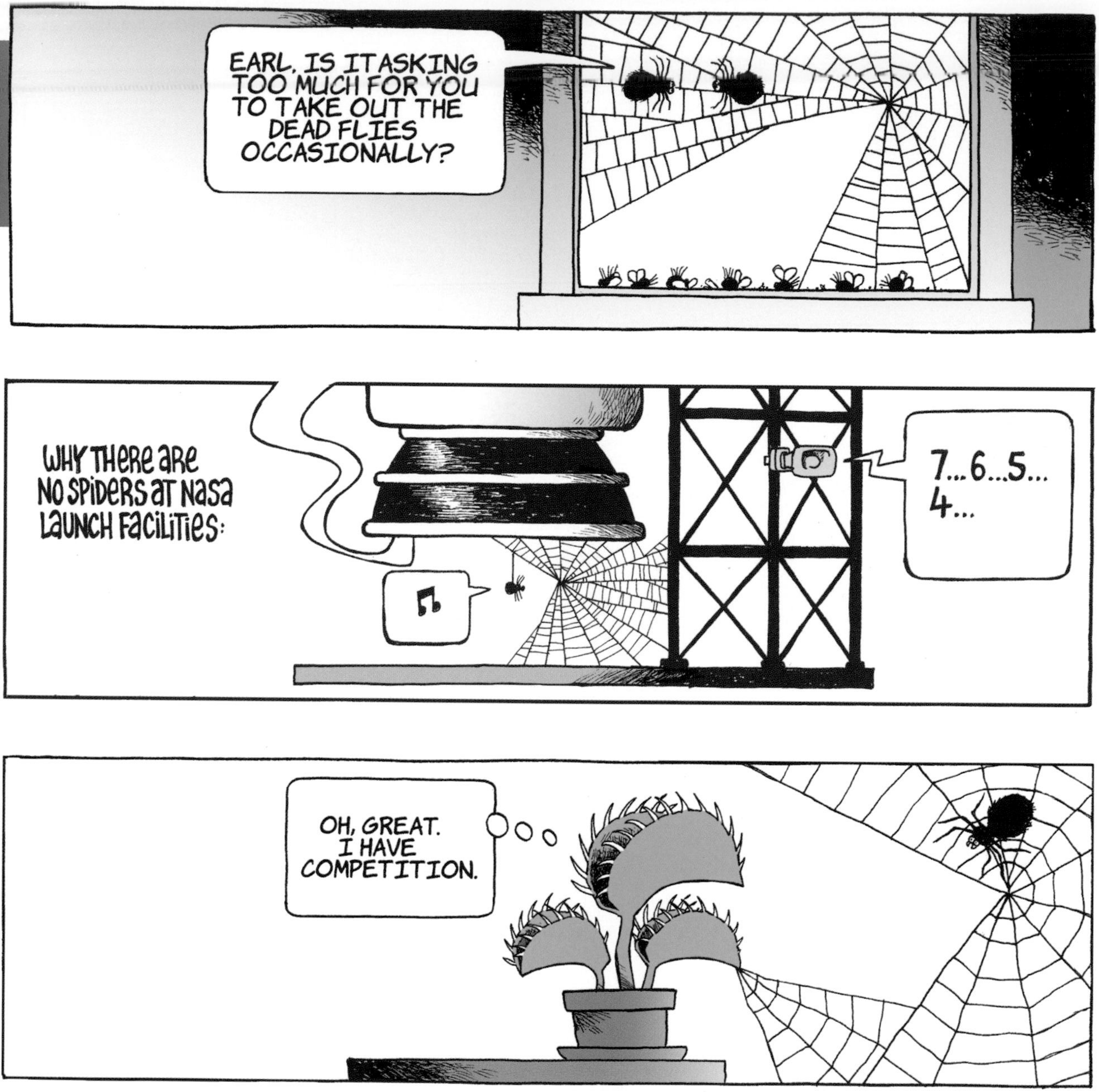
EARL, IS IT ASKING TOO MUCH FOR YOU TO TAKE OUT THE DEAD FLIES OCCASIONALLY?
WHY THERE ARE NO SPIDERS AT NASA LAUNCH FACILITIES:
7...6...5... 4...
OH, GREAT. I HAVE COMPETITION.

WATER DWELLERS 3

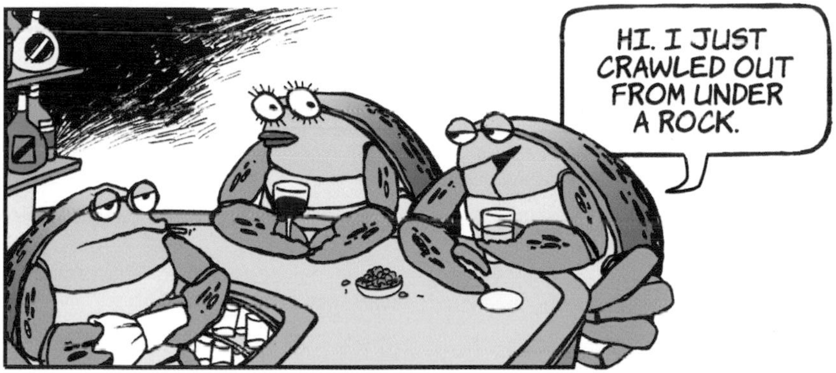
HI. I JUST CRAWLED OUT FROM UNDER A ROCK.

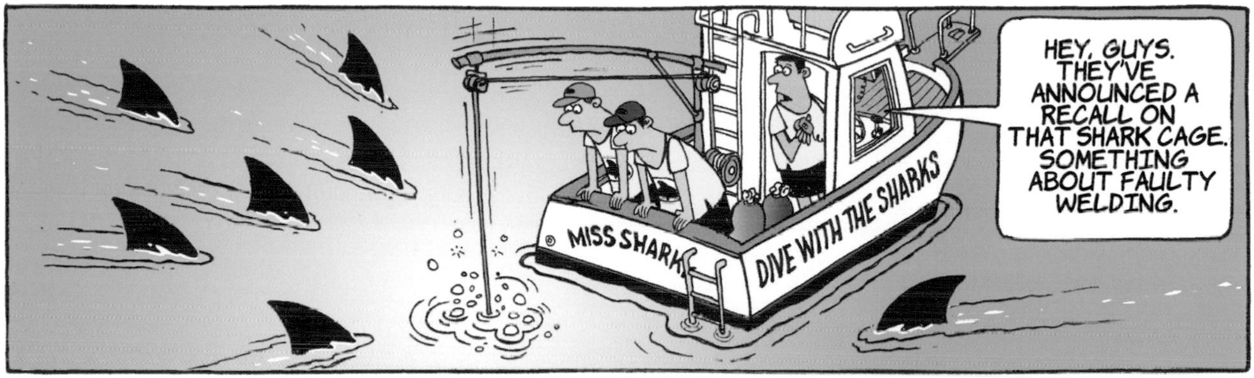
MISS SHARK
DIVE WITH THE SHARKS
HEY, GUYS. THEY'VE ANNOUNCED A RECALL ON THAT SHARK CAGE. SOMETHING ABOUT FAULTY WELDING.

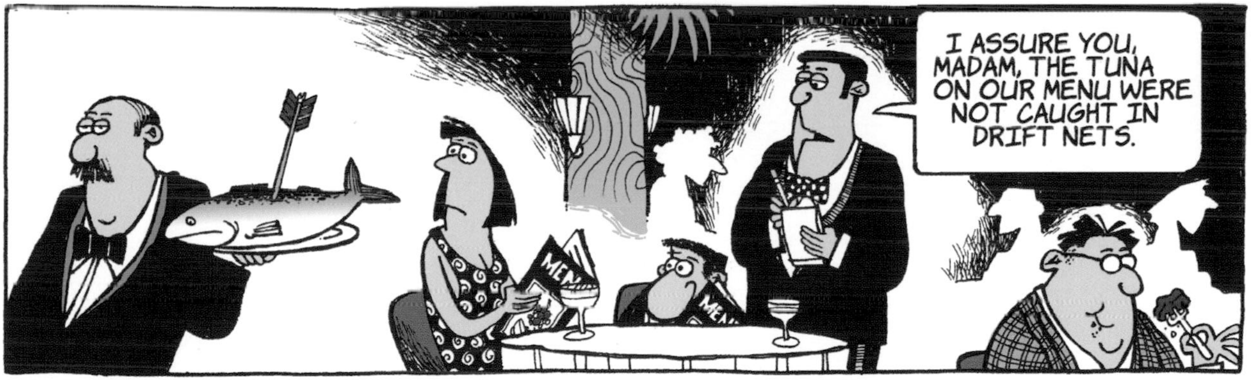
I ASSURE YOU, MADAM, THE TUNA ON OUR MENU WERE NOT CAUGHT IN DRIFT NETS.

GOLDFISH FUNERAL NOTICES:

SAMMY THE GOLDFISH WILL BE FLUSHED DOWN THE TOILET 2 P.M. SATURDAY.

NORRY THE NEON FLUSH...

GERRY GOLDFISH CEREMONIAL TOILET FLUSHING 1 P.M. FRIDAY.

GERALDO THE GUPPY WILL BE FLUSHED DOWN TOILET FRIDAY 6 P.M.

BOB THE GOLDFISH WILL BE FLUSHED DOWN THE TOILET 3 P.M. MONDAY.

HAROLD THE GUPPY, TOILET FLUSHING MONDAY. FAMILY ONLY, PLEASE.

COMING THIS FALL ON DISCOVERY, PLANKTON WEEK.

I THINK WE CAN SAFELY SAY OUR OCEANS HAVE BEEN WELL AND TRULY OVERFISHED.

AWWW. PHOOEY!

TUNA

WELL, THIS IS AN AWKWARD PREDICAMENT...

BUT I EXPECT I'LL END UP IN A 5 STAR RESTAURANT, SERVED ON A BED OF CAVIAR AND ACCOMPANIED BY A FINE FRENCH CHAMPAGNE.

AWWW. PHOOEY!

CAT FOOD

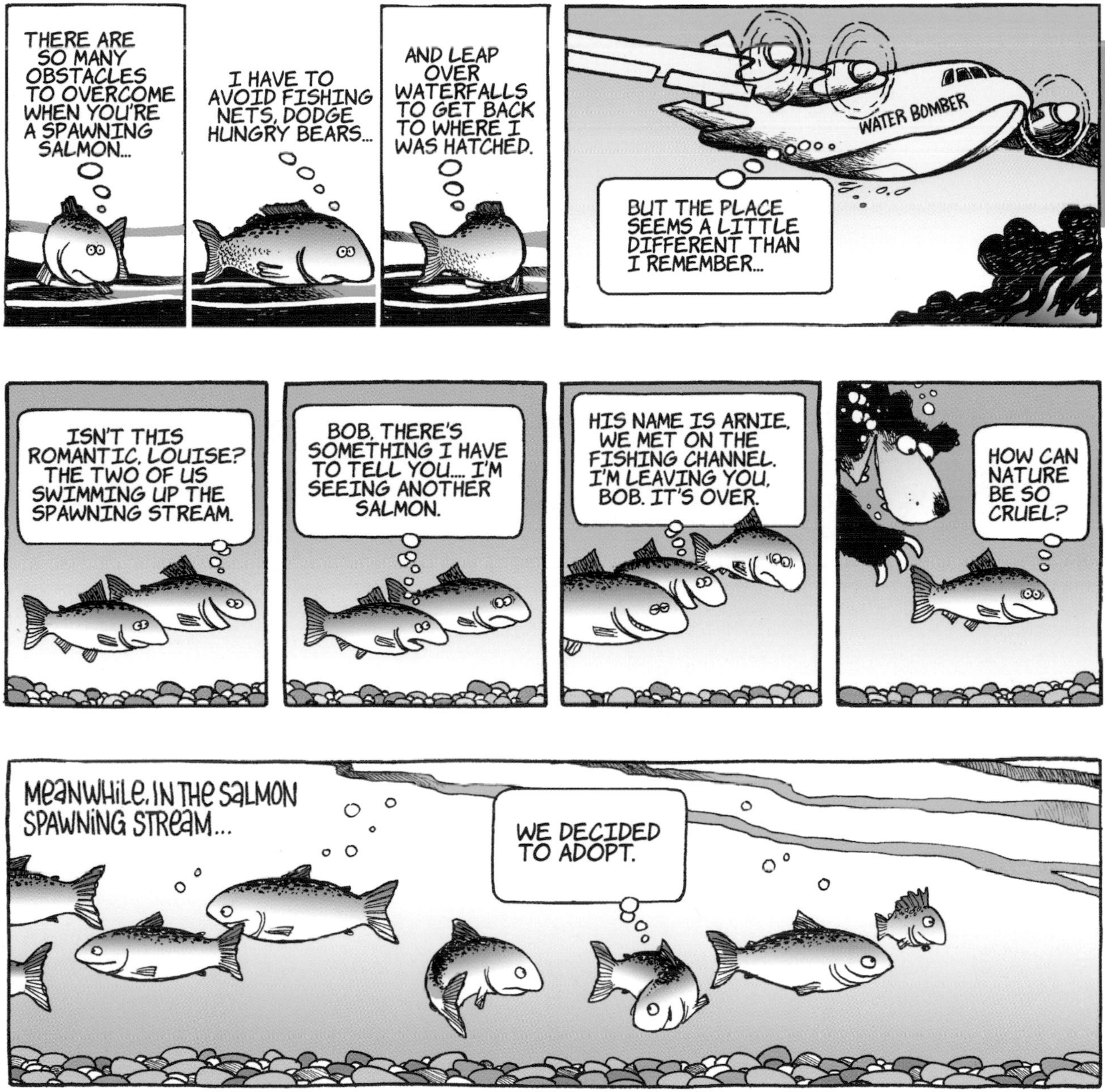

THERE ARE SO MANY OBSTACLES TO OVERCOME WHEN YOU'RE A SPAWNING SALMON...
I HAVE TO AVOID FISHING NETS, DODGE HUNGRY BEARS...
AND LEAP OVER WATERFALLS TO GET BACK TO WHERE I WAS HATCHED.
WATER BOMBER
BUT THE PLACE SEEMS A LITTLE DIFFERENT THAN I REMEMBER...
ISN'T THIS ROMANTIC, LOUISE? THE TWO OF US SWIMMING UP THE SPAWNING STREAM.
BOB, THERE'S SOMETHING I HAVE TO TELL YOU.... I'M SEEING ANOTHER SALMON.
HIS NAME IS ARNIE. WE MET ON THE FISHING CHANNEL. I'M LEAVING YOU, BOB. IT'S OVER.
HOW CAN NATURE BE SO CRUEL?
MEANWHILE, IN THE SALMON SPAWNING STREAM...
WE DECIDED TO ADOPT.

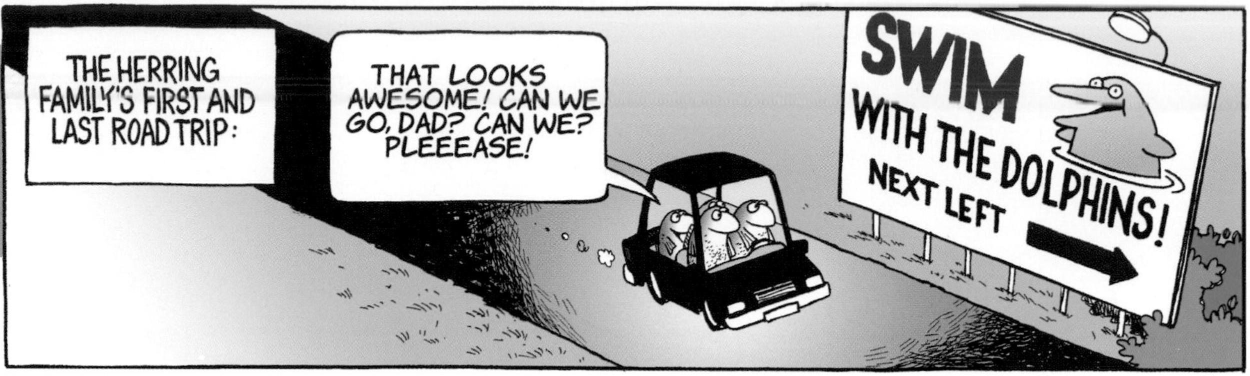
THE HERRING FAMILY'S FIRST AND LAST ROAD TRIP:
THAT LOOKS AWESOME! CAN WE GO, DAD? CAN WE? PLEEEASE!
SWIM WITH THE DOLPHINS!
NEXT LEFT

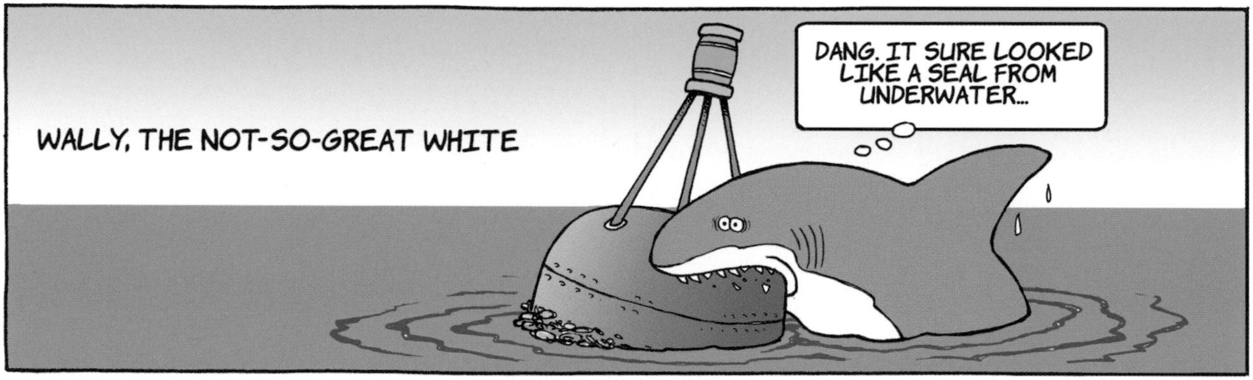
WALLY, THE NOT-SO-GREAT WHITE
DANG. IT SURE LOOKED LIKE A SEAL FROM UNDERWATER...

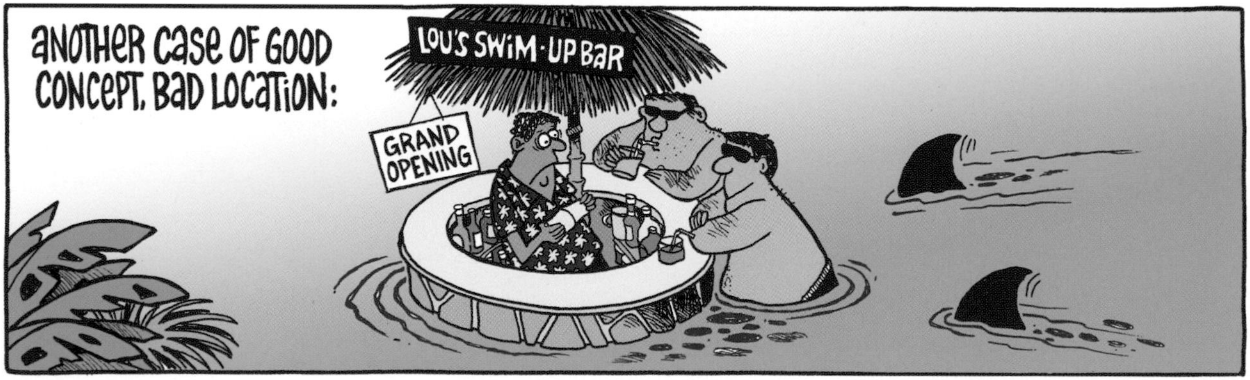
ANOTHER CASE OF GOOD CONCEPT, BAD LOCATION:
LOU'S SWIM-UP BAR
GRAND OPENING

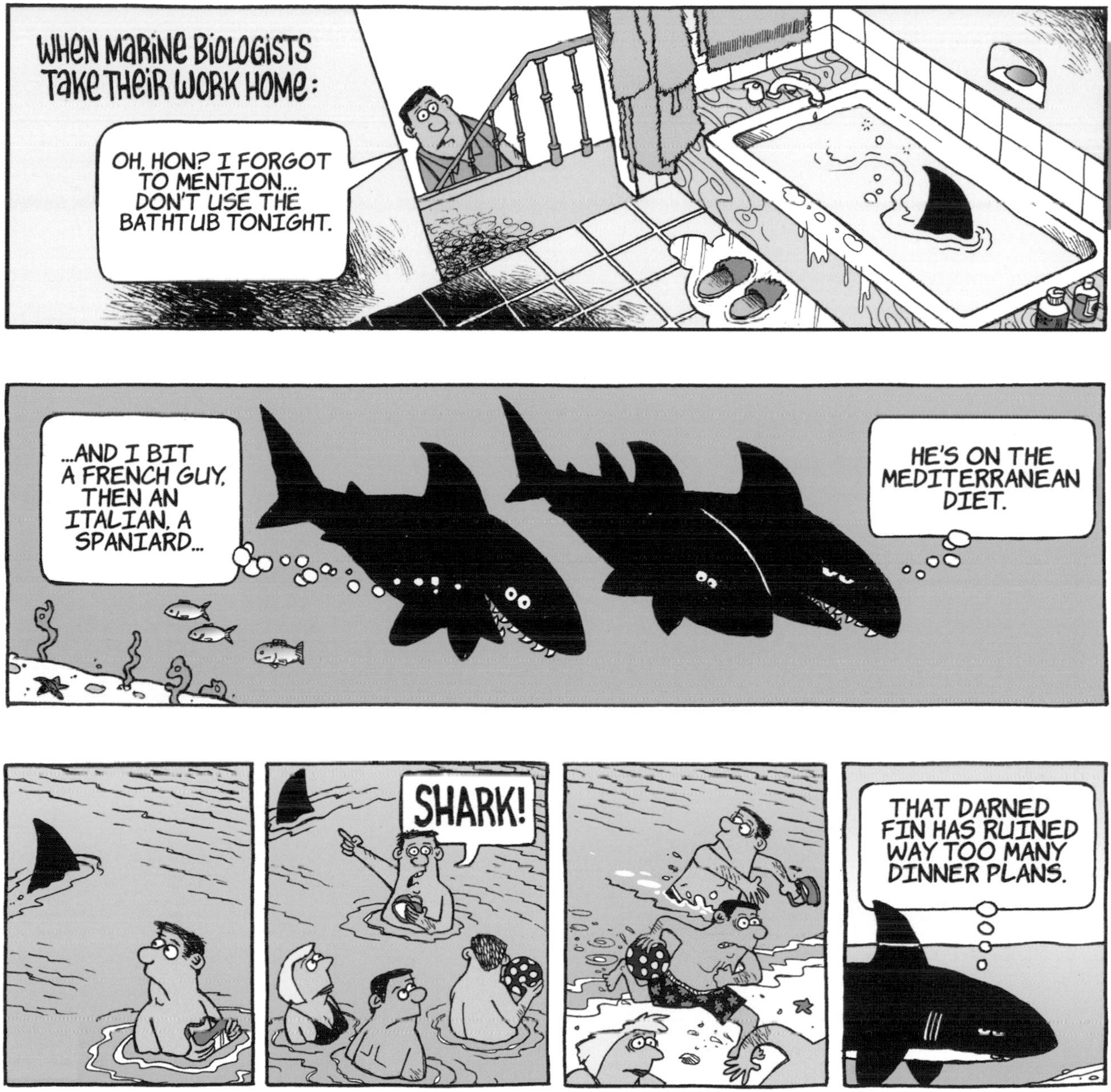
WHEN MARINE BIOLOGISTS TAKE THEIR WORK HOME:
OH, HON? I FORGOT TO MENTION... DON'T USE THE BATHTUB TONIGHT.
...AND I BIT A FRENCH GUY, THEN AN ITALIAN, A SPANIARD...
HE'S ON THE MEDITERRANEAN DIET.
SHARK!
THAT DARNED FIN HAS RUINED WAY TOO MANY DINNER PLANS.

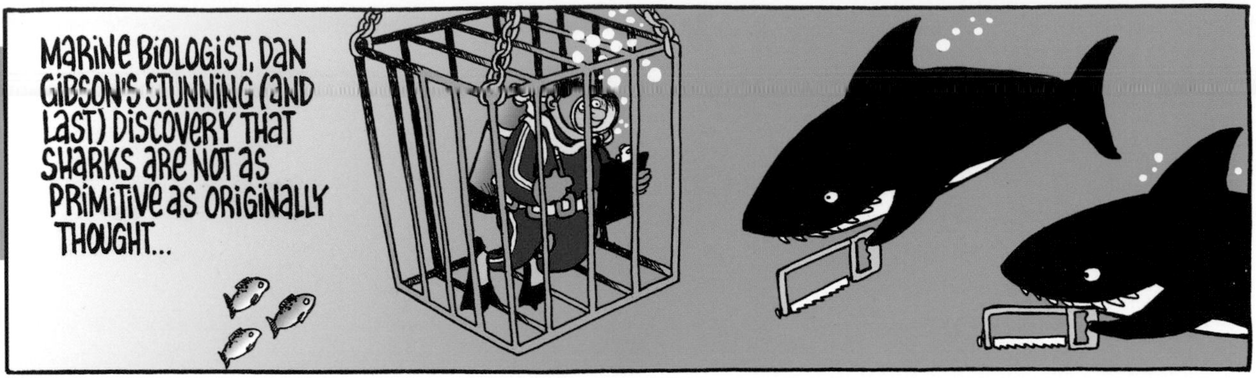
MARINE BIOLOGIST, DAN GIBSON'S STUNNING (AND LAST) DISCOVERY THAT SHARKS ARE NOT AS PRIMITIVE AS ORIGINALLY THOUGHT...

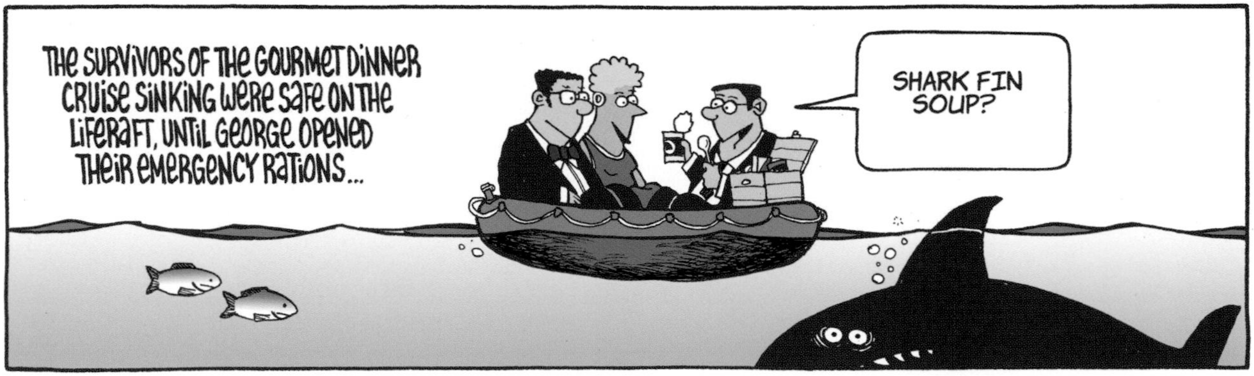
THE SURVIVORS OF THE GOURMET DINNER CRUISE SINKING WERE SAFE ON THE LIFERAFT, UNTIL GEORGE OPENED THEIR EMERGENCY RATIONS...
SHARK FIN SOUP?

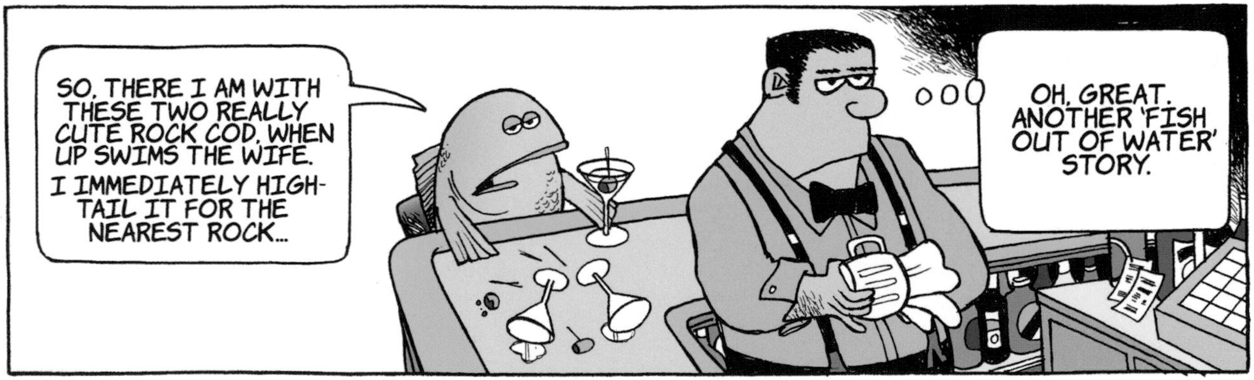
SO, THERE I AM WITH THESE TWO REALLY CUTE ROCK COD, WHEN UP SWIMS THE WIFE.
I IMMEDIATELY HIGH-TAIL IT FOR THE NEAREST ROCK...
OH, GREAT. ANOTHER 'FISH OUT OF WATER' STORY.

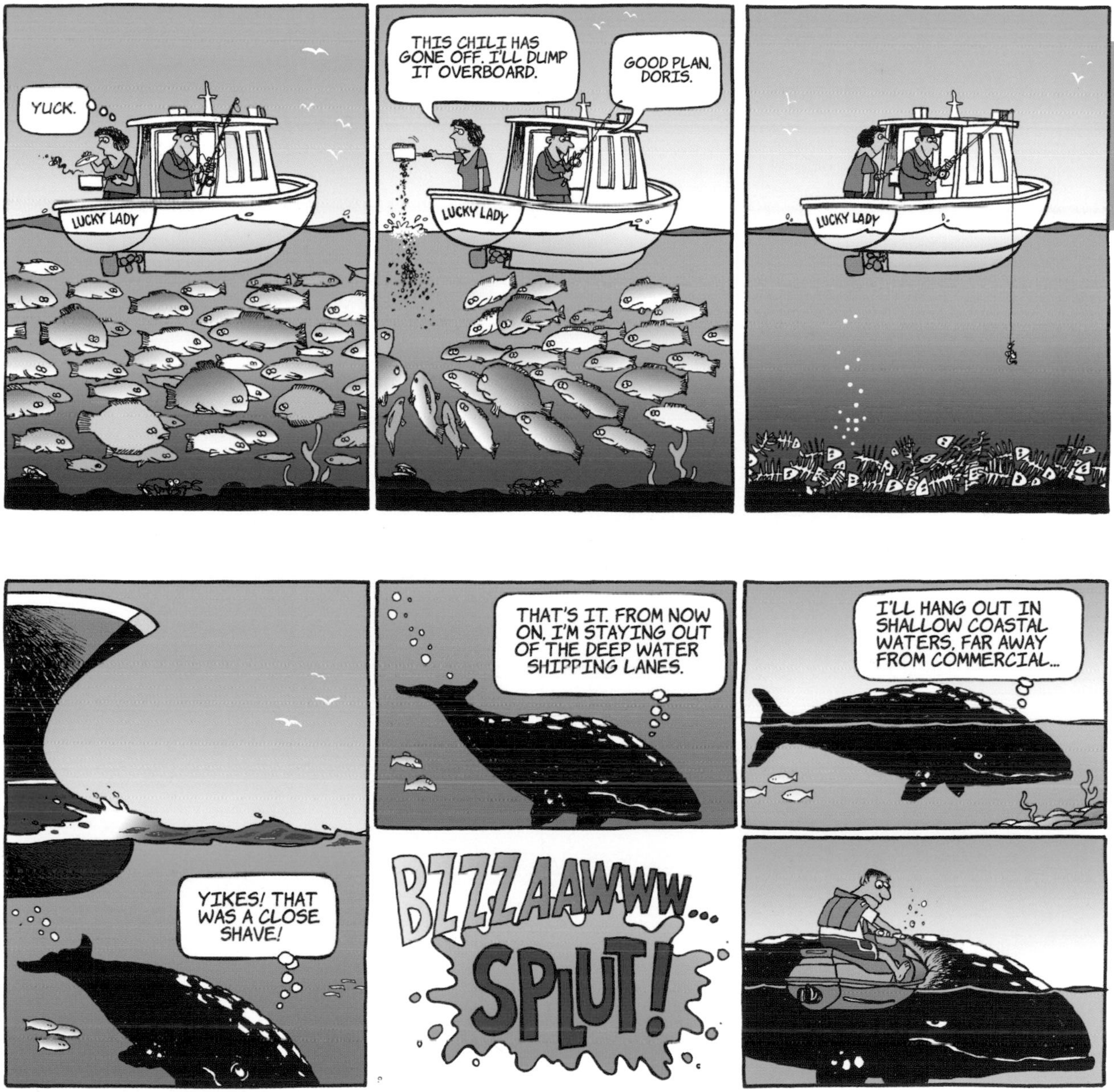
YUCK.
THIS CHILI HAS GONE OFF. I'LL DUMP IT OVERBOARD.
GOOD PLAN, DORIS.
LUCKY LADY
YIKES! THAT WAS A CLOSE SHAVE!
THAT'S IT. FROM NOW ON, I'M STAYING OUT OF THE DEEP WATER SHIPPING LANES.
I'LL HANG OUT IN SHALLOW COASTAL WATERS, FAR AWAY FROM COMMERCIAL...
BZZZAAWWW...
SPLUT!

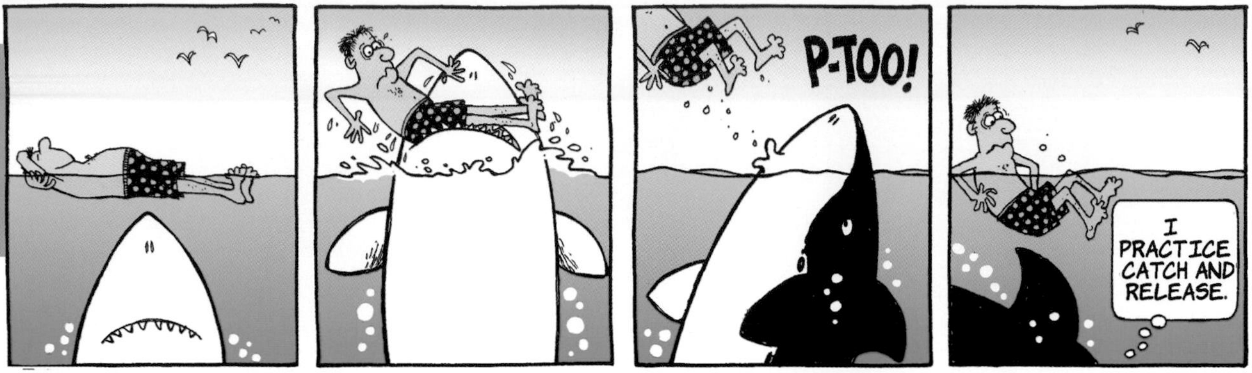
P-TOO!
I PRACTICE CATCH AND RELEASE.

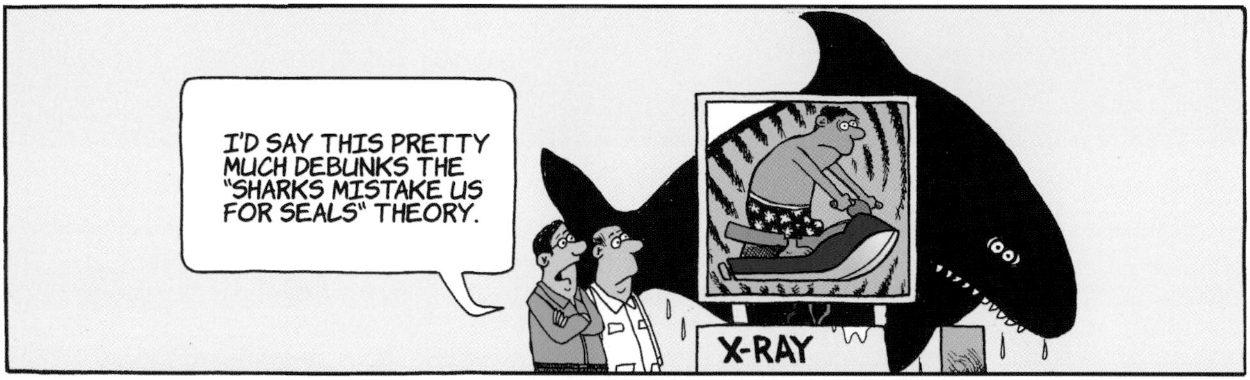
I'D SAY THIS PRETTY MUCH DEBUNKS THE "SHARKS MISTAKE US FOR SEALS" THEORY.
X-RAY

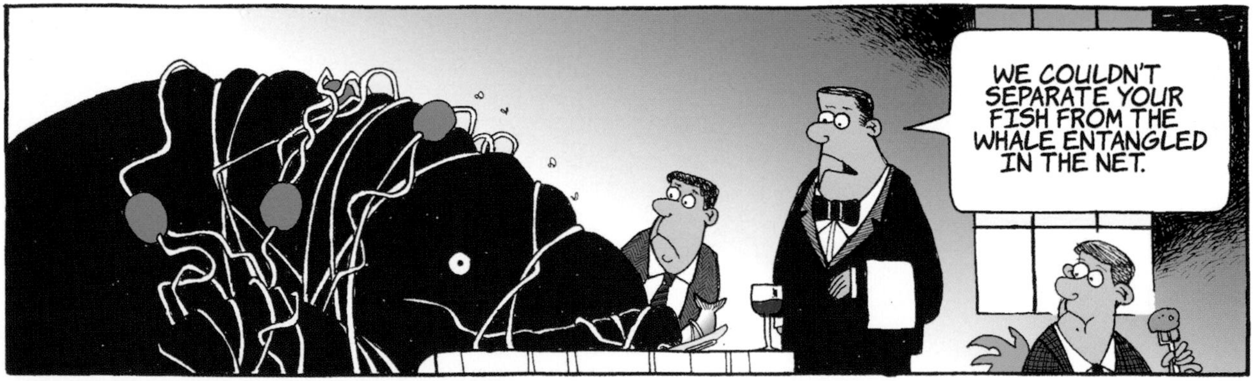
WE COULDN'T SEPARATE YOUR FISH FROM THE WHALE ENTANGLED IN THE NET.

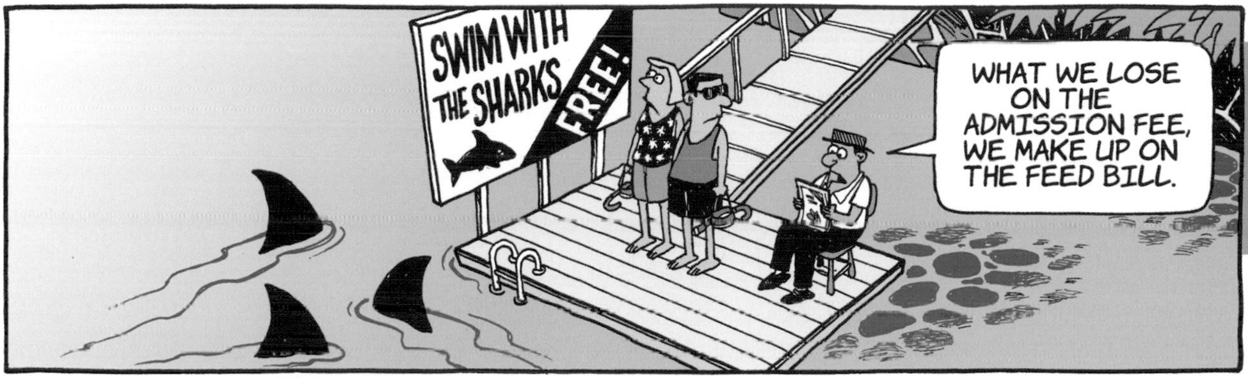
SWIM WITH THE SHARKS
FREE!
WHAT WE LOSE ON THE ADMISSION FEE, WE MAKE UP ON THE FEED BILL.

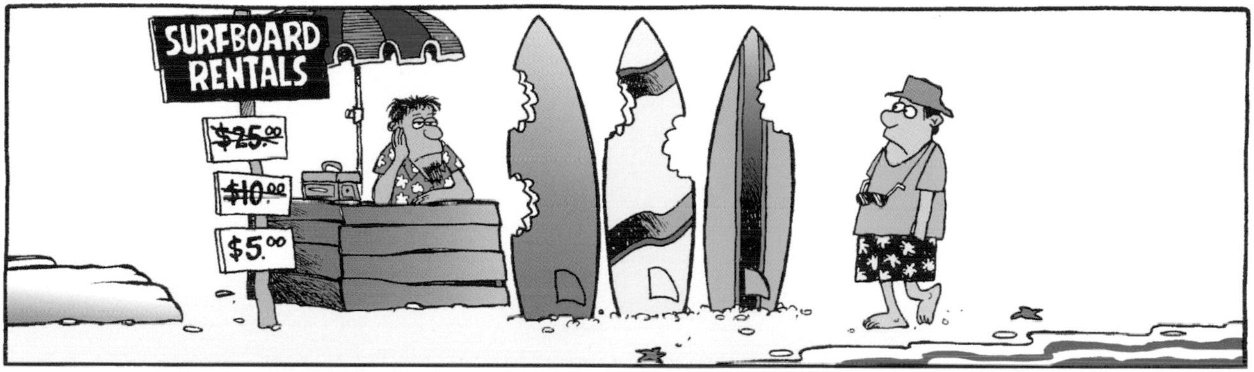
SURFBOARD RENTALS
$25.00
$10.00
$5.00

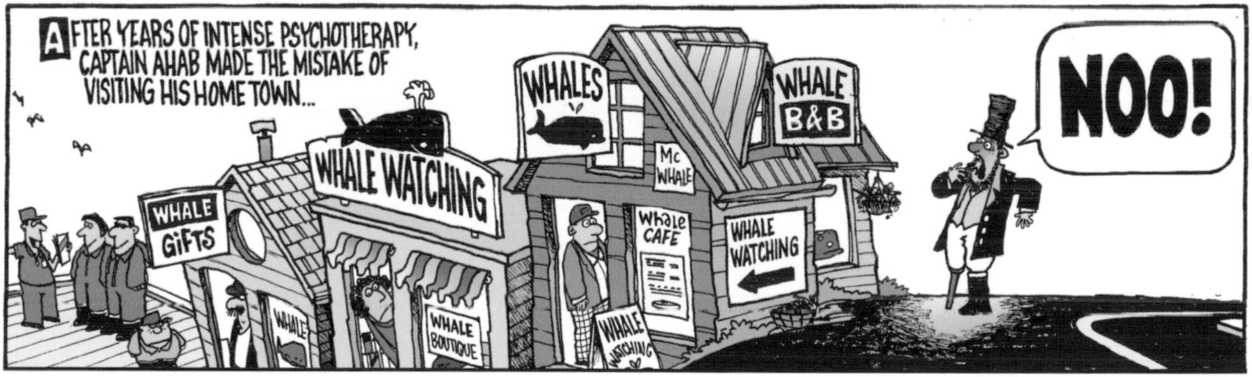
AFTER YEARS OF INTENSE PSYCHOTHERAPY, CAPTAIN AHAB MADE THE MISTAKE OF VISITING HIS HOME TOWN...
WHALES
WHALE B&B
WHALE WATCHING
Mc WHALE
WHALE GIFTS
Whale CAFE
WHALE WATCHING
WHALE BOUTIQUE
WHALE WATCHING
NOO!

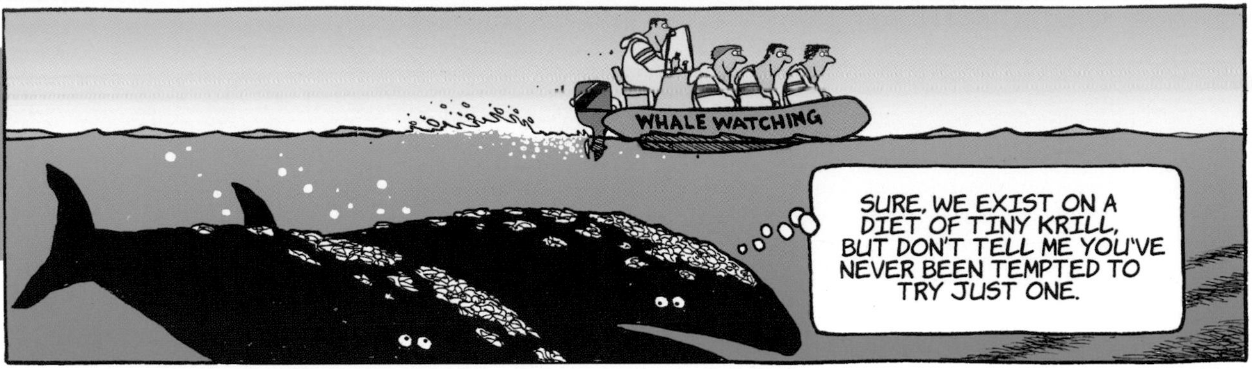
WHALE WATCHING
SURE, WE EXIST ON A DIET OF TINY KRILL, BUT DON'T TELL ME YOU'VE NEVER BEEN TEMPTED TO TRY JUST ONE.

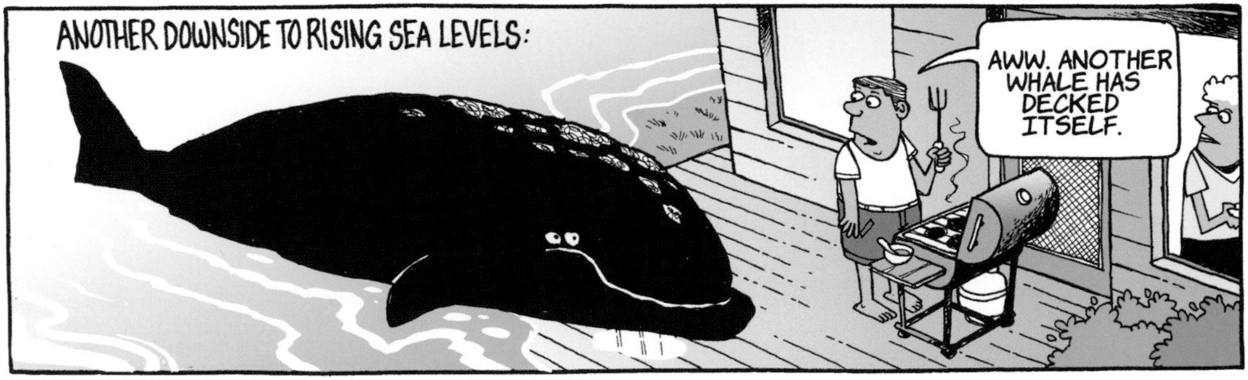
ANOTHER DOWNSIDE TO RISING SEA LEVELS:
AWW. ANOTHER WHALE HAS DECKED ITSELF.

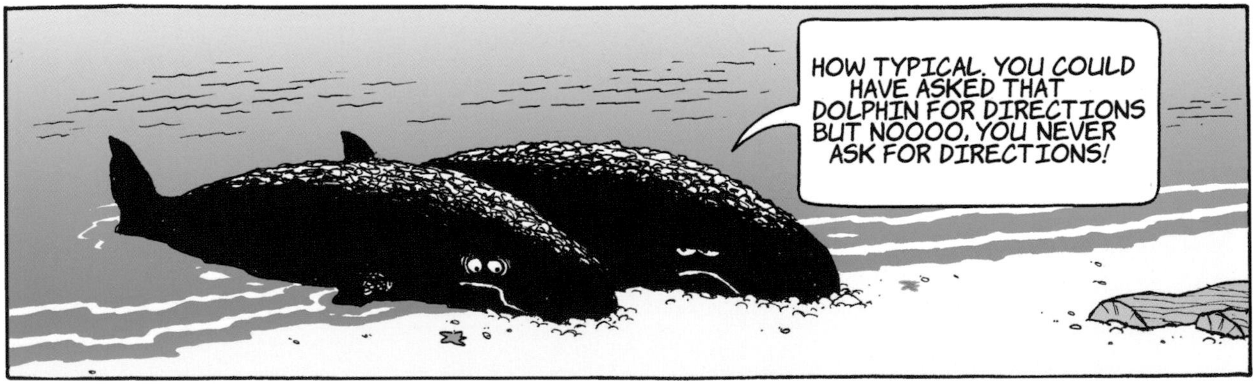
HOW TYPICAL. YOU COULD HAVE ASKED THAT DOLPHIN FOR DIRECTIONS BUT NOOOO, YOU NEVER ASK FOR DIRECTIONS!

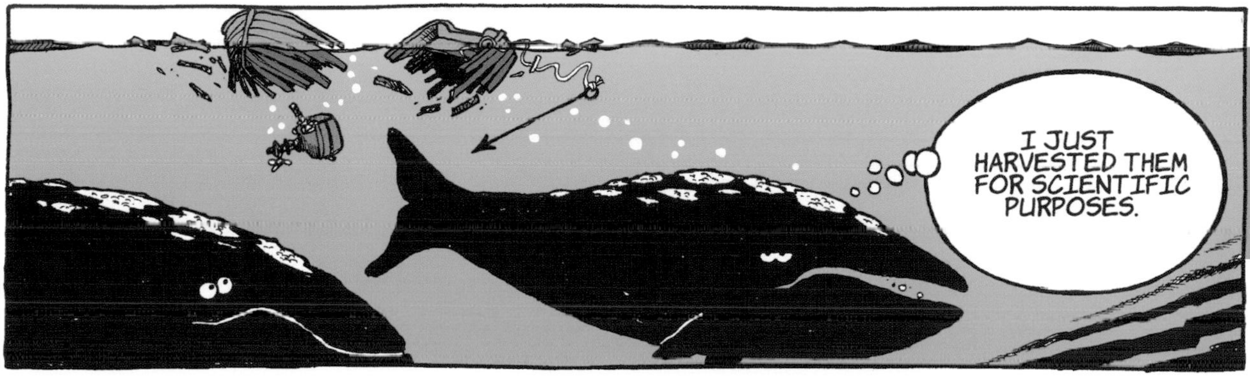
I JUST HARVESTED THEM FOR SCIENTIFIC PURPOSES.

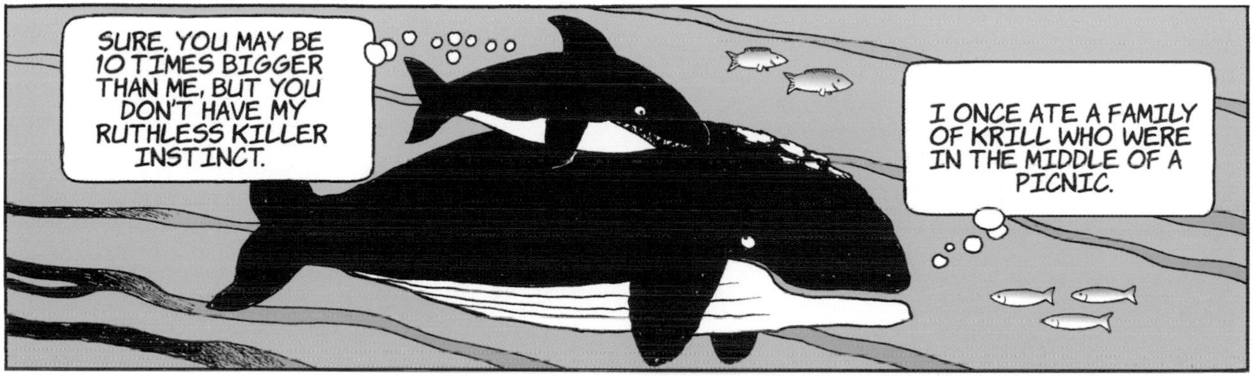
SURE, YOU MAY BE 10 TIMES BIGGER THAN ME, BUT YOU DON'T HAVE MY RUTHLESS KILLER INSTINCT.
I ONCE ATE A FAMILY OF KRILL WHO WERE IN THE MIDDLE OF A PICNIC.

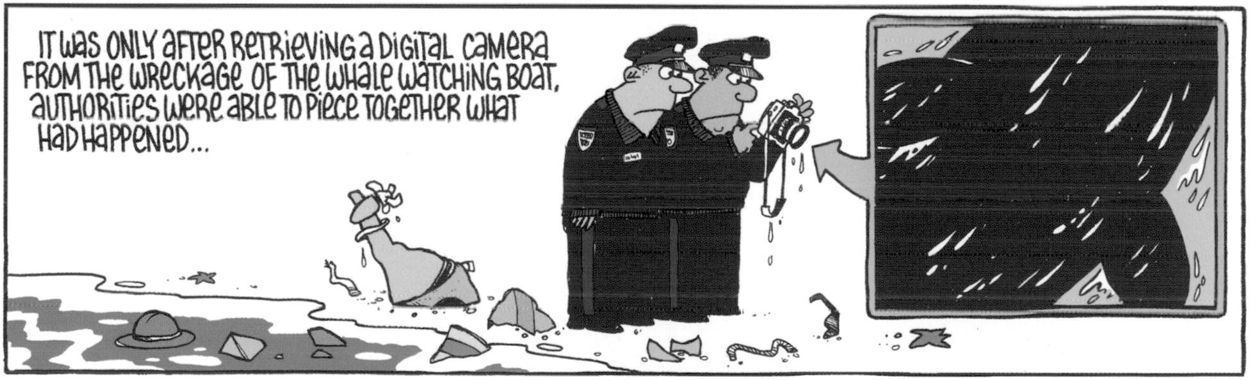
IT WAS ONLY AFTER RETRIEVING A DIGITAL CAMERA FROM THE WRECKAGE OF THE WHALE WATCHING BOAT, AUTHORITIES WERE ABLE TO PIECE TOGETHER WHAT HAD HAPPENED...

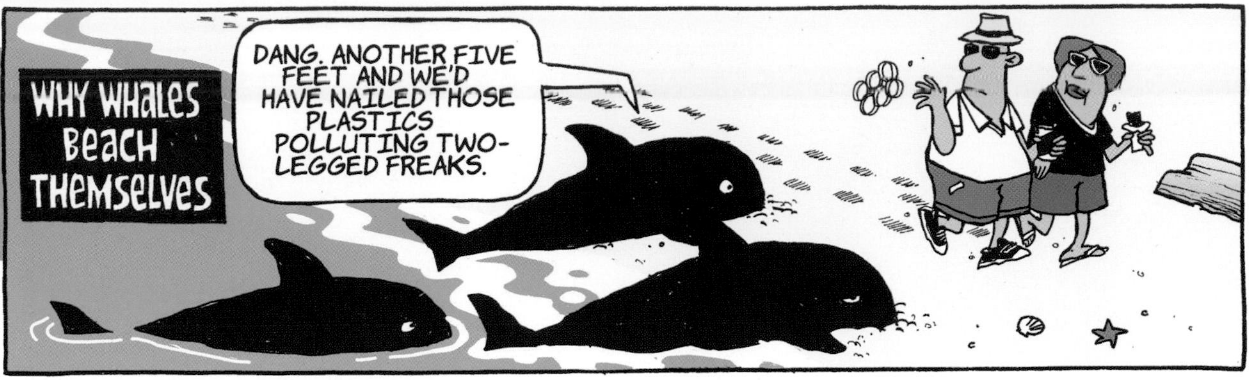
WHY WHALES BEACH THEMSELVES
DANG. ANOTHER FIVE FEET AND WE'D HAVE NAILED THOSE PLASTICS POLLUTING TWO-LEGGED FREAKS.

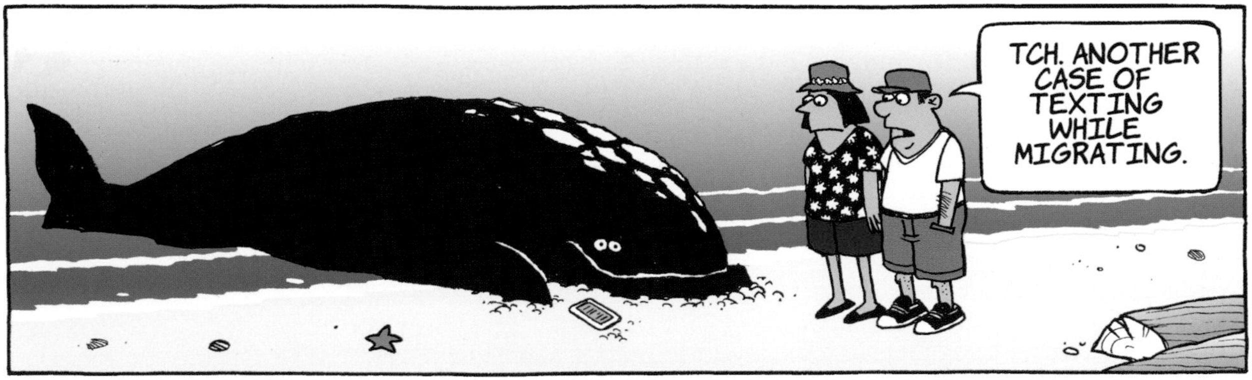
TCH. ANOTHER CASE OF TEXTING WHILE MIGRATING.

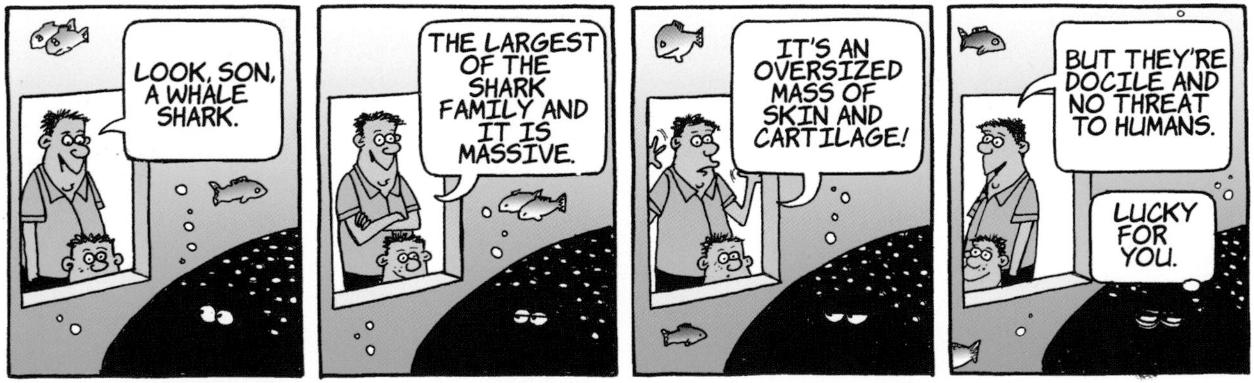
LOOK, SON, A WHALE SHARK.
THE LARGEST OF THE SHARK FAMILY AND IT IS MASSIVE.
IT'S AN OVERSIZED MASS OF SKIN AND CARTILAGE!
BUT THEY'RE DOCILE AND NO THREAT TO HUMANS.
LUCKY FOR YOU.

RAKISH REPTILES 4

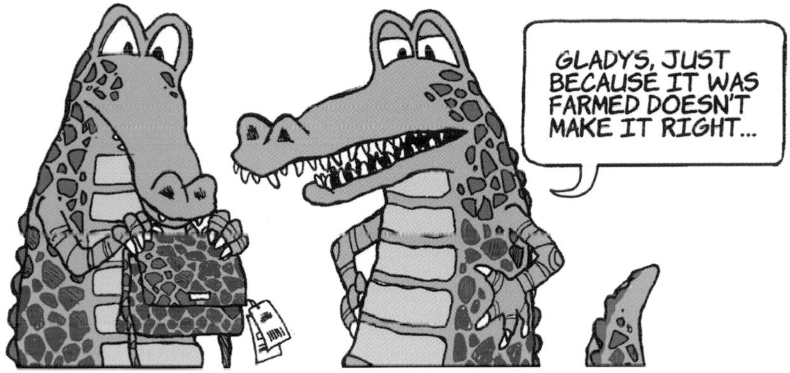

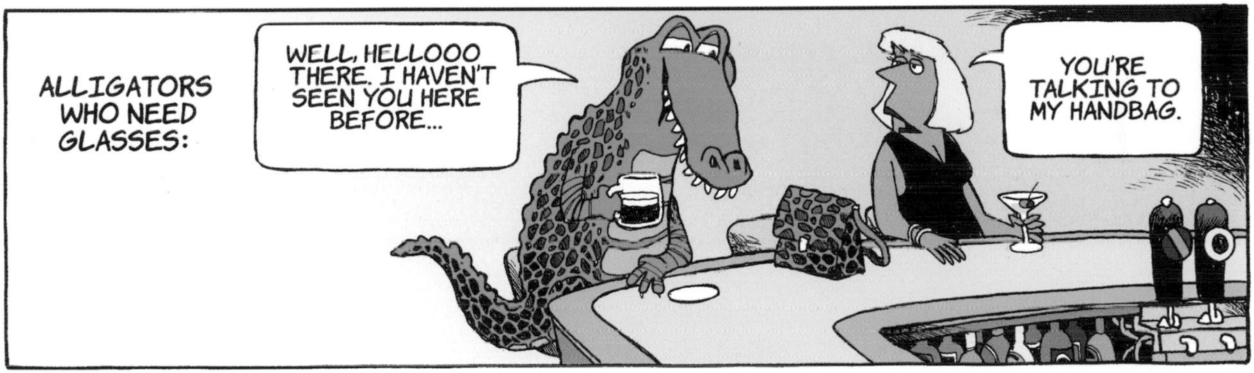

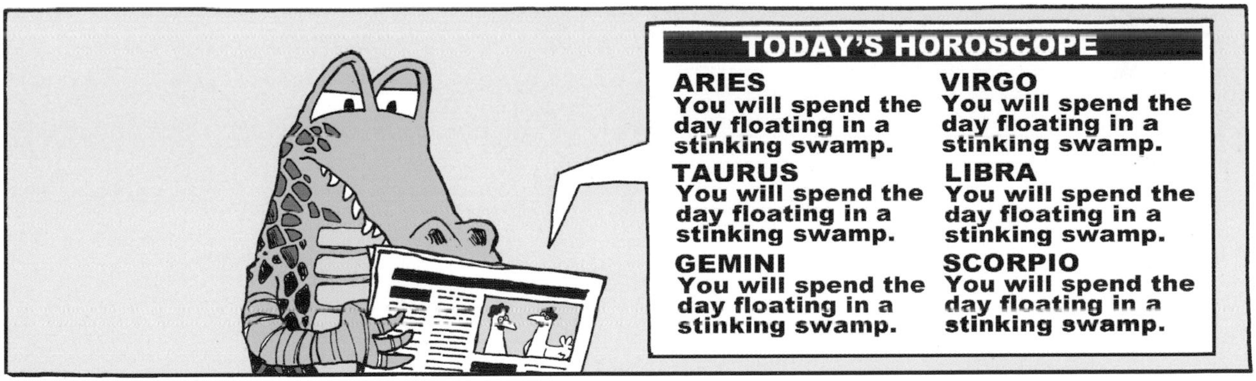

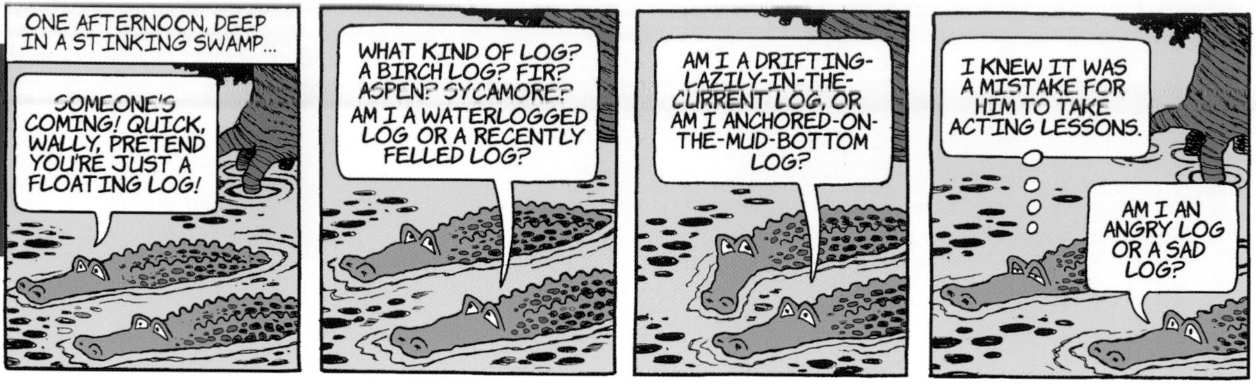
ONE AFTERNOON, DEEP IN A STINKING SWAMP...
SOMEONE'S COMING! QUICK, WALLY, PRETEND YOU'RE JUST A FLOATING LOG!
WHAT KIND OF LOG? A BIRCH LOG? FIR? ASPEN? SYCAMORE?
AM I A WATERLOGGED LOG OR A RECENTLY FELLED LOG?
AM I A DRIFTING-LAZILY-IN-THE-CURRENT LOG, OR AM I ANCHORED-ON-THE-MUD-BOTTOM LOG?
I KNEW IT WAS A MISTAKE FOR HIM TO TAKE ACTING LESSONS.
AM I AN ANGRY LOG OR A SAD LOG?

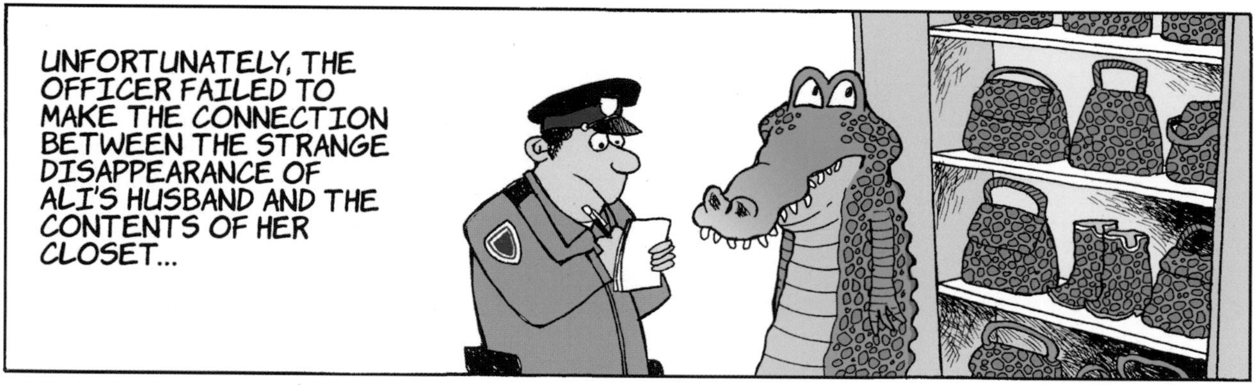
UNFORTUNATELY, THE OFFICER FAILED TO MAKE THE CONNECTION BETWEEN THE STRANGE DISAPPEARANCE OF ALI'S HUSBAND AND THE CONTENTS OF HER CLOSET...

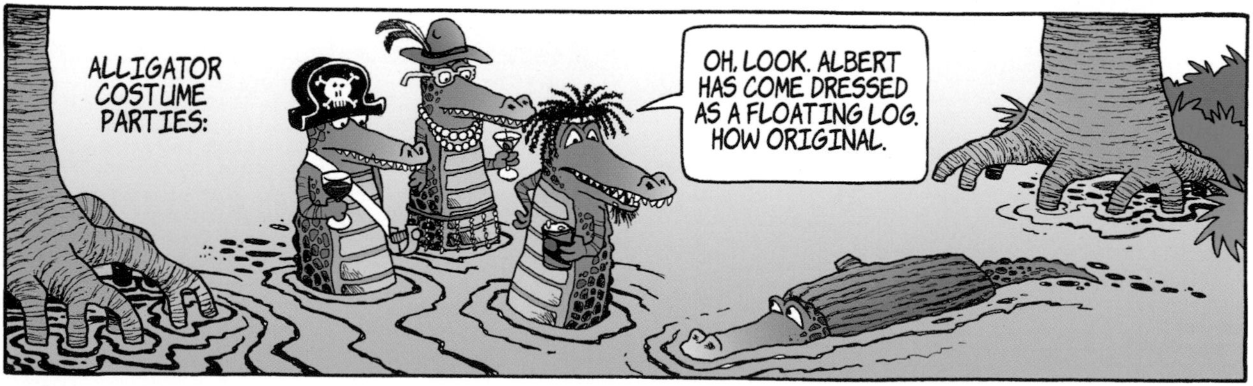
ALLIGATOR COSTUME PARTIES:
OH, LOOK. ALBERT HAS COME DRESSED AS A FLOATING LOG. HOW ORIGINAL.

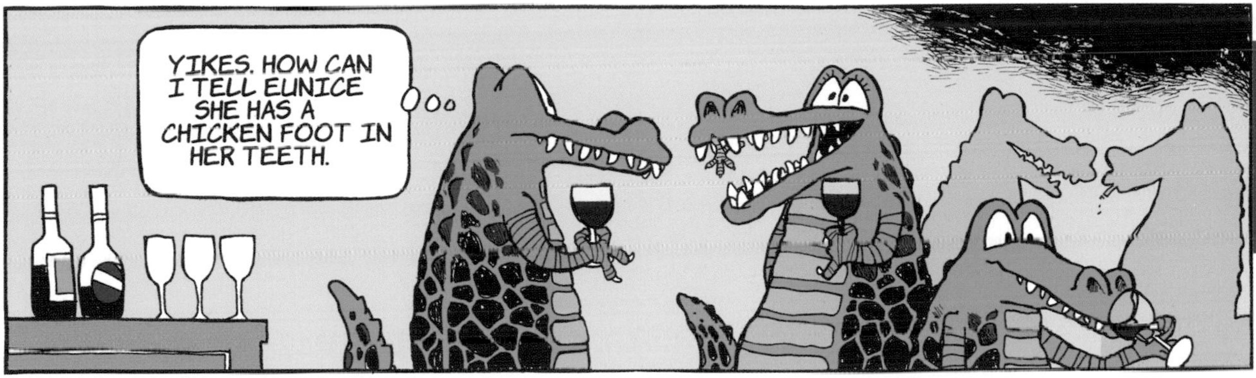
YIKES. HOW CAN I TELL EUNICE SHE HAS A CHICKEN FOOT IN HER TEETH.

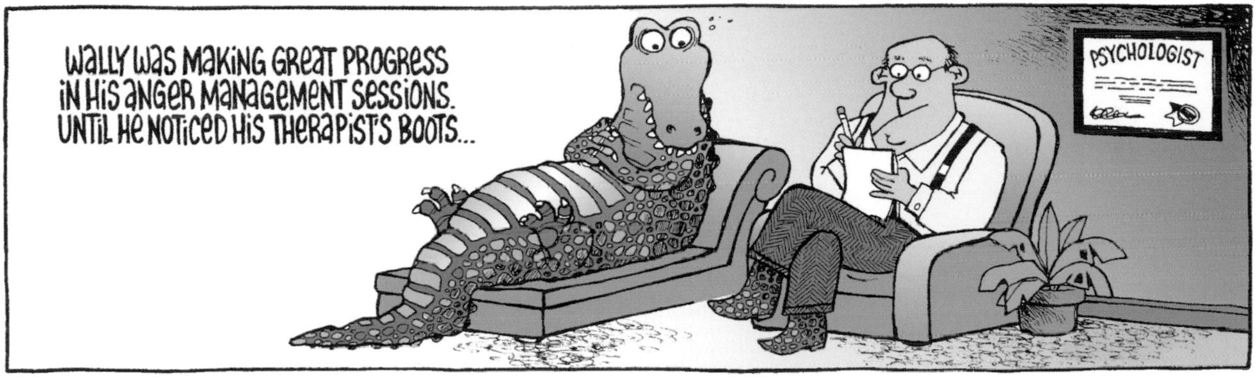
WALLY WAS MAKING GREAT PROGRESS IN HIS ANGER MANAGEMENT SESSIONS. UNTIL HE NOTICED HIS THERAPIST'S BOOTS...
PSYCHOLOGIST

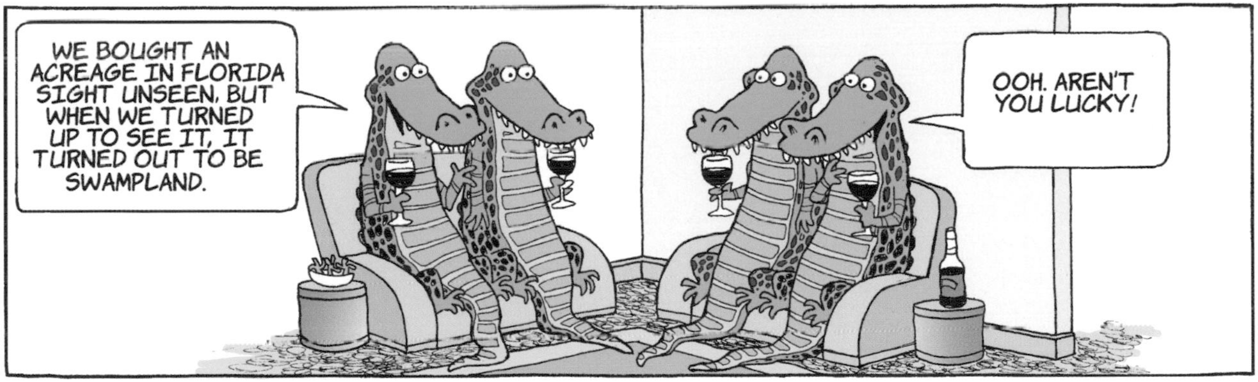
WE BOUGHT AN ACREAGE IN FLORIDA SIGHT UNSEEN, BUT WHEN WE TURNED UP TO SEE IT, IT TURNED OUT TO BE SWAMPLAND.
OOH. AREN'T YOU LUCKY!

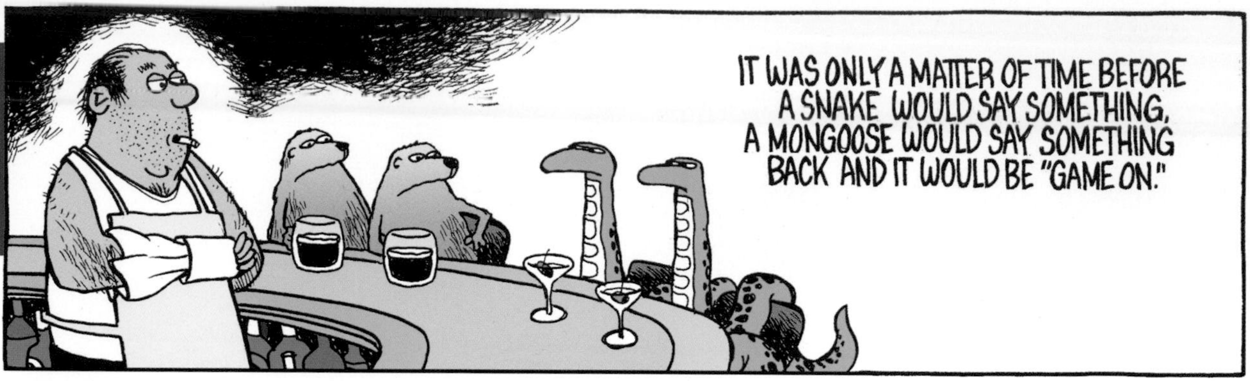
IT WAS ONLY A MATTER OF TIME BEFORE A SNAKE WOULD SAY SOMETHING, A MONGOOSE WOULD SAY SOMETHING BACK AND IT WOULD BE "GAME ON."

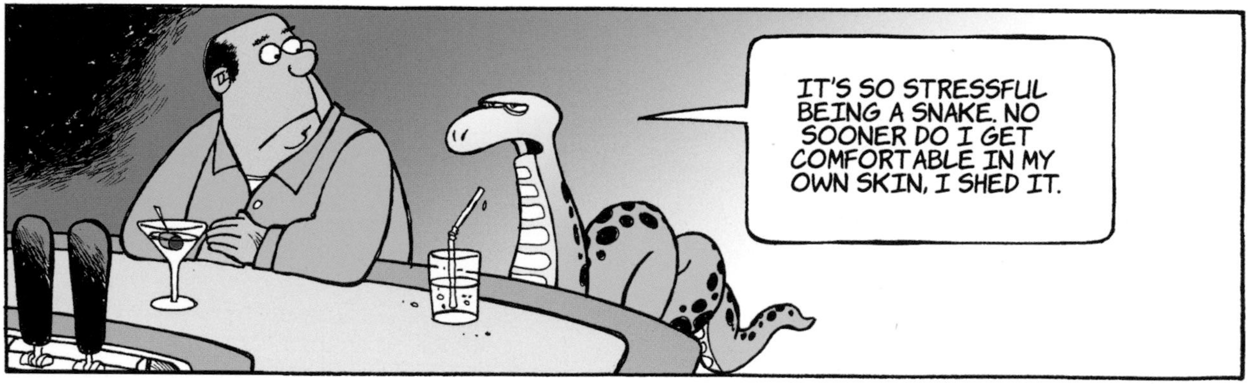
IT'S SO STRESSFUL BEING A SNAKE. NO SOONER DO I GET COMFORTABLE IN MY OWN SKIN, I SHED IT.

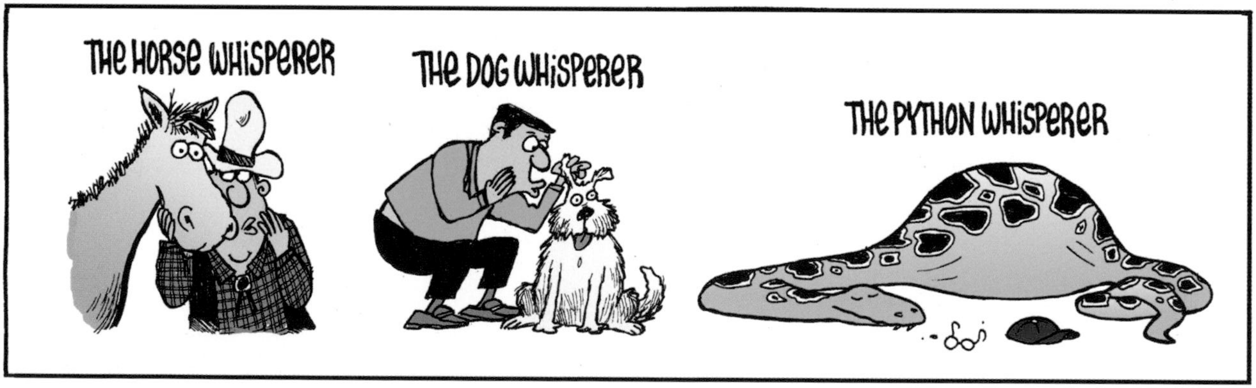
THE HORSE WHISPERER
THE DOG WHISPERER
THE PYTHON WHISPERER

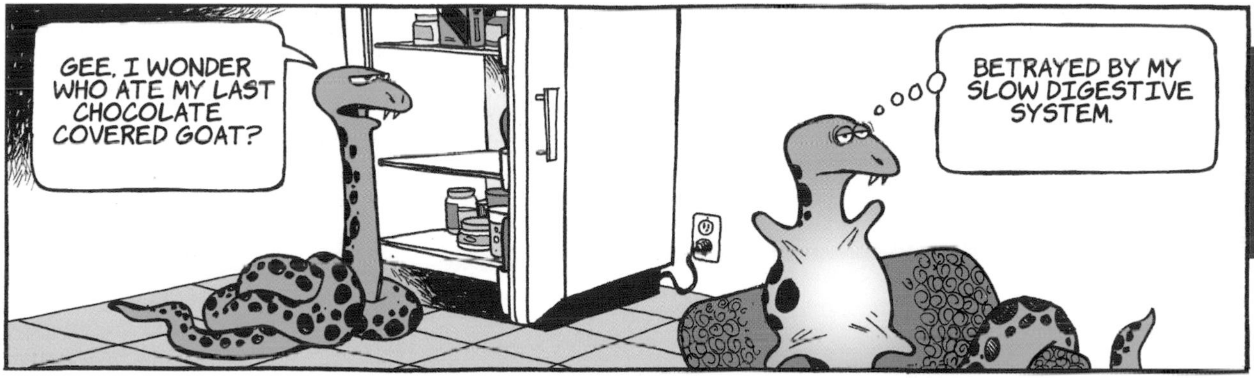
GEE, I WONDER WHO ATE MY LAST CHOCOLATE COVERED GOAT?
BETRAYED BY MY SLOW DIGESTIVE SYSTEM.

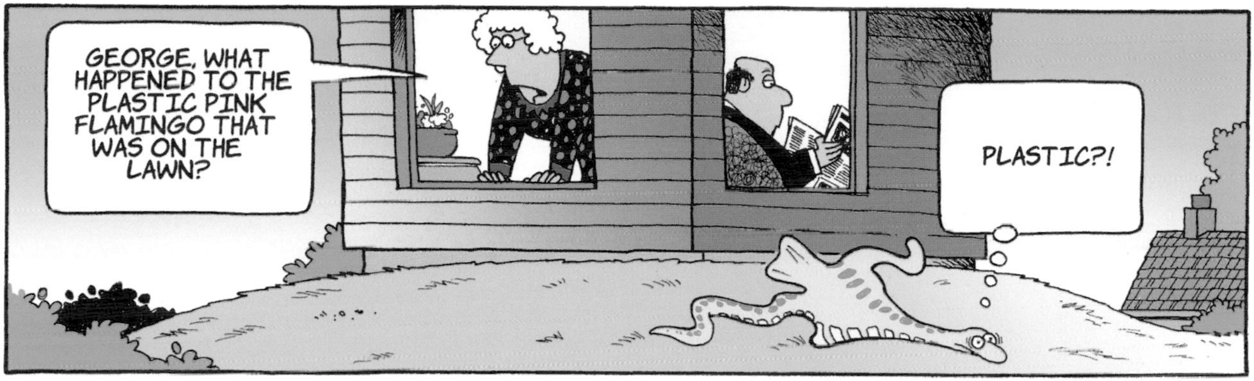
GEORGE, WHAT HAPPENED TO THE PLASTIC PINK FLAMINGO THAT WAS ON THE LAWN?
PLASTIC?!

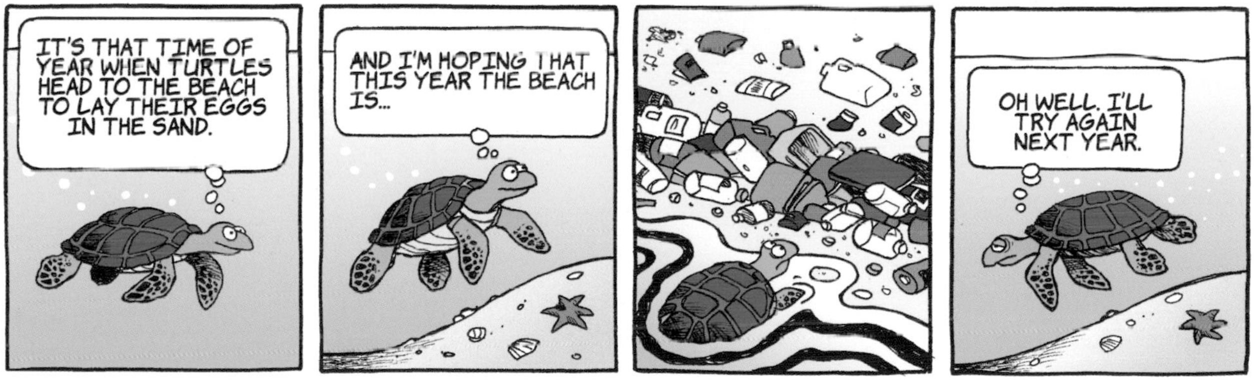
IT'S THAT TIME OF YEAR WHEN TURTLES HEAD TO THE BEACH TO LAY THEIR EGGS IN THE SAND.
AND I'M HOPING THAT THIS YEAR THE BEACH IS...
OH WELL. I'LL TRY AGAIN NEXT YEAR.

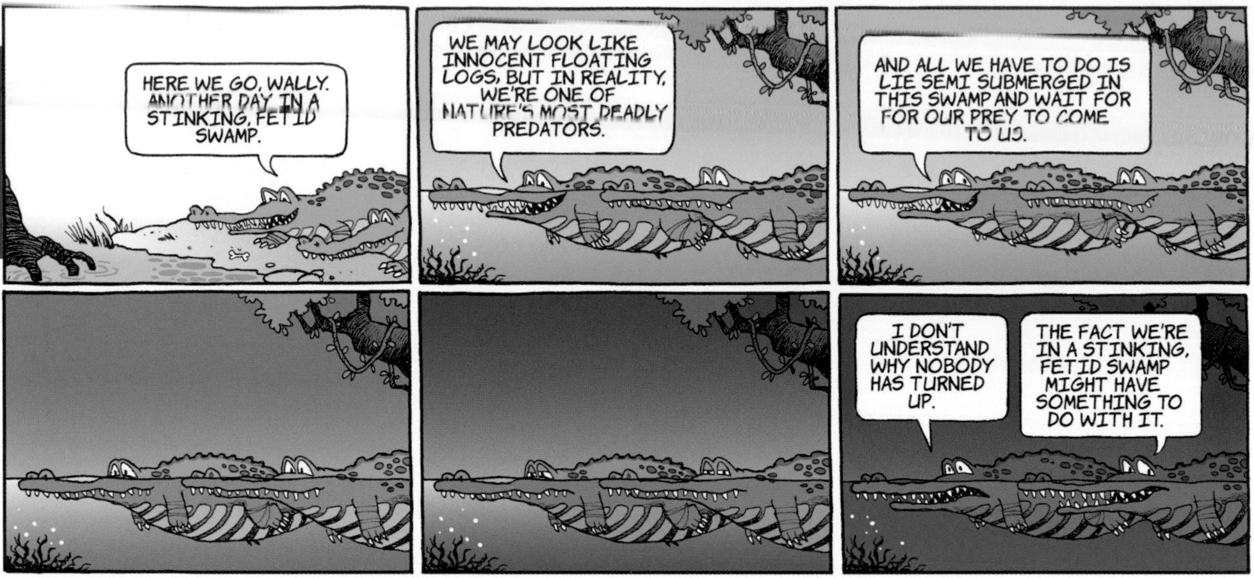
HERE WE GO, WALLY. ANOTHER DAY IN A STINKING, FETID SWAMP.
WE MAY LOOK LIKE INNOCENT FLOATING LOGS, BUT IN REALITY, WE'RE ONE OF NATURE'S MOST DEADLY PREDATORS.
AND ALL WE HAVE TO DO IS LIE SEMI SUBMERGED IN THIS SWAMP AND WAIT FOR FOR OUR PREY TO COME TO US.
I DON'T UNDERSTAND WHY NOBODY HAS TURNED UP.
THE FACT WE'RE IN A STINKING, FETID SWAMP MIGHT HAVE SOMETHING TO DO WITH IT.

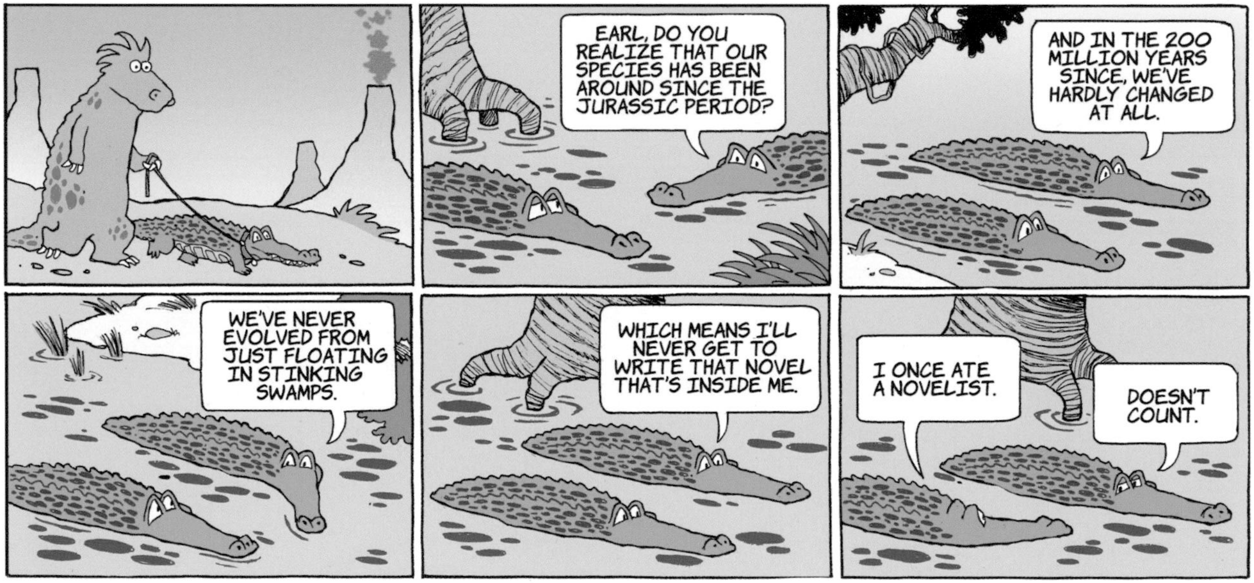
EARL, DO YOU REALIZE THAT OUR SPECIES HAS BEEN AROUND SINCE THE JURASSIC PERIOD?
AND IN THE 200 MILLION YEARS SINCE, WE'VE HARDLY CHANGED AT ALL.
WE'VE NEVER EVOLVED FROM JUST FLOATING IN STINKING SWAMPS.
WHICH MEANS I'LL NEVER GET TO WRITE THAT NOVEL THAT'S INSIDE ME.
I ONCE ATE A NOVELIST.
DOESN'T COUNT.

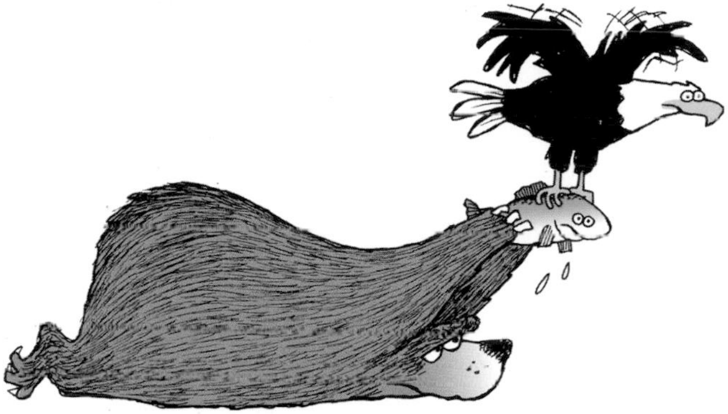

EXUBERANT EAGLES 5

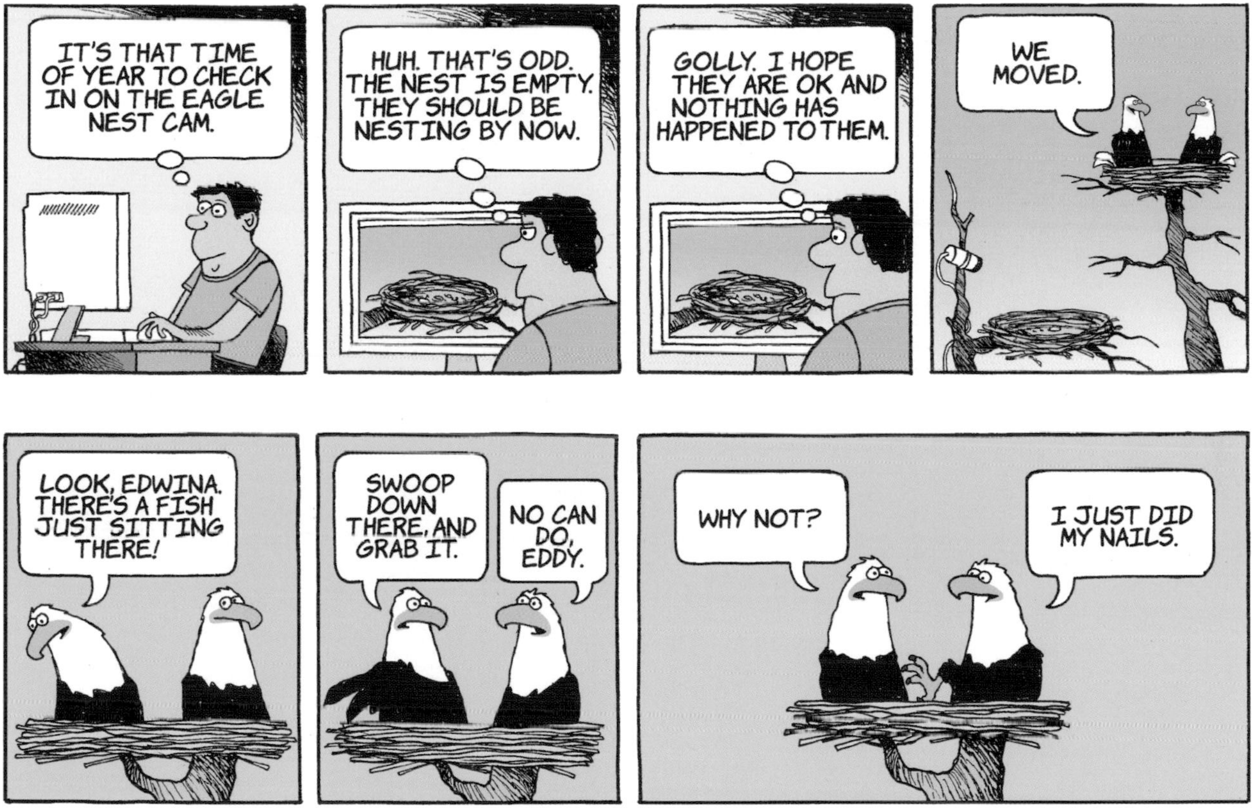

IT'S THAT TIME OF YEAR TO CHECK IN ON THE EAGLE NEST CAM.
HUH. THAT'S ODD. THE NEST IS EMPTY. THEY SHOULD BE NESTING BY NOW.
GOLLY. I HOPE THEY ARE OK AND NOTHING HAS HAPPENED TO THEM.
WE MOVED.
LOOK, EDWINA. THERE'S A FISH JUST SITTING THERE!
SWOOP DOWN THERE, AND GRAB IT.
NO CAN DO, EDDY.
WHY NOT?
I JUST DID MY NAILS.

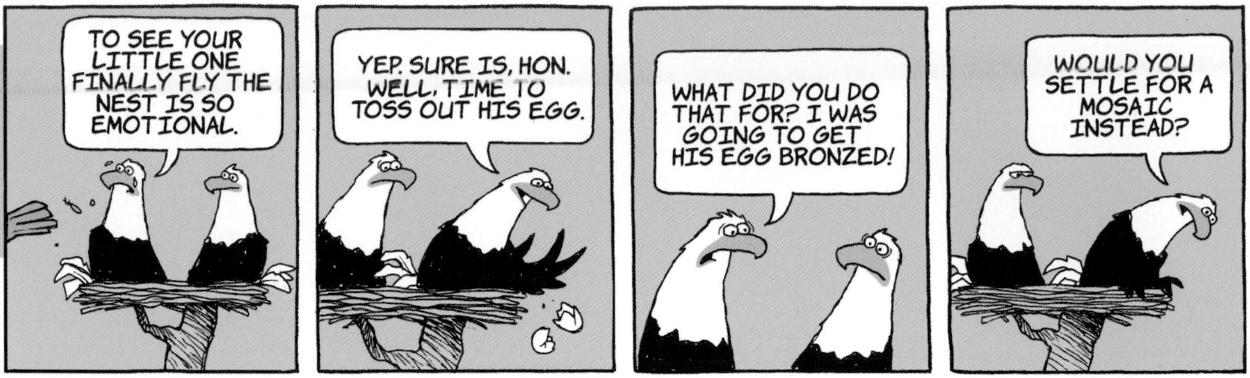
TO SEE YOUR LITTLE ONE FINALLY FLY THE NEST IS SO EMOTIONAL.
YEP. SURE IS, HON. WELL, TIME TO TOSS OUT HIS EGG.
WHAT DID YOU DO THAT FOR? I WAS GOING TO GET HIS EGG BRONZED!
WOULD YOU SETTLE FOR A MOSAIC INSTEAD?

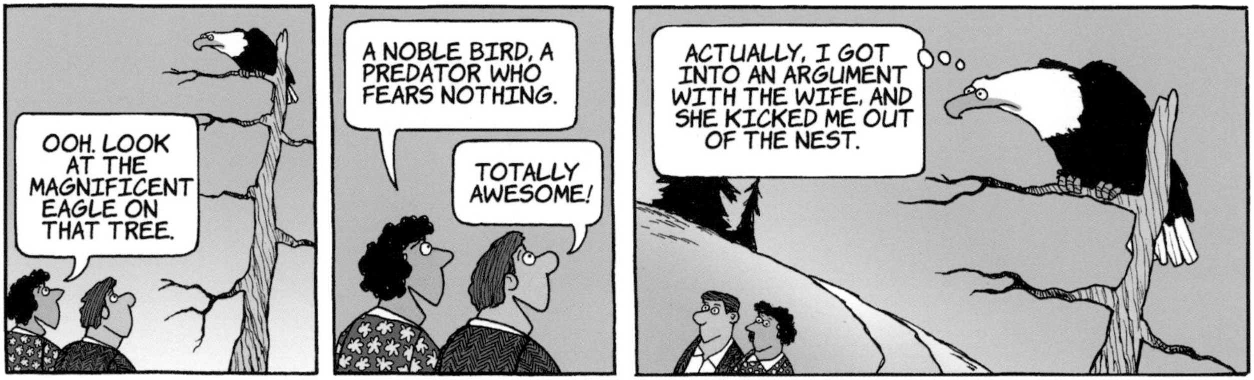
OOH. LOOK AT THE MAGNIFICENT EAGLE ON THAT TREE.
A NOBLE BIRD, A PREDATOR WHO FEARS NOTHING.
TOTALLY AWESOME!
ACTUALLY, I GOT INTO AN ARGUMENT WITH THE WIFE, AND SHE KICKED ME OUT OF THE NEST.

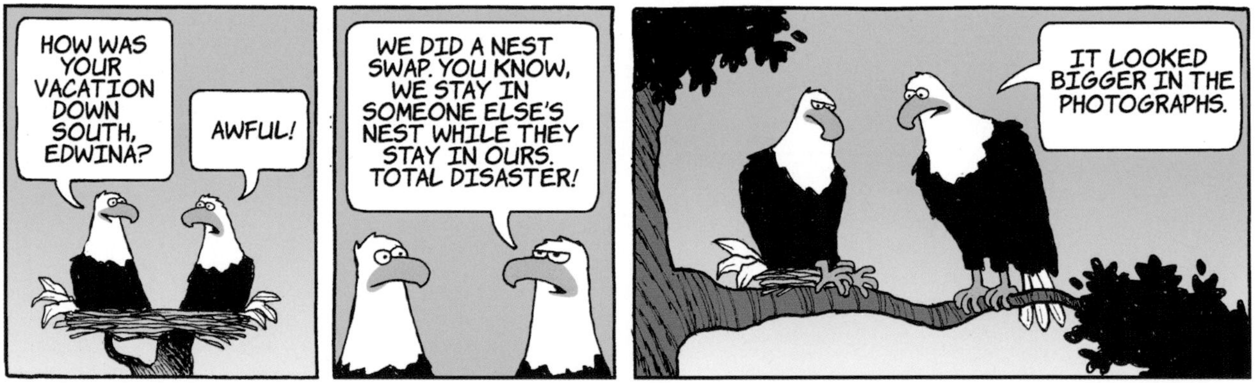
HOW WAS YOUR VACATION DOWN SOUTH, EDWINA?
AWFUL!
WE DID A NEST SWAP. YOU KNOW, WE STAY IN SOMEONE ELSE'S NEST WHILE THEY STAY IN OURS. TOTAL DISASTER!
IT LOOKED BIGGER IN THE PHOTOGRAPHS.

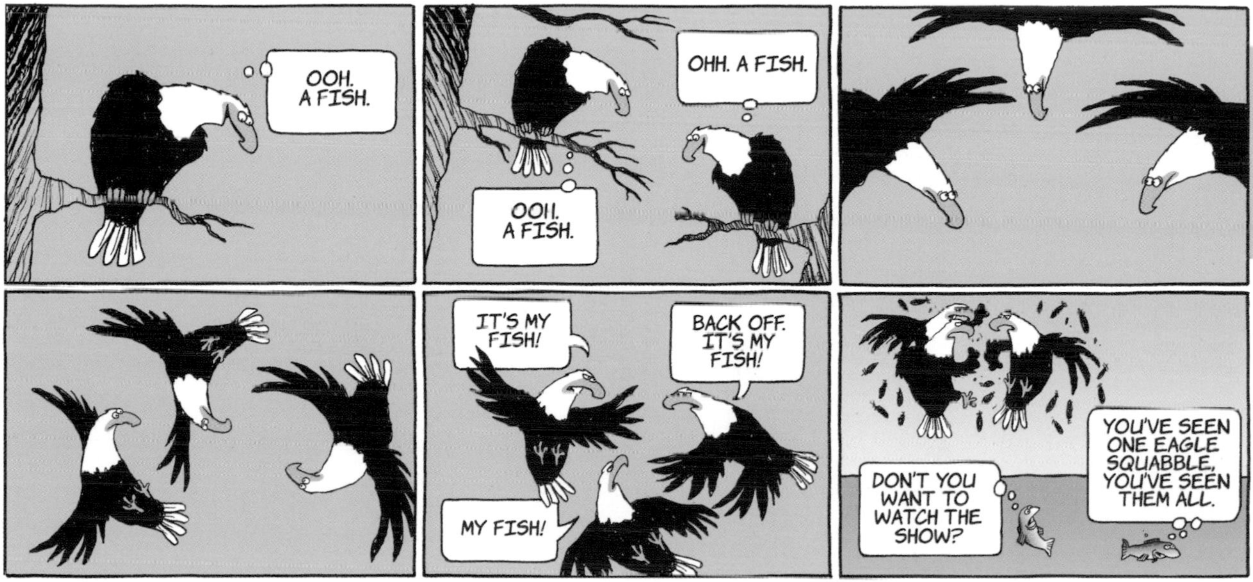
OOH. A FISH.
OHH. A FISH.
OOH. A FISH.
IT'S MY FISH!
BACK OFF. IT'S MY FISH!
MY FISH!
DON'T YOU WANT TO WATCH THE SHOW?
YOU'VE SEEN ONE EAGLE SQUABBLE, YOU'VE SEEN THEM ALL.

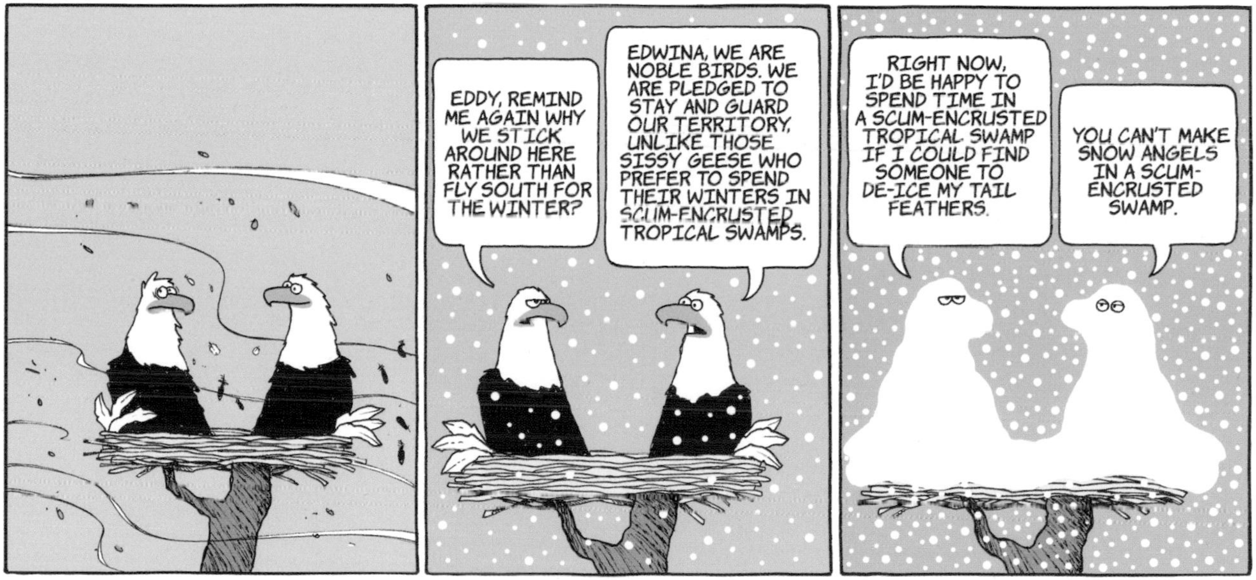
EDDY, REMIND ME AGAIN WHY WE STICK AROUND HERE RATHER THAN FLY SOUTH FOR THE WINTER?
EDWINA, WE ARE NOBLE BIRDS. WE ARE PLEDGED TO STAY AND GUARD OUR TERRITORY, UNLIKE THOSE SISSY GEESE WHO PREFER TO SPEND THEIR WINTERS IN SCUM-ENCRUSTED TROPICAL SWAMPS.
RIGHT NOW, I'D BE HAPPY TO SPEND TIME IN A SCUM-ENCRUSTED TROPICAL SWAMP IF I COULD FIND SOMEONE TO DE-ICE MY TAIL FEATHERS.
YOU CAN'T MAKE SNOW ANGELS IN A SCUM-ENCRUSTED SWAMP.

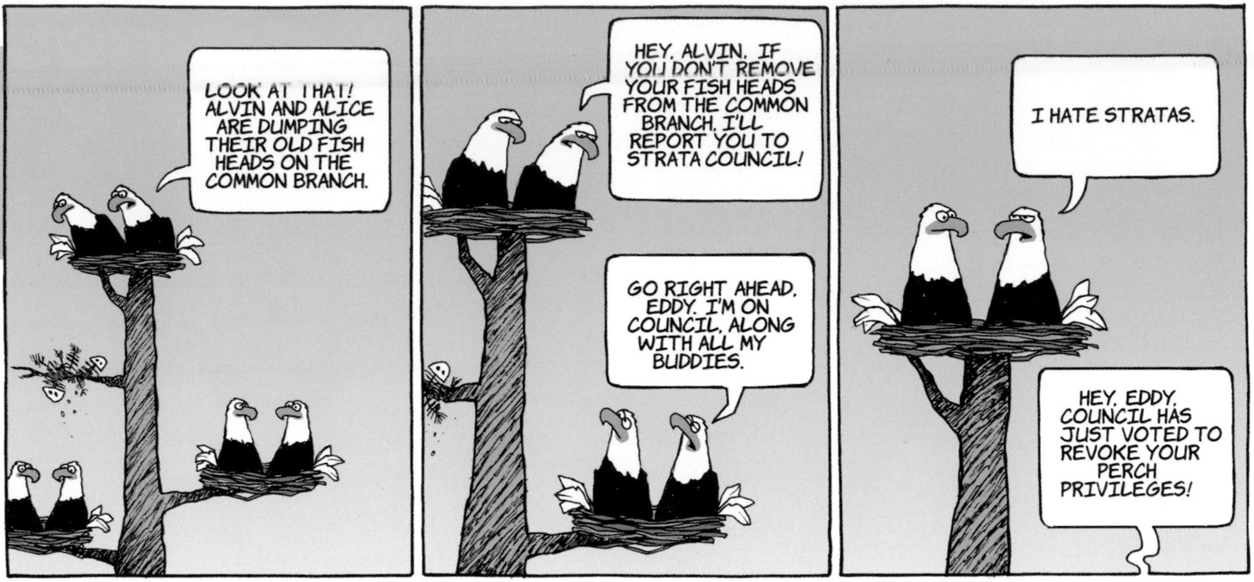
LOOK AT THAT! ALVIN AND ALICE ARE DUMPING THEIR OLD FISH HEADS ON THE COMMON BRANCH.
HEY, ALVIN, IF YOU DON'T REMOVE YOUR FISH HEADS FROM THE COMMON BRANCH, I'LL REPORT YOU TO STRATA COUNCIL!
GO RIGHT AHEAD, EDDY. I'M ON COUNCIL, ALONG WITH ALL MY BUDDIES.
I HATE STRATAS.
HEY, EDDY, COUNCIL HAS JUST VOTED TO REVOKE YOUR PERCH PRIVILEGES!

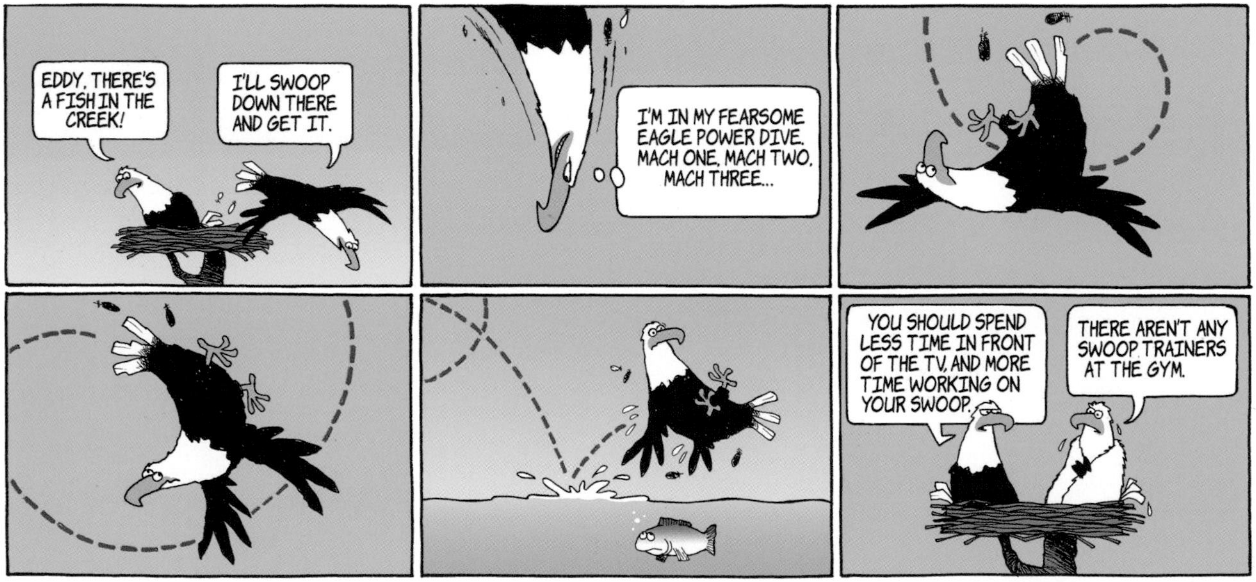
EDDY, THERE'S A FISH IN THE CREEK!
I'LL SWOOP DOWN THERE AND GET IT.
I'M IN MY FEARSOME EAGLE POWER DIVE. MACH ONE, MACH TWO, MACH THREE...
YOU SHOULD SPEND LESS TIME IN FRONT OF THE TV, AND MORE TIME WORKING ON YOUR SWOOP.
THERE AREN'T ANY SWOOP TRAINERS AT THE GYM.

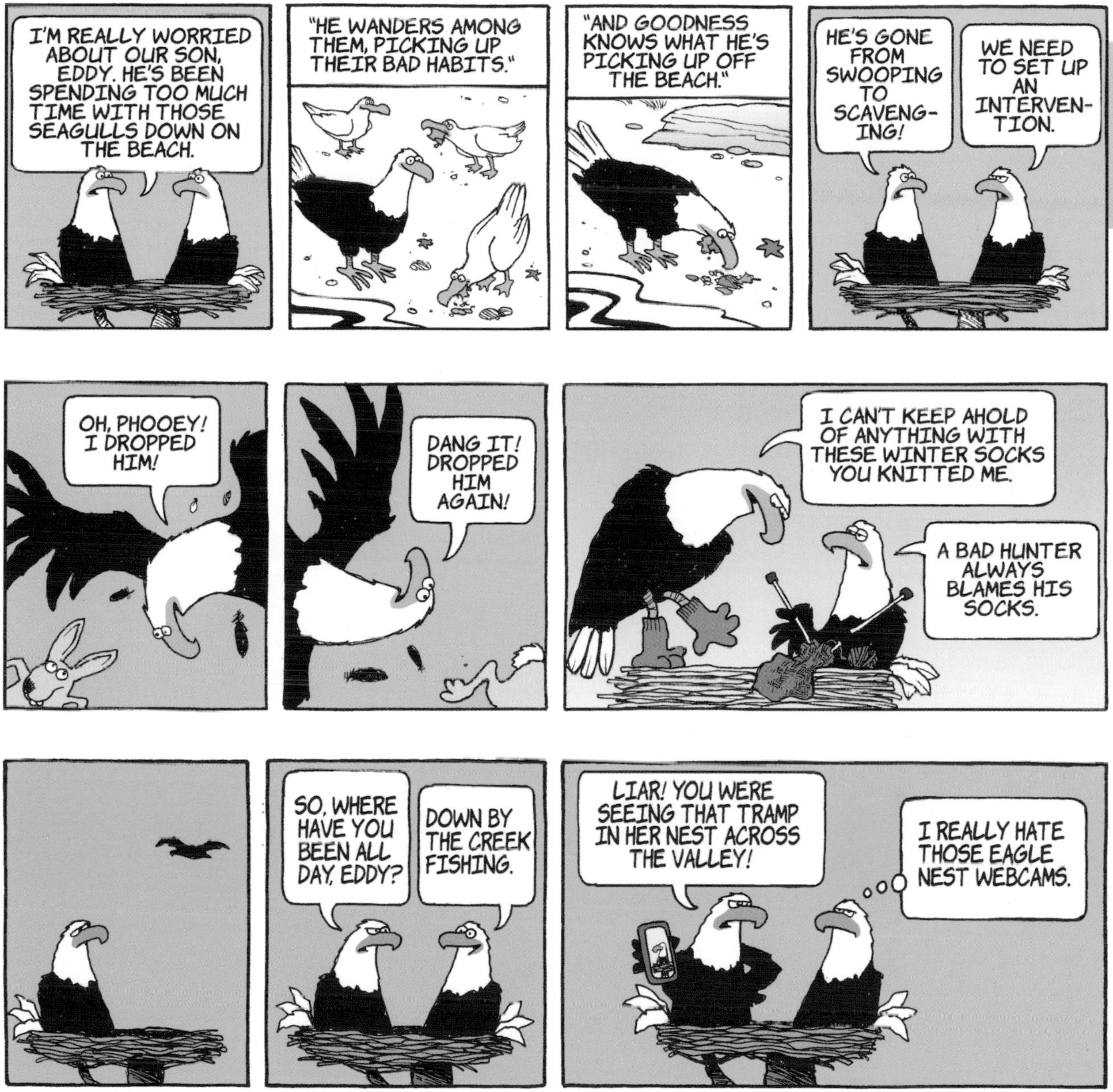
I'M REALLY WORRIED ABOUT OUR SON, EDDY. HE'S BEEN SPENDING TOO MUCH TIME WITH THOSE SEAGULLS DOWN ON THE BEACH.
"HE WANDERS AMONG THEM, PICKING UP THEIR BAD HABITS."
"AND GOODNESS KNOWS WHAT HE'S PICKING UP OFF THE BEACH."
HE'S GONE FROM SWOOPING TO SCAVENG-ING!
WE NEED TO SET UP AN INTERVEN-TION.
OH, PHOOEY! I DROPPED HIM!
DANG IT! DROPPED HIM AGAIN!
I CAN'T KEEP AHOLD OF ANYTHING WITH THESE WINTER SOCKS YOU KNITTED ME.
A BAD HUNTER ALWAYS BLAMES HIS SOCKS.
SO, WHERE HAVE YOU BEEN ALL DAY, EDDY?
DOWN BY THE CREEK FISHING.
LIAR! YOU WERE SEEING THAT TRAMP IN HER NEST ACROSS THE VALLEY!
I REALLY HATE THOSE EAGLE NEST WEBCAMS.

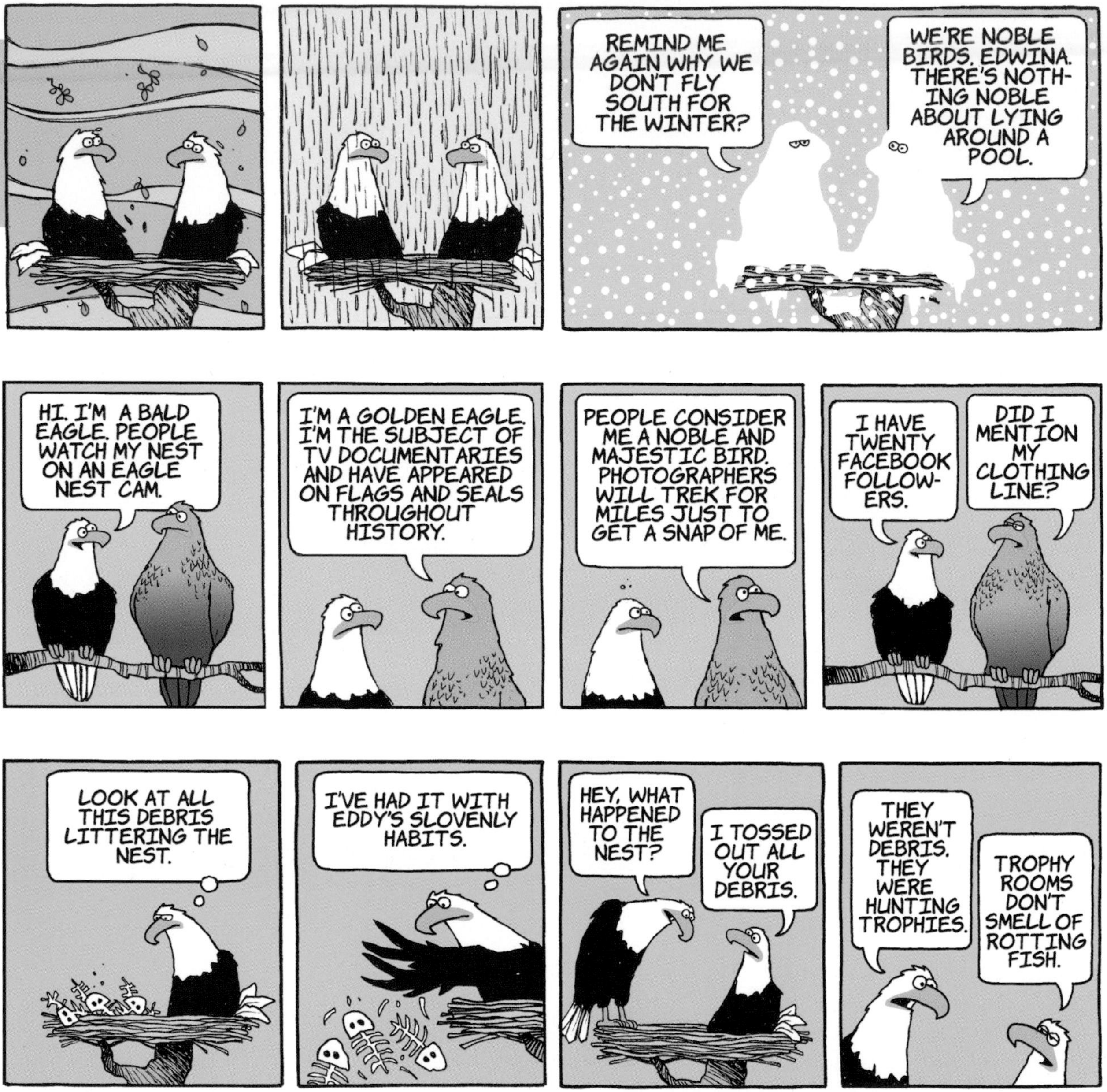
REMIND ME AGAIN WHY WE DON'T FLY SOUTH FOR THE WINTER?
WE'RE NOBLE BIRDS, EDWINA. THERE'S NOTHING NOBLE ABOUT LYING AROUND A POOL.
HI. I'M A BALD EAGLE. PEOPLE WATCH MY NEST ON AN EAGLE NEST CAM.
I'M A GOLDEN EAGLE. I'M THE SUBJECT OF TV DOCUMENTARIES AND HAVE APPEARED ON FLAGS AND SEALS THROUGHOUT HISTORY.
PEOPLE CONSIDER ME A NOBLE AND MAJESTIC BIRD. PHOTOGRAPHERS WILL TREK FOR MILES JUST TO GET A SNAP OF ME.
I HAVE TWENTY FACEBOOK FOLLOWERS.
DID I MENTION MY CLOTHING LINE?
LOOK AT ALL THIS DEBRIS LITTERING THE NEST.
I'VE HAD IT WITH EDDY'S SLOVENLY HABITS.
HEY, WHAT HAPPENED TO THE NEST?
I TOSSED OUT ALL YOUR DEBRIS.
THEY WEREN'T DEBRIS. THEY WERE HUNTING TROPHIES.
TROPHY ROOMS DON'T SMELL OF ROTTING FISH.

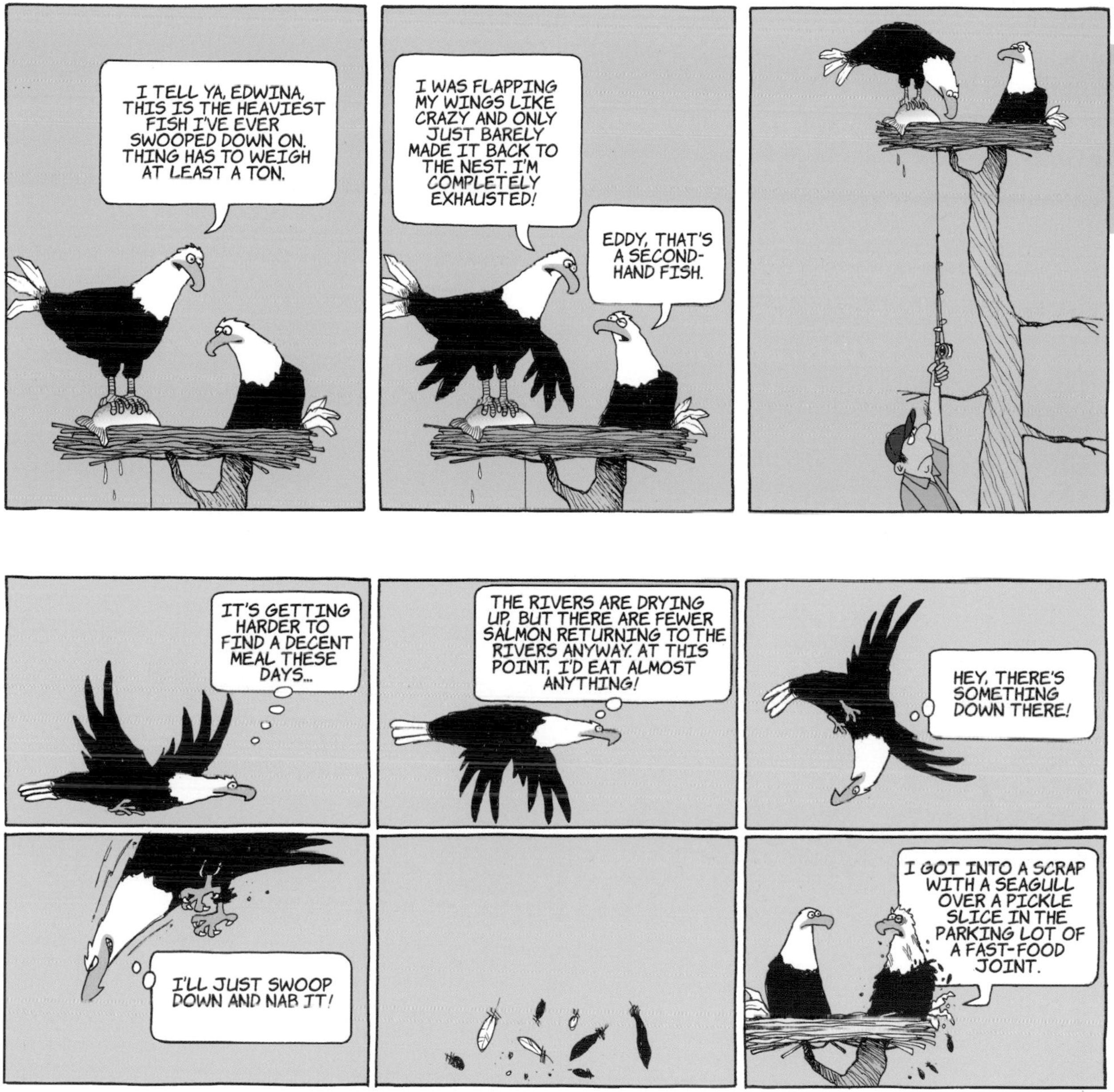
I TELL YA, EDWINA, THIS IS THE HEAVIEST FISH I'VE EVER SWOOPED DOWN ON. THING HAS TO WEIGH AT LEAST A TON.
I WAS FLAPPING MY WINGS LIKE CRAZY AND ONLY JUST BARELY MADE IT BACK TO THE NEST. I'M COMPLETELY EXHAUSTED!
EDDY, THAT'S A SECOND-HAND FISH.
IT'S GETTING HARDER TO FIND A DECENT MEAL THESE DAYS...
THE RIVERS ARE DRYING UP, BUT THERE ARE FEWER SALMON RETURNING TO THE RIVERS ANYWAY. AT THIS POINT, I'D EAT ALMOST ANYTHING!
HEY, THERE'S SOMETHING DOWN THERE!
I'LL JUST SWOOP DOWN AND NAB IT!
I GOT INTO A SCRAP WITH A SEAGULL OVER A PICKLE SLICE IN THE PARKING LOT OF A FAST-FOOD JOINT.

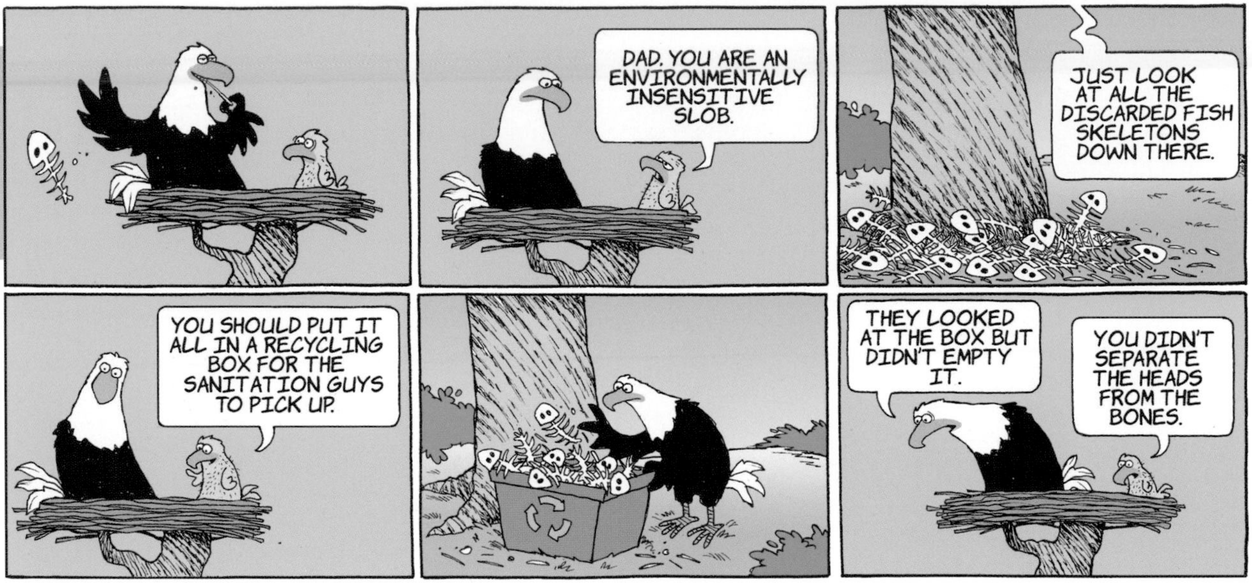
DAD. YOU ARE AN ENVIRONMENTALLY INSENSITIVE SLOB.
JUST LOOK AT ALL THE DISCARDED FISH SKELETONS DOWN THERE.
YOU SHOULD PUT IT ALL IN A RECYCLING BOX FOR THE SANITATION GUYS TO PICK UP.
THEY LOOKED AT THE BOX BUT DIDN'T EMPTY IT.
YOU DIDN'T SEPARATE THE HEADS FROM THE BONES.

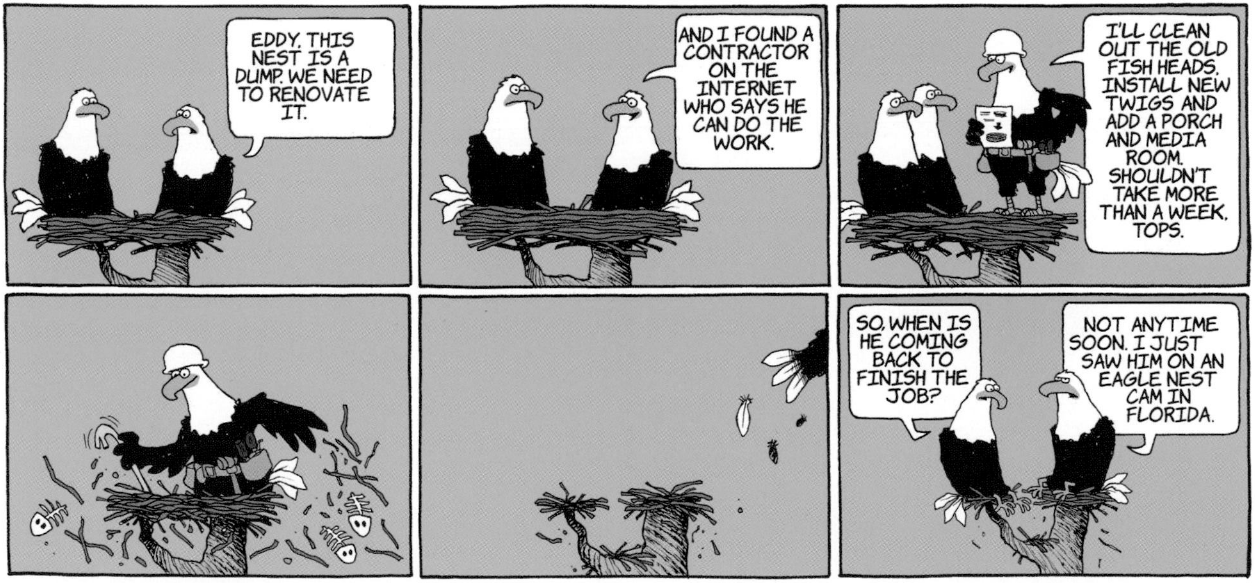
EDDY. THIS NEST IS A DUMP. WE NEED TO RENOVATE IT.
AND I FOUND A CONTRACTOR ON THE INTERNET WHO SAYS HE CAN DO THE WORK.
I'LL CLEAN OUT THE OLD FISH HEADS. INSTALL NEW TWIGS AND ADD A PORCH AND MEDIA ROOM. SHOULDN'T TAKE MORE THAN A WEEK. TOPS.
SO, WHEN IS HE COMING BACK TO FINISH THE JOB?
NOT ANYTIME SOON. I JUST SAW HIM ON AN EAGLE NEST CAM IN FLORIDA.

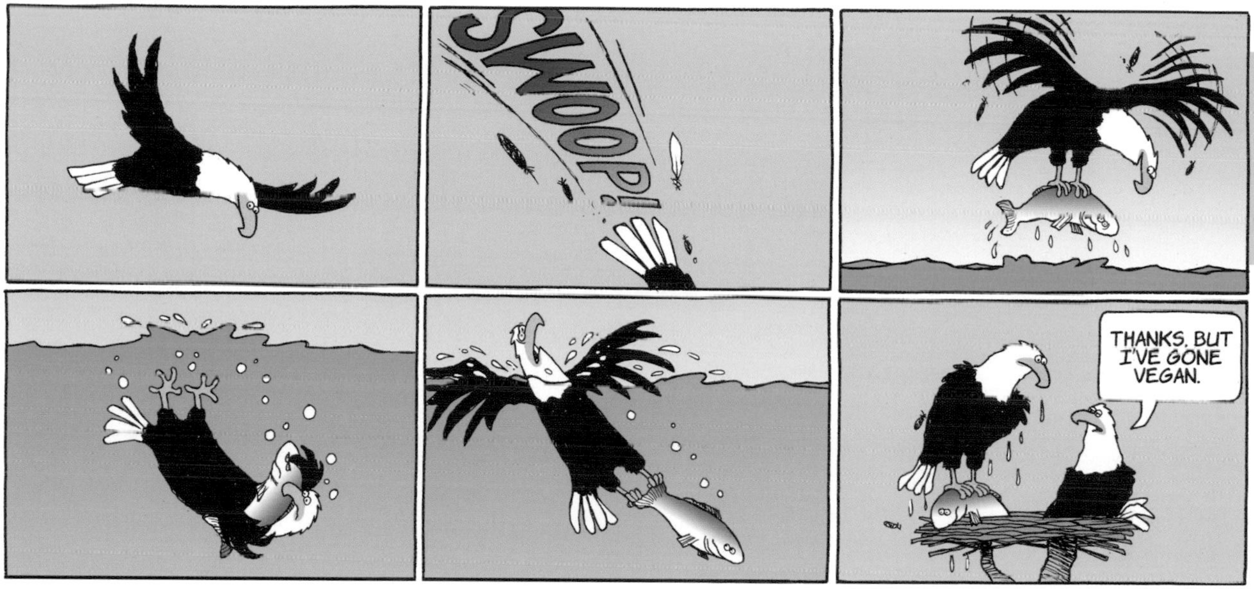
SWOOP!!
THANKS, BUT I'VE GONE VEGAN.

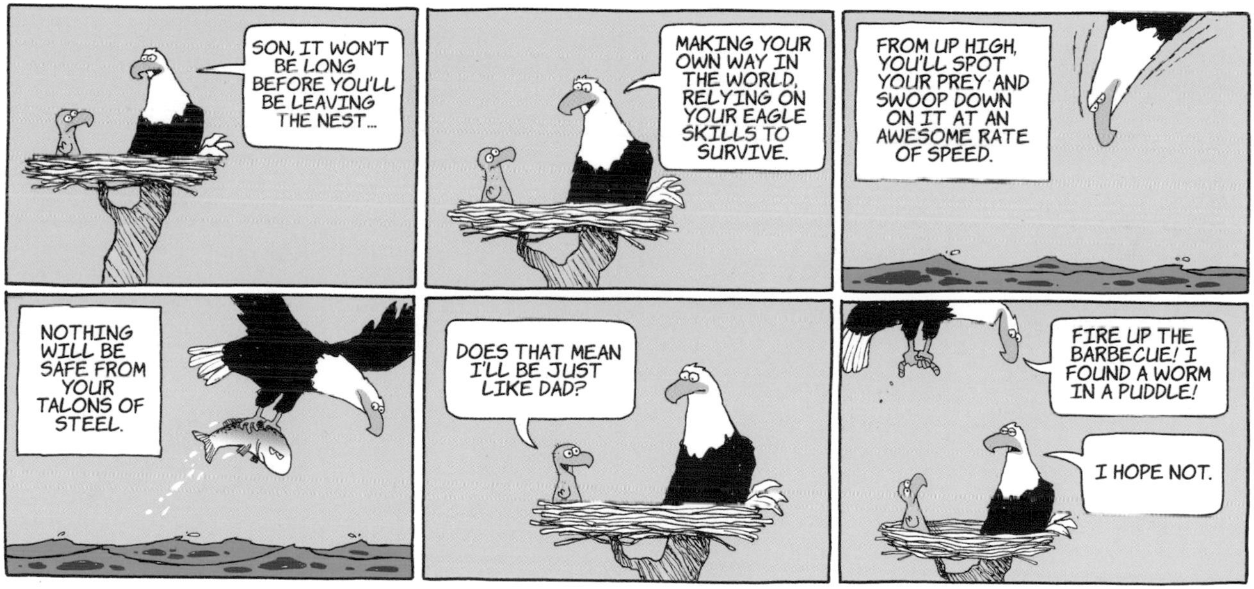
SON, IT WON'T BE LONG BEFORE YOU'LL BE LEAVING THE NEST...
MAKING YOUR OWN WAY IN THE WORLD, RELYING ON YOUR EAGLE SKILLS TO SURVIVE.
FROM UP HIGH, YOU'LL SPOT YOUR PREY AND SWOOP DOWN ON IT AT AN AWESOME RATE OF SPEED.
NOTHING WILL BE SAFE FROM YOUR TALONS OF STEEL.
DOES THAT MEAN I'LL BE JUST LIKE DAD?
FIRE UP THE BARBECUE! I FOUND A WORM IN A PUDDLE!
I HOPE NOT.

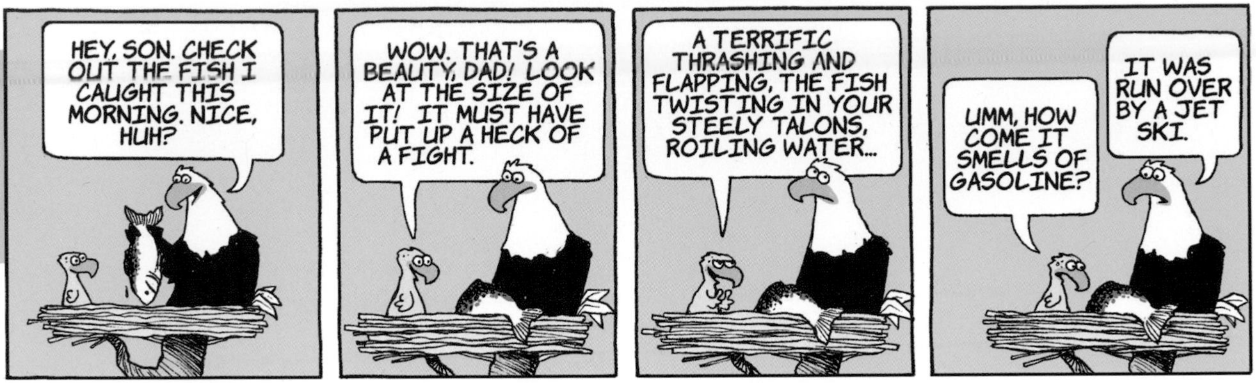
HEY, SON. CHECK OUT THE FISH I CAUGHT THIS MORNING. NICE, HUH?
WOW. THAT'S A BEAUTY, DAD! LOOK AT THE SIZE OF IT! IT MUST HAVE PUT UP A HECK OF A FIGHT.
A TERRIFIC THRASHING AND FLAPPING, THE FISH TWISTING IN YOUR STEELY TALONS, ROILING WATER...
UMM, HOW COME IT SMELLS OF GASOLINE?
IT WAS RUN OVER BY A JET SKI.

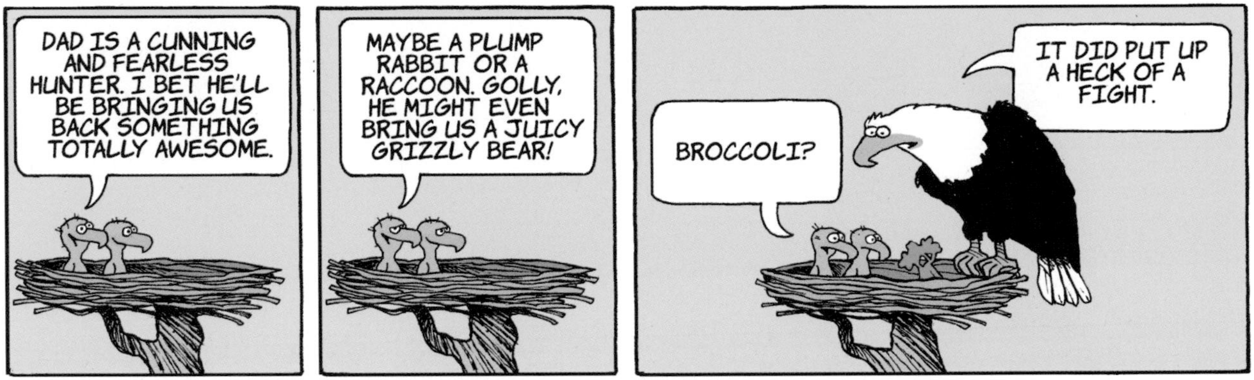
DAD IS A CUNNING AND FEARLESS HUNTER. I BET HE'LL BE BRINGING US BACK SOMETHING TOTALLY AWESOME.
MAYBE A PLUMP RABBIT OR A RACCOON. GOLLY, HE MIGHT EVEN BRING US A JUICY GRIZZLY BEAR!
BROCCOLI?
IT DID PUT UP A HECK OF A FIGHT.

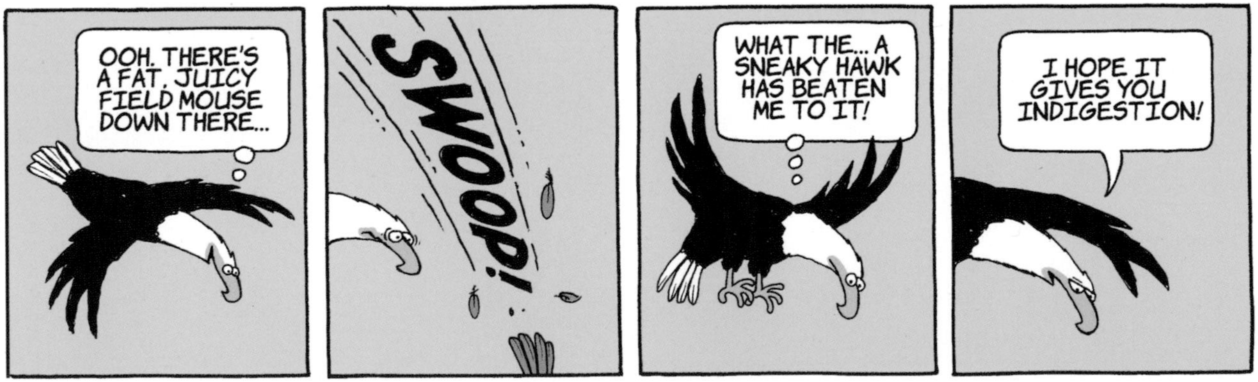
OOH. THERE'S A FAT, JUICY FIELD MOUSE DOWN THERE...
SWOOP!
WHAT THE... A SNEAKY HAWK HAS BEATEN ME TO IT!
I HOPE IT GIVES YOU INDIGESTION!

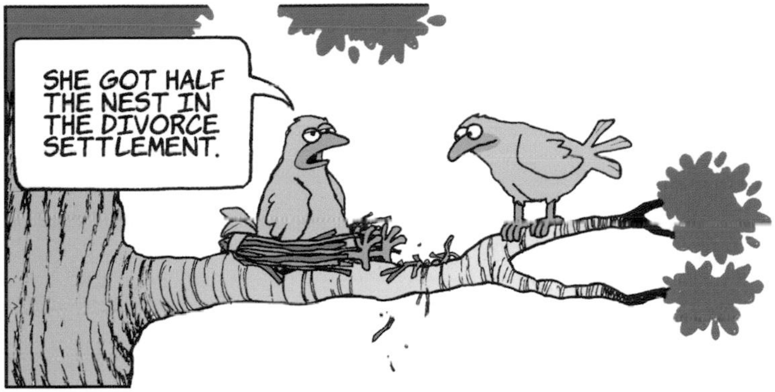
SHE GOT HALF THE NEST IN THE DIVORCE SETTLEMENT.

OTHER WINGED WONDERS 6

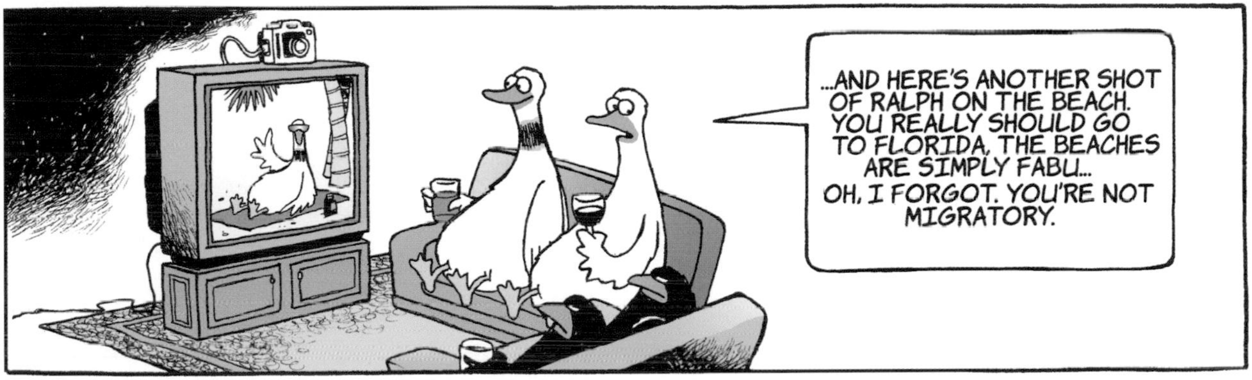
...AND HERE'S ANOTHER SHOT OF RALPH ON THE BEACH. YOU REALLY SHOULD GO TO FLORIDA, THE BEACHES ARE SIMPLY FABU... OH, I FORGOT. YOU'RE NOT MIGRATORY.

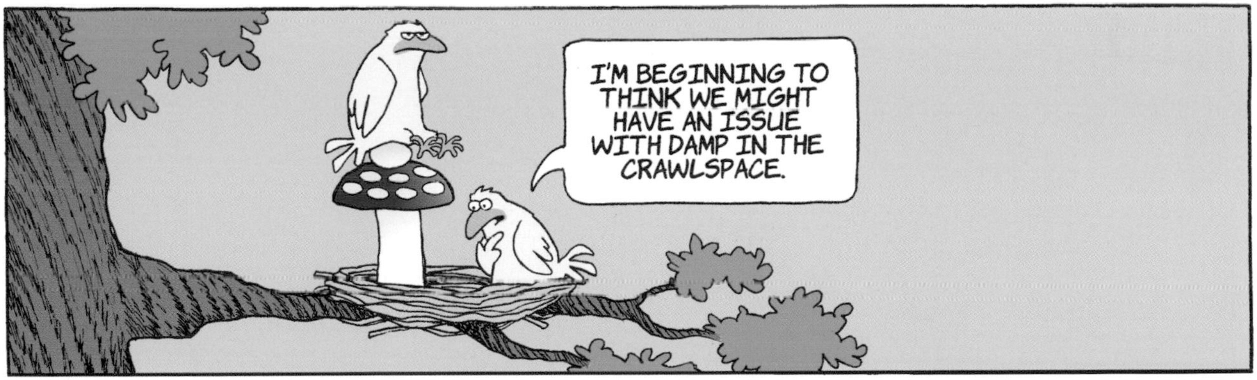
I'M BEGINNING TO THINK WE MIGHT HAVE AN ISSUE WITH DAMP IN THE CRAWLSPACE.

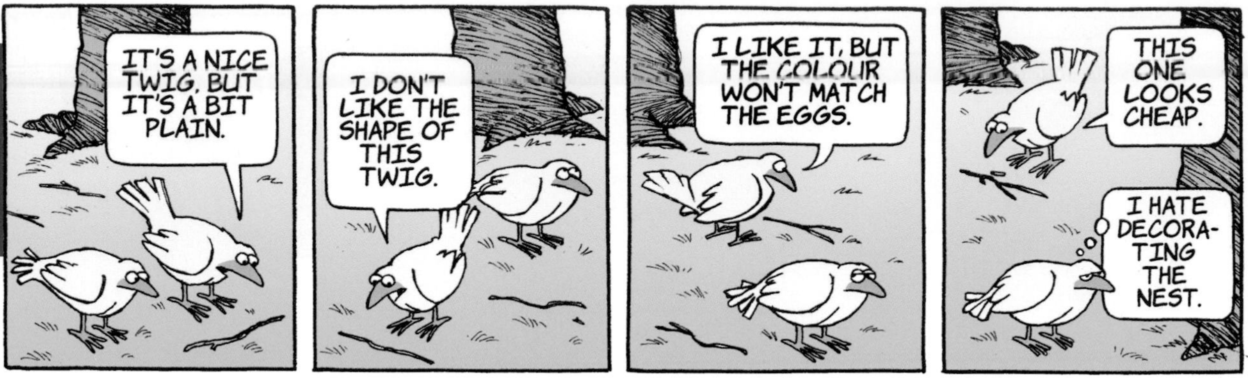
IT'S A NICE TWIG, BUT IT'S A BIT PLAIN.
I DON'T LIKE THE SHAPE OF THIS TWIG.
I LIKE IT, BUT THE COLOUR WON'T MATCH THE EGGS.
THIS ONE LOOKS CHEAP.
I HATE DECORATING THE NEST.

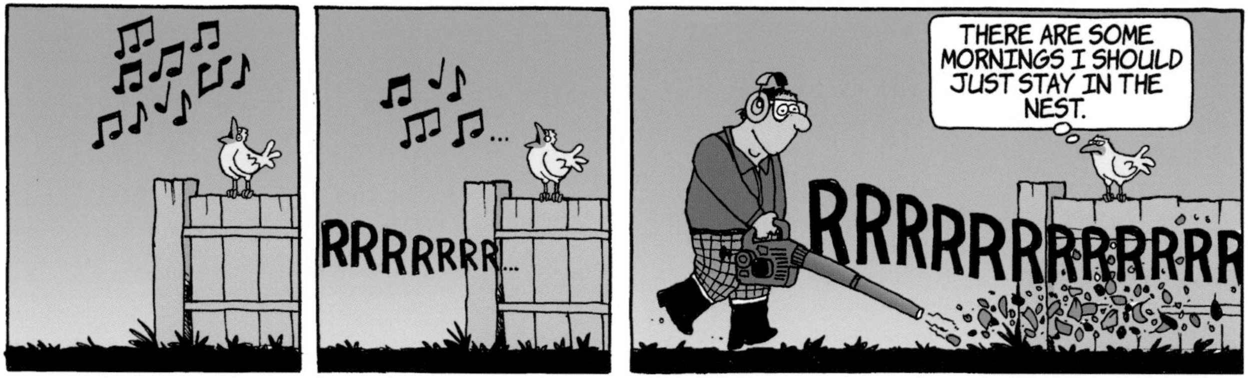
RRRRRRRR...
RRRRRRRRRRRRRR
THERE ARE SOME MORNINGS I SHOULD JUST STAY IN THE NEST.

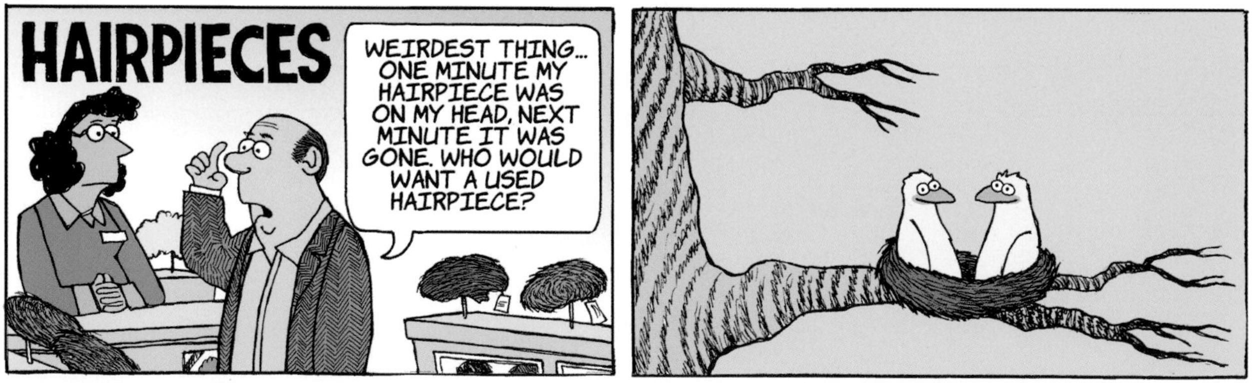
HAIRPIECES
WEIRDEST THING... ONE MINUTE MY HAIRPIECE WAS ON MY HEAD, NEXT MINUTE IT WAS GONE. WHO WOULD WANT A USED HAIRPIECE?

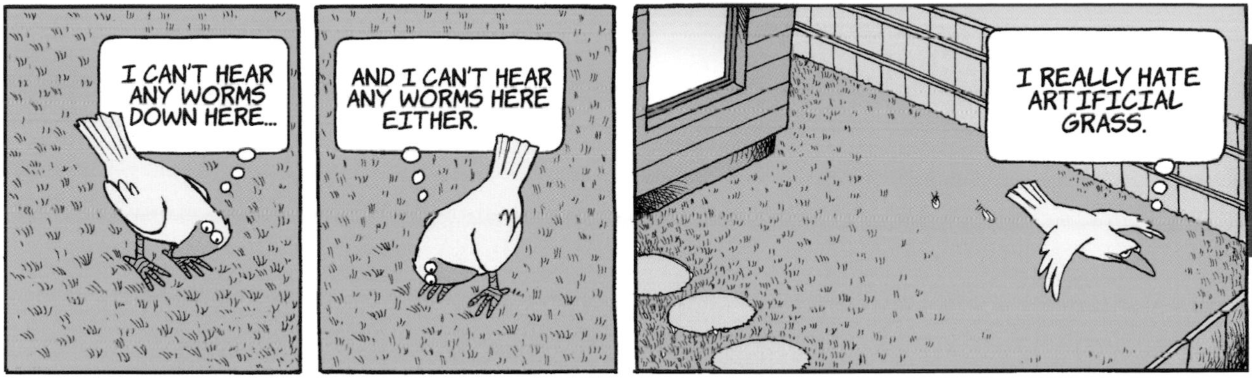
I CAN'T HEAR ANY WORMS DOWN HERE...
AND I CAN'T HEAR ANY WORMS HERE EITHER.
I REALLY HATE ARTIFICIAL GRASS.

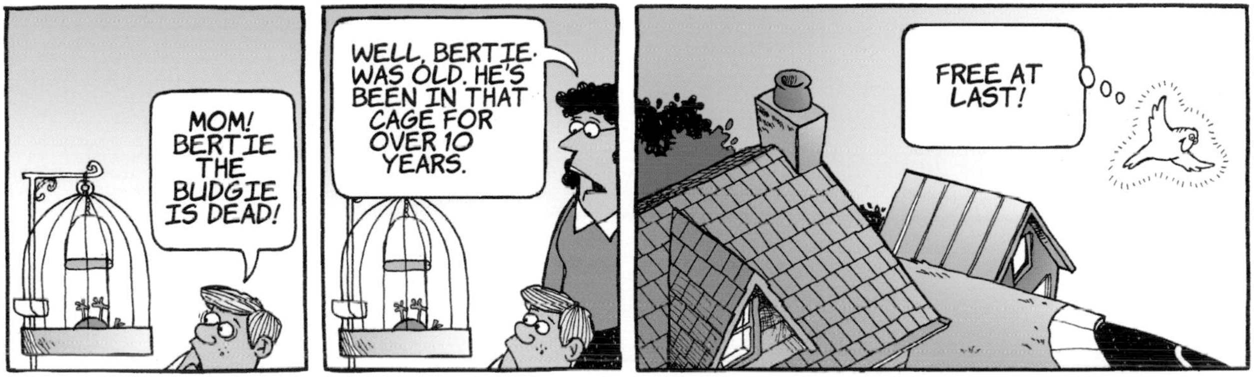
MOM! BERTIE THE BUDGIE IS DEAD!
WELL, BERTIE WAS OLD. HE'S BEEN IN THAT CAGE FOR OVER 10 YEARS.
FREE AT LAST!

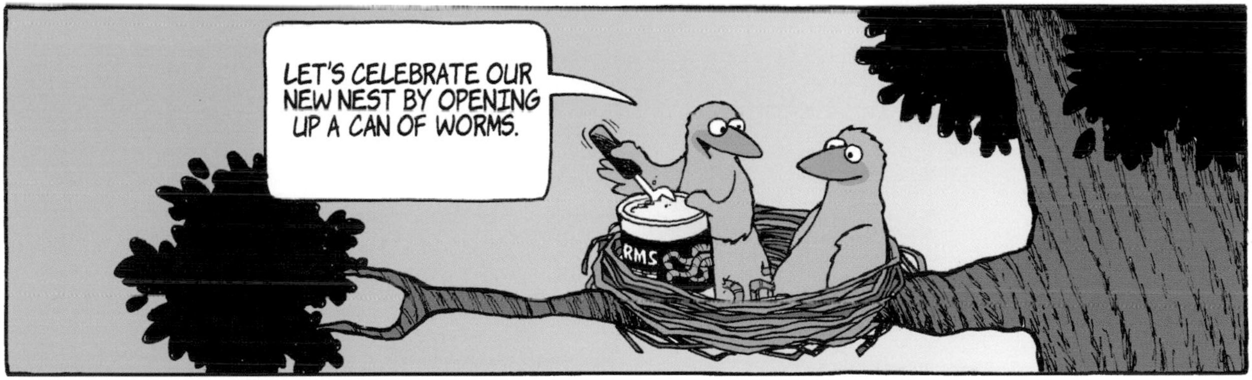
LET'S CELEBRATE OUR NEW NEST BY OPENING UP A CAN OF WORMS.
RMS

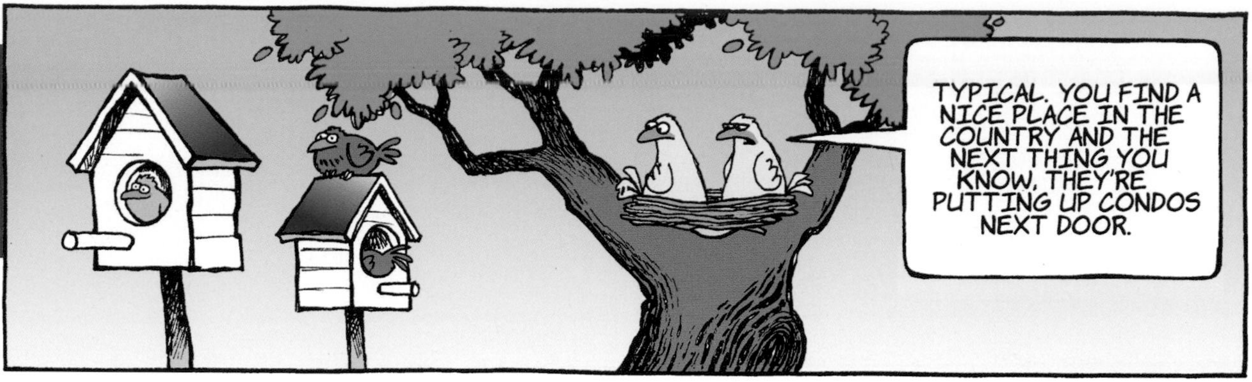
TYPICAL. YOU FIND A NICE PLACE IN THE COUNTRY AND THE NEXT THING YOU KNOW, THEY'RE PUTTING UP CONDOS NEXT DOOR.

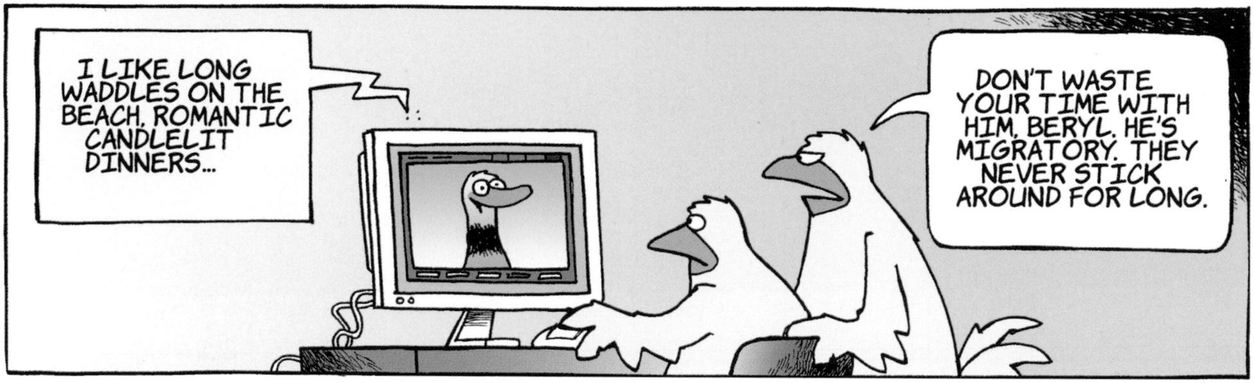
I LIKE LONG WADDLES ON THE BEACH, ROMANTIC CANDLELIT DINNERS...
DON'T WASTE YOUR TIME WITH HIM, BERYL. HE'S MIGRATORY. THEY NEVER STICK AROUND FOR LONG.

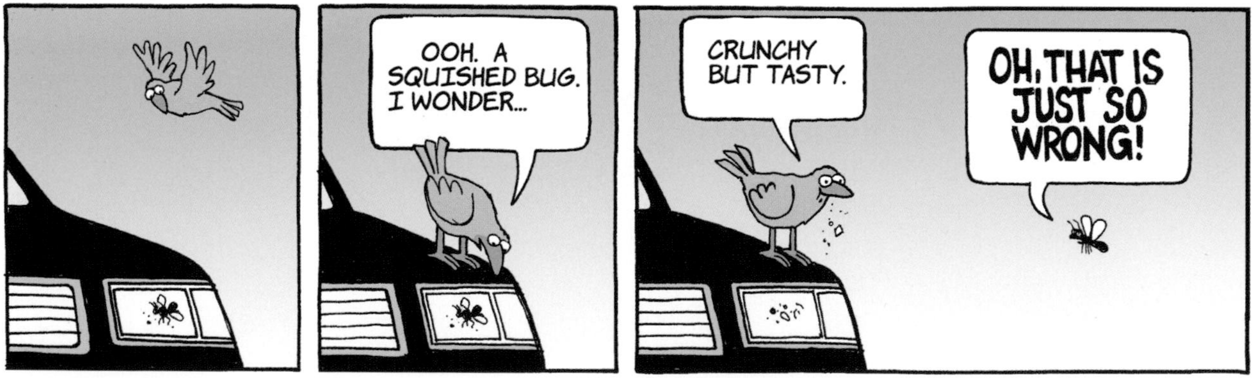
OOH. A SQUISHED BUG. I WONDER...
CRUNCHY BUT TASTY.
OH, THAT IS JUST SO WRONG!

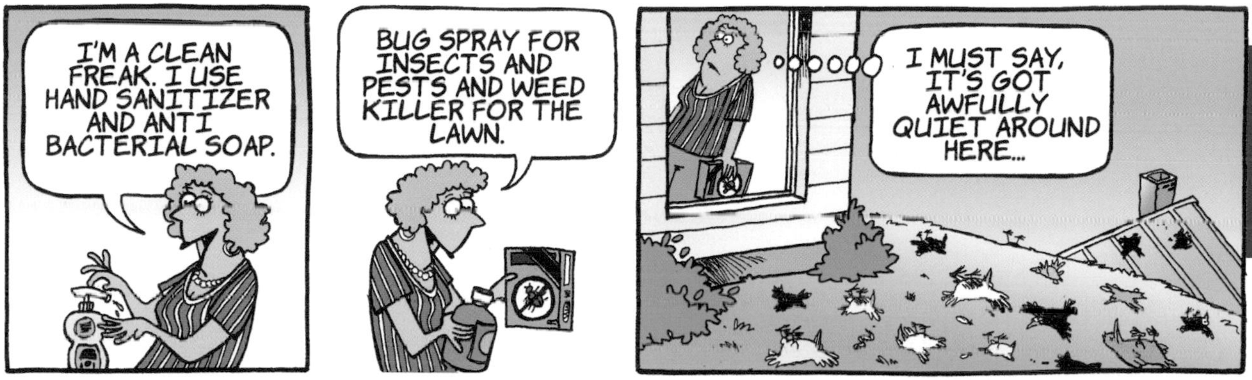
I'M A CLEAN FREAK. I USE HAND SANITIZER AND ANTI BACTERIAL SOAP.
BUG SPRAY FOR INSECTS AND PESTS AND WEED KILLER FOR THE LAWN.
I MUST SAY, IT'S GOT AWFULLY QUIET AROUND HERE...

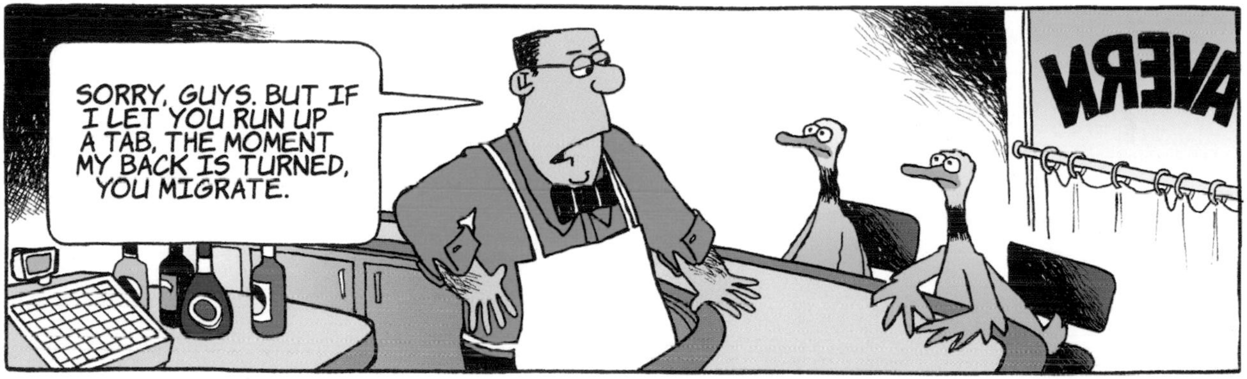
SORRY, GUYS. BUT IF I LET YOU RUN UP A TAB, THE MOMENT MY BACK IS TURNED, YOU MIGRATE.
AVERN

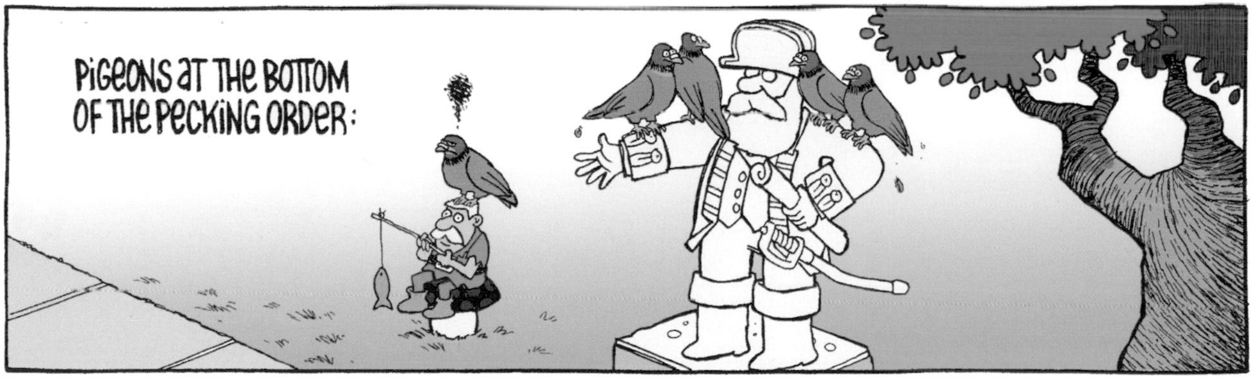
PIGEONS AT THE BOTTOM OF THE PECKING ORDER:

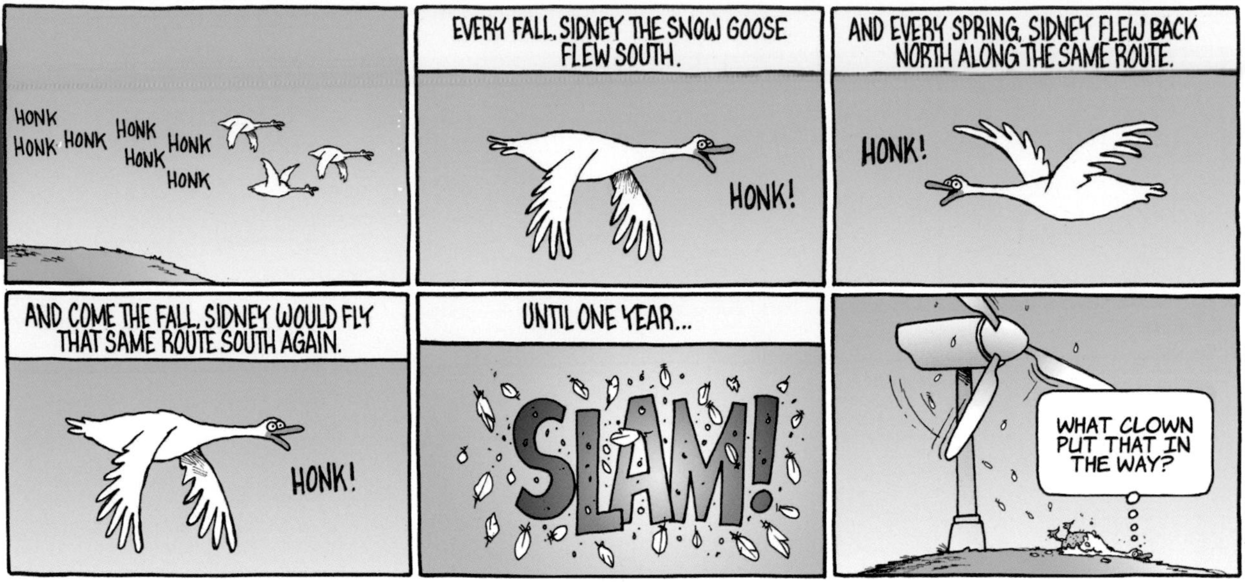
HONK HONK HONK HONK HONK HONK HONK HONK
EVERY FALL, SIDNEY THE SNOW GOOSE FLEW SOUTH.
HONK!
AND EVERY SPRING, SIDNEY FLEW BACK NORTH ALONG THE SAME ROUTE.
HONK!
AND COME THE FALL, SIDNEY WOULD FLY THAT SAME ROUTE SOUTH AGAIN.
HONK!
UNTIL ONE YEAR...
SLAM!
WHAT CLOWN PUT THAT IN THE WAY?

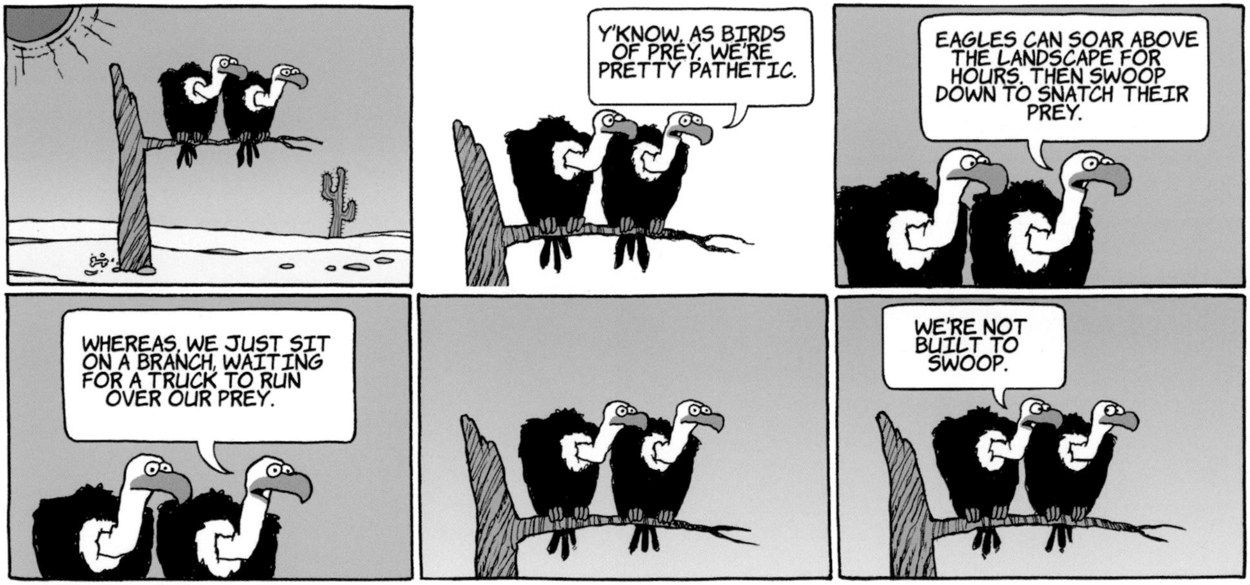
Y'KNOW, AS BIRDS OF PREY, WE'RE PRETTY PATHETIC.
EAGLES CAN SOAR ABOVE THE LANDSCAPE FOR HOURS, THEN SWOOP DOWN TO SNATCH THEIR PREY.
WHEREAS, WE JUST SIT ON A BRANCH, WAITING FOR A TRUCK TO RUN OVER OUR PREY.
WE'RE NOT BUILT TO SWOOP.

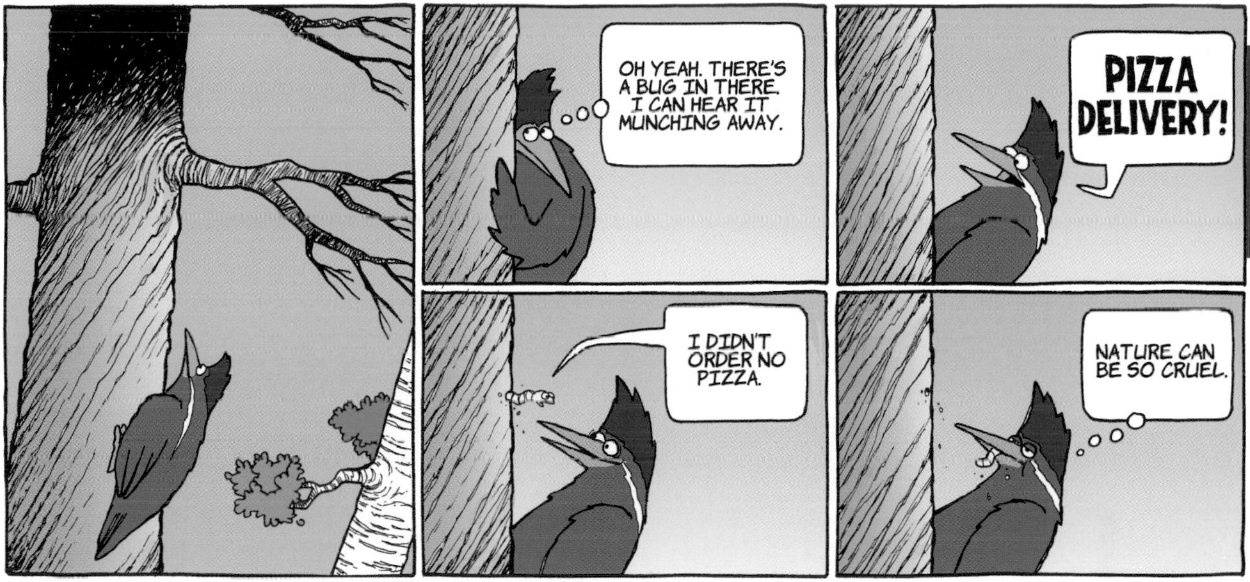
OH YEAH. THERE'S A BUG IN THERE. I CAN HEAR IT MUNCHING AWAY.
PIZZA DELIVERY!
I DIDN'T ORDER NO PIZZA.
NATURE CAN BE SO CRUEL.

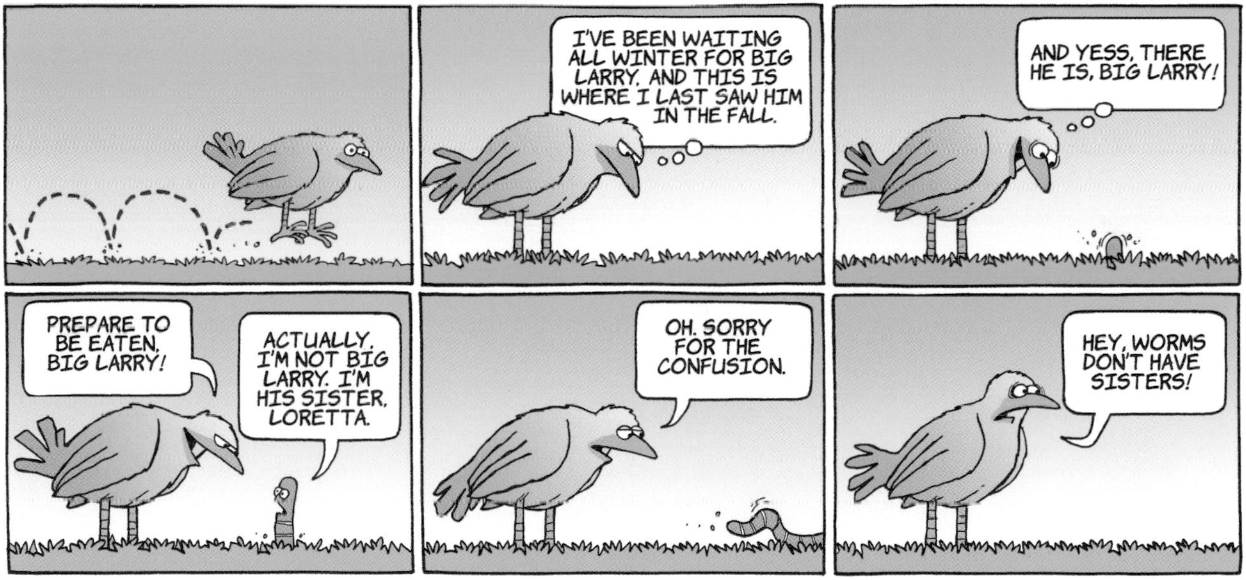
I'VE BEEN WAITING ALL WINTER FOR BIG LARRY, AND THIS IS WHERE I LAST SAW HIM IN THE FALL.
AND YESS, THERE HE IS, BIG LARRY!
PREPARE TO BE EATEN, BIG LARRY!
ACTUALLY, I'M NOT BIG LARRY. I'M HIS SISTER, LORETTA.
OH. SORRY FOR THE CONFUSION.
HEY, WORMS DON'T HAVE SISTERS!

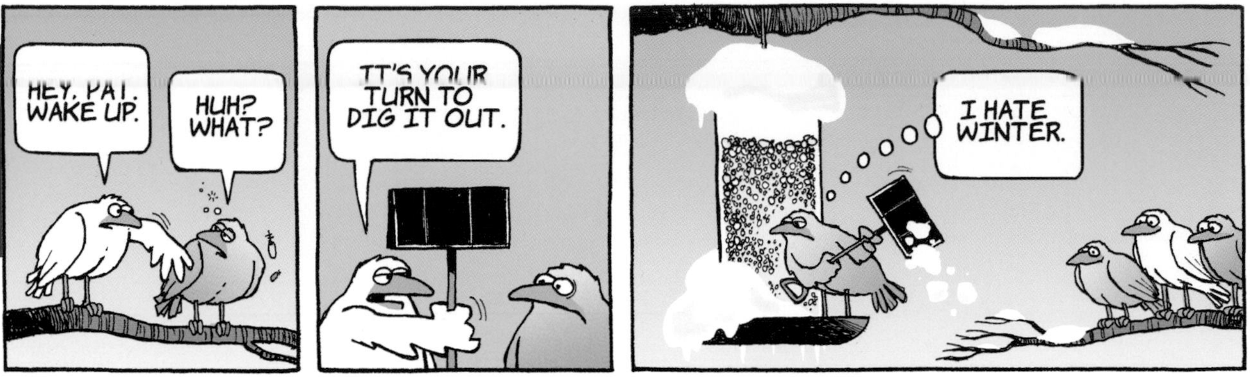
HEY, PAT. WAKE UP.
HUH? WHAT?
IT'S YOUR TURN TO DIG IT OUT.
I HATE WINTER.

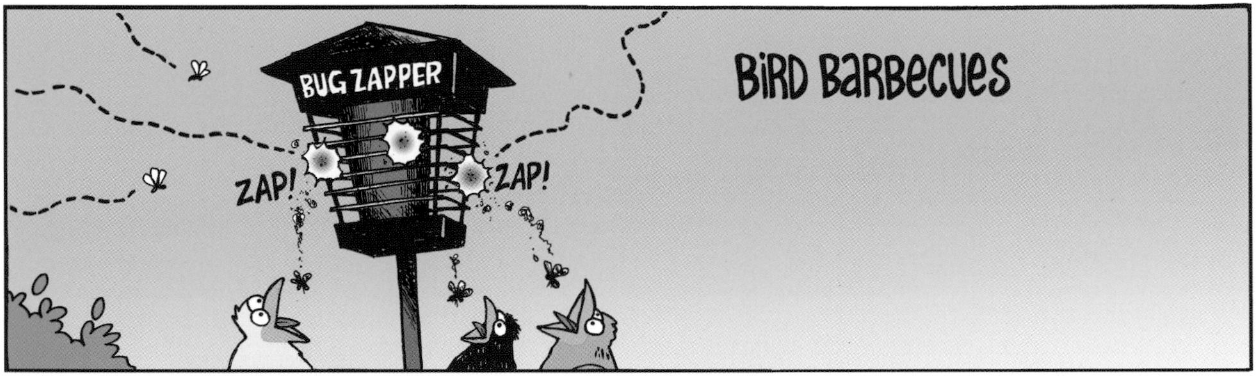
BUG ZAPPER
ZAP!
ZAP!
BIRD BARBECUES

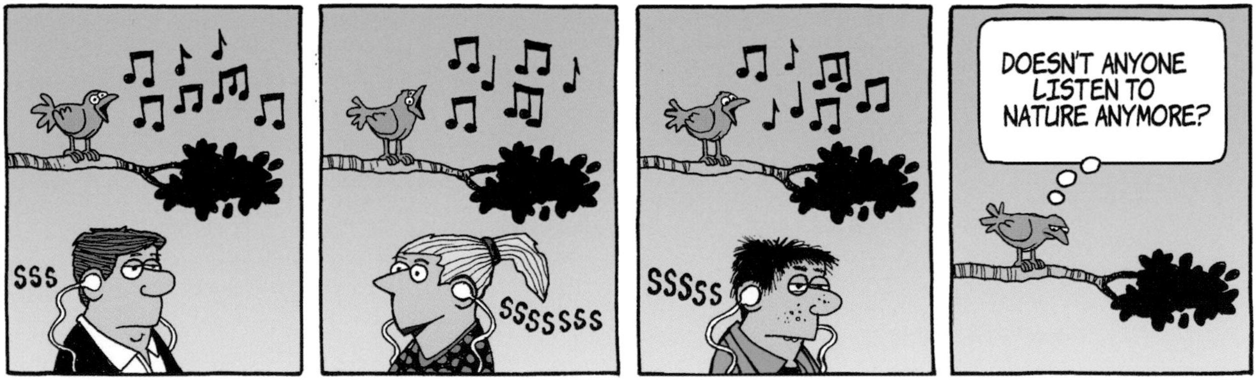
SSS
SSSSSSS
SSSSS
DOESN'T ANYONE LISTEN TO NATURE ANYMORE?

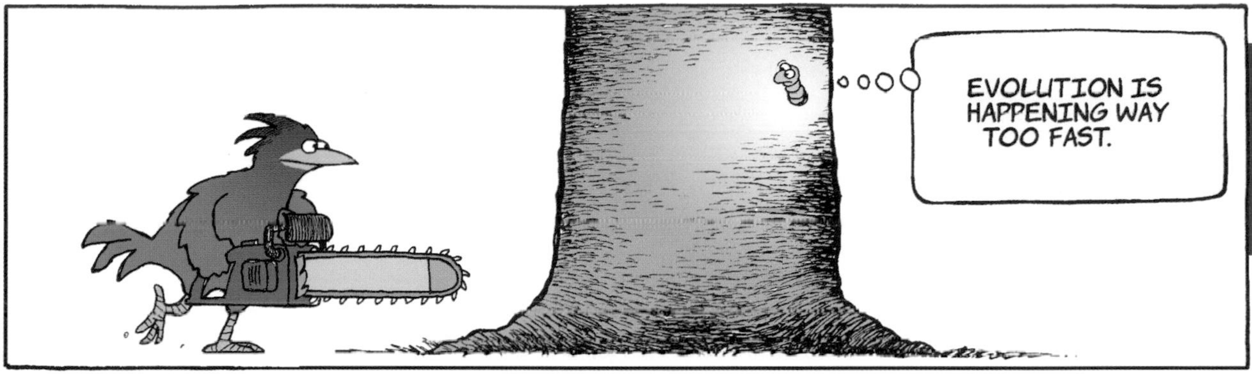
EVOLUTION IS HAPPENING WAY TOO FAST.

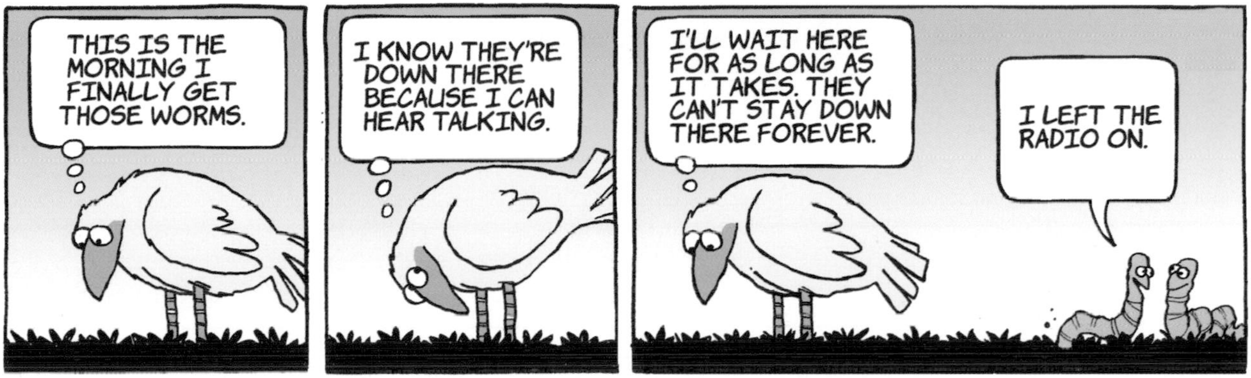
THIS IS THE MORNING I FINALLY GET THOSE WORMS.
I KNOW THEY'RE DOWN THERE BECAUSE I CAN HEAR TALKING.
I'LL WAIT HERE FOR AS LONG AS IT TAKES. THEY CAN'T STAY DOWN THERE FOREVER.
I LEFT THE RADIO ON.

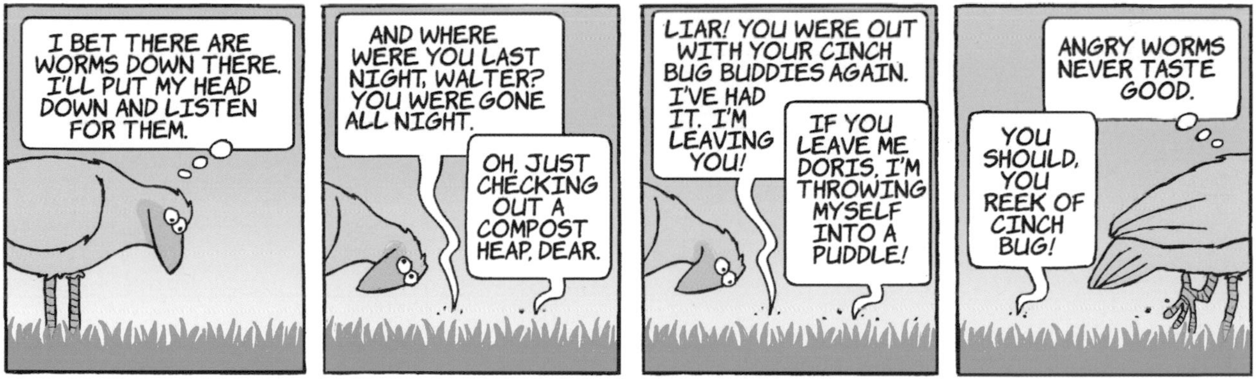
I BET THERE ARE WORMS DOWN THERE. I'LL PUT MY HEAD DOWN AND LISTEN FOR THEM.
AND WHERE WERE YOU LAST NIGHT, WALTER? YOU WERE GONE ALL NIGHT.
OH, JUST CHECKING OUT A COMPOST HEAP, DEAR.
LIAR! YOU WERE OUT WITH YOUR CINCH BUG BUDDIES AGAIN. I'VE HAD IT. I'M LEAVING YOU!
IF YOU LEAVE ME DORIS, I'M THROWING MYSELF INTO A PUDDLE!
ANGRY WORMS NEVER TASTE GOOD.
YOU SHOULD, YOU REEK OF CINCH BUG!

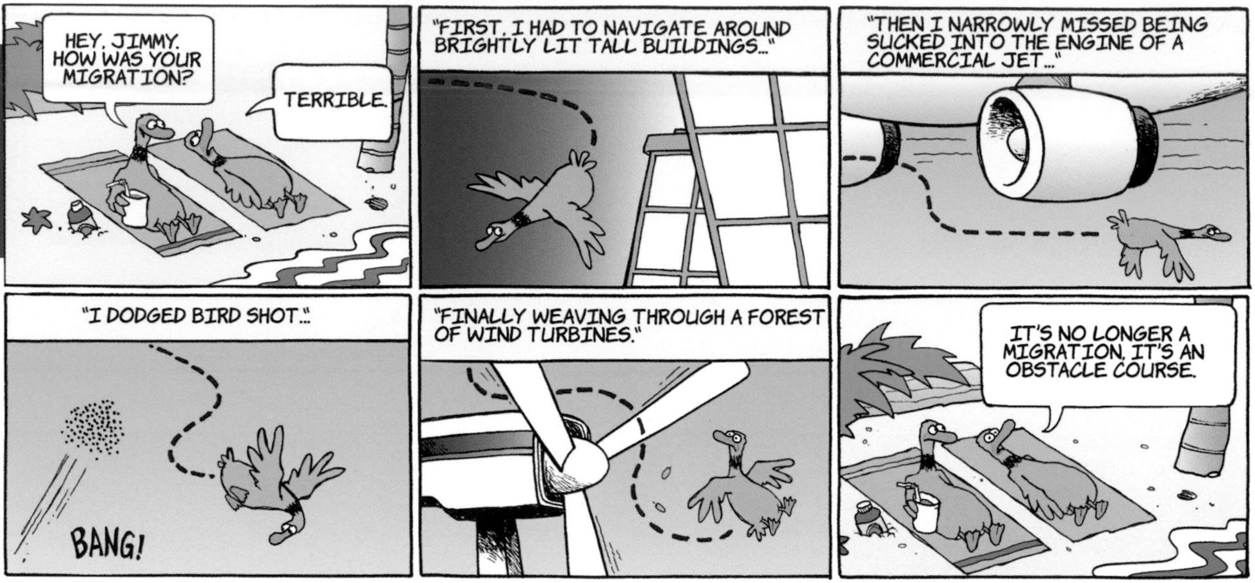
HEY, JIMMY. HOW WAS YOUR MIGRATION?
TERRIBLE.
"FIRST, I HAD TO NAVIGATE AROUND BRIGHTLY LIT TALL BUILDINGS..."
"THEN I NARROWLY MISSED BEING SUCKED INTO THE ENGINE OF A COMMERCIAL JET..."
"I DODGED BIRD SHOT..."
BANG!
"FINALLY WEAVING THROUGH A FOREST OF WIND TURBINES."
IT'S NO LONGER A MIGRATION, IT'S AN OBSTACLE COURSE.

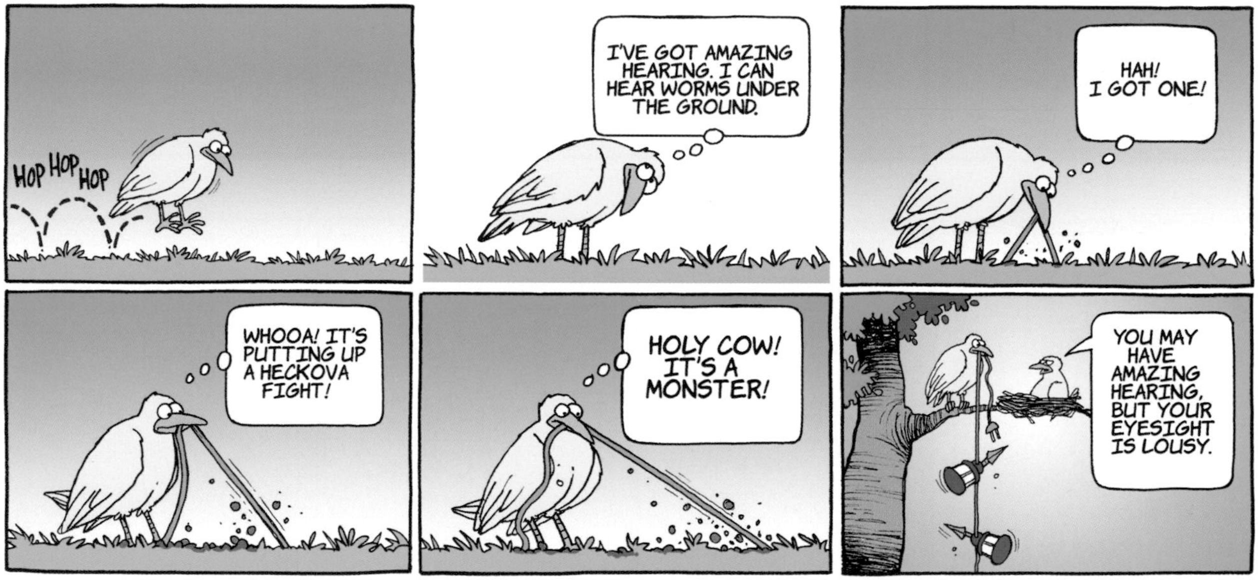
HOP HOP HOP
I'VE GOT AMAZING HEARING. I CAN HEAR WORMS UNDER THE GROUND.
HAH! I GOT ONE!
WHOOA! IT'S PUTTING UP A HECKOVA FIGHT!
HOLY COW! IT'S A MONSTER!
YOU MAY HAVE AMAZING HEARING, BUT YOUR EYESIGHT IS LOUSY.

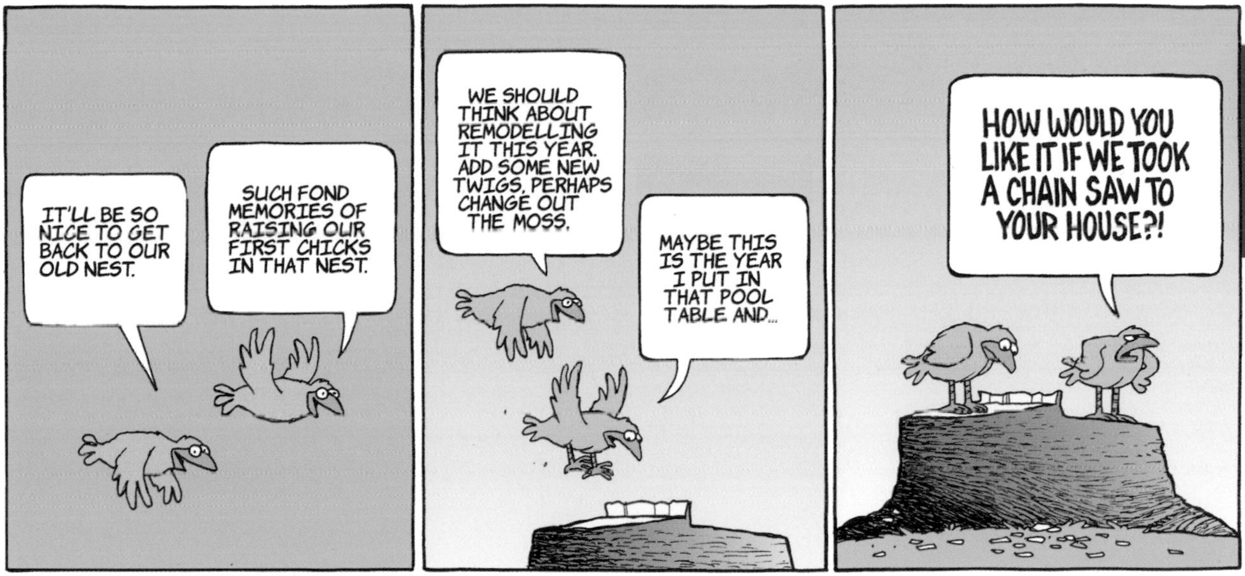
IT'LL BE SO NICE TO GET BACK TO OUR OLD NEST.
SUCH FOND MEMORIES OF RAISING OUR FIRST CHICKS IN THAT NEST.
WE SHOULD THINK ABOUT REMODELLING IT THIS YEAR. ADD SOME NEW TWIGS. PERHAPS CHANGE OUT THE MOSS.
MAYBE THIS IS THE YEAR I PUT IN THAT POOL TABLE AND...
HOW WOULD YOU LIKE IT IF WE TOOK A CHAIN SAW TO YOUR HOUSE?!

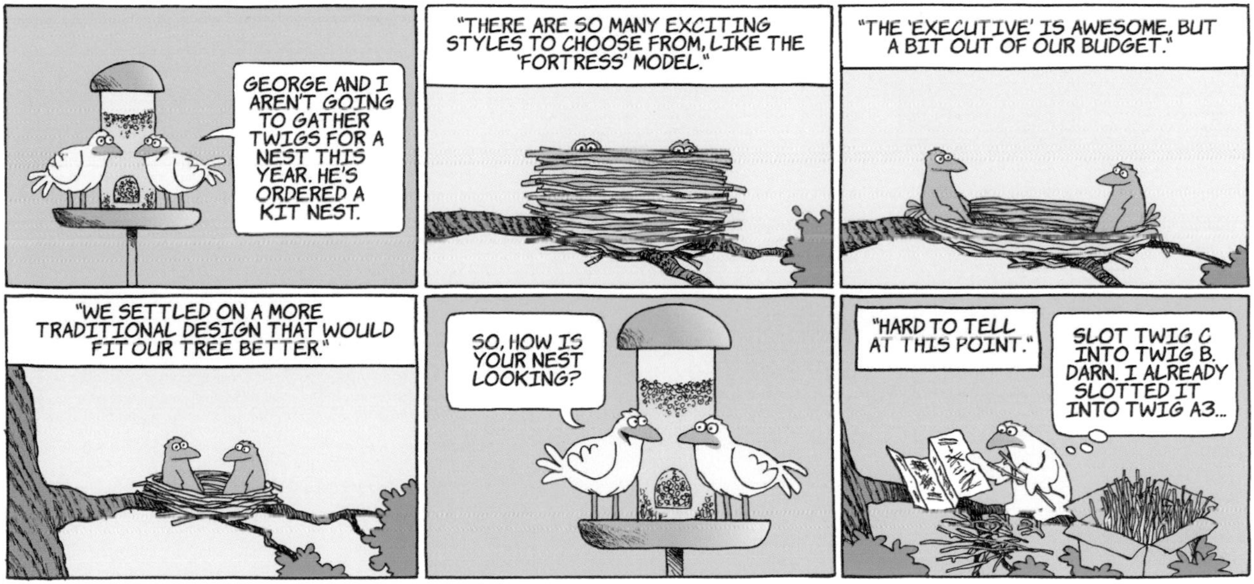
GEORGE AND I AREN'T GOING TO GATHER TWIGS FOR A NEST THIS YEAR. HE'S ORDERED A KIT NEST.
"THERE ARE SO MANY EXCITING STYLES TO CHOOSE FROM, LIKE THE 'FORTRESS' MODEL."
"THE 'EXECUTIVE' IS AWESOME, BUT A BIT OUT OF OUR BUDGET."
"WE SETTLED ON A MORE TRADITIONAL DESIGN THAT WOULD FIT OUR TREE BETTER."
SO, HOW IS YOUR NEST LOOKING?
"HARD TO TELL AT THIS POINT."
SLOT TWIG C INTO TWIG B. DARN. I ALREADY SLOTTED IT INTO TWIG A3...

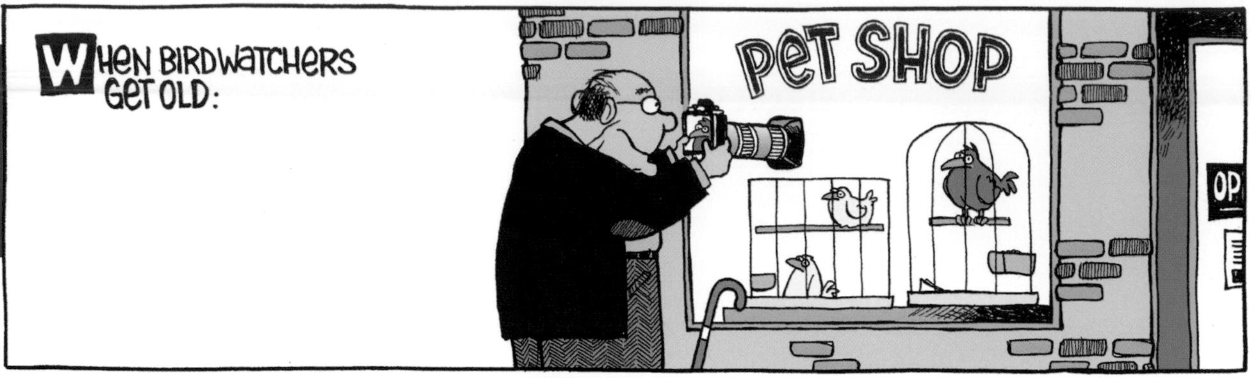
WHEN BIRDWATCHERS GET OLD:
PET SHOP
OP

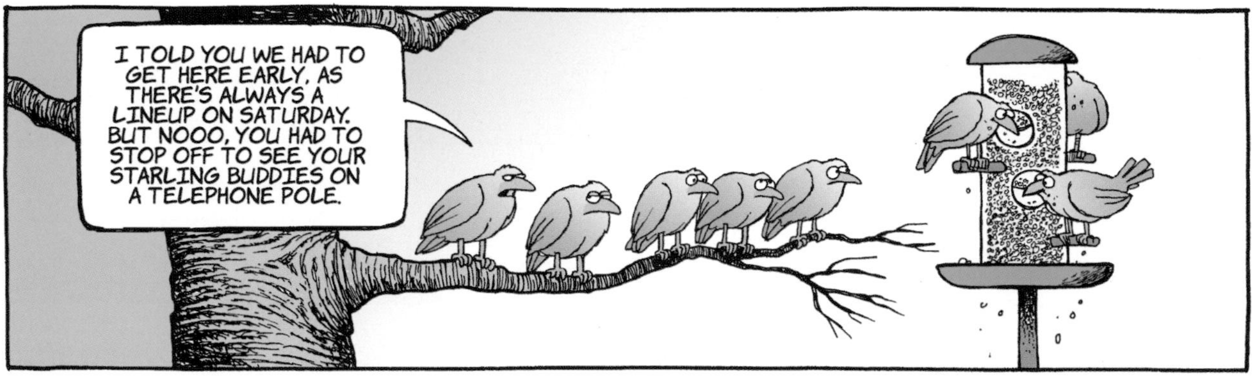
I TOLD YOU WE HAD TO GET HERE EARLY, AS THERE'S ALWAYS A LINEUP ON SATURDAY. BUT NOOO, YOU HAD TO STOP OFF TO SEE YOUR STARLING BUDDIES ON A TELEPHONE POLE.

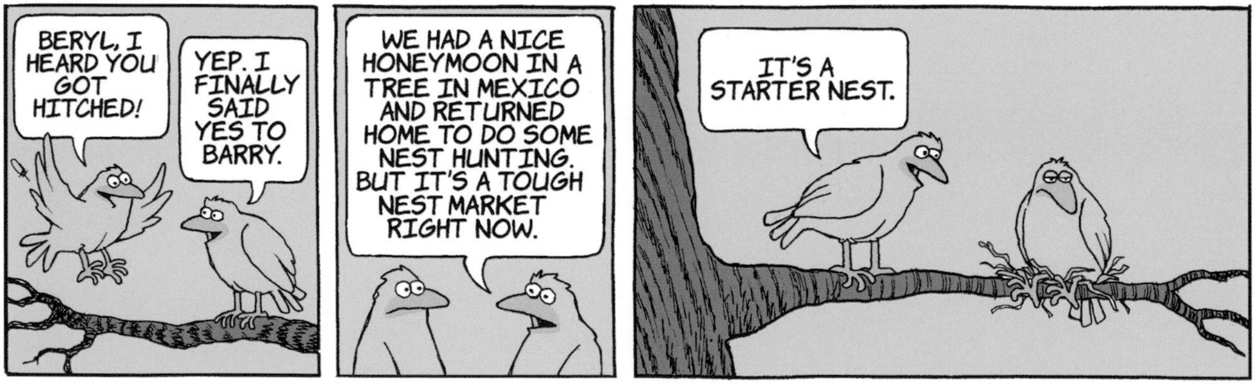
BERYL, I HEARD YOU GOT HITCHED!
YEP. I FINALLY SAID YES TO BARRY.
WE HAD A NICE HONEYMOON IN A TREE IN MEXICO AND RETURNED HOME TO DO SOME NEST HUNTING. BUT IT'S A TOUGH NEST MARKET RIGHT NOW.
IT'S A STARTER NEST.

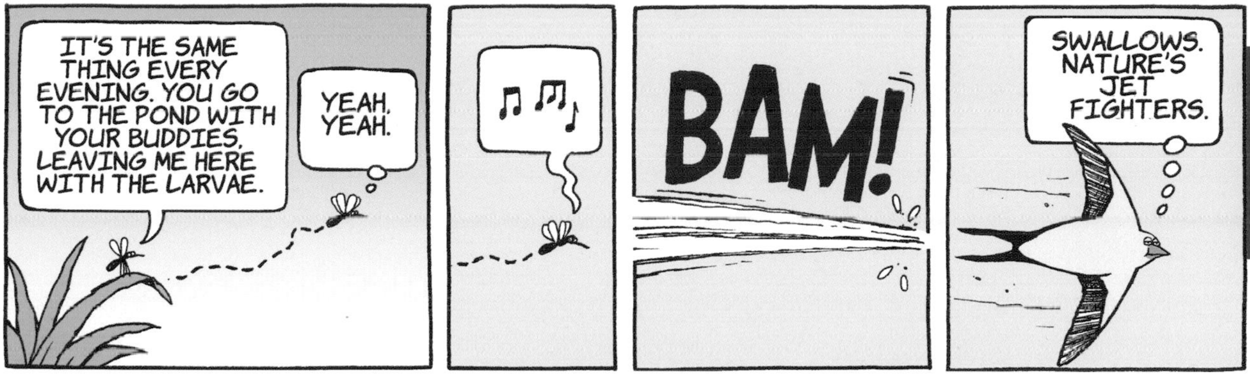
IT'S THE SAME THING EVERY EVENING. YOU GO TO THE POND WITH YOUR BUDDIES, LEAVING ME HERE WITH THE LARVAE.
YEAH, YEAH.
BAM!
SWALLOWS. NATURE'S JET FIGHTERS.

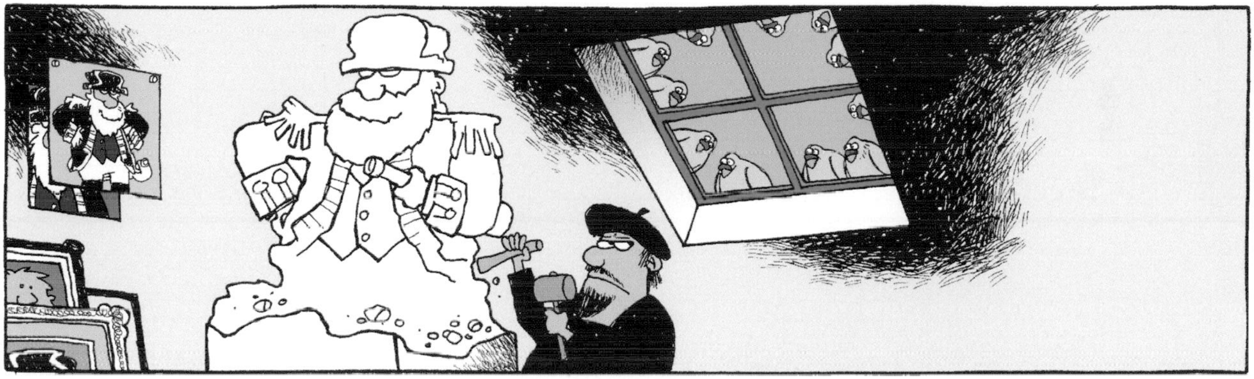

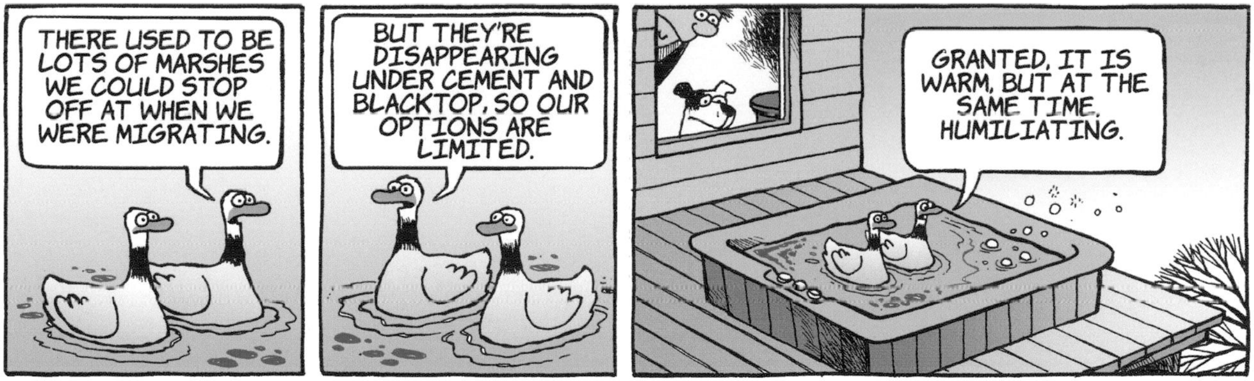
THERE USED TO BE LOTS OF MARSHES WE COULD STOP OFF AT WHEN WE WERE MIGRATING.
BUT THEY'RE DISAPPEARING UNDER CEMENT AND BLACKTOP, SO OUR OPTIONS ARE LIMITED.
GRANTED, IT IS WARM, BUT AT THE SAME TIME, HUMILIATING.

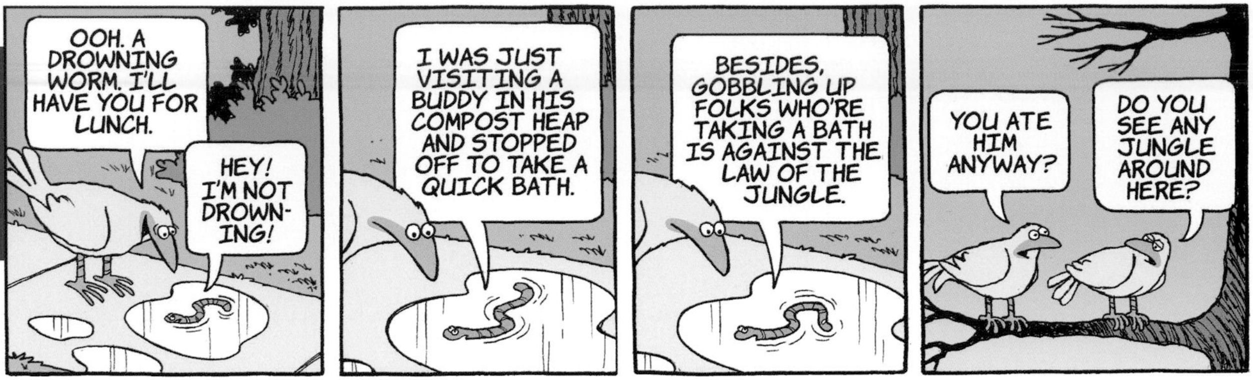
OOH. A DROWNING WORM. I'LL HAVE YOU FOR LUNCH.
HEY! I'M NOT DROWNING!
I WAS JUST VISITING A BUDDY IN HIS COMPOST HEAP AND STOPPED OFF TO TAKE A QUICK BATH.
BESIDES, GOBBLING UP FOLKS WHO'RE TAKING A BATH IS AGAINST THE LAW OF THE JUNGLE.
YOU ATE HIM ANYWAY?
DO YOU SEE ANY JUNGLE AROUND HERE?

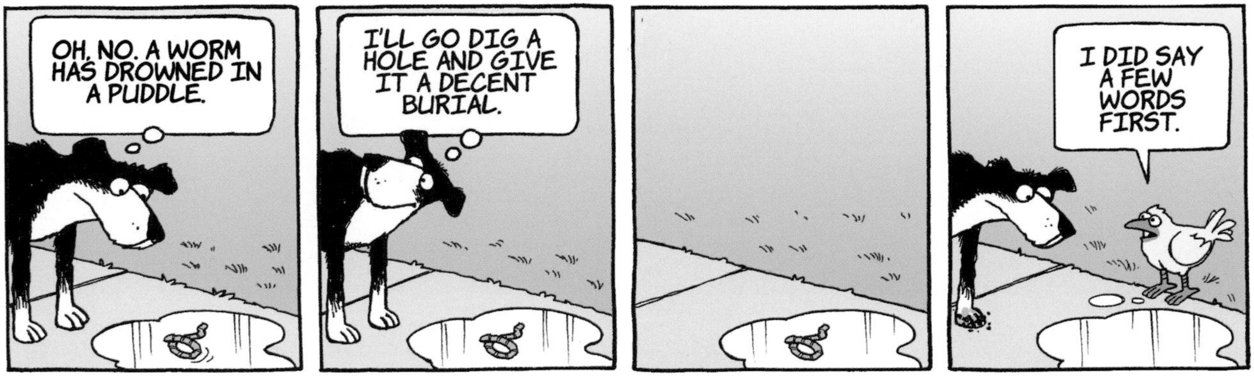
OH, NO. A WORM HAS DROWNED IN A PUDDLE.
I'LL GO DIG A HOLE AND GIVE IT A DECENT BURIAL.
I DID SAY A FEW WORDS FIRST.

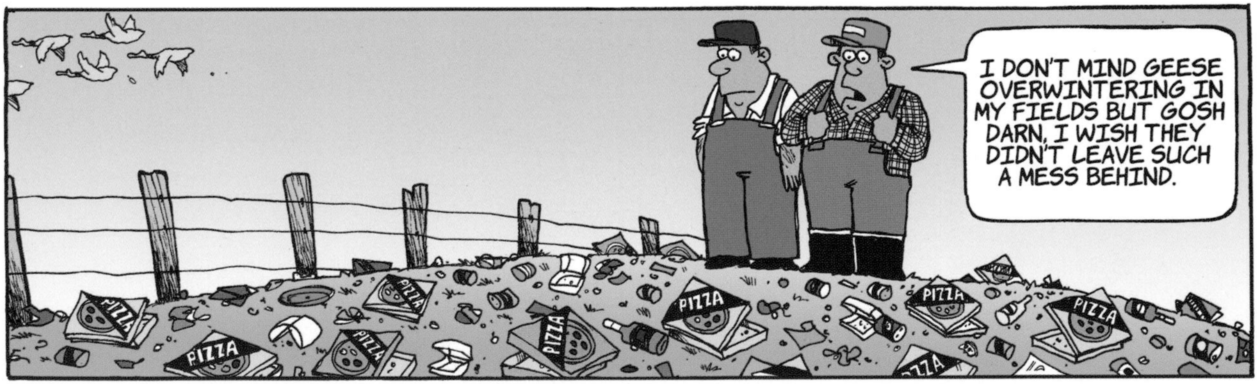
I DON'T MIND GEESE OVERWINTERING IN MY FIELDS BUT GOSH DARN, I WISH THEY DIDN'T LEAVE SUCH A MESS BEHIND.

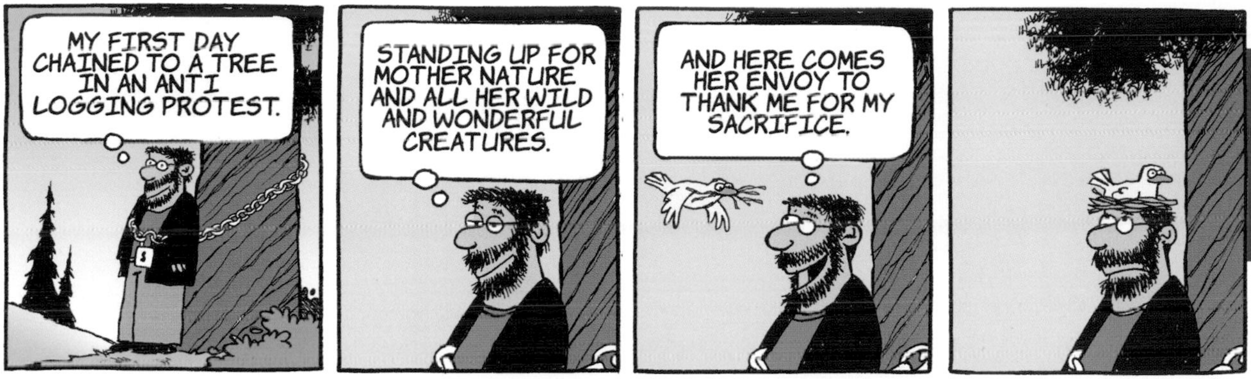
MY FIRST DAY CHAINED TO A TREE IN AN ANTI LOGGING PROTEST.
STANDING UP FOR MOTHER NATURE AND ALL HER WILD AND WONDERFUL CREATURES.
AND HERE COMES HER ENVOY TO THANK ME FOR MY SACRIFICE.

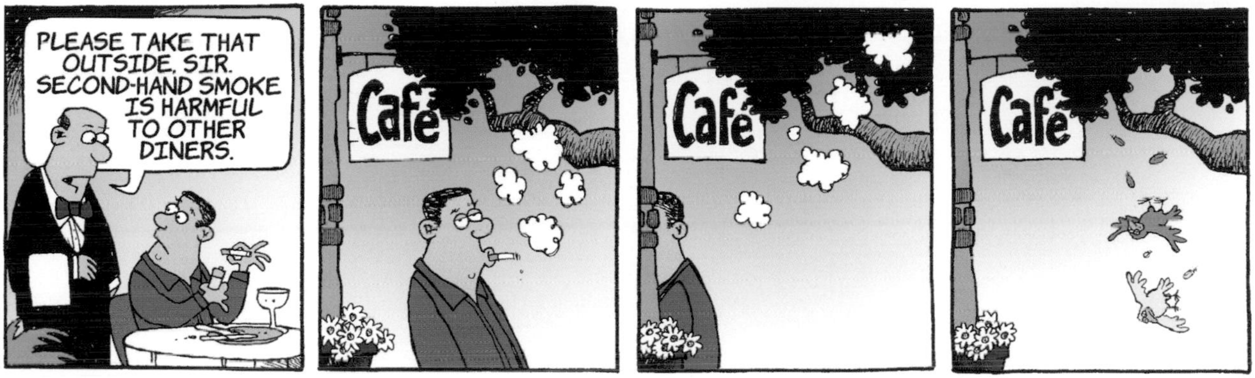
PLEASE TAKE THAT OUTSIDE, SIR. SECOND-HAND SMOKE IS HARMFUL TO OTHER DINERS.
Café
Café
Café

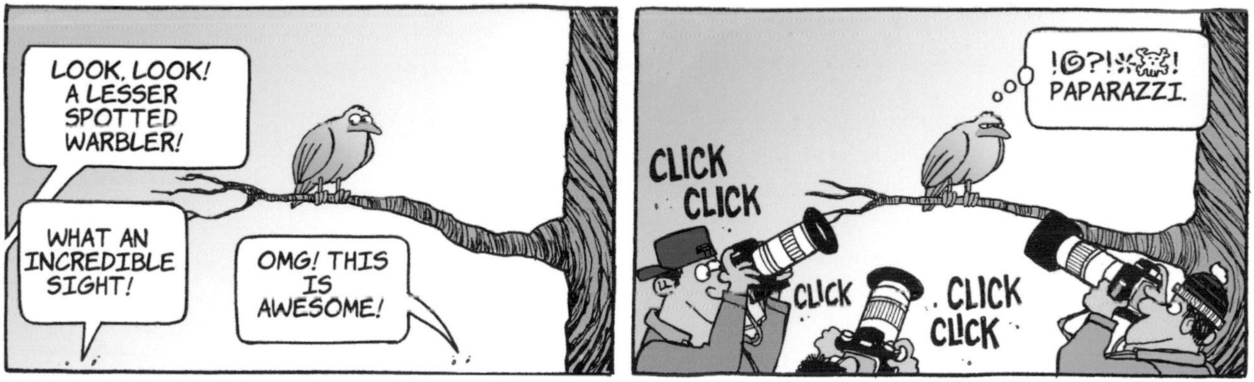
LOOK, LOOK! A LESSER SPOTTED WARBLER!
WHAT AN INCREDIBLE SIGHT!
OMG! THIS IS AWESOME!
CLICK
CLICK
CLICK
CLICK
CLICK
PAPARAZZI.

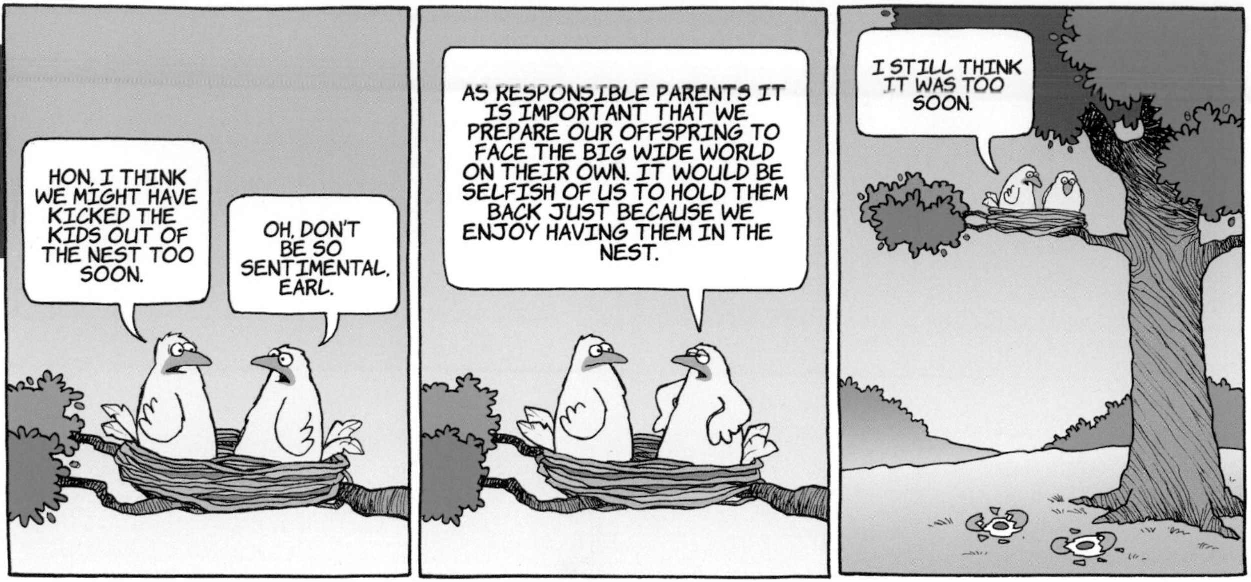
HON, I THINK WE MIGHT HAVE KICKED THE KIDS OUT OF THE NEST TOO SOON.
OH, DON'T BE SO SENTIMENTAL, EARL.
AS RESPONSIBLE PARENTS IT IS IMPORTANT THAT WE PREPARE OUR OFFSPRING TO FACE THE BIG WIDE WORLD ON THEIR OWN. IT WOULD BE SELFISH OF US TO HOLD THEM BACK JUST BECAUSE WE ENJOY HAVING THEM IN THE NEST.
I STILL THINK IT WAS TOO SOON.

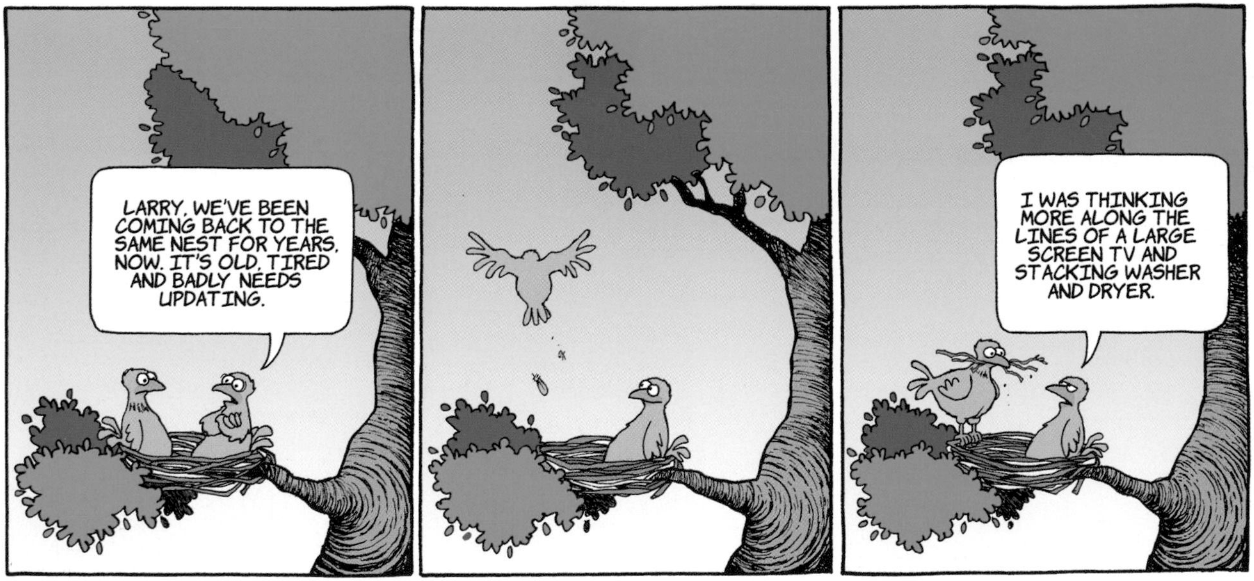
LARRY, WE'VE BEEN COMING BACK TO THE SAME NEST FOR YEARS, NOW. IT'S OLD, TIRED AND BADLY NEEDS UPDATING.
I WAS THINKING MORE ALONG THE LINES OF A LARGE SCREEN TV AND STACKING WASHER AND DRYER.

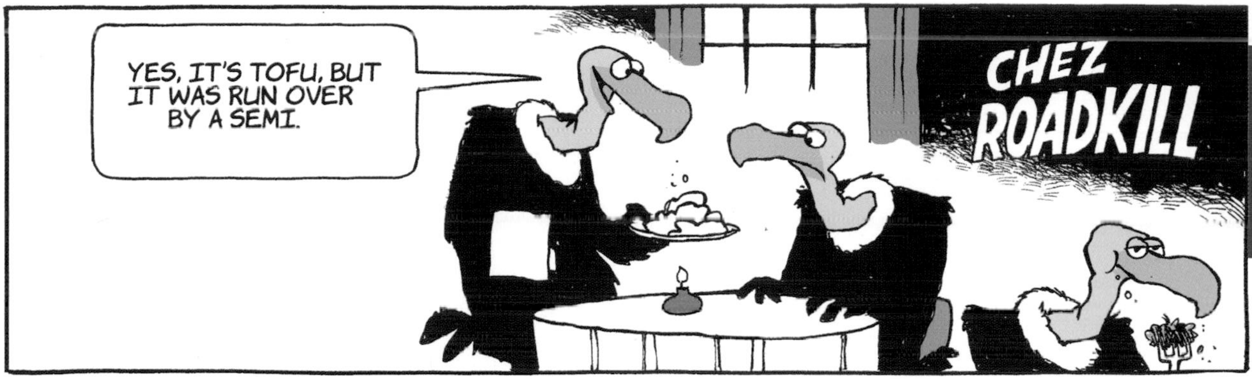
YES, IT'S TOFU, BUT IT WAS RUN OVER BY A SEMI.
CHEZ ROADKILL

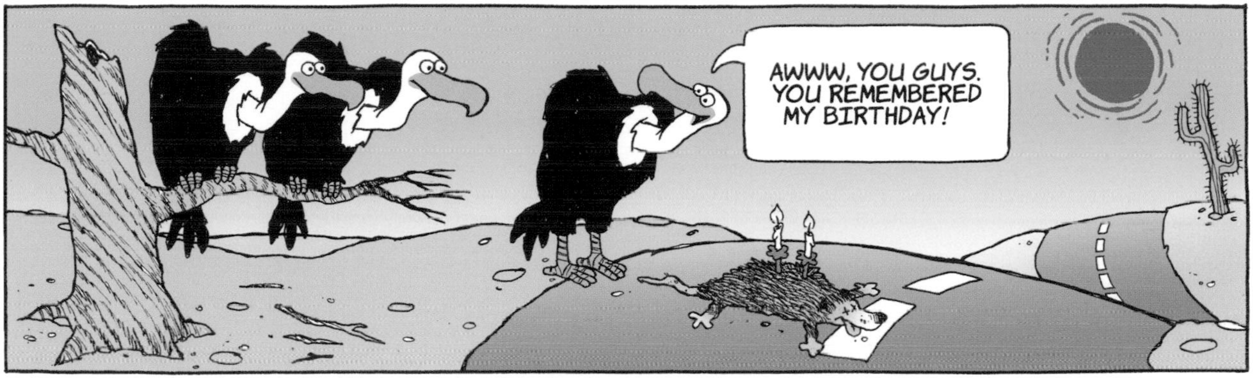
AWWW, YOU GUYS. YOU REMEMBERED MY BIRTHDAY!

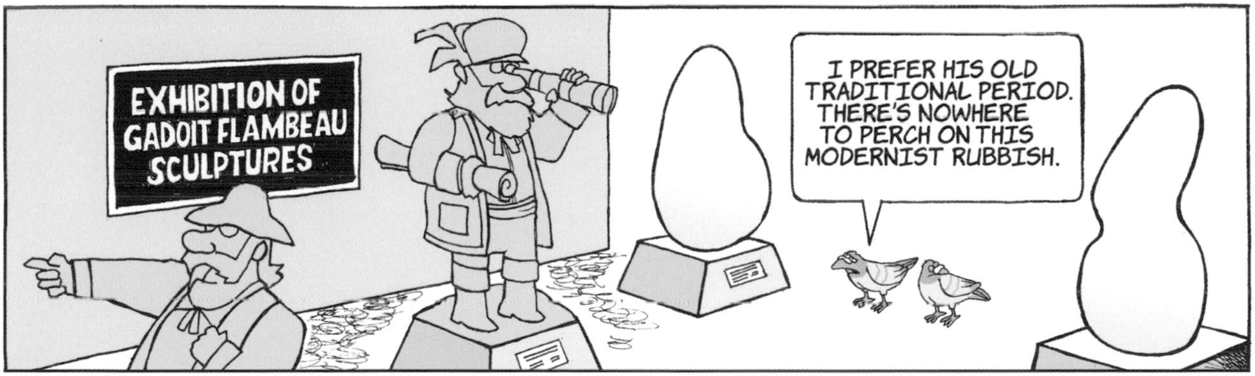
EXHIBITION OF GADOIT FLAMBEAU SCULPTURES
I PREFER HIS OLD TRADITIONAL PERIOD. THERE'S NOWHERE TO PERCH ON THIS MODERNIST RUBBISH.

7 RAMPANT RODENTS

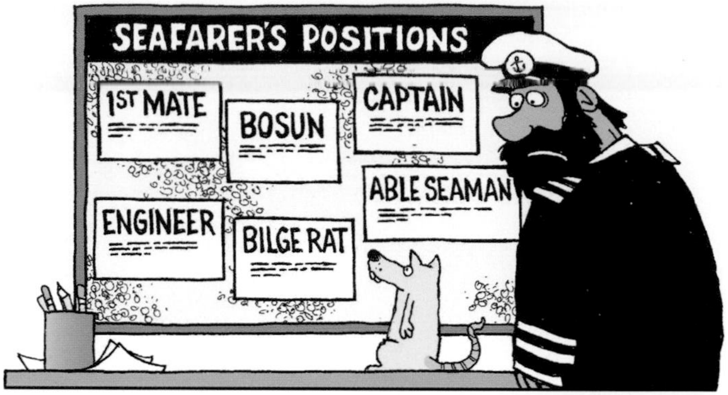
SEAFARER'S POSITIONS
1ST MATE
BOSUN
CAPTAIN
ABLE SEAMAN
ENGINEER
BILGE RAT

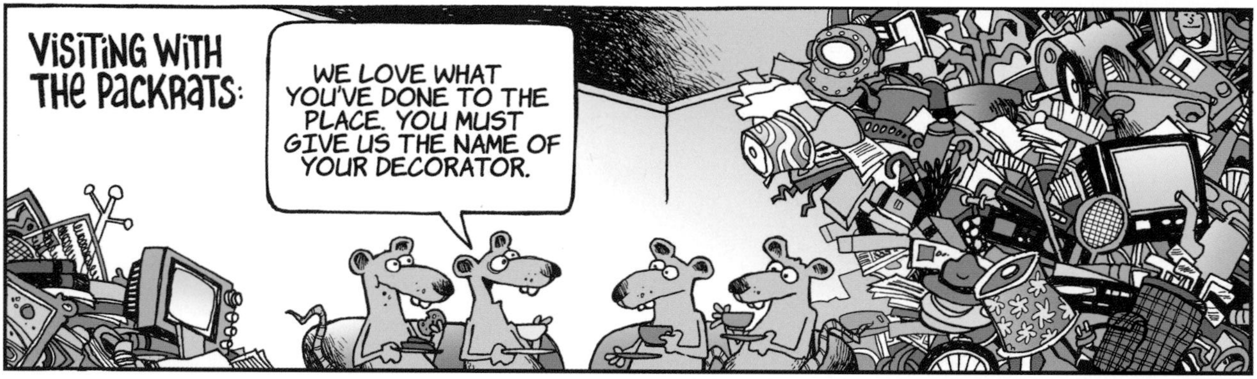
VISITING WITH THE PACKRATS:
WE LOVE WHAT YOU'VE DONE TO THE PLACE. YOU MUST GIVE US THE NAME OF YOUR DECORATOR.

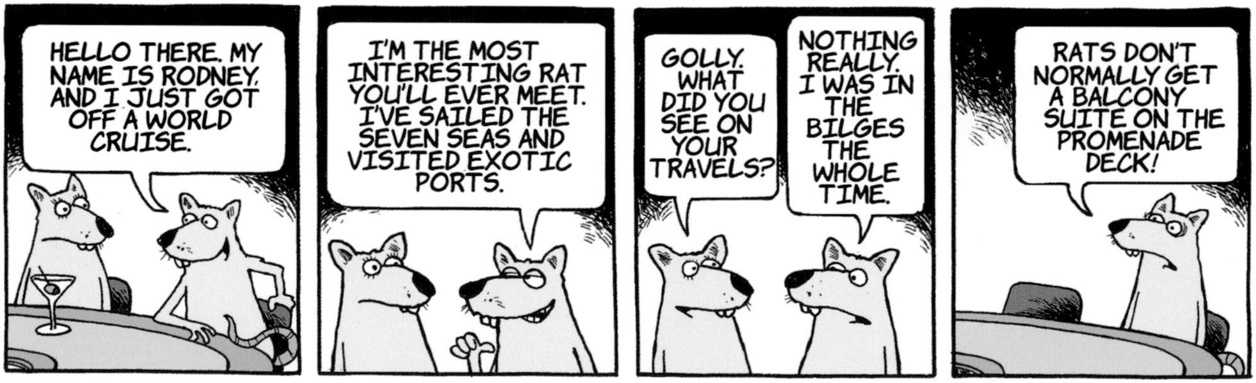
HELLO THERE. MY NAME IS RODNEY. AND I JUST GOT OFF A WORLD CRUISE.
I'M THE MOST INTERESTING RAT YOU'LL EVER MEET. I'VE SAILED THE SEVEN SEAS AND VISITED EXOTIC PORTS.
GOLLY. WHAT DID YOU SEE ON YOUR TRAVELS?
NOTHING REALLY. I WAS IN THE BILGES THE WHOLE TIME.
RATS DON'T NORMALLY GET A BALCONY SUITE ON THE PROMENADE DECK!

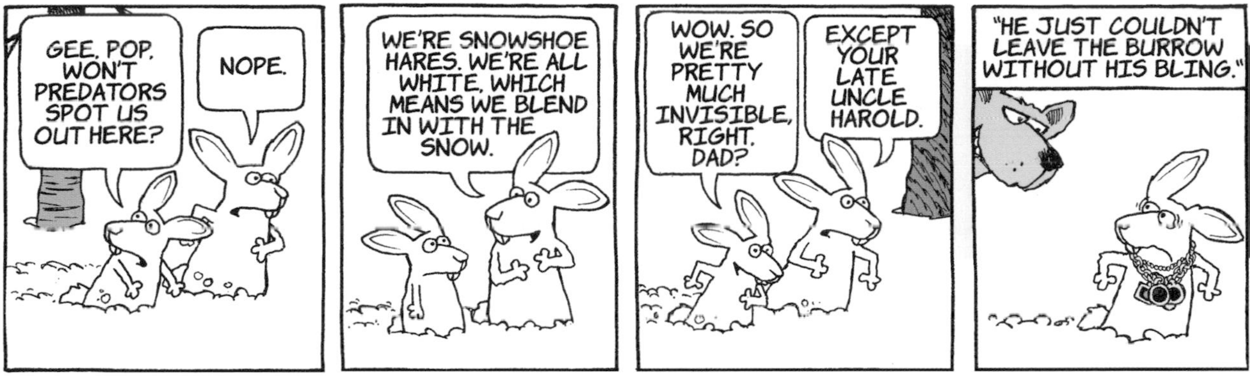
GEE, POP, WON'T PREDATORS SPOT US OUT HERE?
NOPE.
WE'RE SNOWSHOE HARES. WE'RE ALL WHITE, WHICH MEANS WE BLEND IN WITH THE SNOW.
WOW. SO WE'RE PRETTY MUCH INVISIBLE, RIGHT, DAD?
EXCEPT YOUR LATE UNCLE HAROLD.
"HE JUST COULDN'T LEAVE THE BURROW WITHOUT HIS BLING."

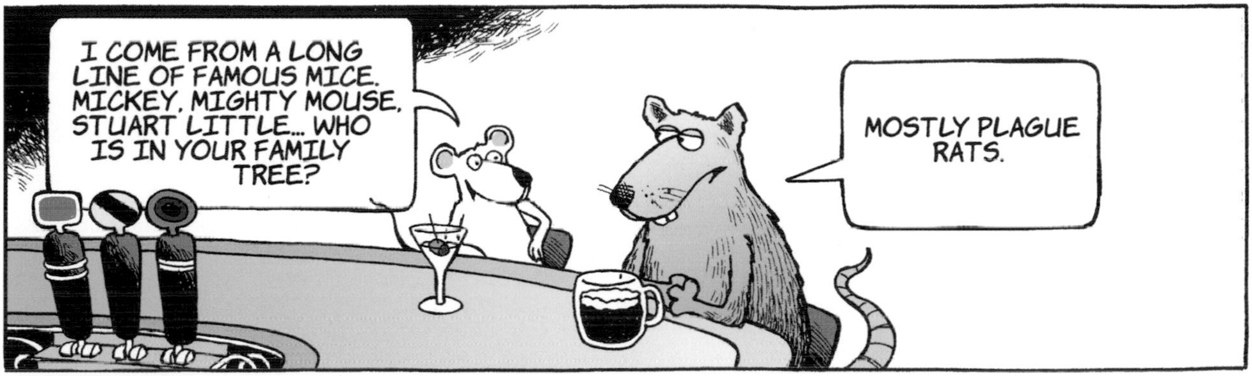
I COME FROM A LONG LINE OF FAMOUS MICE. MICKEY, MIGHTY MOUSE, STUART LITTLE... WHO IS IN YOUR FAMILY TREE?
MOSTLY PLAGUE RATS.

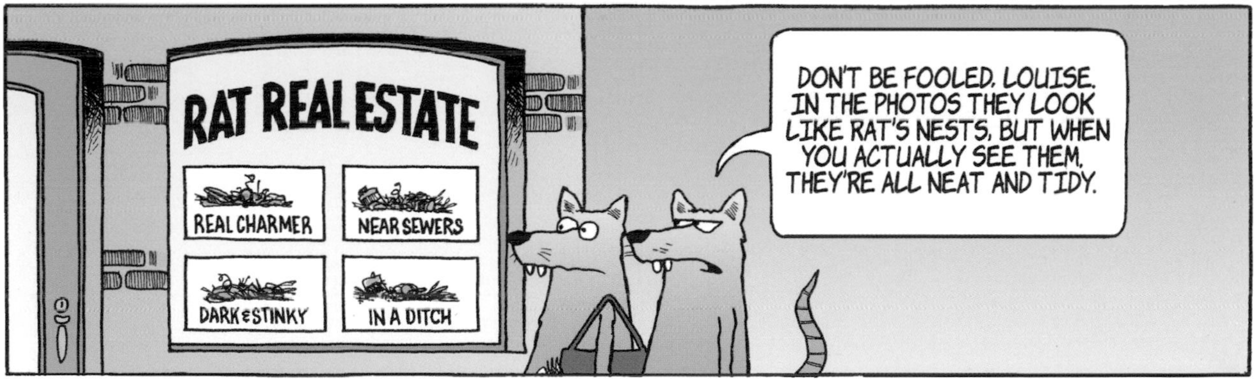
RAT REAL ESTATE
REAL CHARMER
NEAR SEWERS
DARK & STINKY
IN A DITCH
DON'T BE FOOLED, LOUISE. IN THE PHOTOS THEY LOOK LIKE RAT'S NESTS, BUT WHEN YOU ACTUALLY SEE THEM, THEY'RE ALL NEAT AND TIDY.

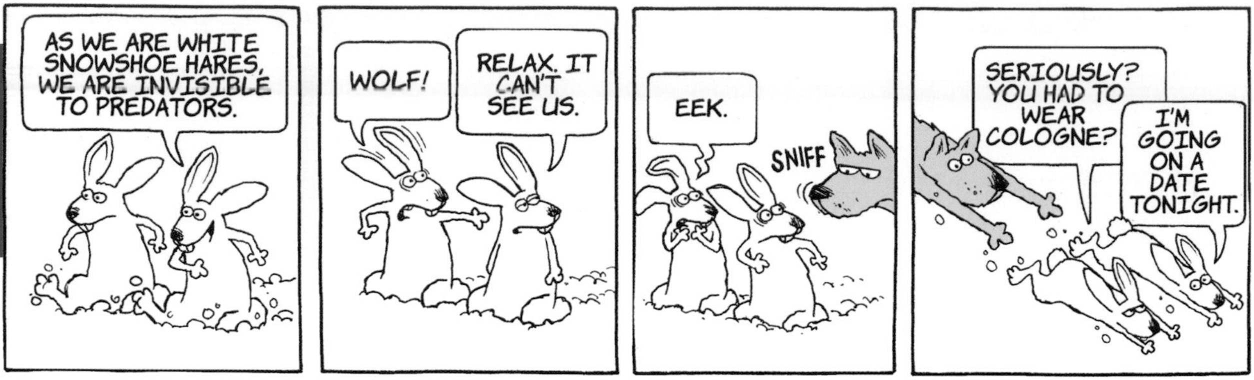
AS WE ARE WHITE SNOWSHOE HARES, WE ARE INVISIBLE TO PREDATORS.
WOLF!
RELAX. IT CAN'T SEE US.
EEK.
SNIFF
SERIOUSLY? YOU HAD TO WEAR COLOGNE?
I'M GOING ON A DATE TONIGHT.

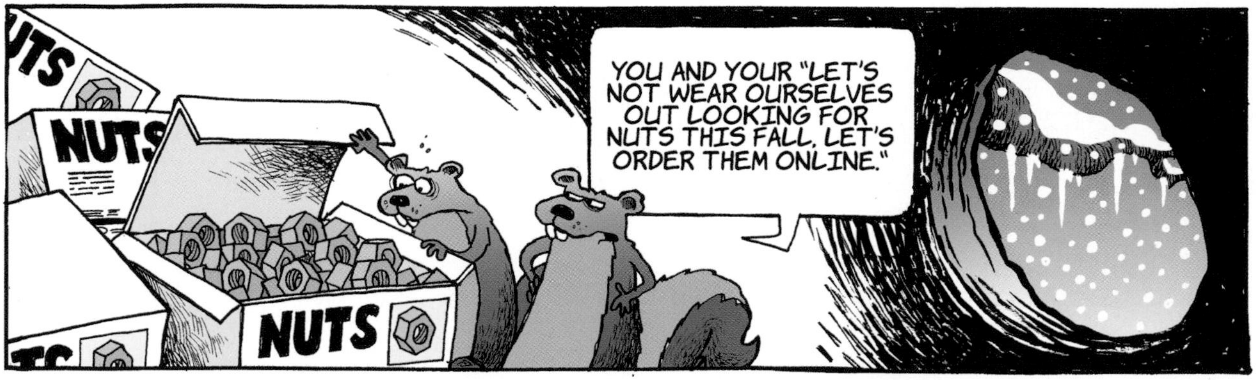
NUTS
NUTS
YOU AND YOUR "LET'S NOT WEAR OURSELVES OUT LOOKING FOR NUTS THIS FALL, LET'S ORDER THEM ONLINE."
NUTS

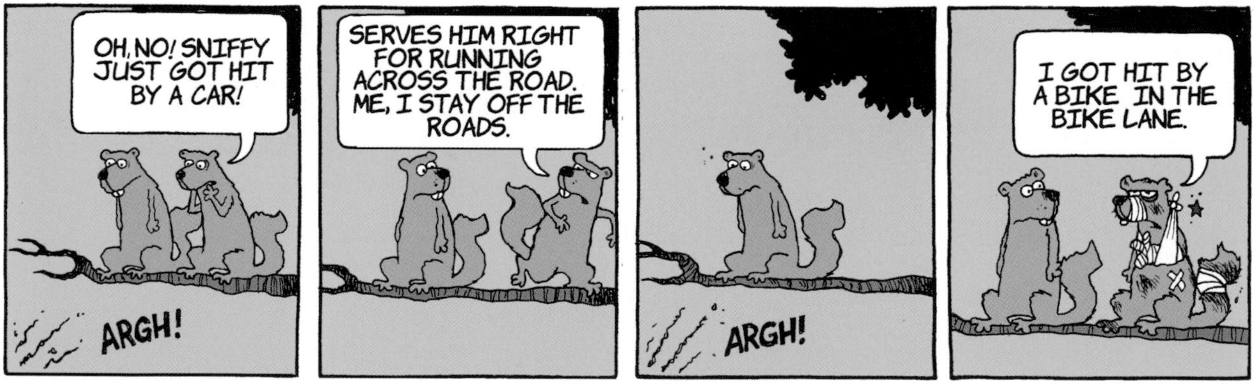
OH, NO! SNIFFY JUST GOT HIT BY A CAR!
ARGH!
SERVES HIM RIGHT FOR RUNNING ACROSS THE ROAD. ME, I STAY OFF THE ROADS.
ARGH!
I GOT HIT BY A BIKE IN THE BIKE LANE.

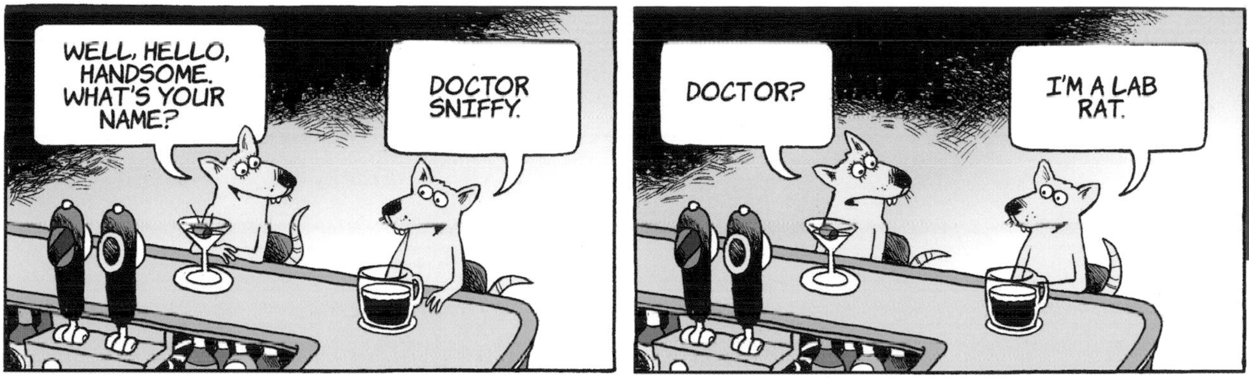
WELL, HELLO, HANDSOME. WHAT'S YOUR NAME?
DOCTOR SNIFFY.
DOCTOR?
I'M A LAB RAT.

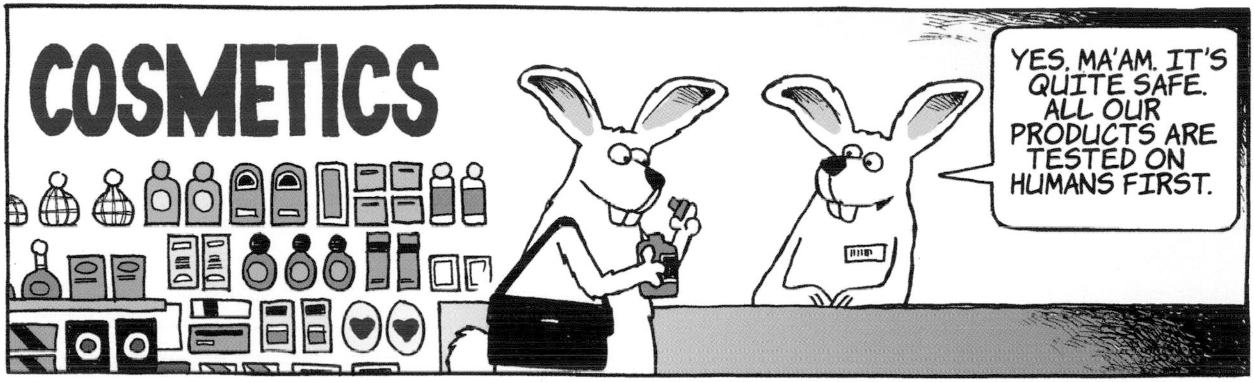
COSMETICS
YES, MA'AM. IT'S QUITE SAFE. ALL OUR PRODUCTS ARE TESTED ON HUMANS FIRST.

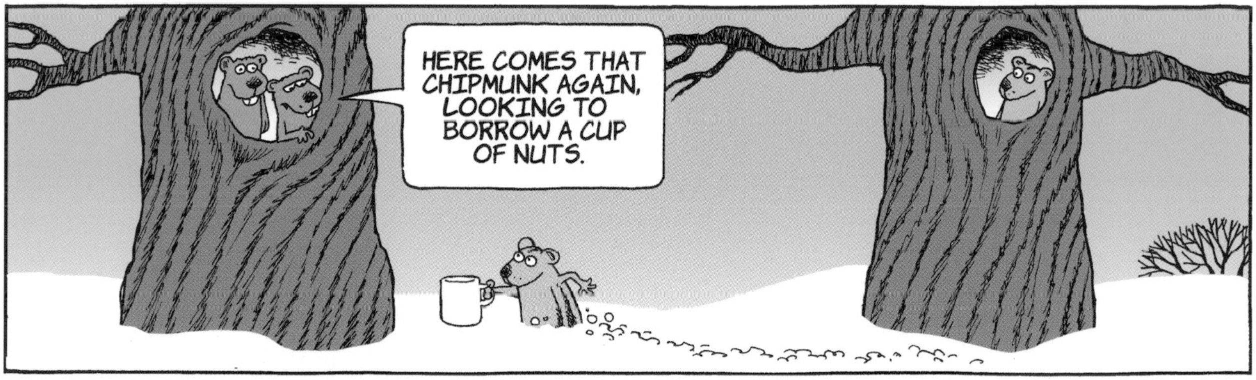
HERE COMES THAT CHIPMUNK AGAIN, LOOKING TO BORROW A CUP OF NUTS.

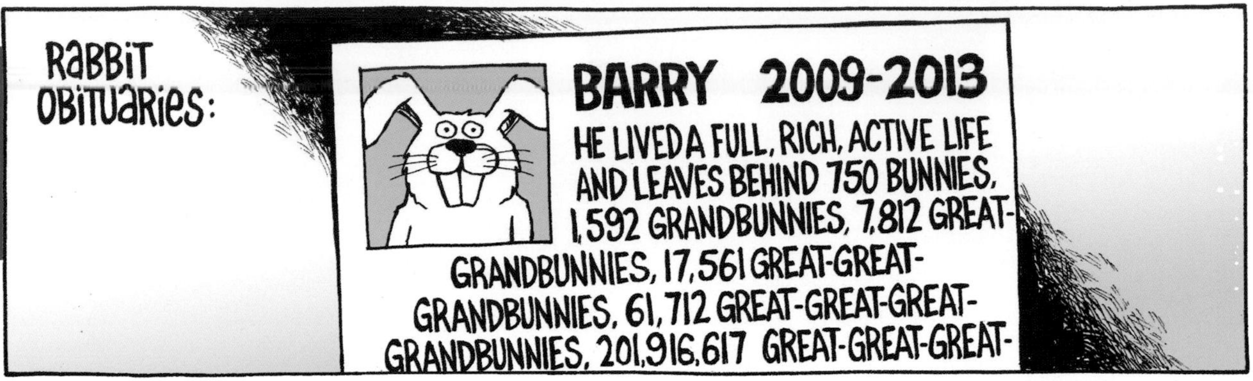
RABBIT OBITUARIES:
BARRY 2009-2013
HE LIVED A FULL, RICH, ACTIVE LIFE AND LEAVES BEHIND 750 BUNNIES, 1,592 GRANDBUNNIES, 7,812 GREAT-GRANDBUNNIES, 17,561 GREAT-GREAT-GRANDBUNNIES, 61,712 GREAT-GREAT-GREAT-GRANDBUNNIES, 201,916,617 GREAT-GREAT-GREAT-

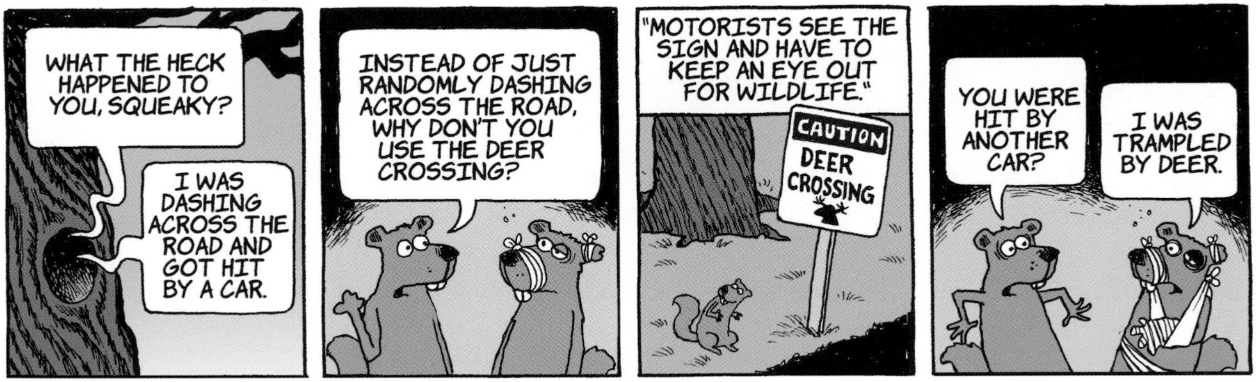
WHAT THE HECK HAPPENED TO YOU, SQUEAKY?
I WAS DASHING ACROSS THE ROAD AND GOT HIT BY A CAR.
INSTEAD OF JUST RANDOMLY DASHING ACROSS THE ROAD, WHY DON'T YOU USE THE DEER CROSSING?
"MOTORISTS SEE THE SIGN AND HAVE TO KEEP AN EYE OUT FOR WILDLIFE."
CAUTION
DEER CROSSING
YOU WERE HIT BY ANOTHER CAR?
I WAS TRAMPLED BY DEER.

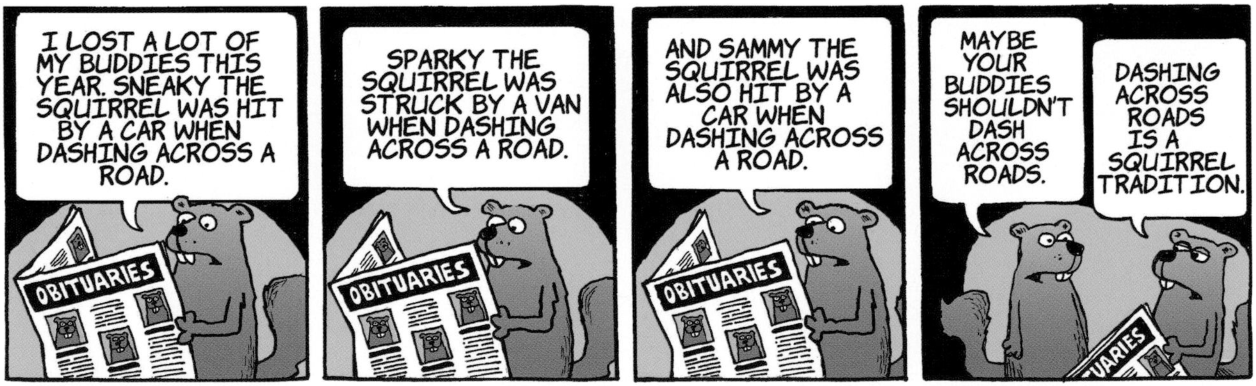
I LOST A LOT OF MY BUDDIES THIS YEAR. SNEAKY THE SQUIRREL WAS HIT BY A CAR WHEN DASHING ACROSS A ROAD.
OBITUARIES
SPARKY THE SQUIRREL WAS STRUCK BY A VAN WHEN DASHING ACROSS A ROAD.
OBITUARIES
AND SAMMY THE SQUIRREL WAS ALSO HIT BY A CAR WHEN DASHING ACROSS A ROAD.
OBITUARIES
MAYBE YOUR BUDDIES SHOULDN'T DASH ACROSS ROADS.
DASHING ACROSS ROADS IS A SQUIRREL TRADITION.

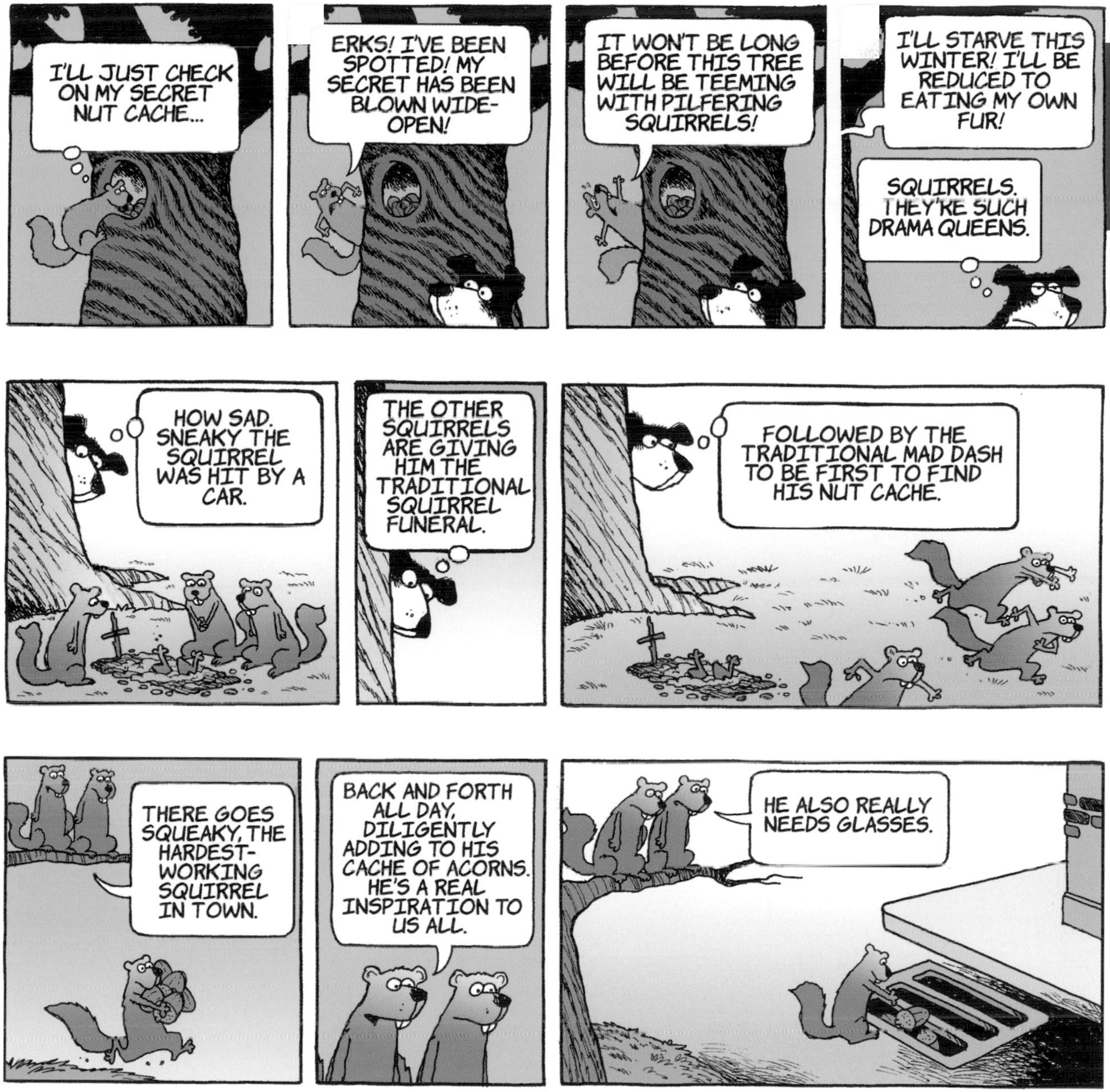
I'LL JUST CHECK ON MY SECRET NUT CACHE...
ERKS! I'VE BEEN SPOTTED! MY SECRET HAS BEEN BLOWN WIDE-OPEN!
IT WON'T BE LONG BEFORE THIS TREE WILL BE TEEMING WITH PILFERING SQUIRRELS!
I'LL STARVE THIS WINTER! I'LL BE REDUCED TO EATING MY OWN FUR!
SQUIRRELS. THEY'RE SUCH DRAMA QUEENS.
HOW SAD. SNEAKY THE SQUIRREL WAS HIT BY A CAR.
THE OTHER SQUIRRELS ARE GIVING HIM THE TRADITIONAL SQUIRREL FUNERAL.
FOLLOWED BY THE TRADITIONAL MAD DASH TO BE FIRST TO FIND HIS NUT CACHE.
THERE GOES SQUEAKY, THE HARDEST-WORKING SQUIRREL IN TOWN.
BACK AND FORTH ALL DAY, DILIGENTLY ADDING TO HIS CACHE OF ACORNS. HE'S A REAL INSPIRATION TO US ALL.
HE ALSO REALLY NEEDS GLASSES.

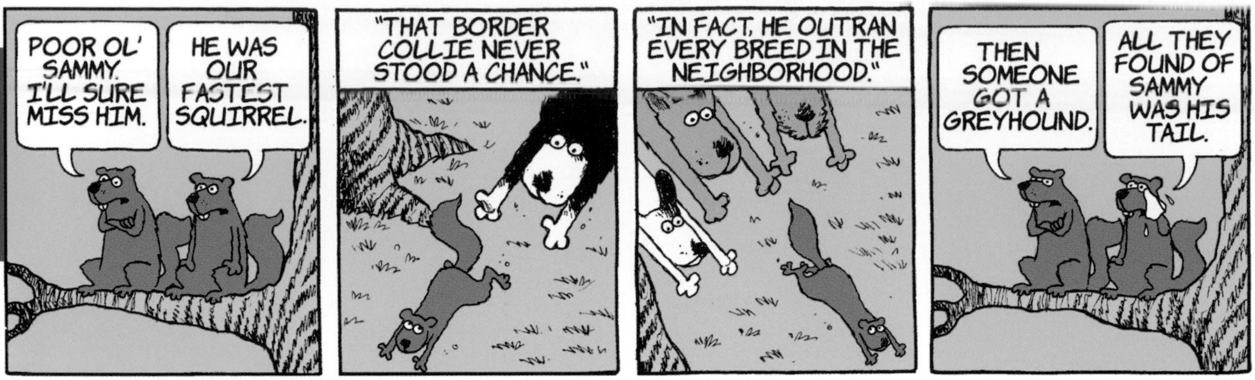
POOR OL' SAMMY. I'LL SURE MISS HIM.
HE WAS OUR FASTEST SQUIRREL.
"THAT BORDER COLLIE NEVER STOOD A CHANCE."
"IN FACT, HE OUTRAN EVERY BREED IN THE NEIGHBORHOOD."
THEN SOMEONE GOT A GREYHOUND.
ALL THEY FOUND OF SAMMY WAS HIS TAIL.

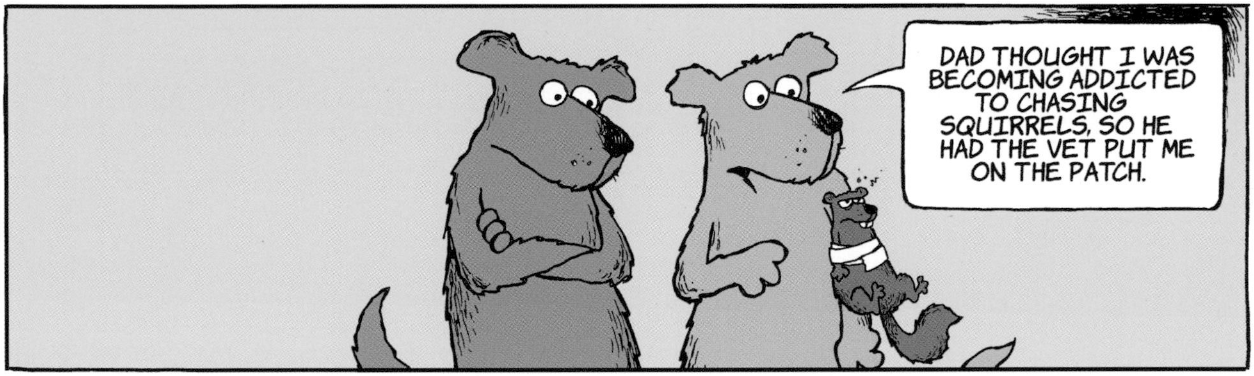
DAD THOUGHT I WAS BECOMING ADDICTED TO CHASING SQUIRRELS, SO HE HAD THE VET PUT ME ON THE PATCH.

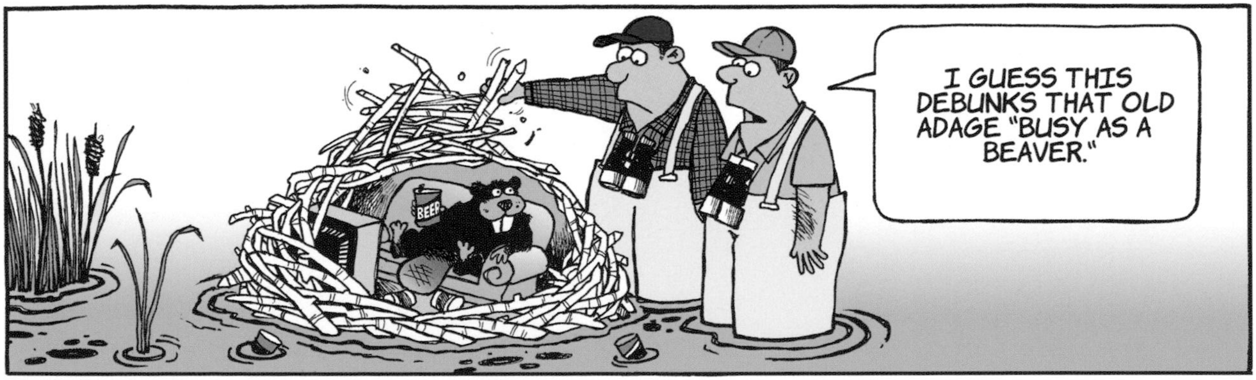
BEER
I GUESS THIS DEBUNKS THAT OLD ADAGE "BUSY AS A BEAVER."

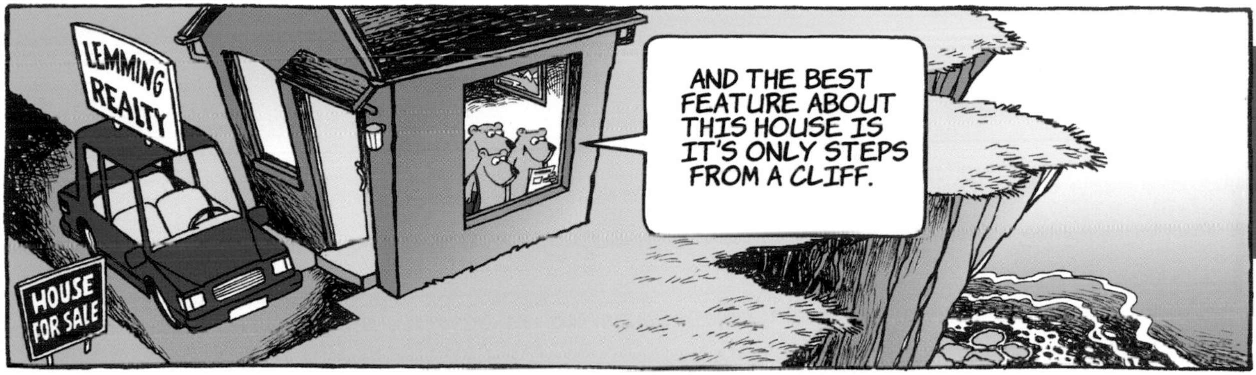
LEMMING REALTY
HOUSE FOR SALE
AND THE BEST FEATURE ABOUT THIS HOUSE IS IT'S ONLY STEPS FROM A CLIFF.

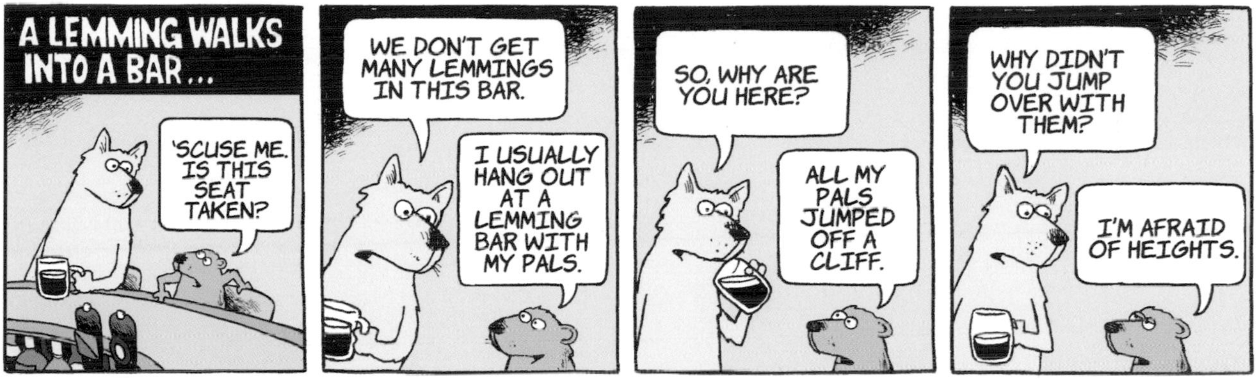
A LEMMING WALKS INTO A BAR...
'SCUSE ME. IS THIS SEAT TAKEN?
WE DON'T GET MANY LEMMINGS IN THIS BAR.
I USUALLY HANG OUT AT A LEMMING BAR WITH MY PALS.
SO, WHY ARE YOU HERE?
ALL MY PALS JUMPED OFF A CLIFF.
WHY DIDN'T YOU JUMP OVER WITH THEM?
I'M AFRAID OF HEIGHTS.

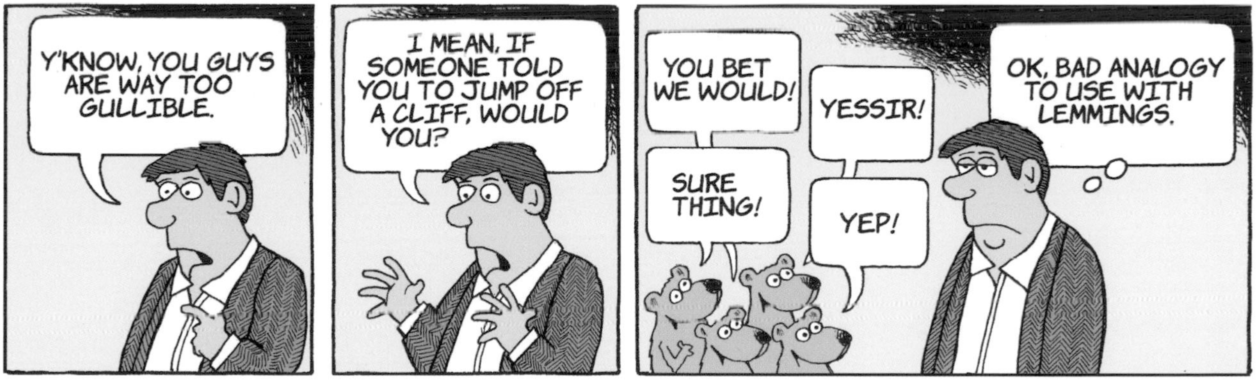
Y'KNOW, YOU GUYS ARE WAY TOO GULLIBLE.
I MEAN, IF SOMEONE TOLD YOU TO JUMP OFF A CLIFF, WOULD YOU?
YOU BET WE WOULD!
YESSIR!
SURE THING!
YEP!
OK, BAD ANALOGY TO USE WITH LEMMINGS.

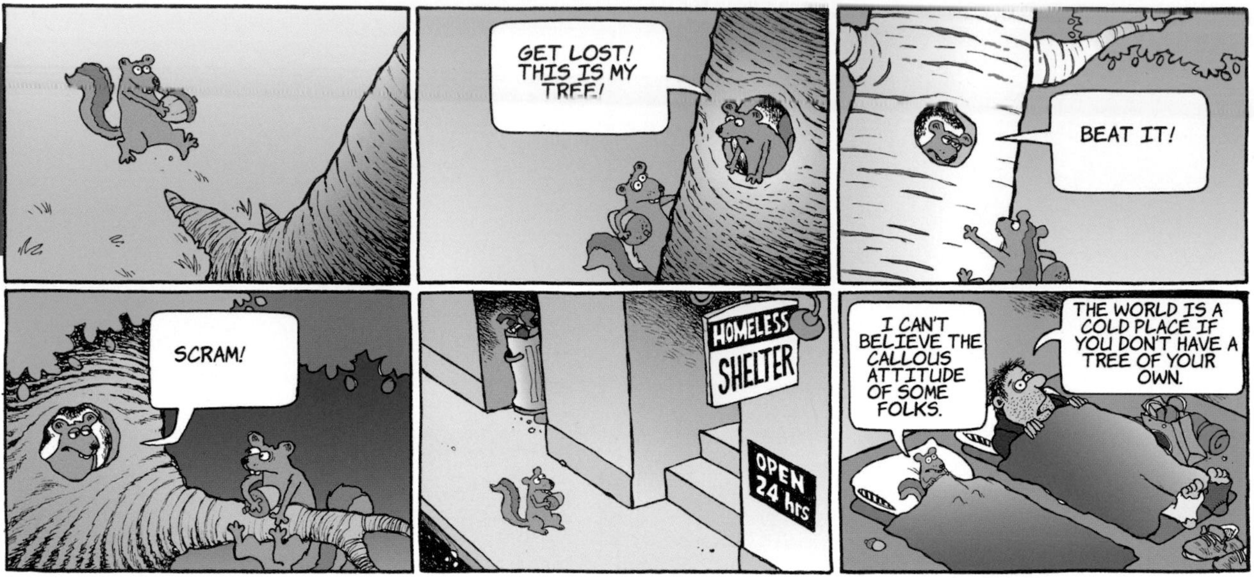
GET LOST! THIS IS MY TREE!
BEAT IT!
SCRAM!
HOMELESS SHELTER
OPEN 24 hrs
I CAN'T BELIEVE THE CALLOUS ATTITUDE OF SOME FOLKS.
THE WORLD IS A COLD PLACE IF YOU DON'T HAVE A TREE OF YOUR OWN.

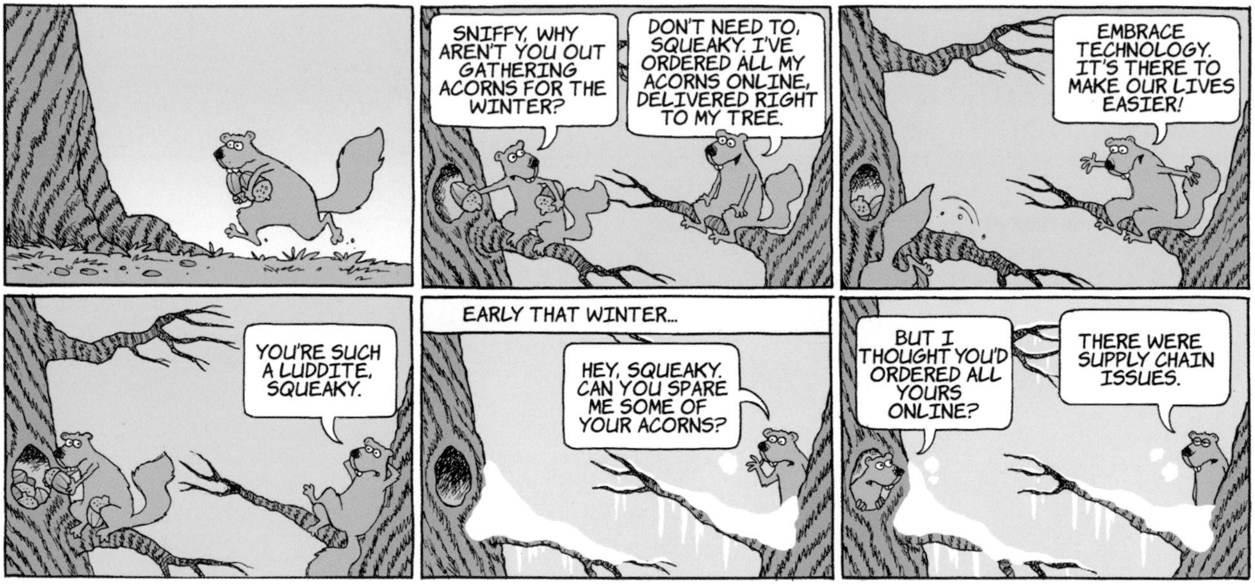
SNIFFY, WHY AREN'T YOU OUT GATHERING ACORNS FOR THE WINTER?
DON'T NEED TO, SQUEAKY. I'VE ORDERED ALL MY ACORNS ONLINE, DELIVERED RIGHT TO MY TREE.
EMBRACE TECHNOLOGY. IT'S THERE TO MAKE OUR LIVES EASIER!
YOU'RE SUCH A LUDDITE, SQUEAKY.
EARLY THAT WINTER...
HEY, SQUEAKY. CAN YOU SPARE ME SOME OF YOUR ACORNS?
BUT I THOUGHT YOU'D ORDERED ALL YOURS ONLINE?
THERE WERE SUPPLY CHAIN ISSUES.

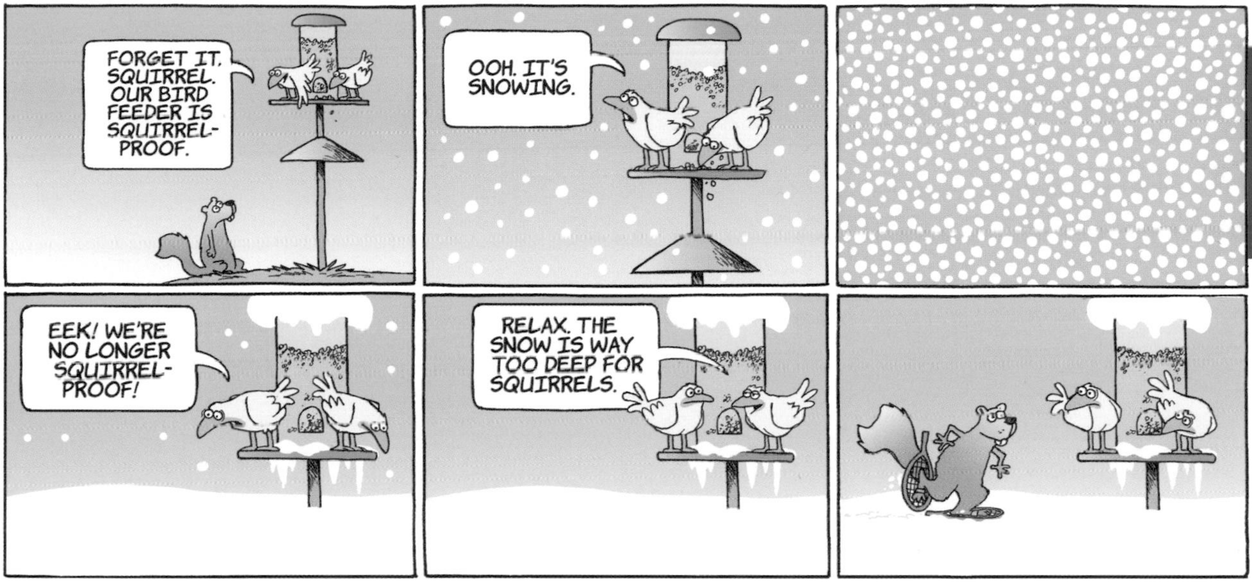
FORGET IT, SQUIRREL. OUR BIRD FEEDER IS SQUIRREL-PROOF.
OOH. IT'S SNOWING.
EEK! WE'RE NO LONGER SQUIRREL-PROOF!
RELAX. THE SNOW IS WAY TOO DEEP FOR SQUIRRELS.

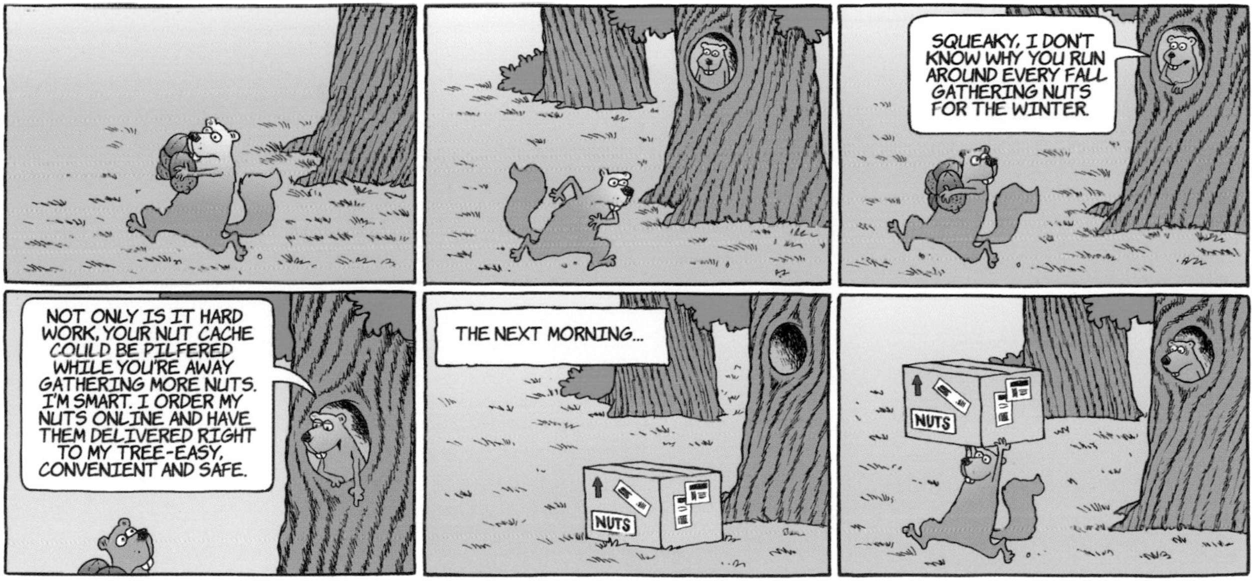
SQUEAKY, I DON'T KNOW WHY YOU RUN AROUND EVERY FALL GATHERING NUTS FOR THE WINTER.
NOT ONLY IS IT HARD WORK, YOUR NUT CACHE COULD BE PILFERED WHILE YOU'RE AWAY GATHERING MORE NUTS. I'M SMART. I ORDER MY NUTS ONLINE AND HAVE THEM DELIVERED RIGHT TO MY TREE-EASY, CONVENIENT AND SAFE.
THE NEXT MORNING...
NUTS
NUTS

8 BODACIOUS BEARS

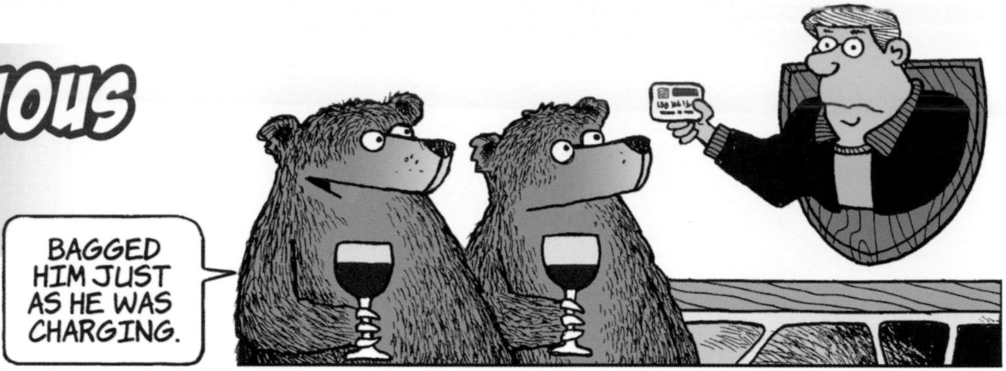
BAGGED HIM JUST AS HE WAS CHARGING.

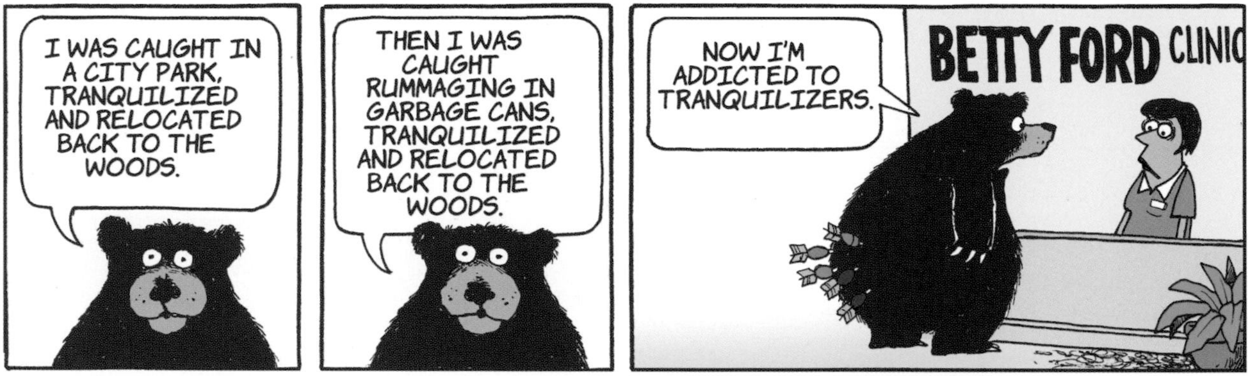
I WAS CAUGHT IN A CITY PARK, TRANQUILIZED AND RELOCATED BACK TO THE WOODS.
THEN I WAS CAUGHT RUMMAGING IN GARBAGE CANS, TRANQUILIZED AND RELOCATED BACK TO THE WOODS.
NOW I'M ADDICTED TO TRANQUILIZERS.
BETTY FORD CLINIC

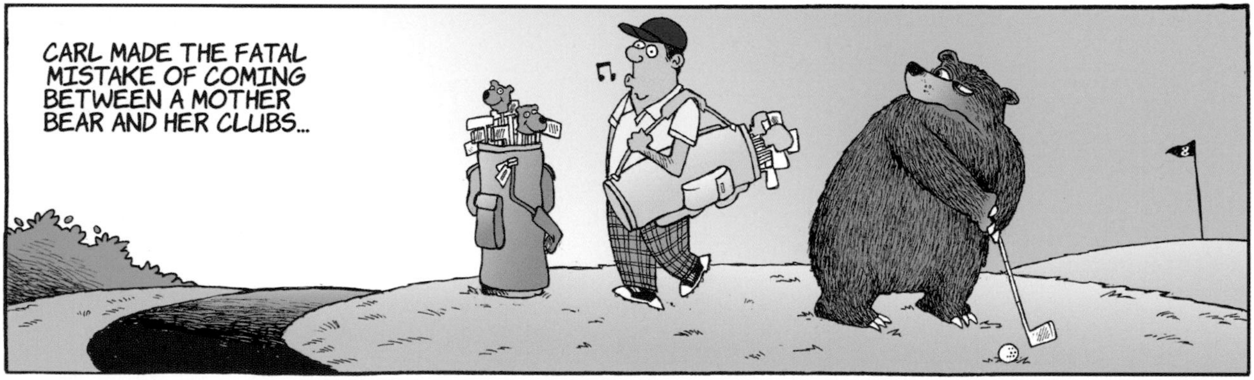
CARL MADE THE FATAL MISTAKE OF COMING BETWEEN A MOTHER BEAR AND HER CLUBS...

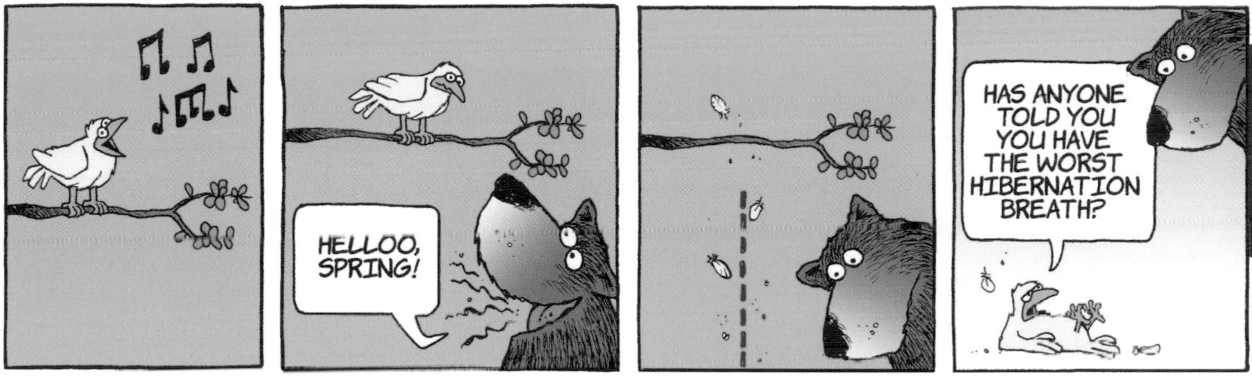
HELLOO, SPRING!
HAS ANYONE TOLD YOU YOU HAVE THE WORST HIBERNATION BREATH?

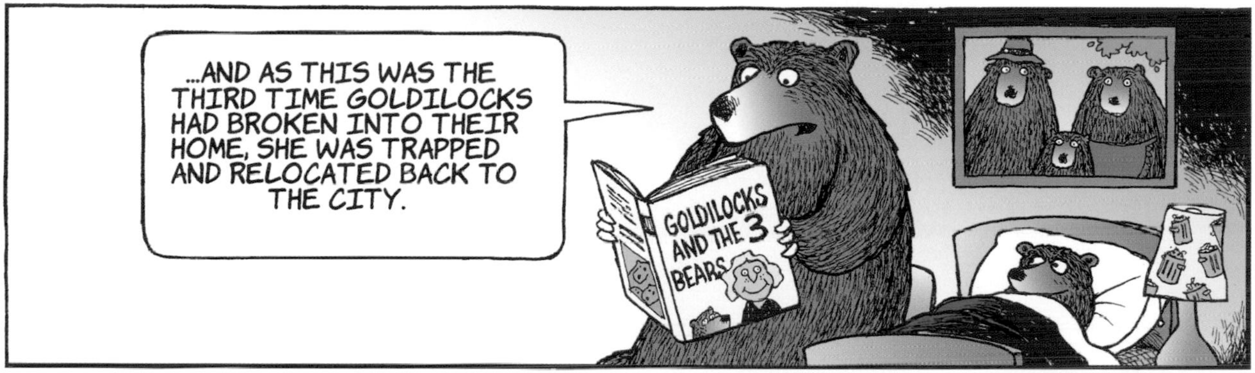
...AND AS THIS WAS THE THIRD TIME GOLDILOCKS HAD BROKEN INTO THEIR HOME, SHE WAS TRAPPED AND RELOCATED BACK TO THE CITY.
GOLDILOCKS AND THE 3 BEARS

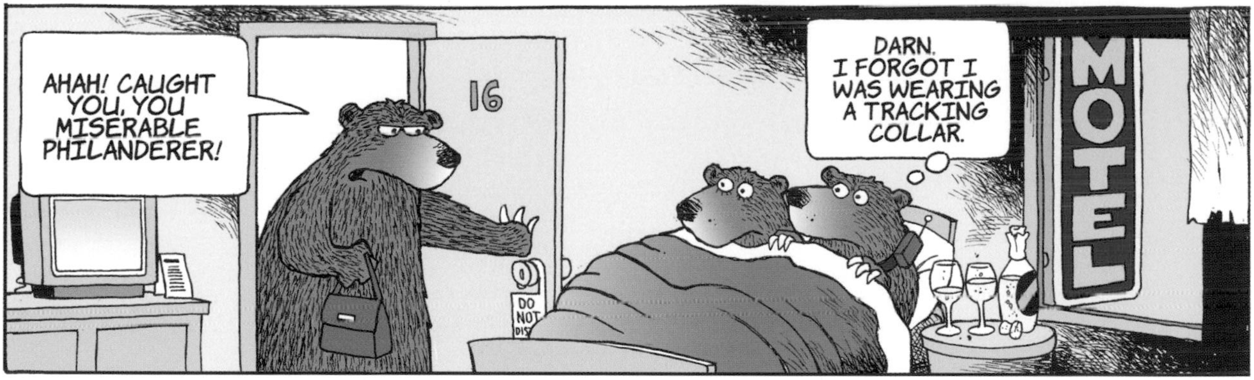
AHAH! CAUGHT YOU, YOU MISERABLE PHILANDERER!
16
DARN. I FORGOT I WAS WEARING A TRACKING COLLAR.
MOTEL

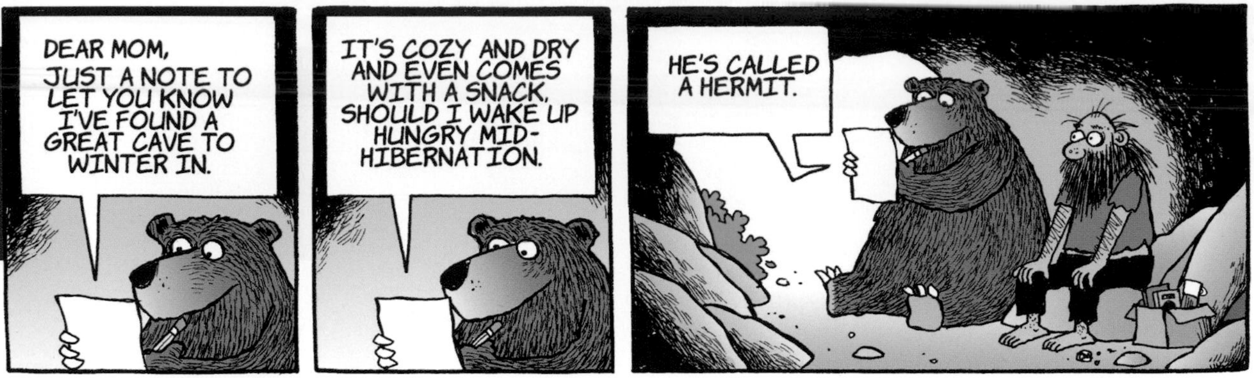
DEAR MOM, JUST A NOTE TO LET YOU KNOW I'VE FOUND A GREAT CAVE TO WINTER IN.
IT'S COZY AND DRY AND EVEN COMES WITH A SNACK, SHOULD I WAKE UP HUNGRY MID-HIBERNATION.
HE'S CALLED A HERMIT.

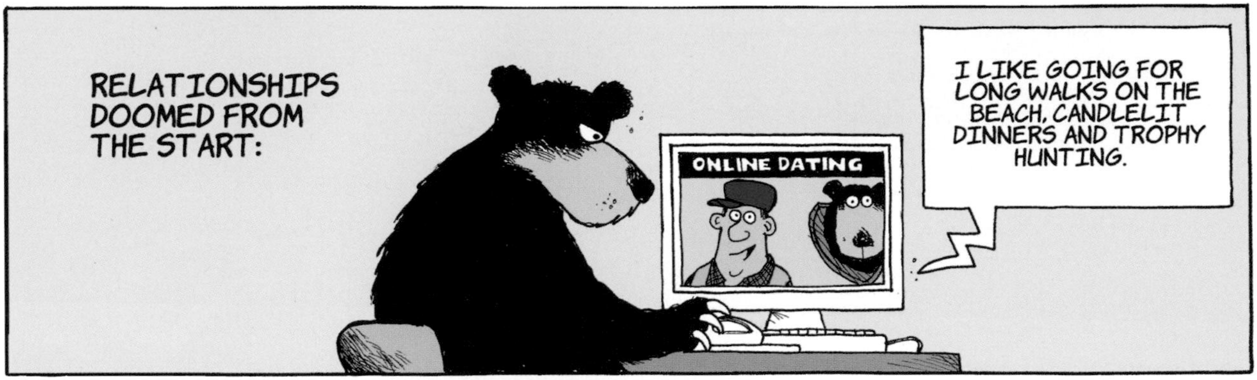
RELATIONSHIPS DOOMED FROM THE START:
ONLINE DATING
I LIKE GOING FOR LONG WALKS ON THE BEACH, CANDLELIT DINNERS AND TROPHY HUNTING.

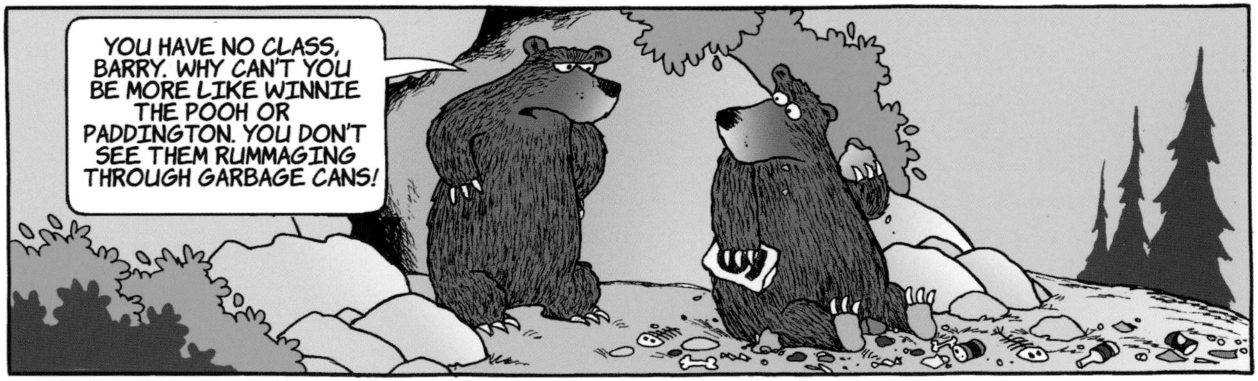
YOU HAVE NO CLASS, BARRY. WHY CAN'T YOU BE MORE LIKE WINNIE THE POOH OR PADDINGTON. YOU DON'T SEE THEM RUMMAGING THROUGH GARBAGE CANS!

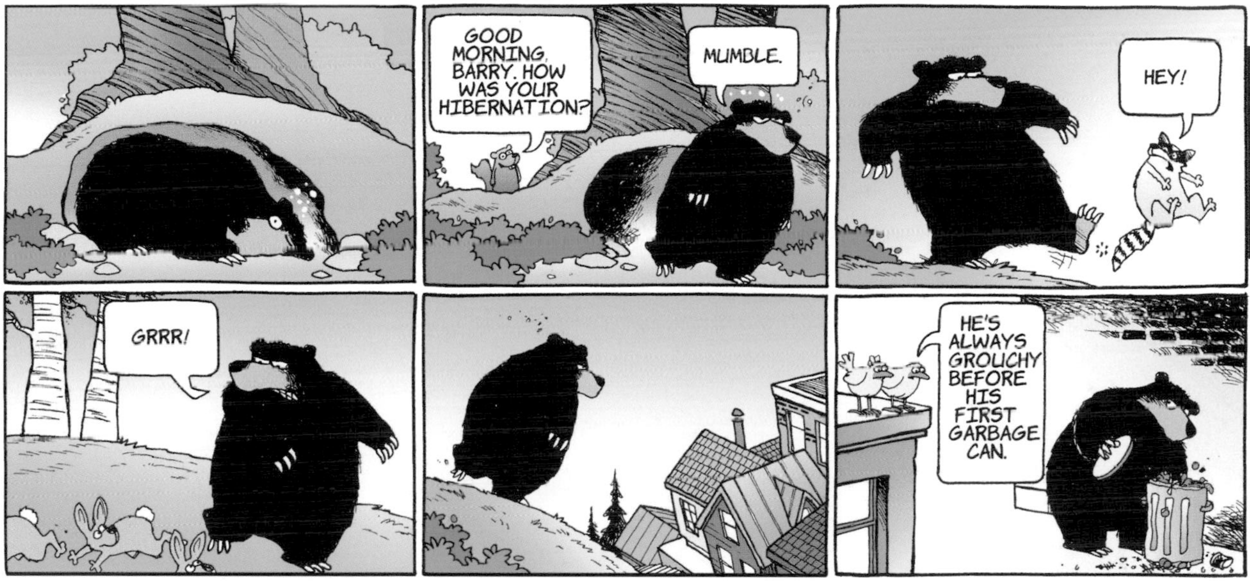
GOOD MORNING, BARRY. HOW WAS YOUR HIBERNATION?
MUMBLE.
HEY!
GRRR!
HE'S ALWAYS GROUCHY BEFORE HIS FIRST GARBAGE CAN.

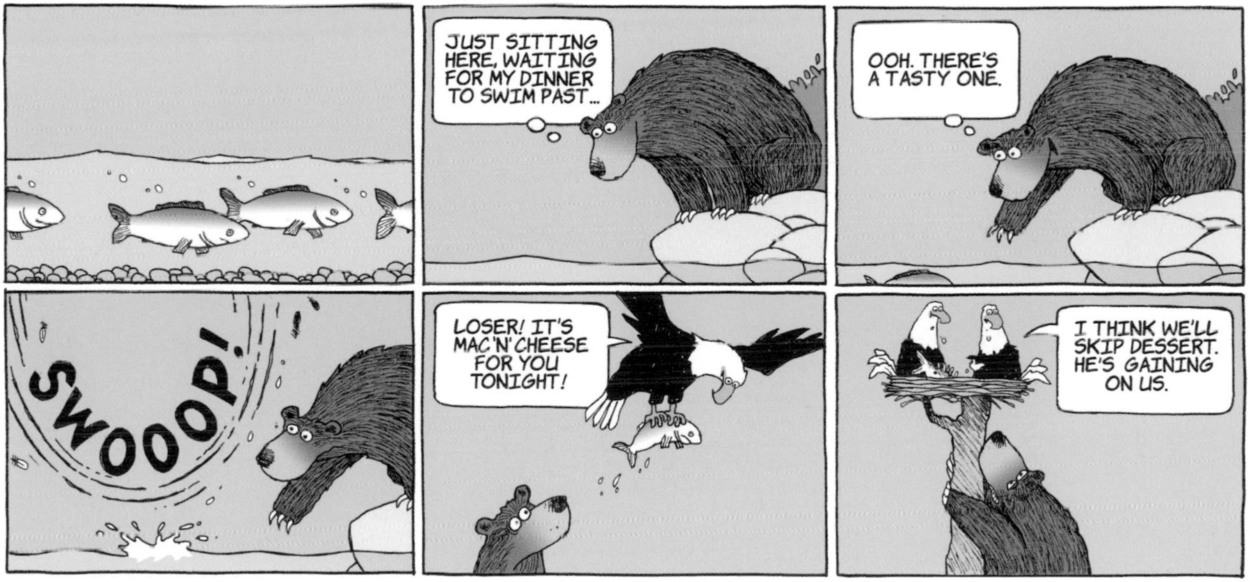
JUST SITTING HERE, WAITING FOR MY DINNER TO SWIM PAST...
OOH. THERE'S A TASTY ONE.
SWOOOP!
LOSER! IT'S MAC'N'CHEESE FOR YOU TONIGHT!
I THINK WE'LL SKIP DESSERT. HE'S GAINING ON US.

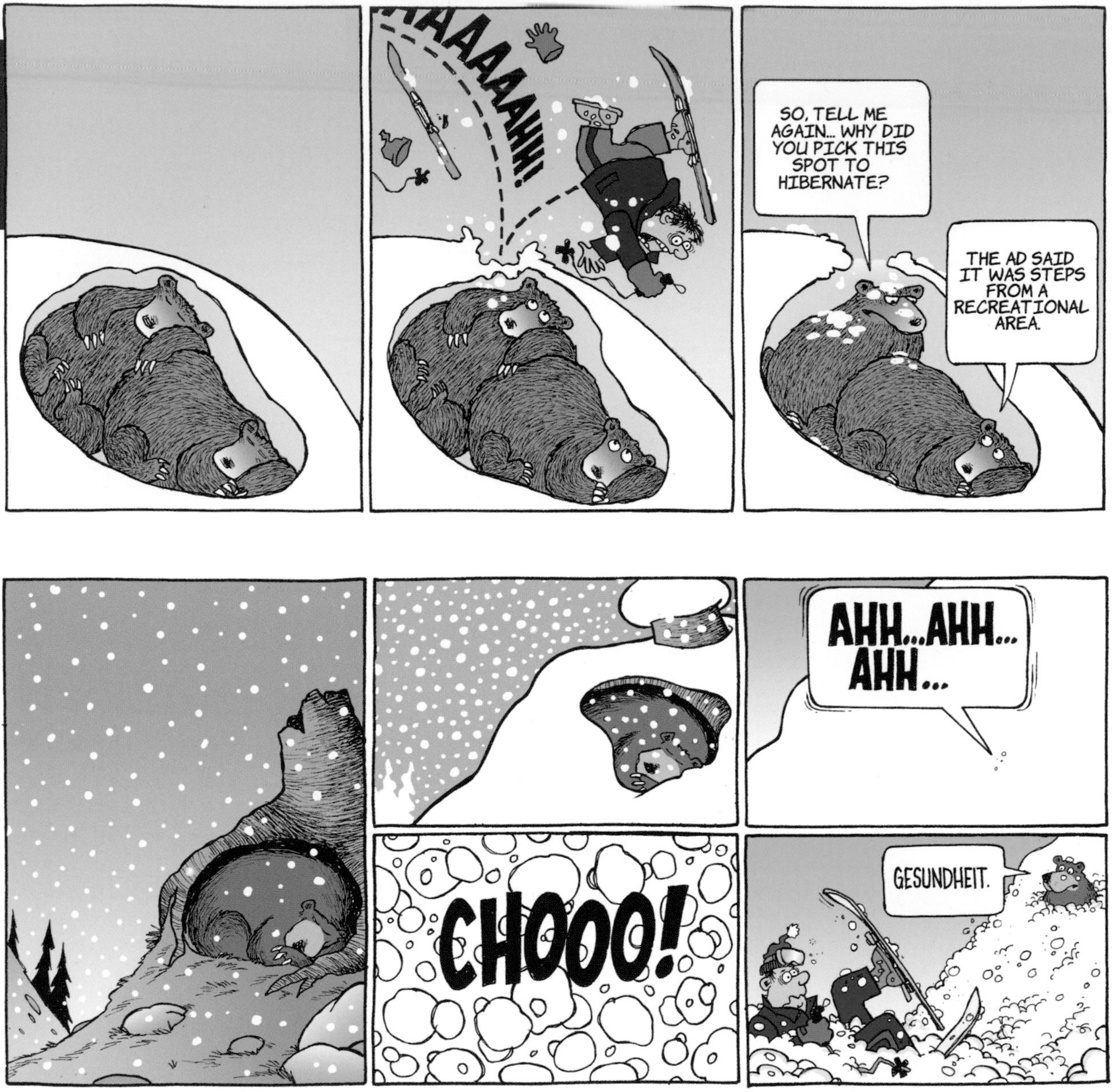
AAAAAAAHH!
SO, TELL ME AGAIN... WHY DID YOU PICK THIS SPOT TO HIBERNATE?
THE AD SAID IT WAS STEPS FROM A RECREATIONAL AREA.
AHH...AHH... AHH...
CHOOO!
GESUNDHEIT.

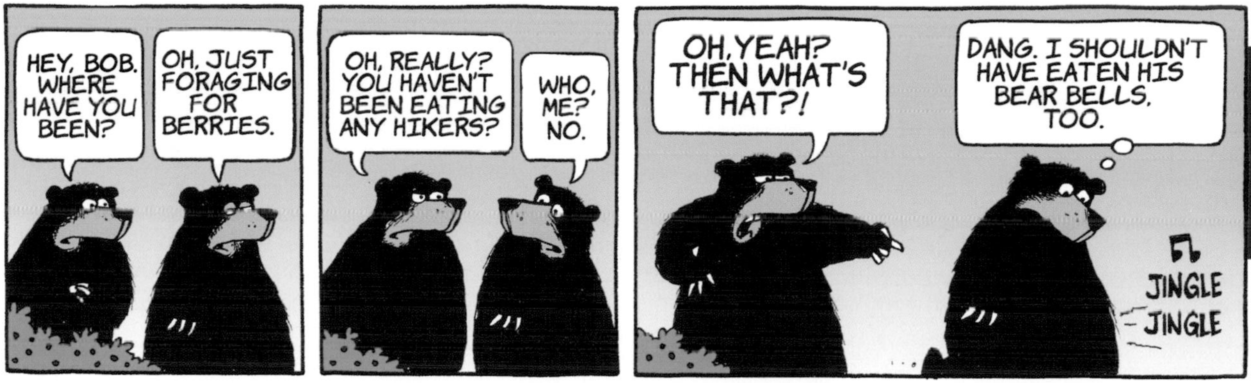
HEY, BOB. WHERE HAVE YOU BEEN?
OH, JUST FORAGING FOR BERRIES.
OH, REALLY? YOU HAVEN'T BEEN EATING ANY HIKERS?
WHO, ME? NO.
OH, YEAH? THEN WHAT'S THAT?!
DANG. I SHOULDN'T HAVE EATEN HIS BEAR BELLS, TOO.
JINGLE
JINGLE

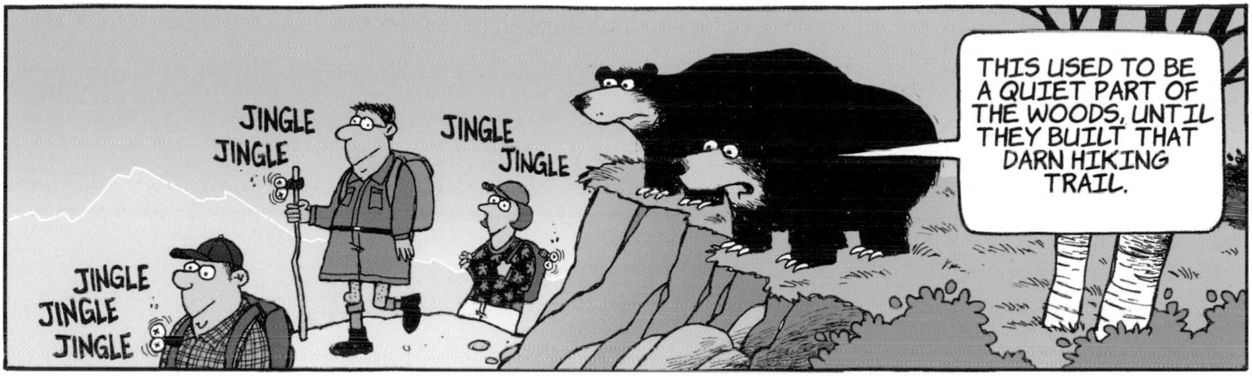
JINGLE
JINGLE
JINGLE
JINGLE
JINGLE
JINGLE
JINGLE
THIS USED TO BE A QUIET PART OF THE WOODS, UNTIL THEY BUILT THAT DARN HIKING TRAIL.

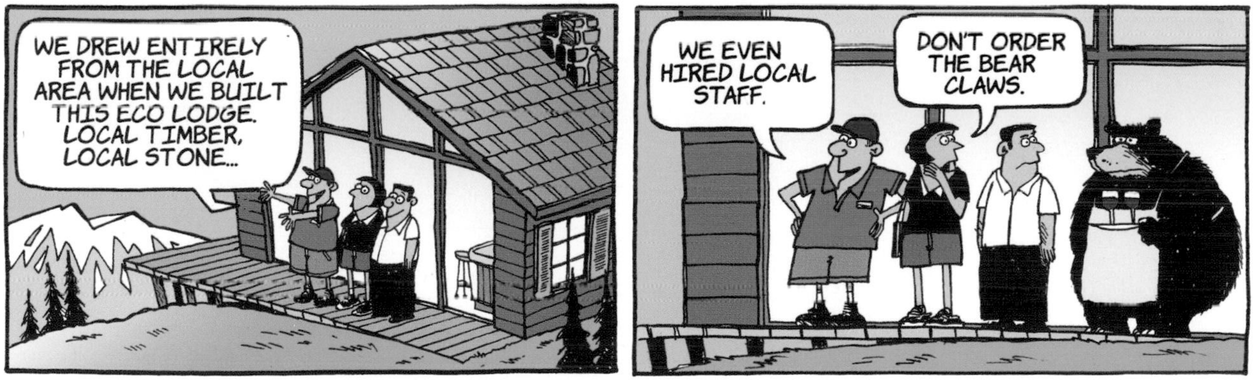
WE DREW ENTIRELY FROM THE LOCAL AREA WHEN WE BUILT THIS ECO LODGE. LOCAL TIMBER, LOCAL STONE...
WE EVEN HIRED LOCAL STAFF.
DON'T ORDER THE BEAR CLAWS.

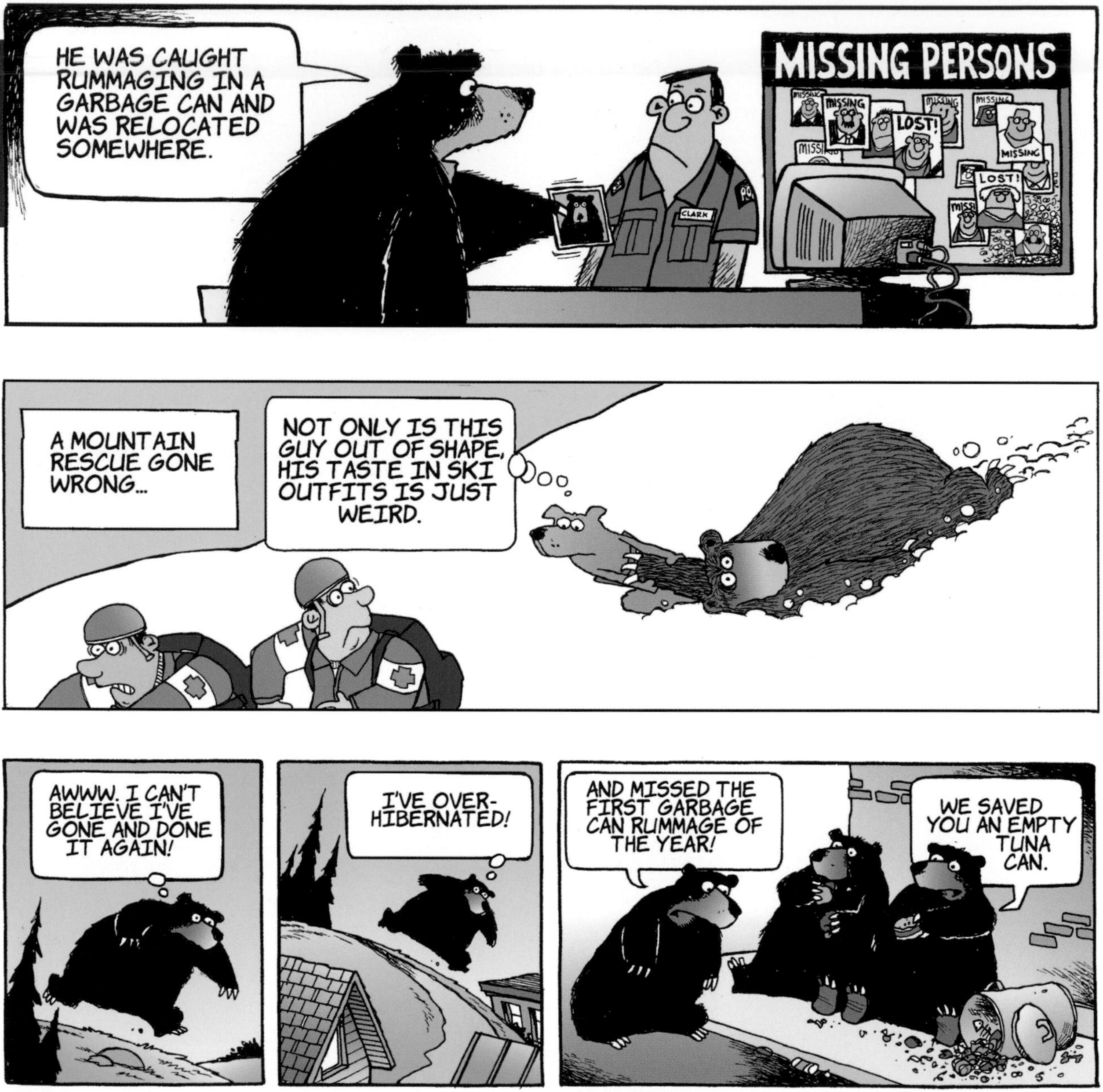
HE WAS CAUGHT RUMMAGING IN A GARBAGE CAN AND WAS RELOCATED SOMEWHERE.
CLARK
MISSING PERSONS
MISSING
LOST!
MISSING
LOST!
A MOUNTAIN RESCUE GONE WRONG...
NOT ONLY IS THIS GUY OUT OF SHAPE, HIS TASTE IN SKI OUTFITS IS JUST WEIRD.
AWWW. I CAN'T BELIEVE I'VE GONE AND DONE IT AGAIN!
I'VE OVER-HIBERNATED!
AND MISSED THE FIRST GARBAGE CAN RUMMAGE OF THE YEAR!
WE SAVED YOU AN EMPTY TUNA CAN.

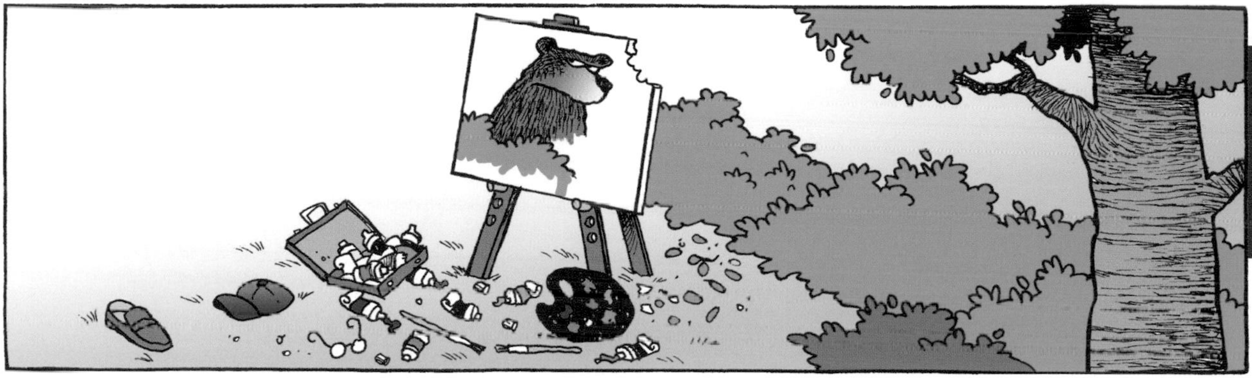

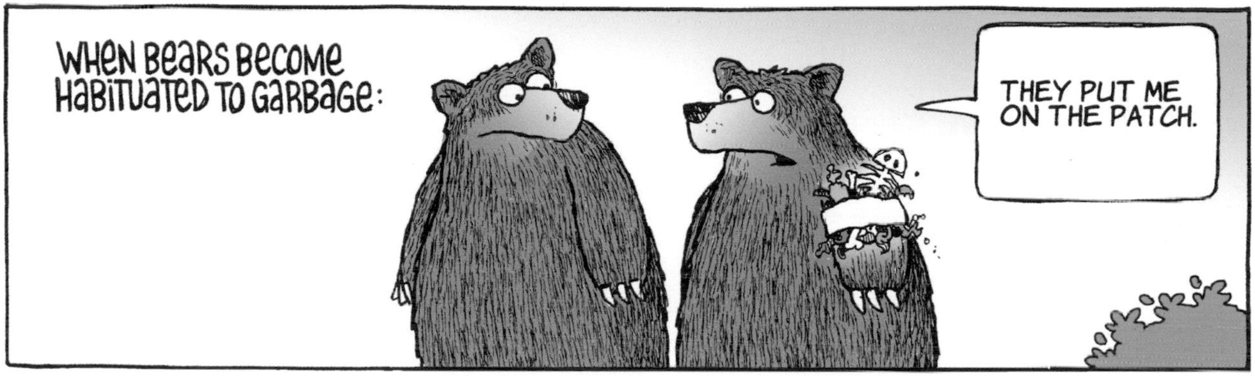
WHEN BEARS BECOME HABITUATED TO GARBAGE:
THEY PUT ME ON THE PATCH.

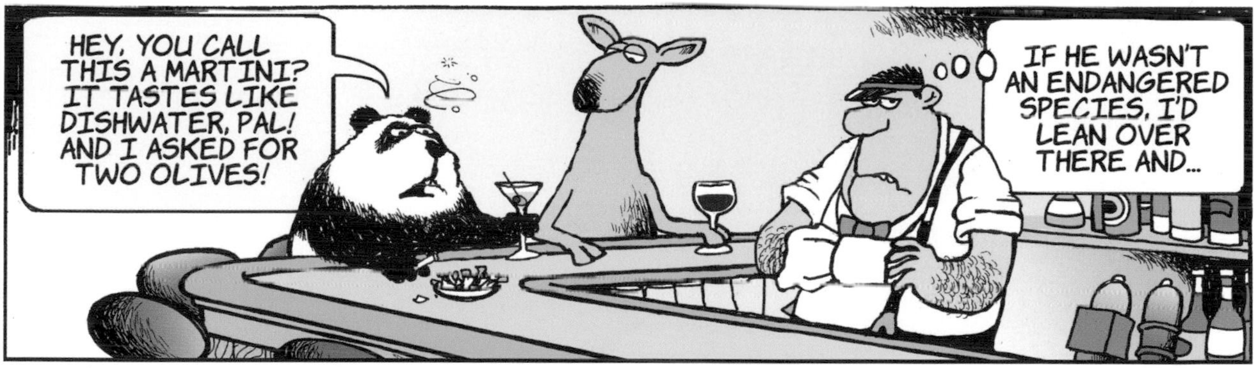
HEY, YOU CALL THIS A MARTINI? IT TASTES LIKE DISHWATER, PAL! AND I ASKED FOR TWO OLIVES!
IF HE WASN'T AN ENDANGERED SPECIES, I'D LEAN OVER THERE AND...

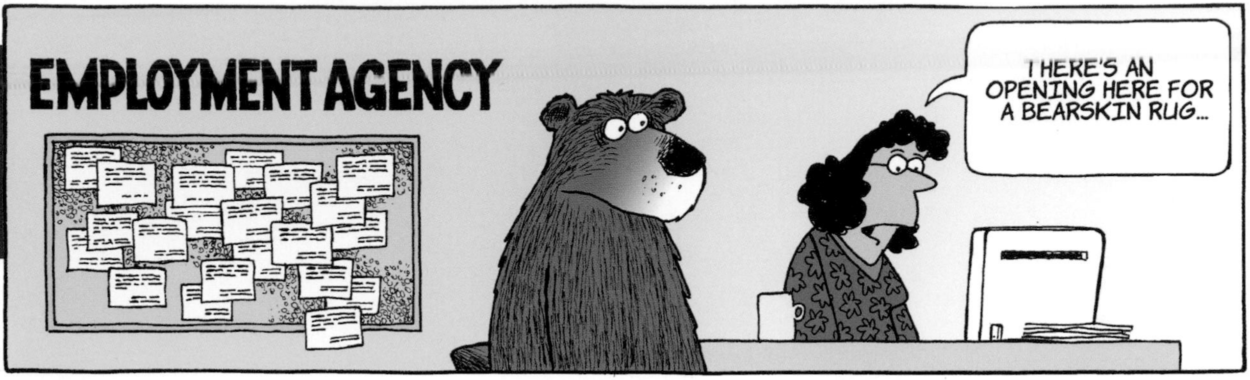
EMPLOYMENT AGENCY
THERE'S AN OPENING HERE FOR A BEARSKIN RUG...

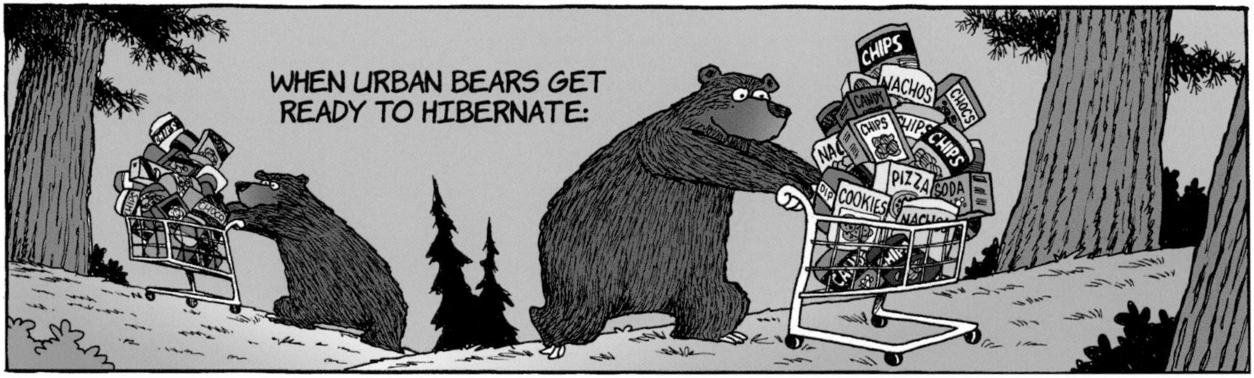
WHEN URBAN BEARS GET READY TO HIBERNATE:
CHIPS
NACHOS
CHOCS
CANDY
PIZZA
SODA
COOKIES
DIP

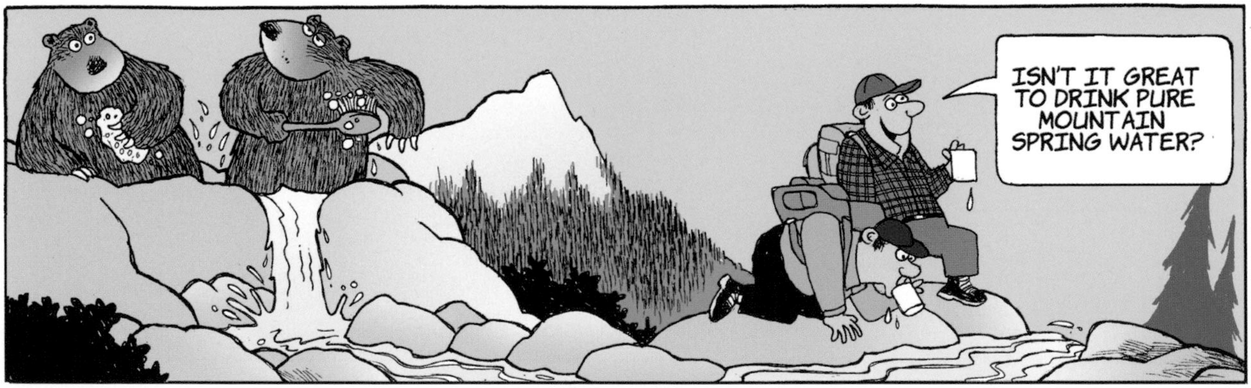
ISN'T IT GREAT TO DRINK PURE MOUNTAIN SPRING WATER?

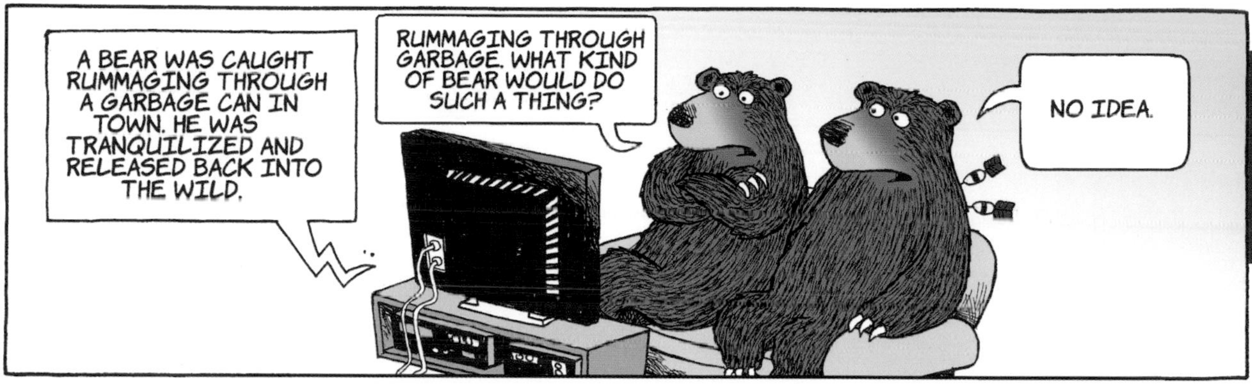
A BEAR WAS CAUGHT RUMMAGING THROUGH A GARBAGE CAN IN TOWN. HE WAS TRANQUILIZED AND RELEASED BACK INTO THE WILD.
RUMMAGING THROUGH GARBAGE. WHAT KIND OF BEAR WOULD DO SUCH A THING?
NO IDEA.

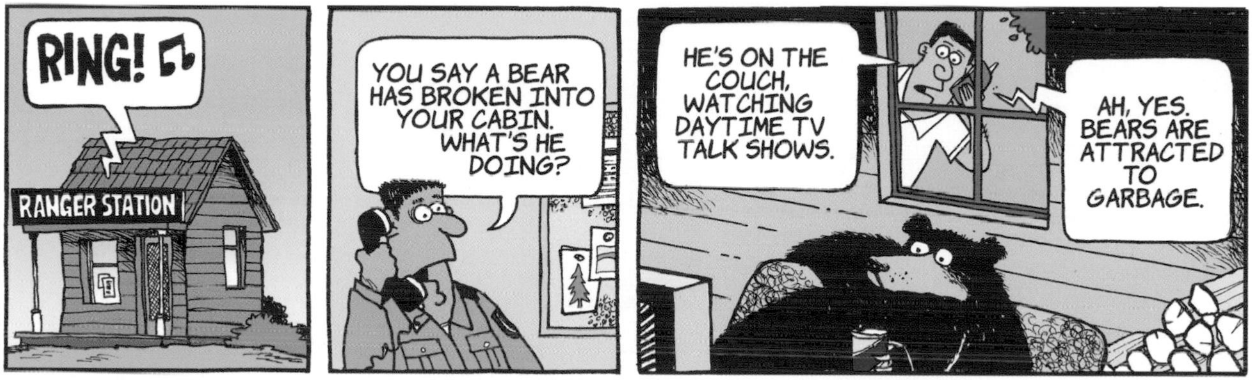
RING!
RANGER STATION
YOU SAY A BEAR HAS BROKEN INTO YOUR CABIN. WHAT'S HE DOING?
HE'S ON THE COUCH, WATCHING DAYTIME TV TALK SHOWS.
AH, YES. BEARS ARE ATTRACTED TO GARBAGE.

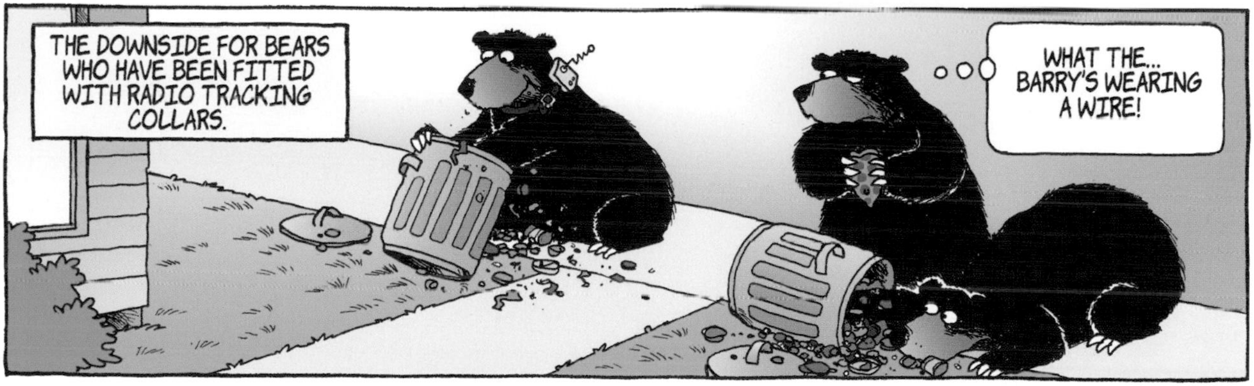
THE DOWNSIDE FOR BEARS WHO HAVE BEEN FITTED WITH RADIO TRACKING COLLARS.
WHAT THE... BARRY'S WEARING A WIRE!

9 WORLDLY WOLVES

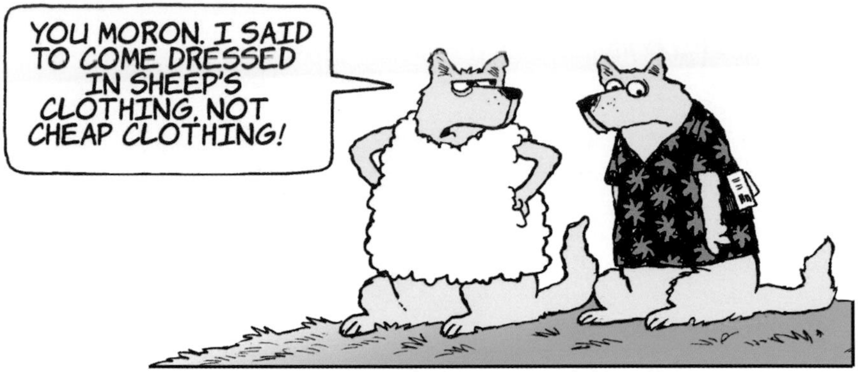
YOU MORON. I SAID TO COME DRESSED IN SHEEP'S CLOTHING, NOT CHEAP CLOTHING!

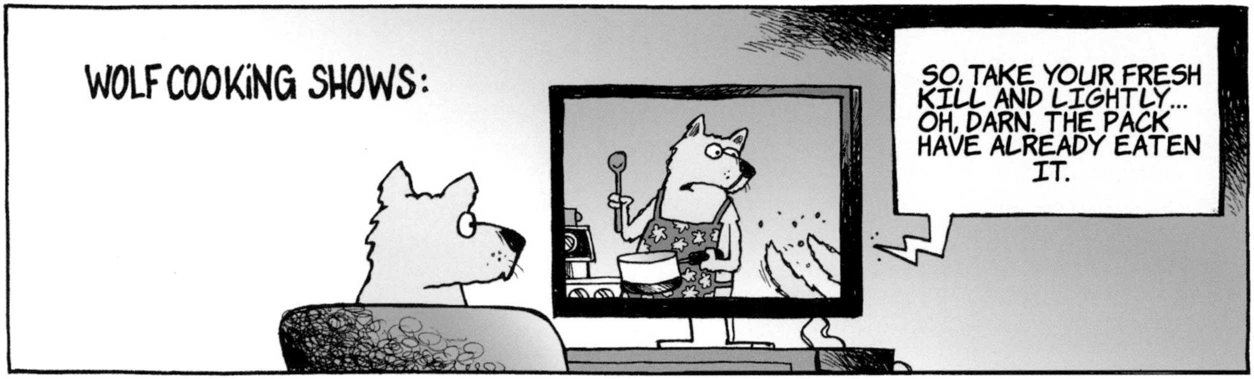
WOLF COOKING SHOWS:
SO, TAKE YOUR FRESH KILL AND LIGHTLY... OH, DARN. THE PACK HAVE ALREADY EATEN IT.

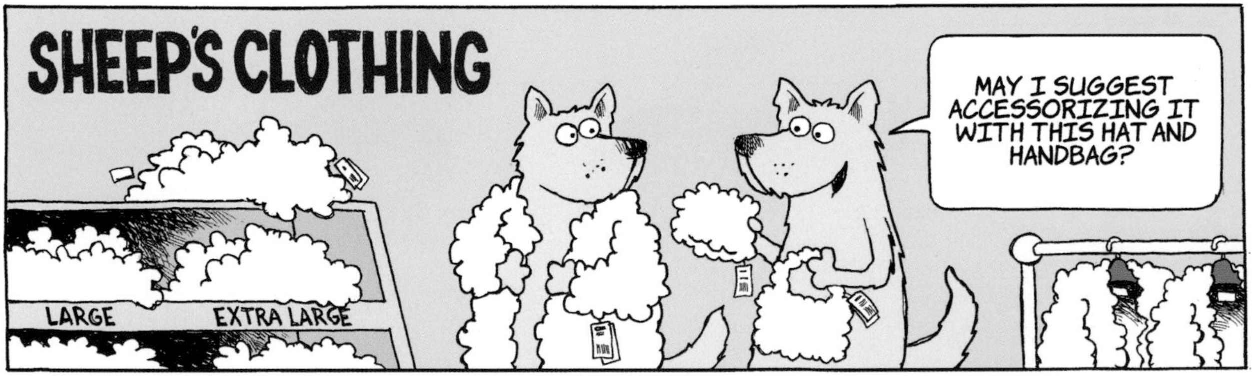
SHEEP'S CLOTHING
MAY I SUGGEST ACCESSORIZING IT WITH THIS HAT AND HANDBAG?
LARGE
EXTRA LARGE

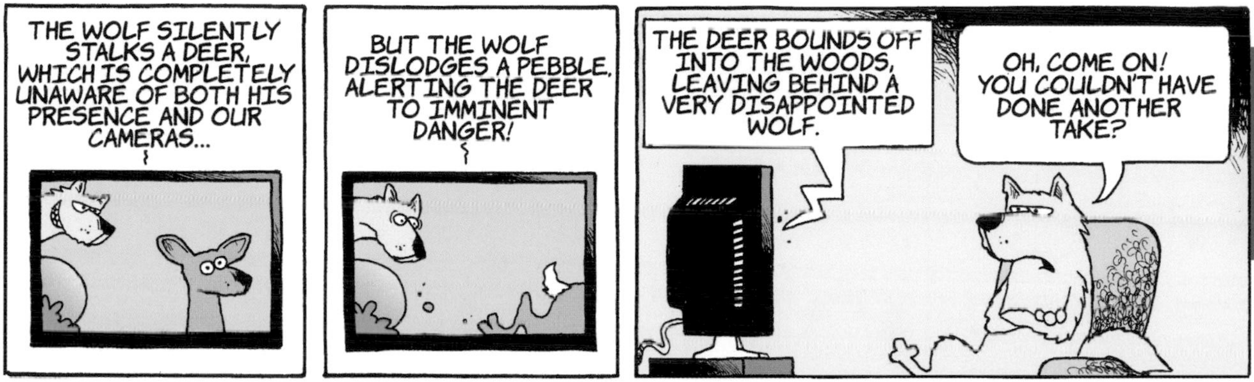
THE WOLF SILENTLY STALKS A DEER, WHICH IS COMPLETELY UNAWARE OF BOTH HIS PRESENCE AND OUR CAMERAS...
BUT THE WOLF DISLODGES A PEBBLE, ALERTING THE DEER TO IMMINENT DANGER!
THE DEER BOUNDS OFF INTO THE WOODS, LEAVING BEHIND A VERY DISAPPOINTED WOLF.
OH, COME ON! YOU COULDN'T HAVE DONE ANOTHER TAKE?

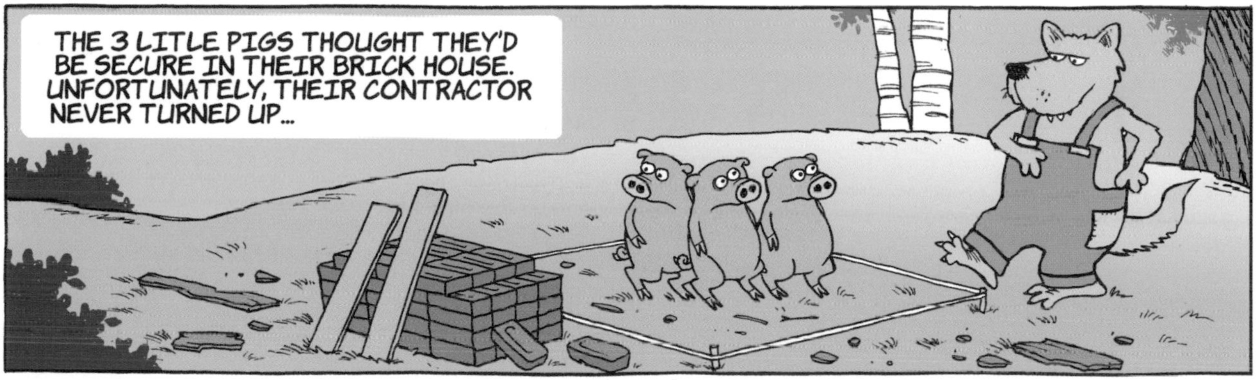
THE 3 LITLE PIGS THOUGHT THEY'D BE SECURE IN THEIR BRICK HOUSE. UNFORTUNATELY, THEIR CONTRACTOR NEVER TURNED UP...

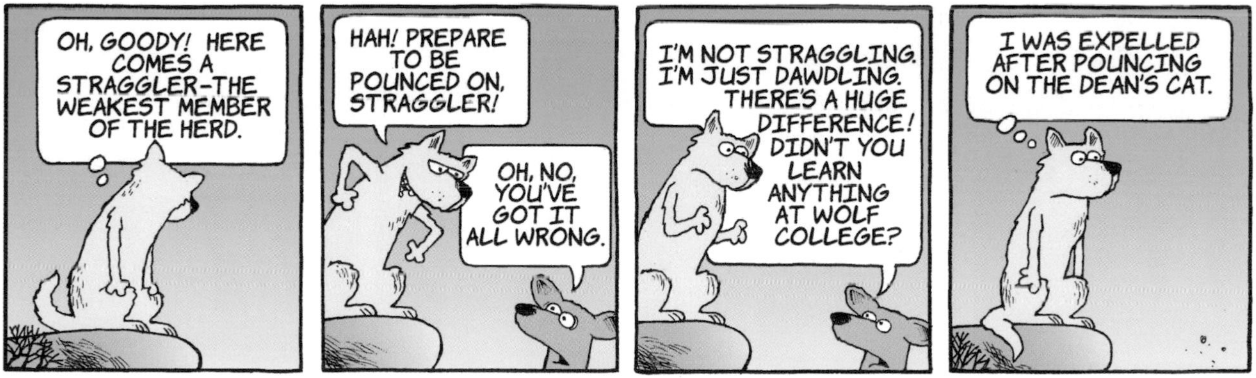
OH, GOODY! HERE COMES A STRAGGLER–THE WEAKEST MEMBER OF THE HERD.
HAH! PREPARE TO BE POUNCED ON, STRAGGLER!
OH, NO, YOU'VE GOT IT ALL WRONG.
I'M NOT STRAGGLING. I'M JUST DAWDLING. THERE'S A HUGE DIFFERENCE! DIDN'T YOU LEARN ANYTHING AT WOLF COLLEGE?
I WAS EXPELLED AFTER POUNCING ON THE DEAN'S CAT.

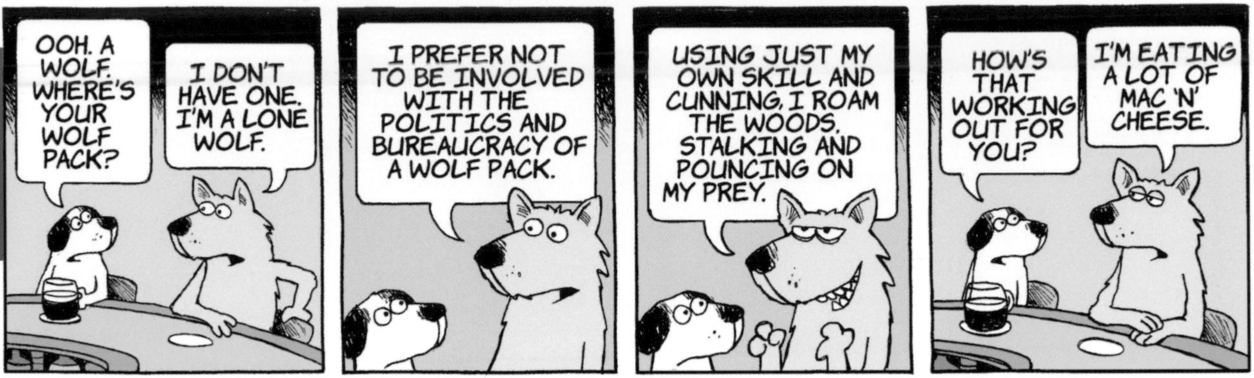
OOH. A WOLF. WHERE'S YOUR WOLF PACK?
I DON'T HAVE ONE. I'M A LONE WOLF.
I PREFER NOT TO BE INVOLVED WITH THE POLITICS AND BUREAUCRACY OF A WOLF PACK.
USING JUST MY OWN SKILL AND CUNNING, I ROAM THE WOODS, STALKING AND POUNCING ON MY PREY.
HOW'S THAT WORKING OUT FOR YOU?
I'M EATING A LOT OF MAC 'N' CHEESE.

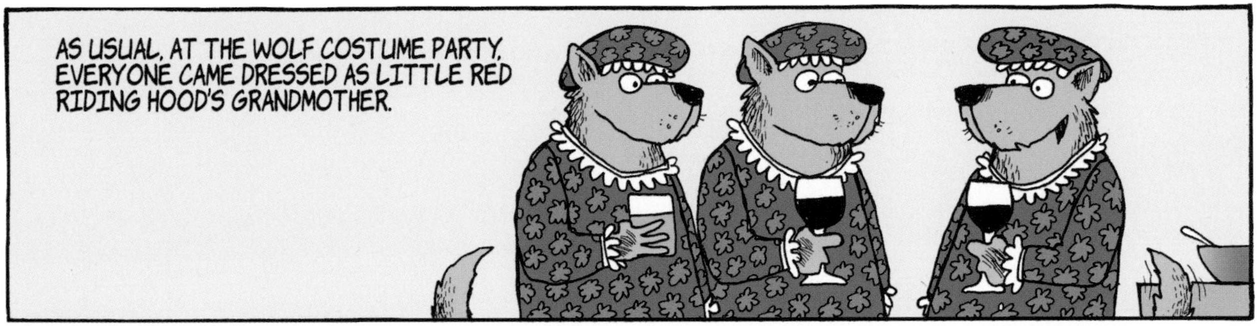
AS USUAL, AT THE WOLF COSTUME PARTY, EVERYONE CAME DRESSED AS LITTLE RED RIDING HOOD'S GRANDMOTHER.

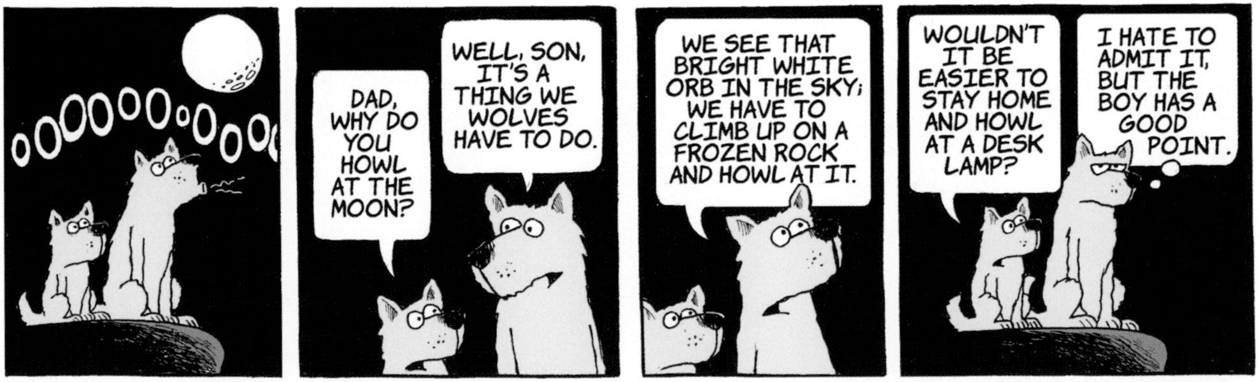
OOOOOOoOOOO
DAD, WHY DO YOU HOWL AT THE MOON?
WELL, SON, IT'S A THING WE WOLVES HAVE TO DO.
WE SEE THAT BRIGHT WHITE ORB IN THE SKY; WE HAVE TO CLIMB UP ON A FROZEN ROCK AND HOWL AT IT.
WOULDN'T IT BE EASIER TO STAY HOME AND HOWL AT A DESK LAMP?
I HATE TO ADMIT IT, BUT THE BOY HAS A GOOD POINT.

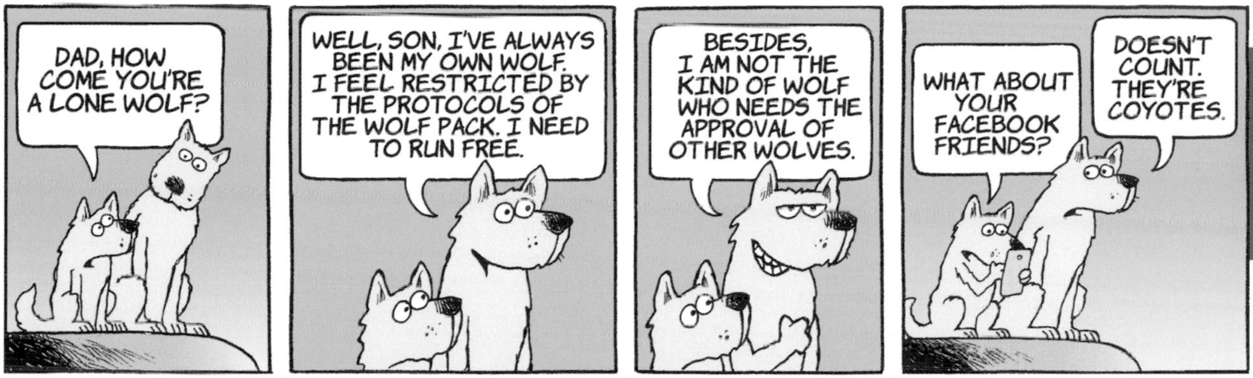
DAD, HOW COME YOU'RE A LONE WOLF?
WELL, SON, I'VE ALWAYS BEEN MY OWN WOLF. I FEEL RESTRICTED BY THE PROTOCOLS OF THE WOLF PACK. I NEED TO RUN FREE.
BESIDES, I AM NOT THE KIND OF WOLF WHO NEEDS THE APPROVAL OF OTHER WOLVES.
WHAT ABOUT YOUR FACEBOOK FRIENDS?
DOESN'T COUNT. THEY'RE COYOTES.

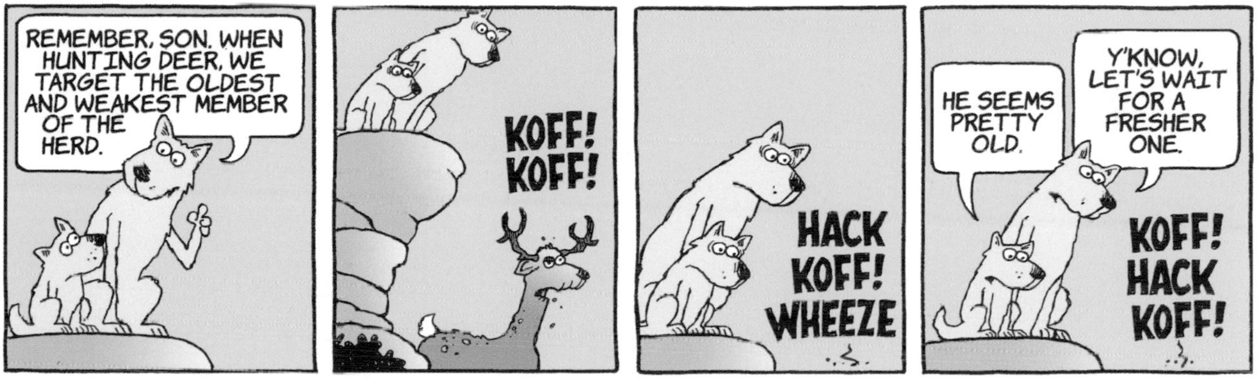
REMEMBER, SON. WHEN HUNTING DEER, WE TARGET THE OLDEST AND WEAKEST MEMBER OF THE HERD.
KOFF! KOFF!
HACK KOFF! WHEEZE
HE SEEMS PRETTY OLD.
Y'KNOW, LET'S WAIT FOR A FRESHER ONE.
KOFF! HACK KOFF!

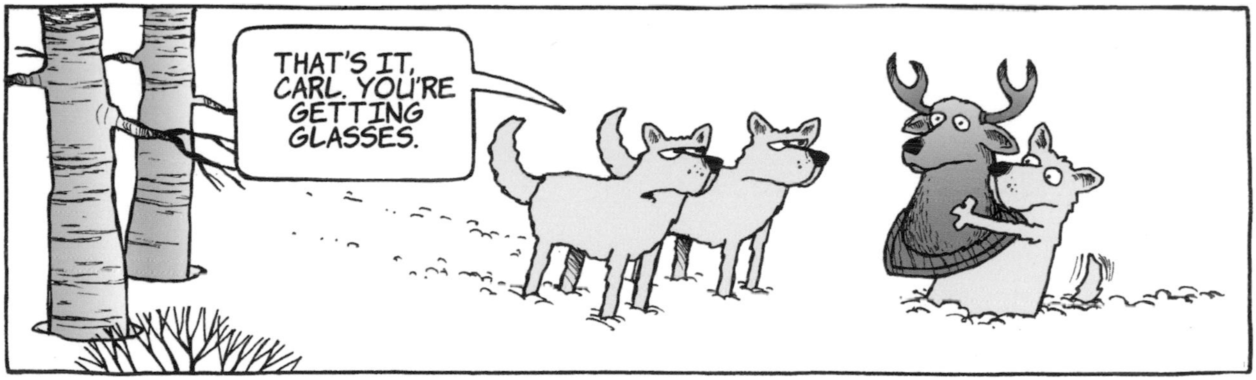
THAT'S IT, CARL. YOU'RE GETTING GLASSES.

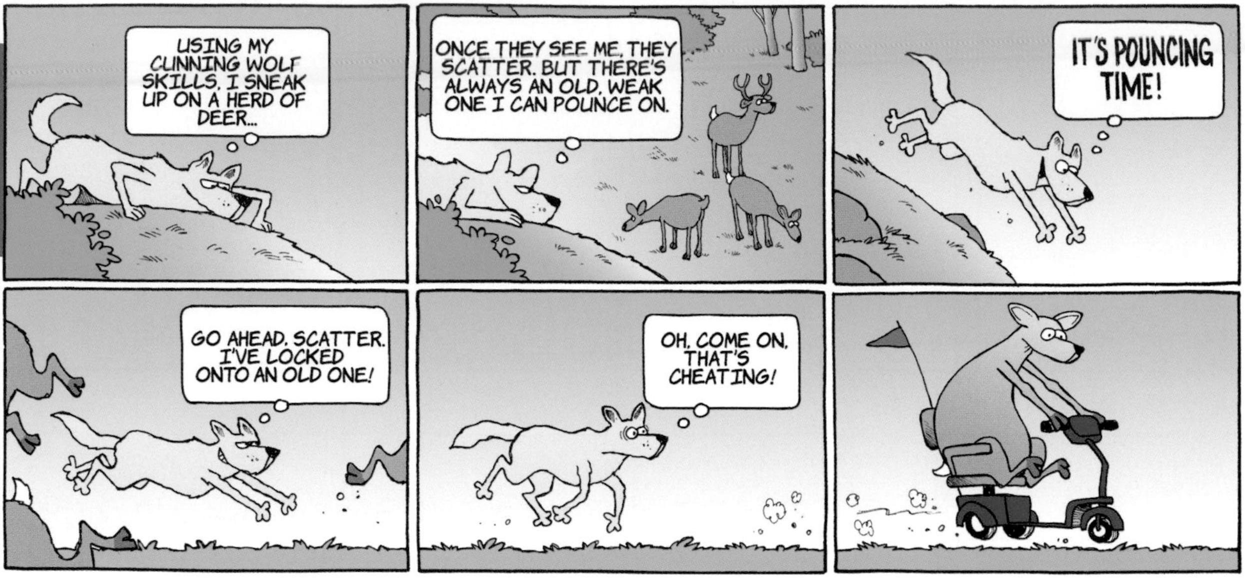
USING MY CUNNING WOLF SKILLS, I SNEAK UP ON A HERD OF DEER...
ONCE THEY SEE ME, THEY SCATTER. BUT THERE'S ALWAYS AN OLD, WEAK ONE I CAN POUNCE ON.
IT'S POUNCING TIME!
GO AHEAD. SCATTER. I'VE LOCKED ONTO AN OLD ONE!
OH, COME ON, THAT'S CHEATING!

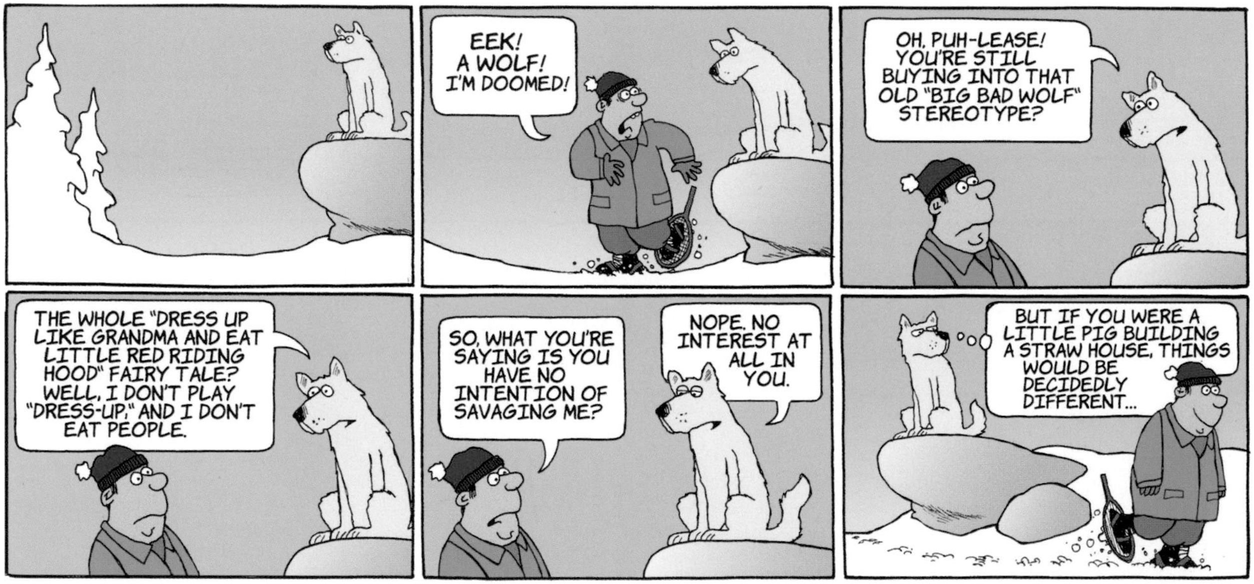
EEK! A WOLF! I'M DOOMED!
OH, PUH-LEASE! YOU'RE STILL BUYING INTO THAT OLD "BIG BAD WOLF" STEREOTYPE?
THE WHOLE "DRESS UP LIKE GRANDMA AND EAT LITTLE RED RIDING HOOD" FAIRY TALE? WELL, I DON'T PLAY "DRESS-UP," AND I DON'T EAT PEOPLE.
SO, WHAT YOU'RE SAYING IS YOU HAVE NO INTENTION OF SAVAGING ME?
NOPE. NO INTEREST AT ALL IN YOU.
BUT IF YOU WERE A LITTLE PIG BUILDING A STRAW HOUSE, THINGS WOULD BE DECIDEDLY DIFFERENT...

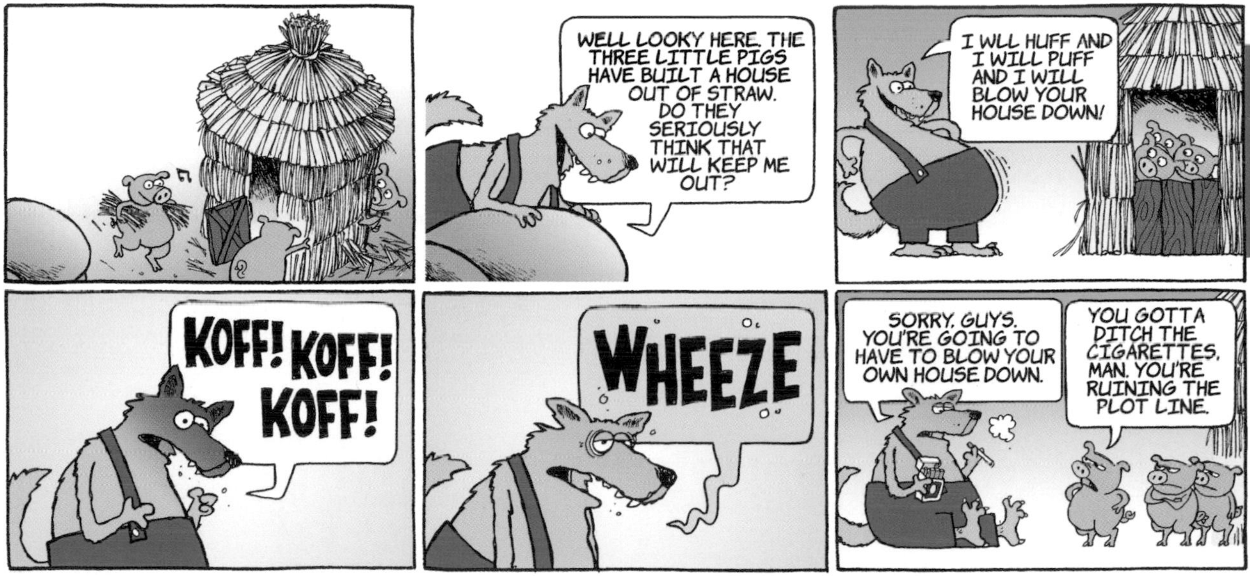
WELL LOOKY HERE. THE THREE LITTLE PIGS HAVE BUILT A HOUSE OUT OF STRAW. DO THEY SERIOUSLY THINK THAT WILL KEEP ME OUT?
I WLL HUFF AND I WILL PUFF AND I WILL BLOW YOUR HOUSE DOWN!
KOFF! KOFF! KOFF!
WHEEZE
SORRY, GUYS. YOU'RE GOING TO HAVE TO BLOW YOUR OWN HOUSE DOWN.
YOU GOTTA DITCH THE CIGARETTES, MAN. YOU'RE RUINING THE PLOT LINE.

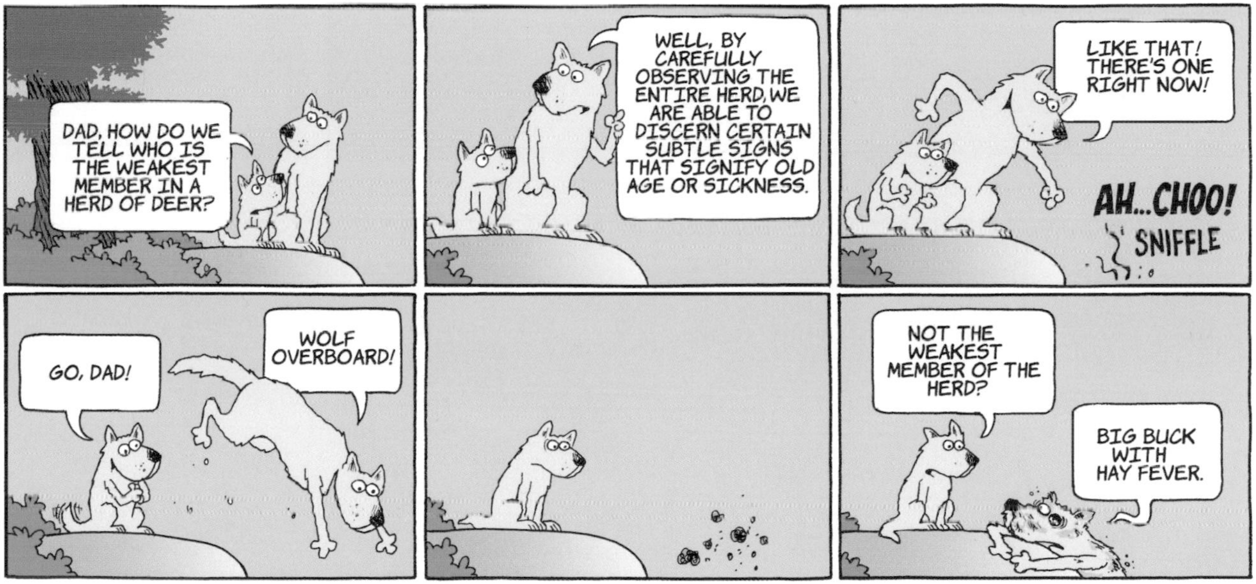
DAD, HOW DO WE TELL WHO IS THE WEAKEST MEMBER IN A HERD OF DEER?
WELL, BY CAREFULLY OBSERVING THE ENTIRE HERD, WE ARE ABLE TO DISCERN CERTAIN SUBTLE SIGNS THAT SIGNIFY OLD AGE OR SICKNESS.
LIKE THAT! THERE'S ONE RIGHT NOW!
AH...CHOO!
SNIFFLE
GO, DAD!
WOLF OVERBOARD!
NOT THE WEAKEST MEMBER OF THE HERD?
BIG BUCK WITH HAY FEVER.

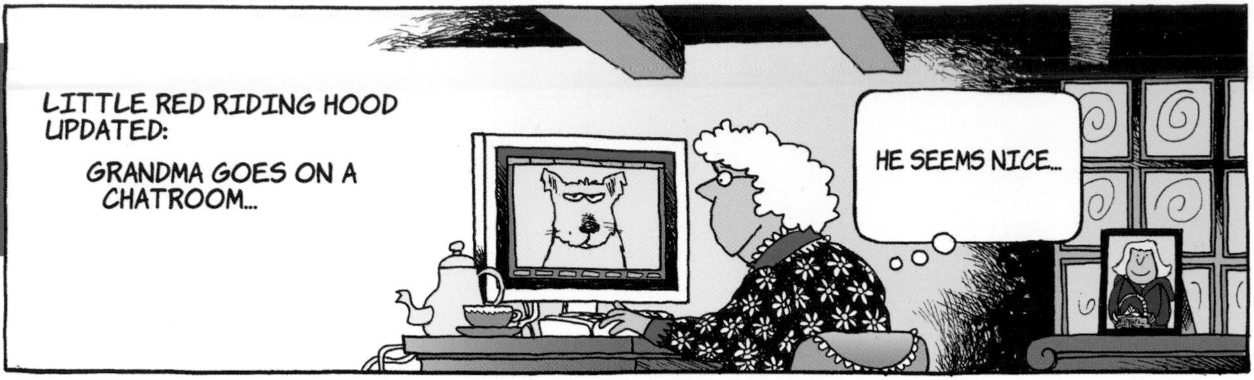
LITTLE RED RIDING HOOD UPDATED:
GRANDMA GOES ON A CHATROOM...
HE SEEMS NICE...

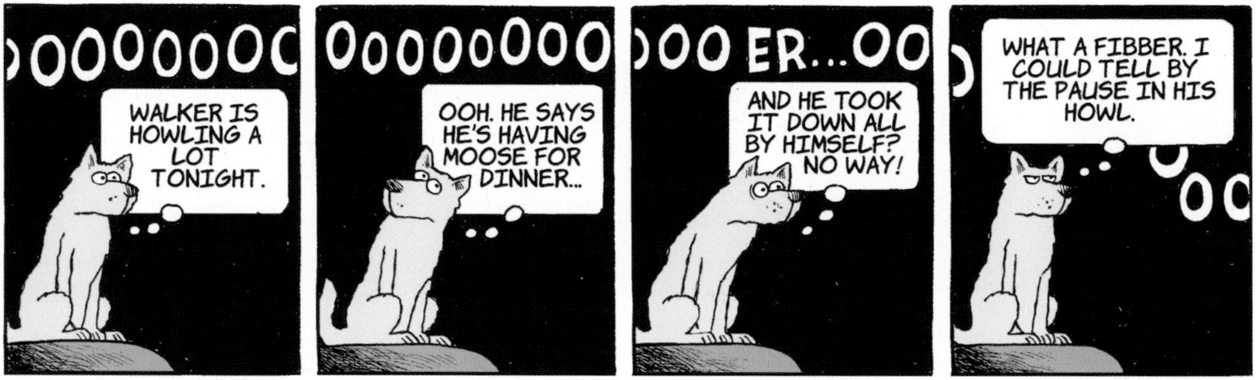
OOOOOOOO
WALKER IS HOWLING A LOT TONIGHT.
OOOOOOOO
OOH. HE SAYS HE'S HAVING MOOSE FOR DINNER...
OOO ER...OO
AND HE TOOK IT DOWN ALL BY HIMSELF? NO WAY!
WHAT A FIBBER. I COULD TELL BY THE PAUSE IN HIS HOWL.
OOO

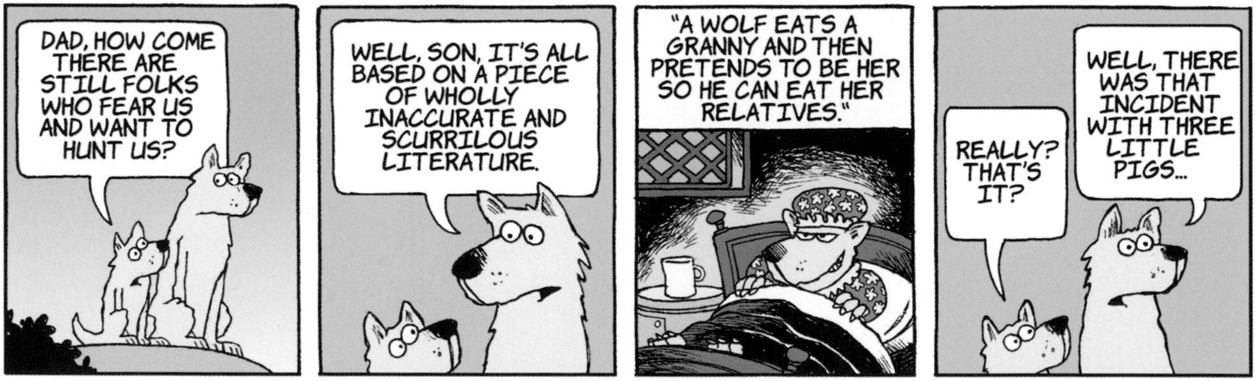
DAD, HOW COME THERE ARE STILL FOLKS WHO FEAR US AND WANT TO HUNT US?
WELL, SON, IT'S ALL BASED ON A PIECE OF WHOLLY INACCURATE AND SCURRILOUS LITERATURE.
"A WOLF EATS A GRANNY AND THEN PRETENDS TO BE HER SO HE CAN EAT HER RELATIVES."
REALLY? THAT'S IT?
WELL, THERE WAS THAT INCIDENT WITH THREE LITTLE PIGS...

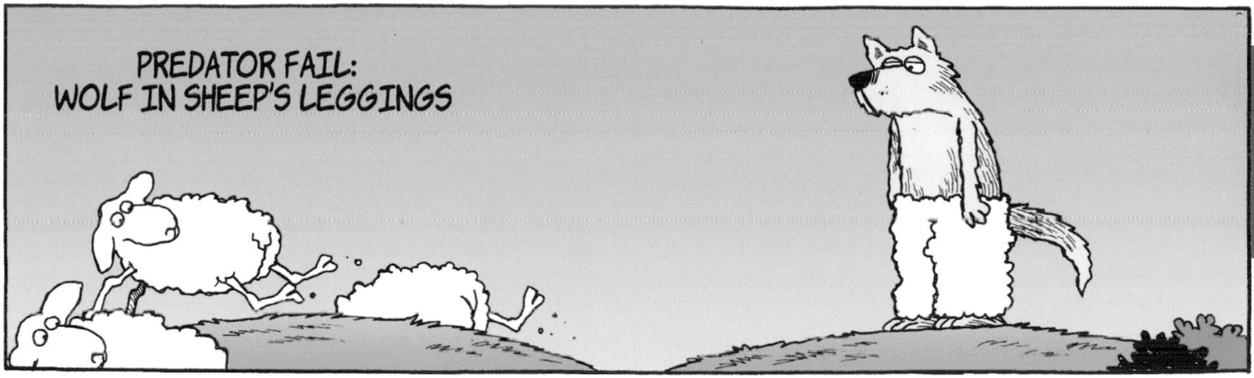
PREDATOR FAIL:
WOLF IN SHEEP'S LEGGINGS

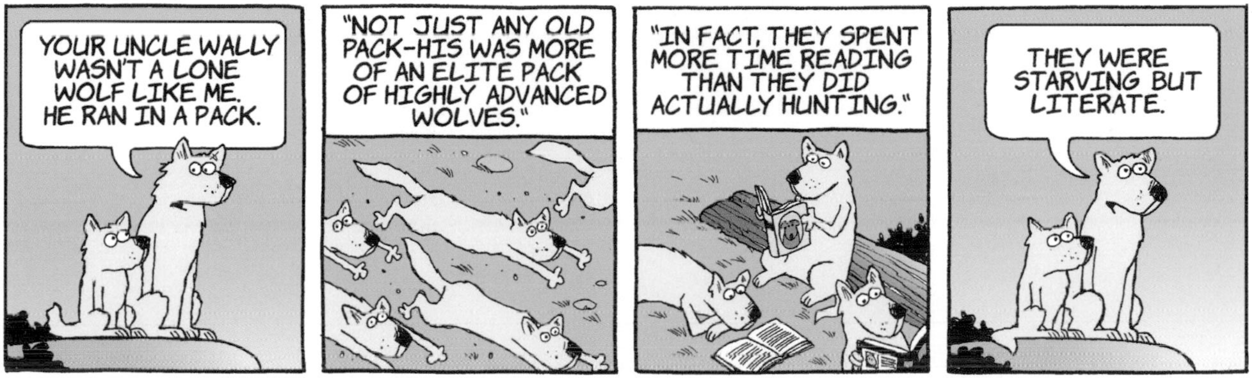
YOUR UNCLE WALLY WASN'T A LONE WOLF LIKE ME. HE RAN IN A PACK.
"NOT JUST ANY OLD PACK—HIS WAS MORE OF AN ELITE PACK OF HIGHLY ADVANCED WOLVES."
"IN FACT, THEY SPENT MORE TIME READING THAN THEY DID ACTUALLY HUNTING."
THEY WERE STARVING BUT LITERATE.

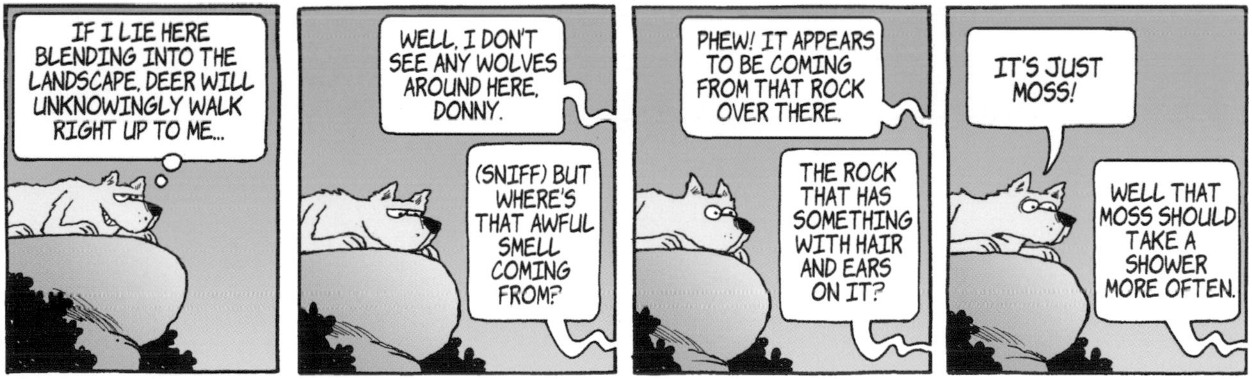
IF I LIE HERE BLENDING INTO THE LANDSCAPE, DEER WILL UNKNOWINGLY WALK RIGHT UP TO ME...
WELL, I DON'T SEE ANY WOLVES AROUND HERE, DONNY.
(SNIFF) BUT WHERE'S THAT AWFUL SMELL COMING FROM?
PHEW! IT APPEARS TO BE COMING FROM THAT ROCK OVER THERE.
THE ROCK THAT HAS SOMETHING WITH HAIR AND EARS ON IT?
IT'S JUST MOSS!
WELL THAT MOSS SHOULD TAKE A SHOWER MORE OFTEN.

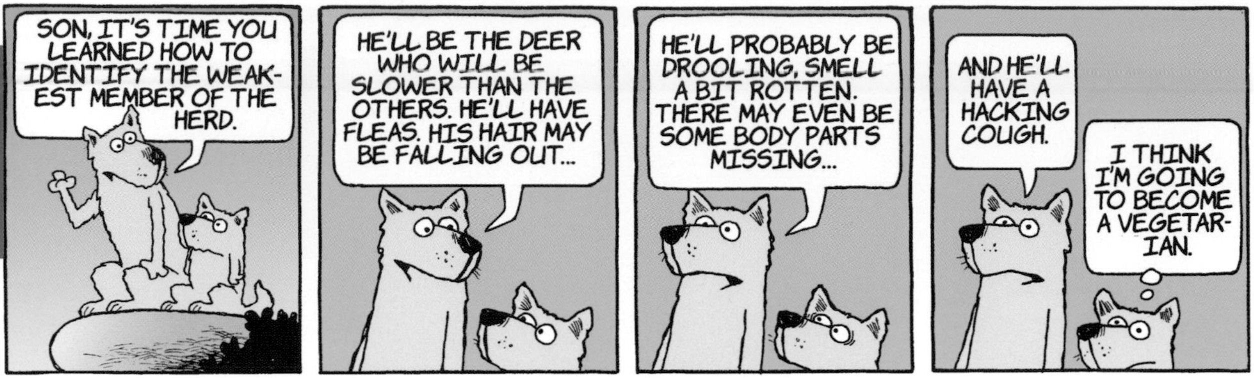
SON, IT'S TIME YOU LEARNED HOW TO IDENTIFY THE WEAKEST MEMBER OF THE HERD.
HE'LL BE THE DEER WHO WILL BE SLOWER THAN THE OTHERS. HE'LL HAVE FLEAS. HIS HAIR MAY BE FALLING OUT...
HE'LL PROBABLY BE DROOLING, SMELL A BIT ROTTEN. THERE MAY EVEN BE SOME BODY PARTS MISSING...
AND HE'LL HAVE A HACKING COUGH.
I THINK I'M GOING TO BECOME A VEGETARIAN.

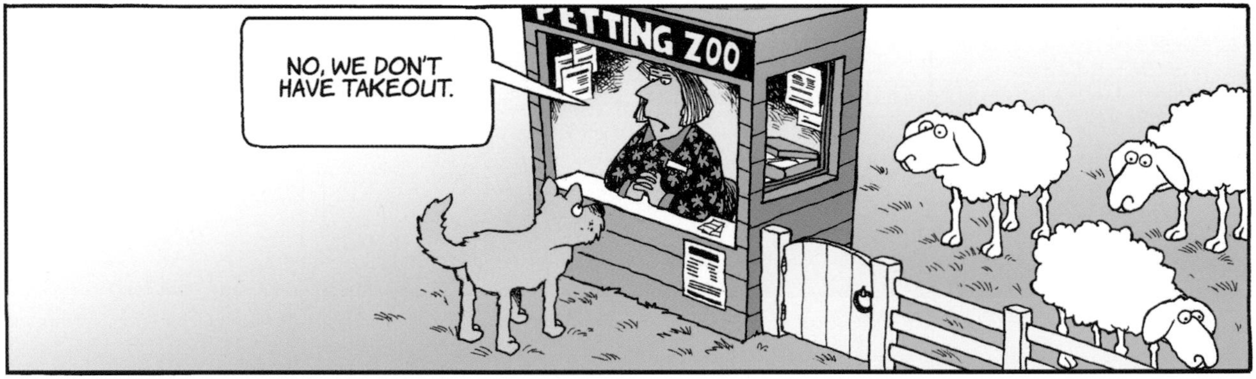
PETTING ZOO
NO, WE DON'T HAVE TAKEOUT.

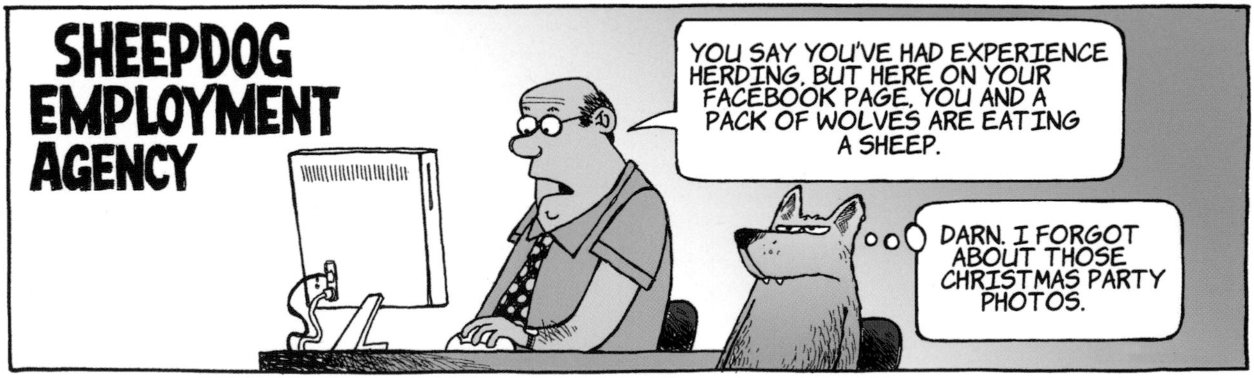
SHEEPDOG EMPLOYMENT AGENCY
YOU SAY YOU'VE HAD EXPERIENCE HERDING, BUT HERE ON YOUR FACEBOOK PAGE, YOU AND A PACK OF WOLVES ARE EATING A SHEEP.
DARN. I FORGOT ABOUT THOSE CHRISTMAS PARTY PHOTOS.

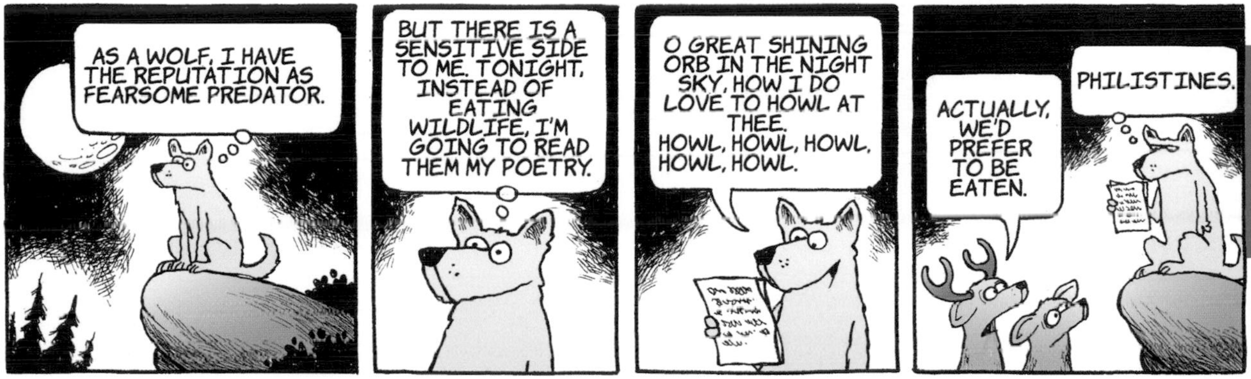
AS A WOLF, I HAVE THE REPUTATION AS FEARSOME PREDATOR.
BUT THERE IS A SENSITIVE SIDE TO ME. TONIGHT, INSTEAD OF EATING WILDLIFE, I'M GOING TO READ THEM MY POETRY.
O GREAT SHINING ORB IN THE NIGHT SKY, HOW I DO LOVE TO HOWL AT THEE. HOWL, HOWL, HOWL, HOWL, HOWL.
ACTUALLY, WE'D PREFER TO BE EATEN.
PHILISTINES.

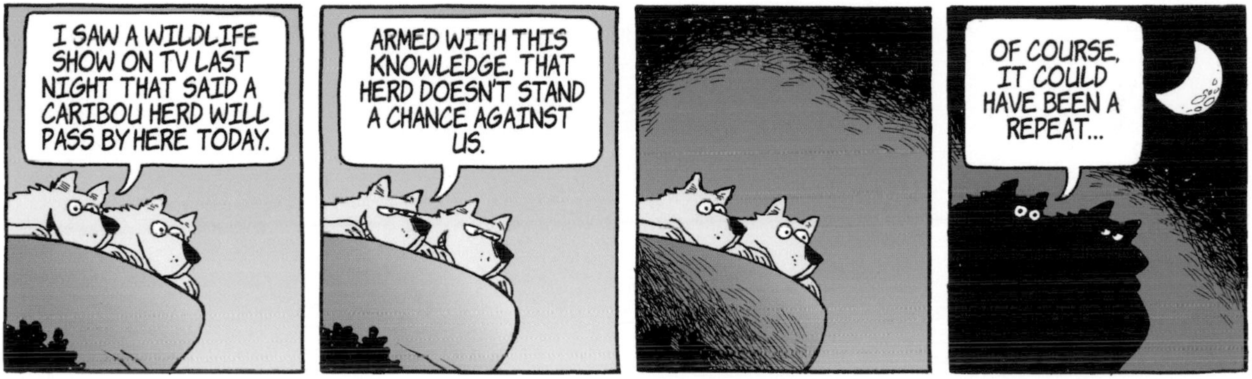
I SAW A WILDLIFE SHOW ON TV LAST NIGHT THAT SAID A CARIBOU HERD WILL PASS BY HERE TODAY.
ARMED WITH THIS KNOWLEDGE, THAT HERD DOESN'T STAND A CHANCE AGAINST US.
OF COURSE, IT COULD HAVE BEEN A REPEAT...

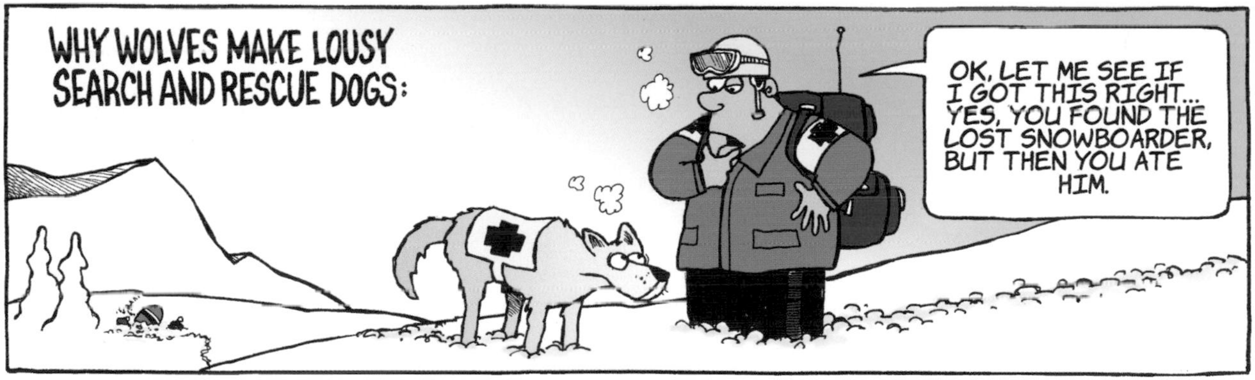
WHY WOLVES MAKE LOUSY SEARCH AND RESCUE DOGS:
OK, LET ME SEE IF I GOT THIS RIGHT... YES, YOU FOUND THE LOST SNOWBOARDER, BUT THEN YOU ATE HIM.

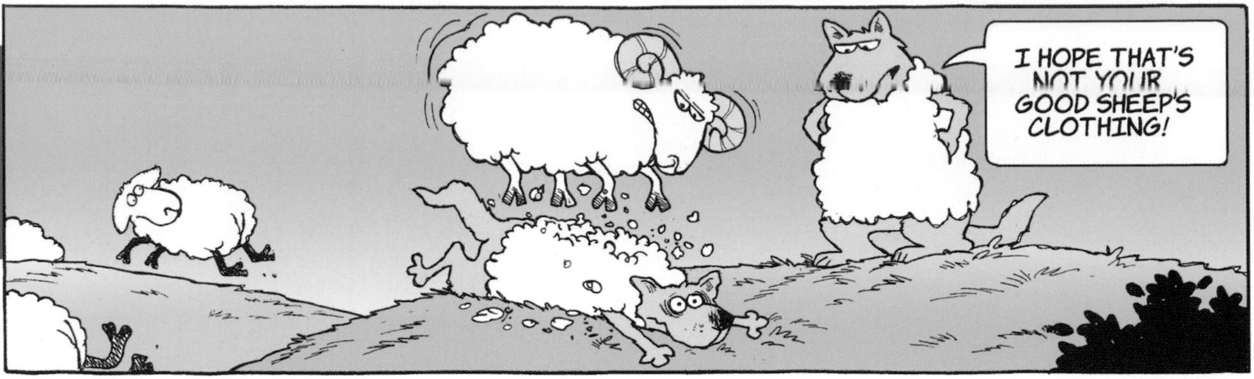
I HOPE THAT'S NOT YOUR GOOD SHEEP'S CLOTHING!

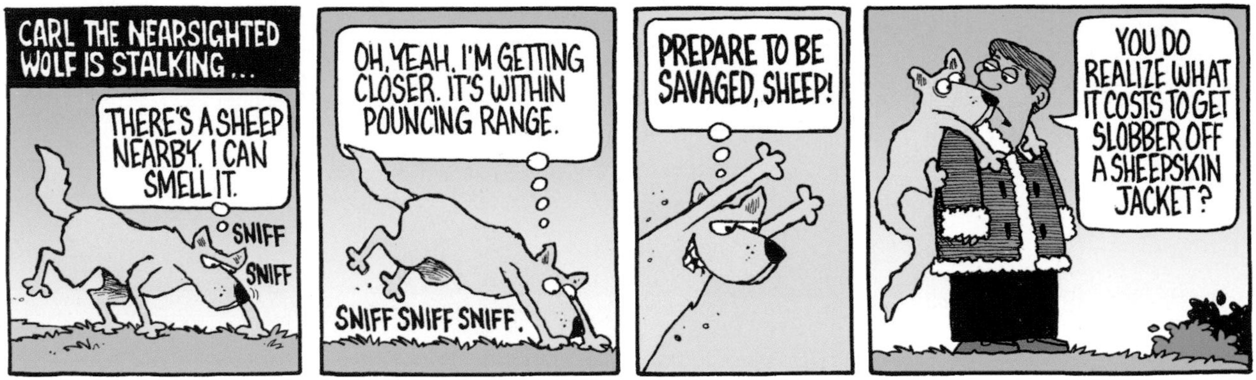
CARL THE NEARSIGHTED WOLF IS STALKING...
THERE'S A SHEEP NEARBY. I CAN SMELL IT.
SNIFF
SNIFF
OH, YEAH. I'M GETTING CLOSER. IT'S WITHIN POUNCING RANGE.
SNIFF SNIFF SNIFF.
PREPARE TO BE SAVAGED, SHEEP!
YOU DO REALIZE WHAT IT COSTS TO GET SLOBBER OFF A SHEEPSKIN JACKET?

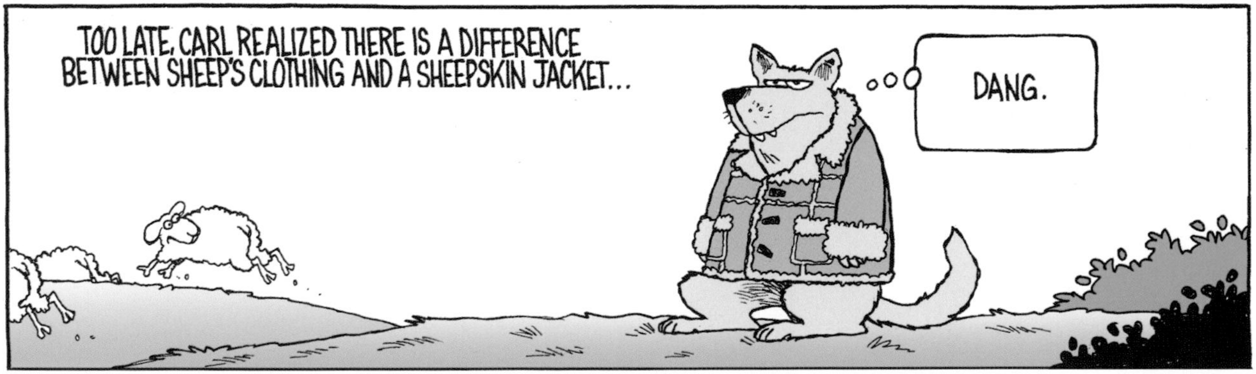
TOO LATE, CARL REALIZED THERE IS A DIFFERENCE BETWEEN SHEEP'S CLOTHING AND A SHEEPSKIN JACKET...
DANG.

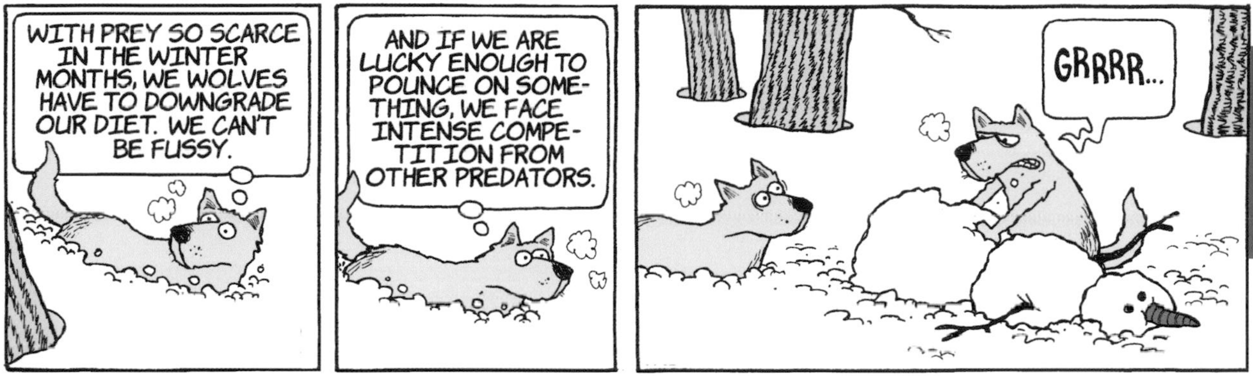
WITH PREY SO SCARCE IN THE WINTER MONTHS, WE WOLVES HAVE TO DOWNGRADE OUR DIET. WE CAN'T BE FUSSY.
AND IF WE ARE LUCKY ENOUGH TO POUNCE ON SOMETHING, WE FACE INTENSE COMPETITION FROM OTHER PREDATORS.
GRRRR...

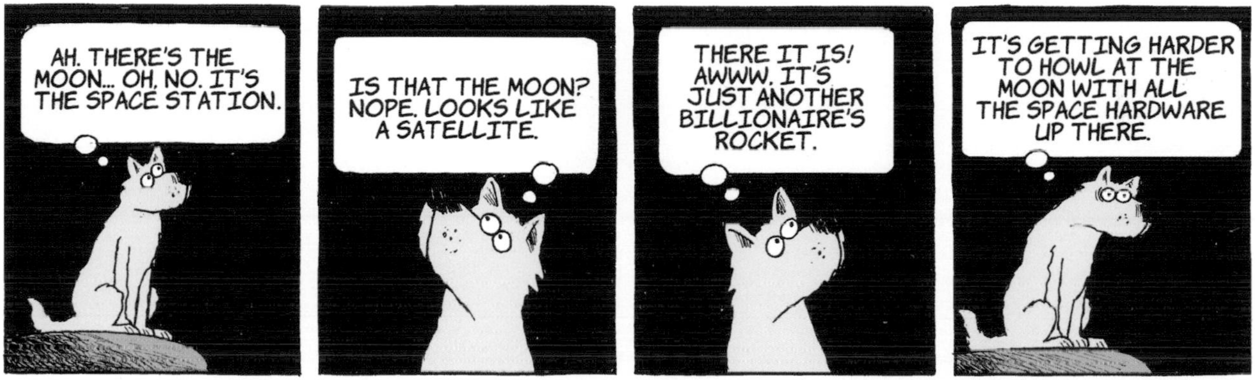
AH. THERE'S THE MOON... OH, NO. IT'S THE SPACE STATION.
IS THAT THE MOON? NOPE. LOOKS LIKE A SATELLITE.
THERE IT IS! AWWW. IT'S JUST ANOTHER BILLIONAIRE'S ROCKET.
IT'S GETTING HARDER TO HOWL AT THE MOON WITH ALL THE SPACE HARDWARE UP THERE.

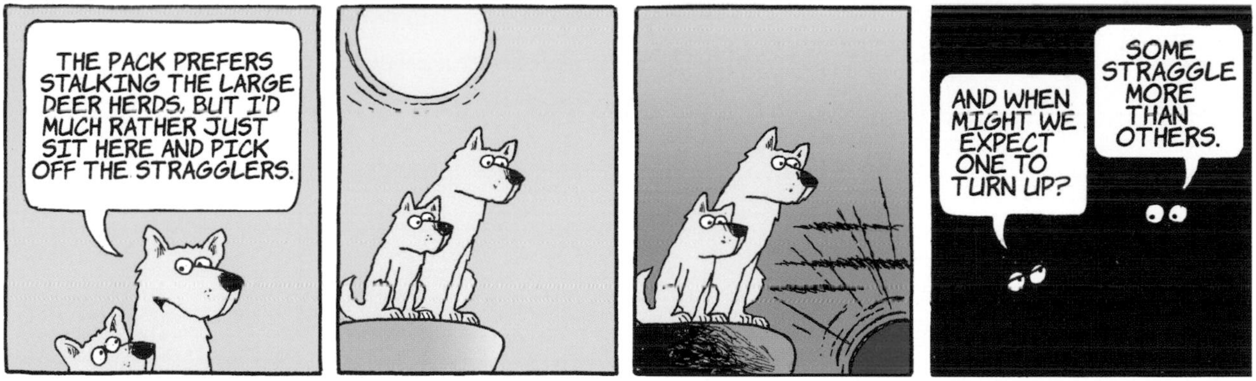
THE PACK PREFERS STALKING THE LARGE DEER HERDS, BUT I'D MUCH RATHER JUST SIT HERE AND PICK OFF THE STRAGGLERS.
AND WHEN MIGHT WE EXPECT ONE TO TURN UP?
SOME STRAGGLE MORE THAN OTHERS.

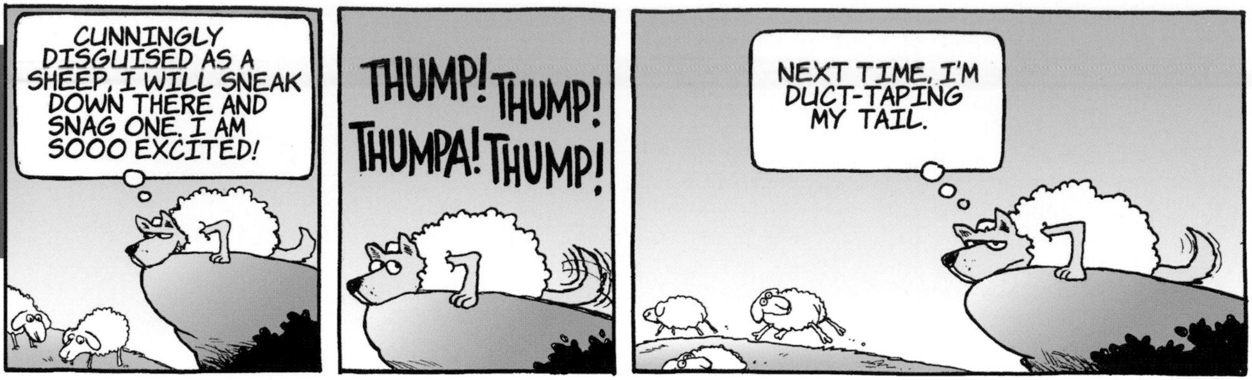
CUNNINGLY DISGUISED AS A SHEEP, I WILL SNEAK DOWN THERE AND SNAG ONE. I AM SOOO EXCITED!
THUMP! THUMP! THUMPA! THUMP!
NEXT TIME, I'M DUCT-TAPING MY TAIL.

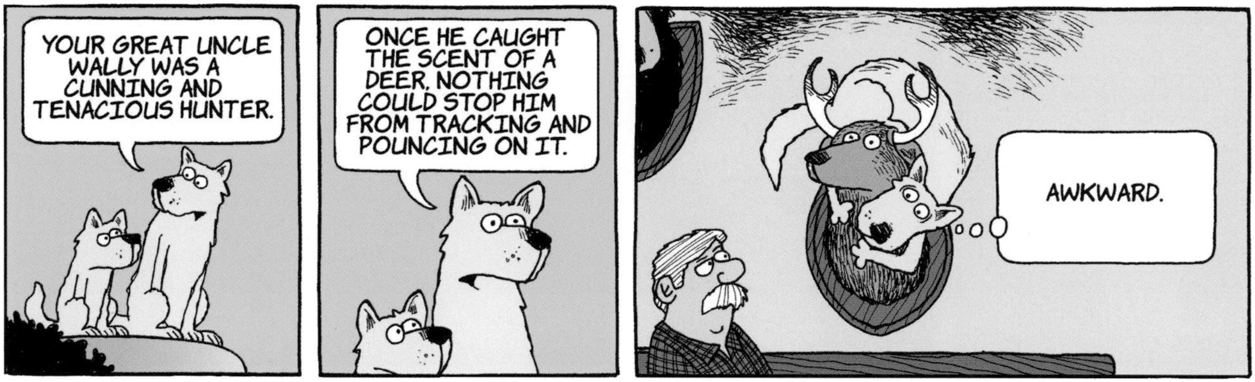
YOUR GREAT UNCLE WALLY WAS A CUNNING AND TENACIOUS HUNTER.
ONCE HE CAUGHT THE SCENT OF A DEER, NOTHING COULD STOP HIM FROM TRACKING AND POUNCING ON IT.
AWKWARD.

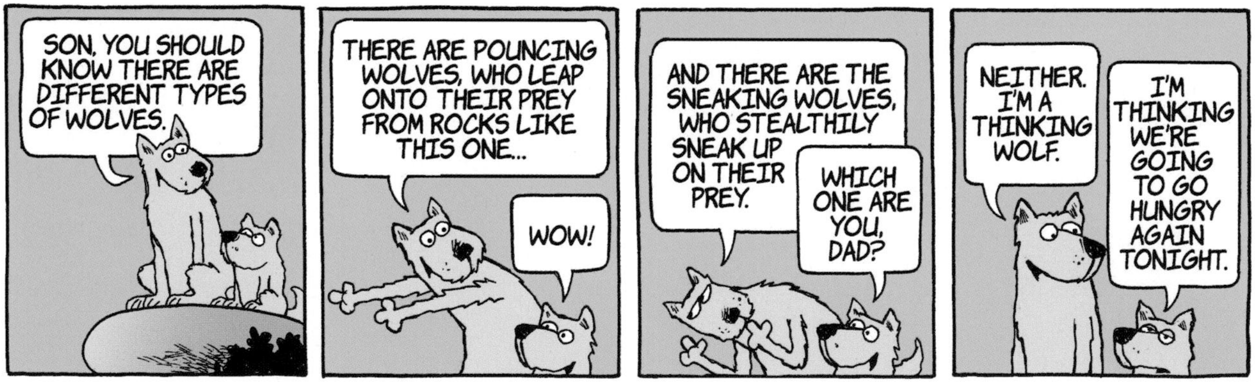
SON, YOU SHOULD KNOW THERE ARE DIFFERENT TYPES OF WOLVES.
THERE ARE POUNCING WOLVES, WHO LEAP ONTO THEIR PREY FROM ROCKS LIKE THIS ONE...
WOW!
AND THERE ARE THE SNEAKING WOLVES, WHO STEALTHILY SNEAK UP ON THEIR PREY.
WHICH ONE ARE YOU, DAD?
NEITHER. I'M A THINKING WOLF.
I'M THINKING WE'RE GOING TO GO HUNGRY AGAIN TONIGHT.

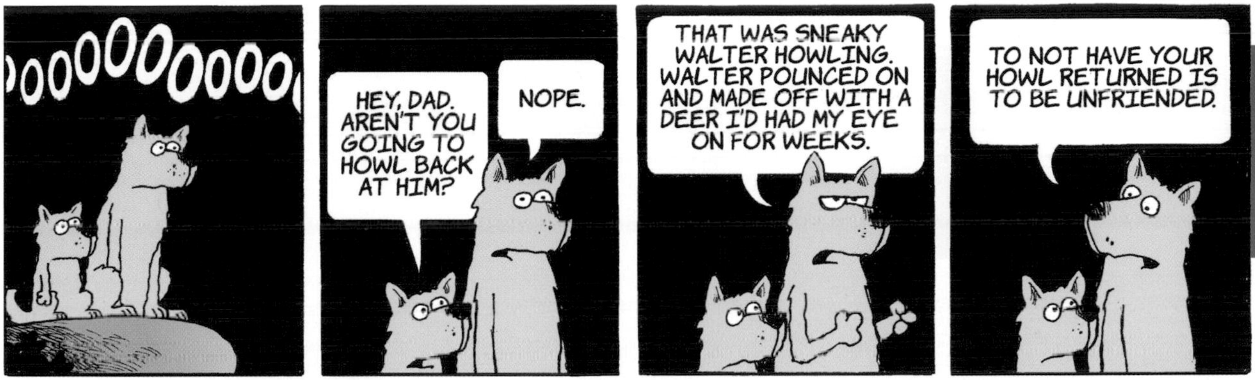
OOOOOOOOOOOO
HEY, DAD. AREN'T YOU GOING TO HOWL BACK AT HIM?
NOPE.
THAT WAS SNEAKY WALTER HOWLING. WALTER POUNCED ON AND MADE OFF WITH A DEER I'D HAD MY EYE ON FOR WEEKS.
TO NOT HAVE YOUR HOWL RETURNED IS TO BE UNFRIENDED.

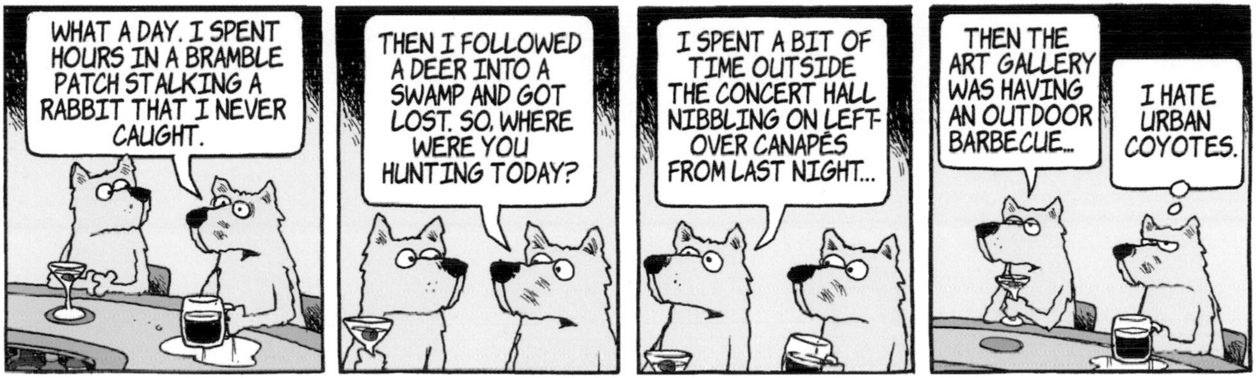
WHAT A DAY. I SPENT HOURS IN A BRAMBLE PATCH STALKING A RABBIT THAT I NEVER CAUGHT.
THEN I FOLLOWED A DEER INTO A SWAMP AND GOT LOST. SO, WHERE WERE YOU HUNTING TODAY?
I SPENT A BIT OF TIME OUTSIDE THE CONCERT HALL NIBBLING ON LEFT-OVER CANAPÉS FROM LAST NIGHT...
THEN THE ART GALLERY WAS HAVING AN OUTDOOR BARBECUE...
I HATE URBAN COYOTES.

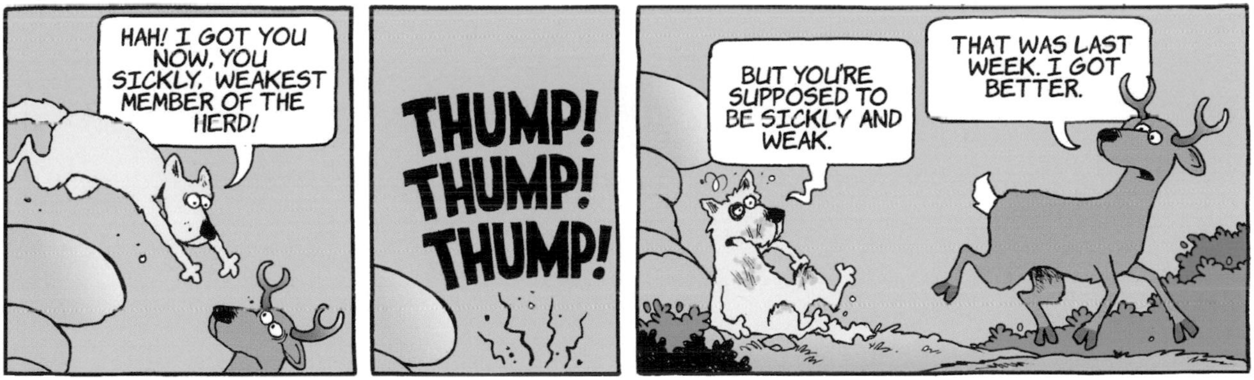
HAH! I GOT YOU NOW, YOU SICKLY, WEAKEST MEMBER OF THE HERD!
THUMP! THUMP! THUMP!
BUT YOU'RE SUPPOSED TO BE SICKLY AND WEAK.
THAT WAS LAST WEEK. I GOT BETTER.

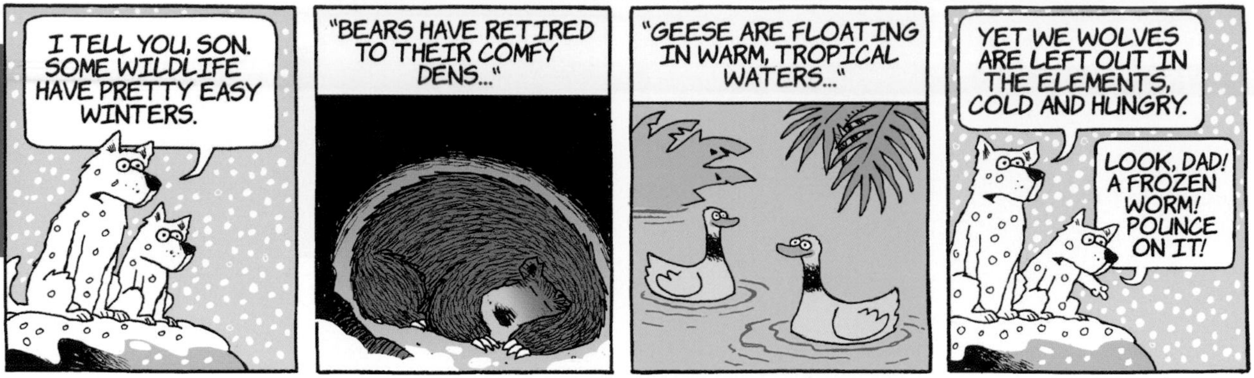
I TELL YOU, SON. SOME WILDLIFE HAVE PRETTY EASY WINTERS.
"BEARS HAVE RETIRED TO THEIR COMFY DENS..."
"GEESE ARE FLOATING IN WARM, TROPICAL WATERS..."
YET WE WOLVES ARE LEFT OUT IN THE ELEMENTS, COLD AND HUNGRY.
LOOK, DAD! A FROZEN WORM! POUNCE ON IT!

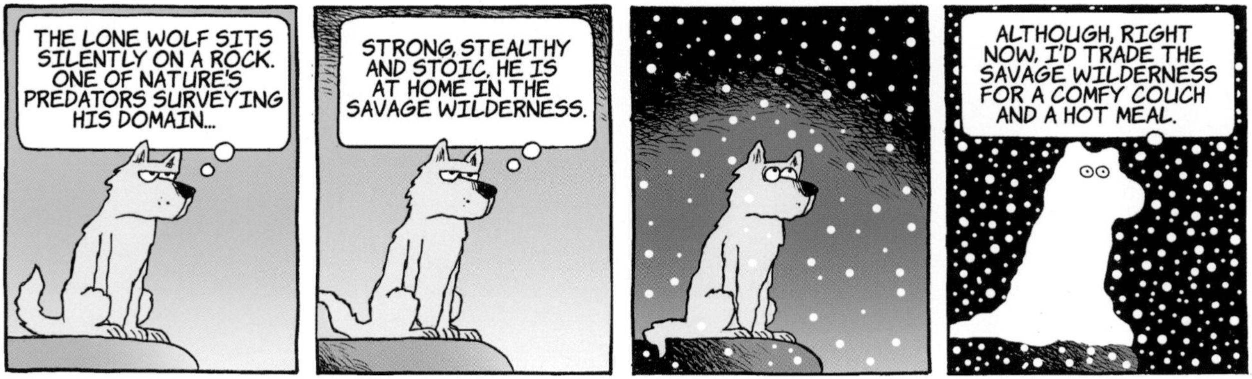
THE LONE WOLF SITS SILENTLY ON A ROCK. ONE OF NATURE'S PREDATORS SURVEYING HIS DOMAIN...
STRONG, STEALTHY AND STOIC, HE IS AT HOME IN THE SAVAGE WILDERNESS.
ALTHOUGH, RIGHT NOW, I'D TRADE THE SAVAGE WILDERNESS FOR A COMFY COUCH AND A HOT MEAL.

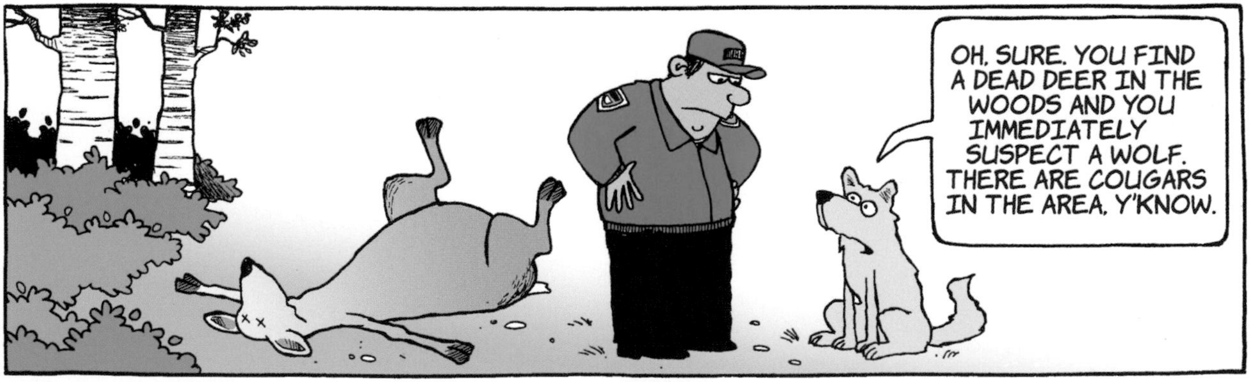
OH, SURE. YOU FIND A DEAD DEER IN THE WOODS AND YOU IMMEDIATELY SUSPECT A WOLF. THERE ARE COUGARS IN THE AREA, Y'KNOW.

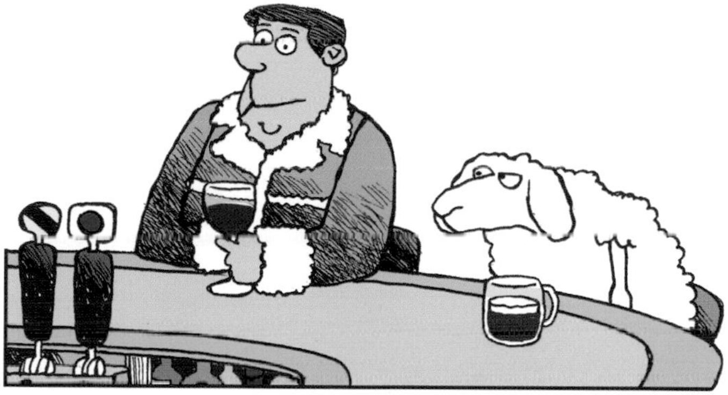

UBIQUITOUS UNGULATES 10

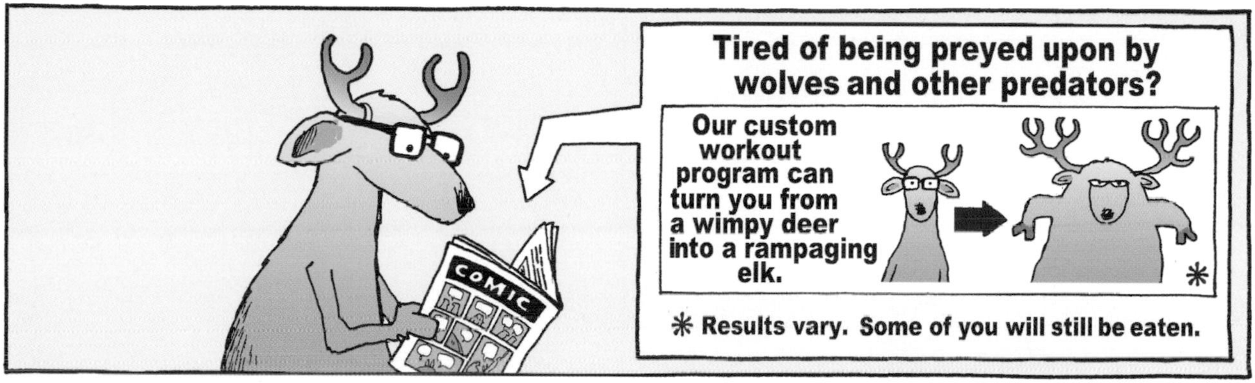
Tired of being preyed upon by wolves and other predators?
Our custom workout program can turn you from a wimpy deer into a rampaging elk.
*
* Results vary. Some of you will still be eaten.
COMIC

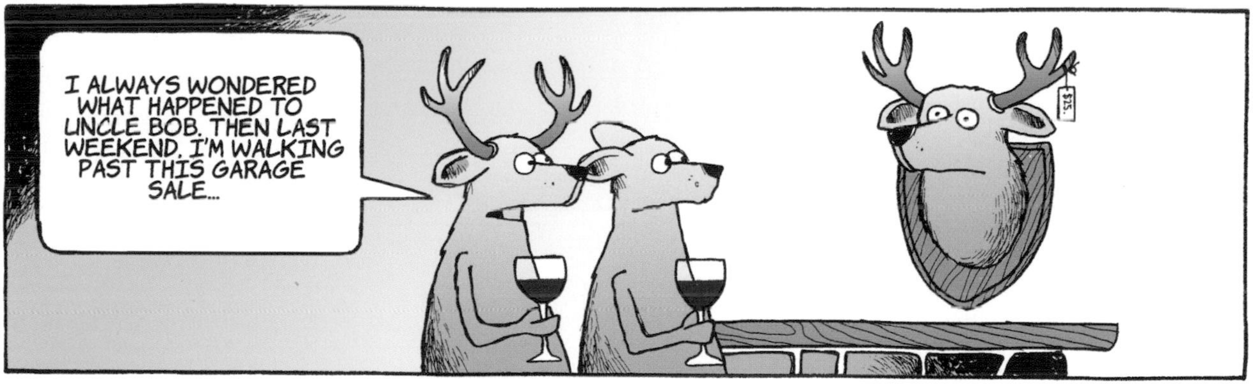
I ALWAYS WONDERED WHAT HAPPENED TO UNCLE BOB. THEN LAST WEEKEND, I'M WALKING PAST THIS GARAGE SALE...

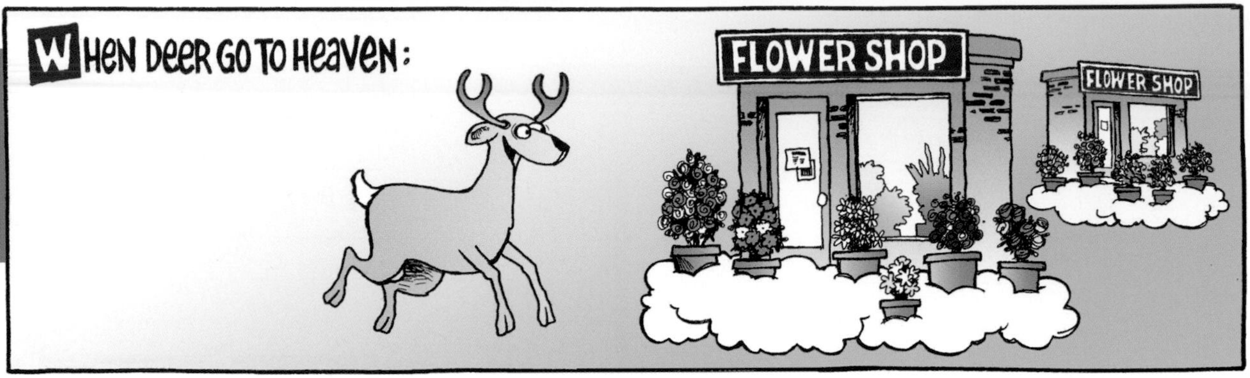
WHEN DEER GO TO HEAVEN:
FLOWER SHOP
FLOWER SHOP

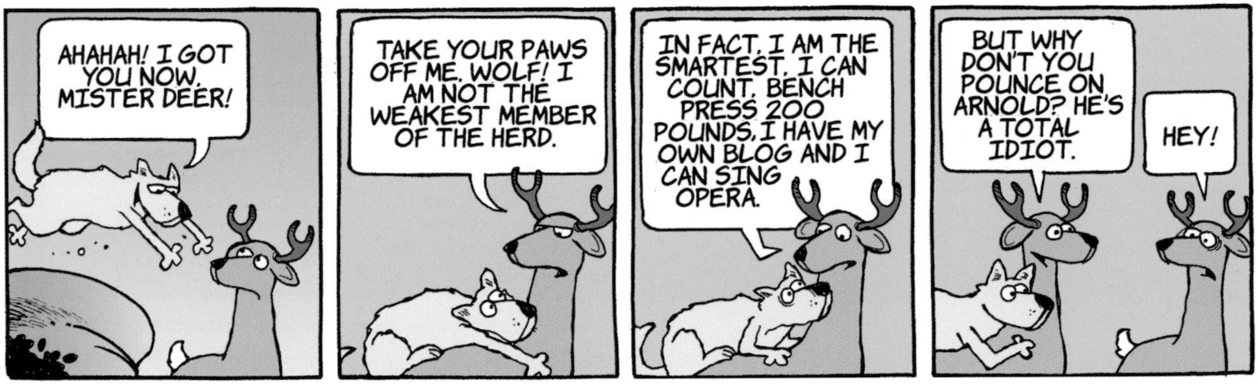
AHAHAH! I GOT YOU NOW, MISTER DEER!
TAKE YOUR PAWS OFF ME, WOLF! I AM NOT THE WEAKEST MEMBER OF THE HERD.
IN FACT, I AM THE SMARTEST. I CAN COUNT, BENCH PRESS 200 POUNDS, I HAVE MY OWN BLOG AND I CAN SING OPERA.
BUT WHY DON'T YOU POUNCE ON ARNOLD? HE'S A TOTAL IDIOT.
HEY!

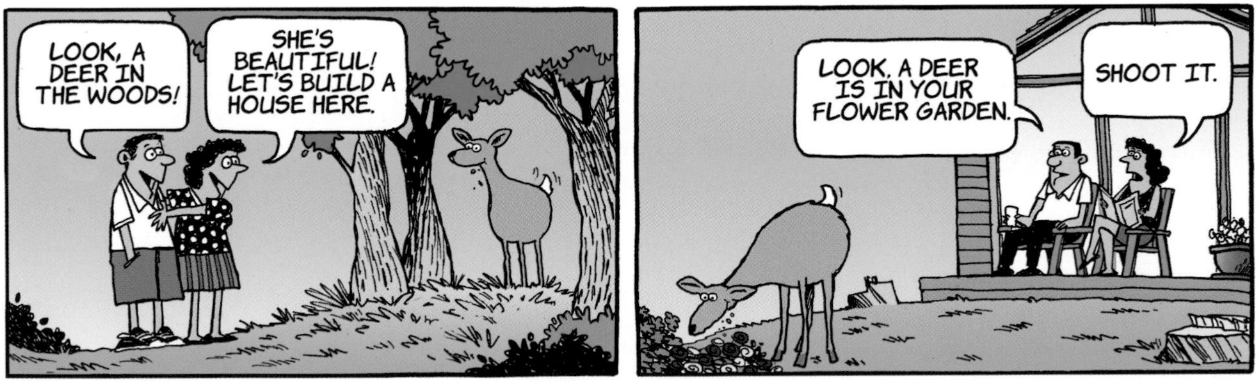
LOOK, A DEER IN THE WOODS!
SHE'S BEAUTIFUL! LET'S BUILD A HOUSE HERE.
LOOK, A DEER IS IN YOUR FLOWER GARDEN.
SHOOT IT.

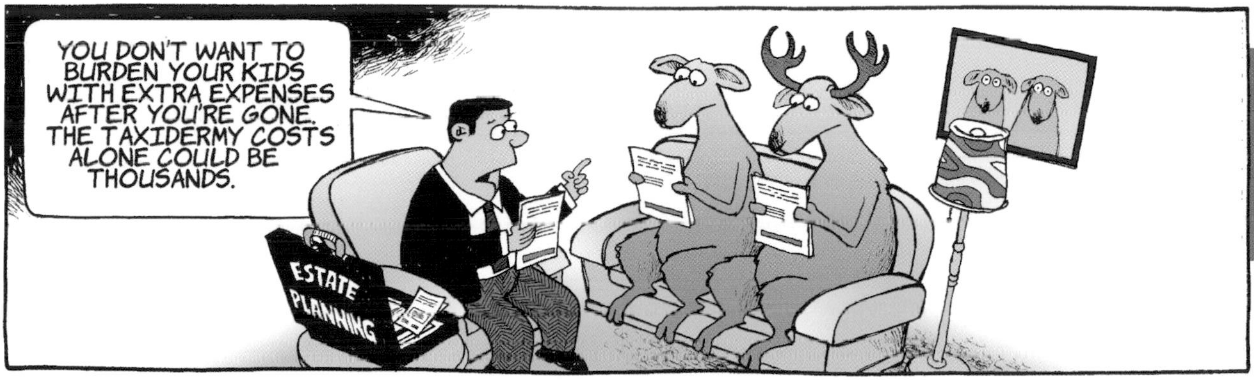
YOU DON'T WANT TO BURDEN YOUR KIDS WITH EXTRA EXPENSES AFTER YOU'RE GONE. THE TAXIDERMY COSTS ALONE COULD BE THOUSANDS.
ESTATE PLANNING

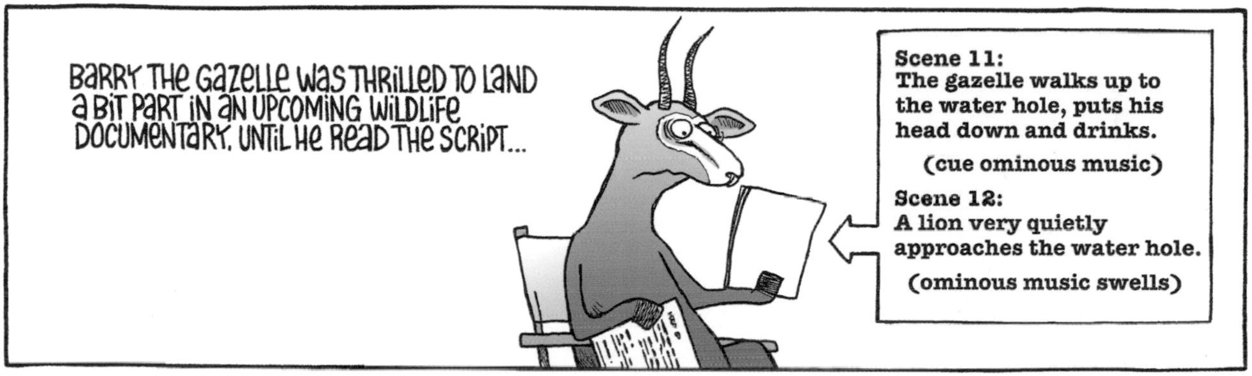
BARRY THE GAZELLE WAS THRILLED TO LAND A BIT PART IN AN UPCOMING WILDLIFE DOCUMENTARY. UNTIL HE READ THE SCRIPT...
Scene 11:
The gazelle walks up to the water hole, puts his head down and drinks.
(cue ominous music)
Scene 12:
A lion very quietly approaches the water hole.
(ominous music swells)

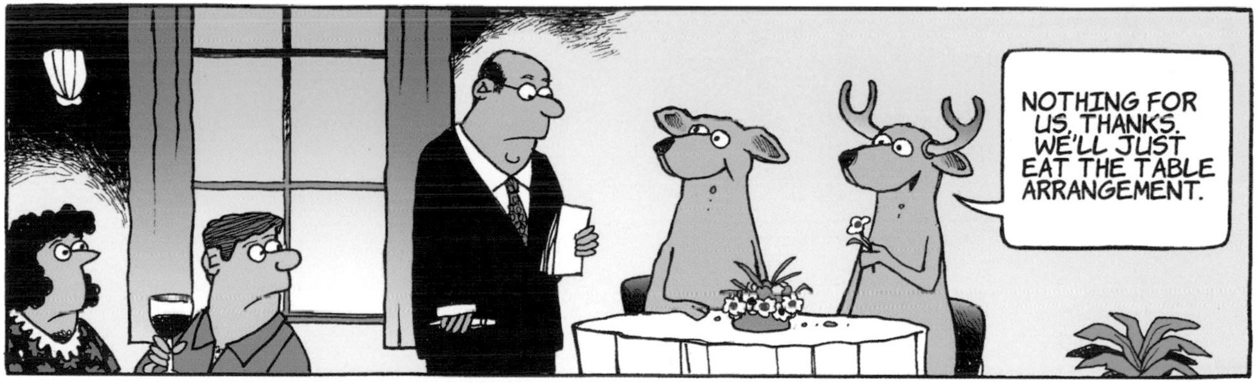
NOTHING FOR US, THANKS. WE'LL JUST EAT THE TABLE ARRANGEMENT.

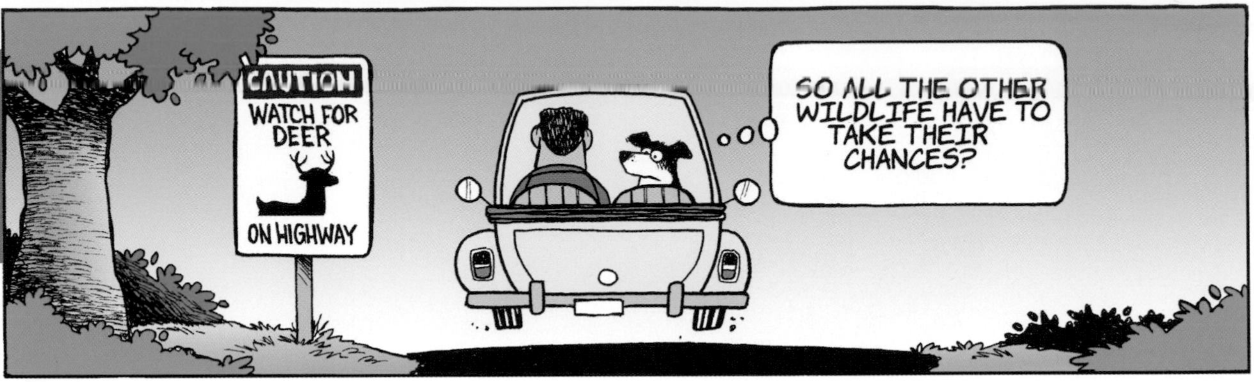
CAUTION
WATCH FOR DEER
ON HIGHWAY
SO ALL THE OTHER WILDLIFE HAVE TO TAKE THEIR CHANCES?

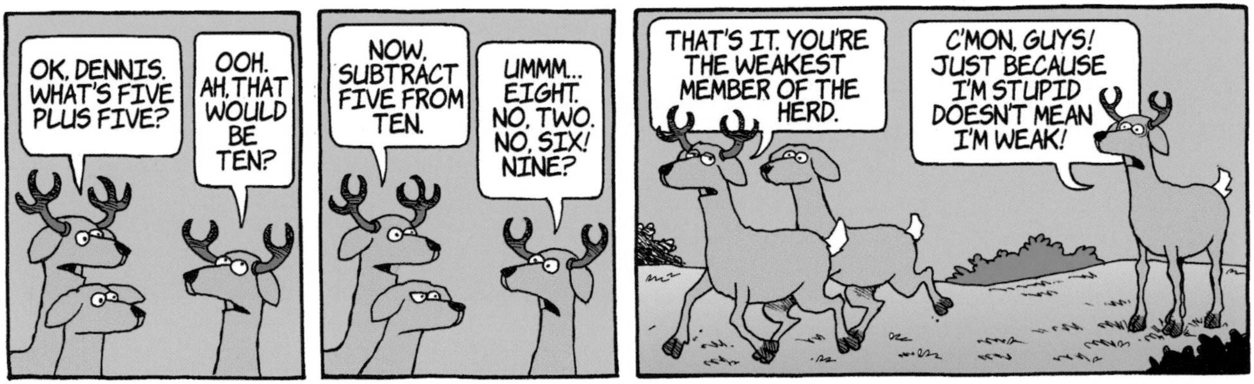
OK, DENNIS. WHAT'S FIVE PLUS FIVE?
OOH. AH, THAT WOULD BE TEN?
NOW, SUBTRACT FIVE FROM TEN.
UMMM... EIGHT. NO, TWO. NO, SIX! NINE?
THAT'S IT. YOU'RE THE WEAKEST MEMBER OF THE HERD.
C'MON, GUYS! JUST BECAUSE I'M STUPID DOESN'T MEAN I'M WEAK!

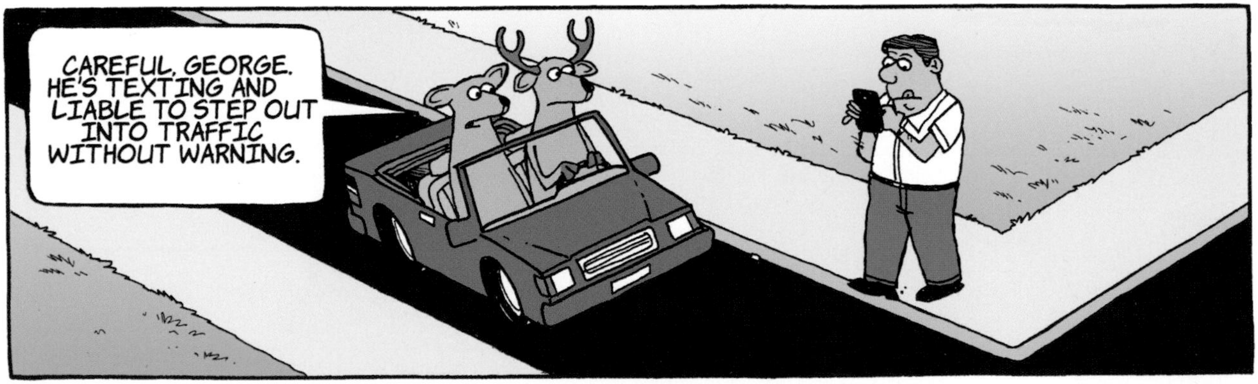
CAREFUL, GEORGE. HE'S TEXTING AND LIABLE TO STEP OUT INTO TRAFFIC WITHOUT WARNING.

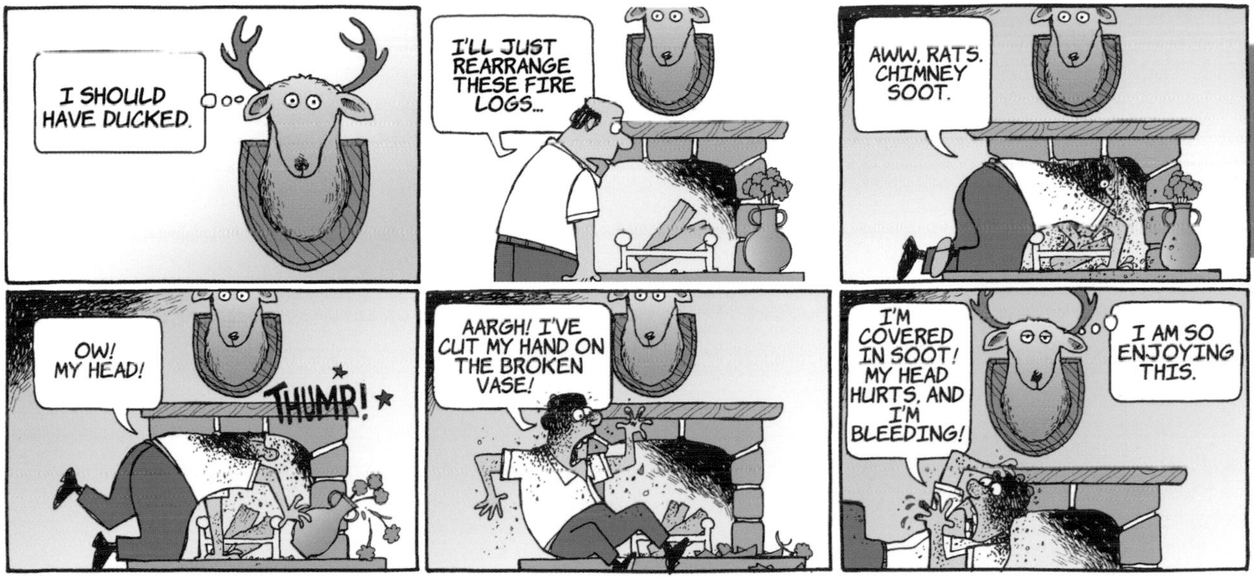
I SHOULD HAVE DUCKED.
I'LL JUST REARRANGE THESE FIRE LOGS...
AWW, RATS. CHIMNEY SOOT.
OW! MY HEAD!
THUMP!
AARGH! I'VE CUT MY HAND ON THE BROKEN VASE!
I'M COVERED IN SOOT! MY HEAD HURTS, AND I'M BLEEDING!
I AM SO ENJOYING THIS.

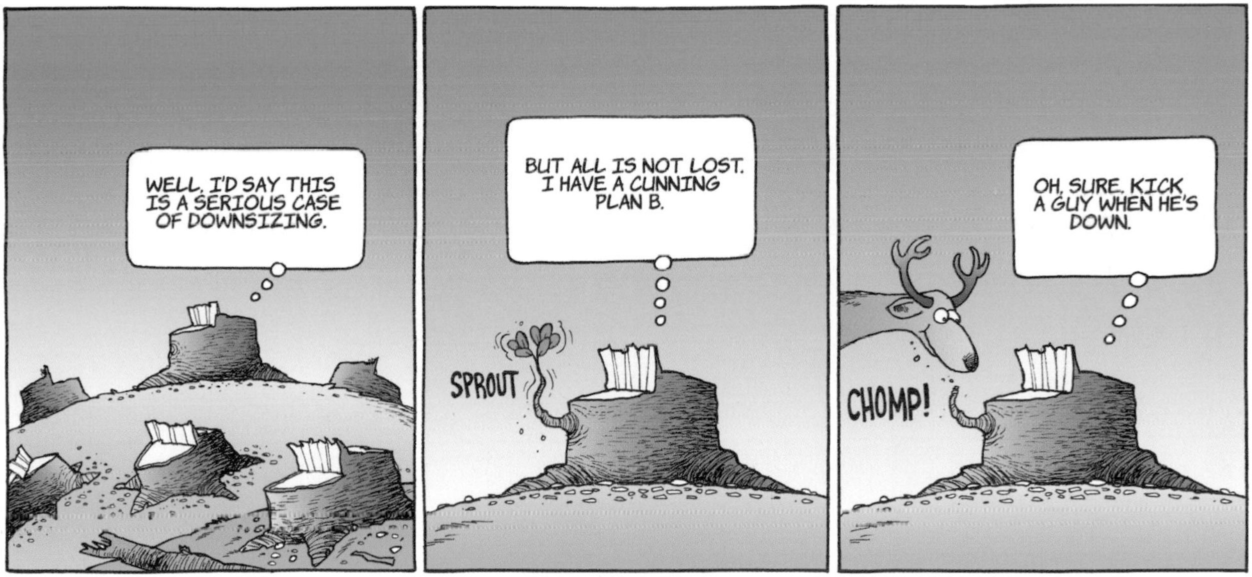
WELL, I'D SAY THIS IS A SERIOUS CASE OF DOWNSIZING.
BUT ALL IS NOT LOST. I HAVE A CUNNING PLAN B.
SPROUT
OH, SURE. KICK A GUY WHEN HE'S DOWN.
CHOMP!

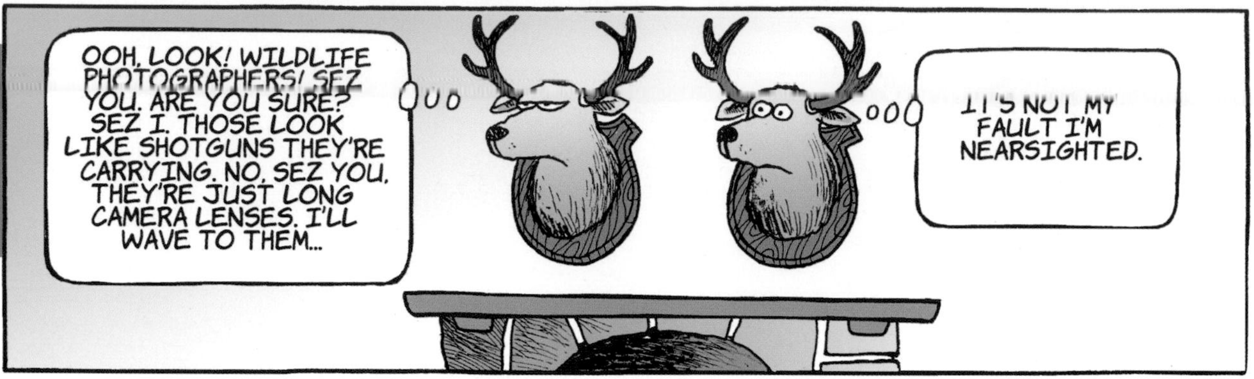
OOH, LOOK! WILDLIFE PHOTOGRAPHERS! SEZ YOU. ARE YOU SURE? SEZ I. THOSE LOOK LIKE SHOTGUNS THEY'RE CARRYING. NO, SEZ YOU. THEY'RE JUST LONG CAMERA LENSES. I'LL WAVE TO THEM...
IT'S NOT MY FAULT I'M NEARSIGHTED.

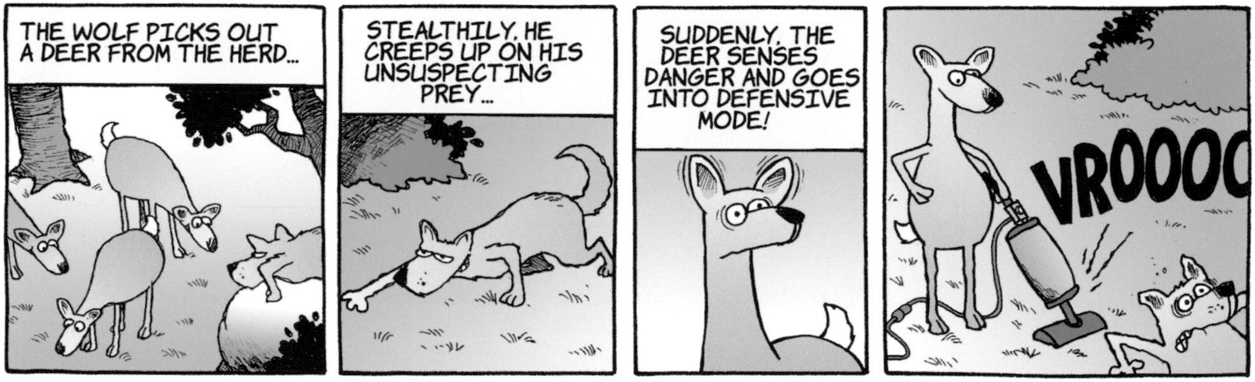
THE WOLF PICKS OUT A DEER FROM THE HERD...
STEALTHILY, HE CREEPS UP ON HIS UNSUSPECTING PREY...
SUDDENLY, THE DEER SENSES DANGER AND GOES INTO DEFENSIVE MODE!
VROOOO

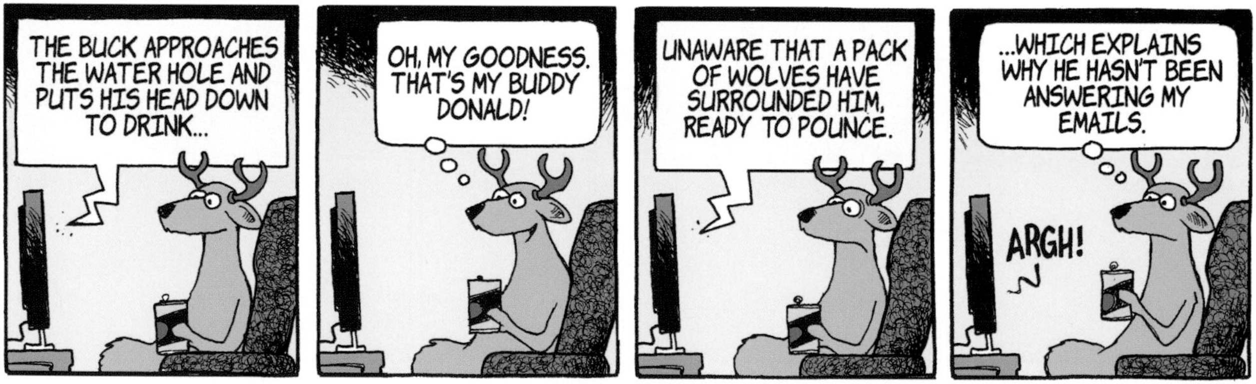
THE BUCK APPROACHES THE WATER HOLE AND PUTS HIS HEAD DOWN TO DRINK...
OH, MY GOODNESS. THAT'S MY BUDDY DONALD!
UNAWARE THAT A PACK OF WOLVES HAVE SURROUNDED HIM, READY TO POUNCE.
...WHICH EXPLAINS WHY HE HASN'T BEEN ANSWERING MY EMAILS.
ARGH!

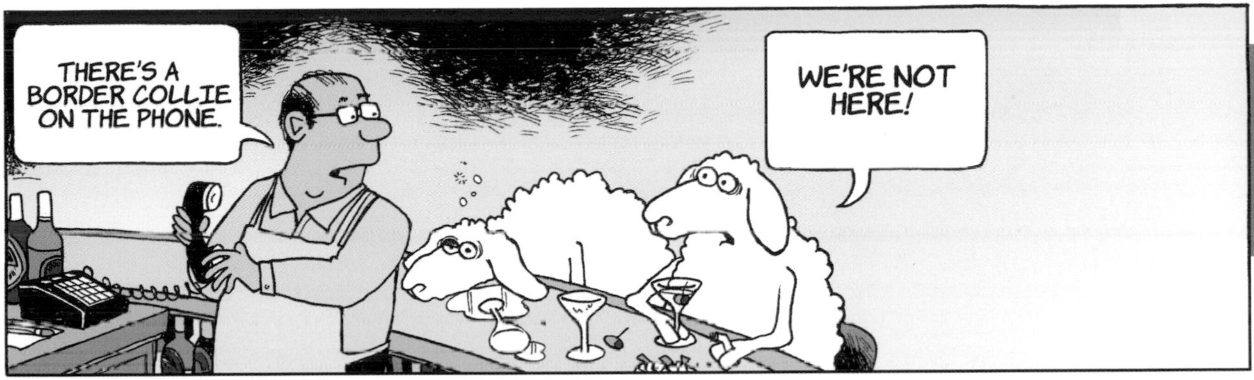
THERE'S A BORDER COLLIE ON THE PHONE.
WE'RE NOT HERE!

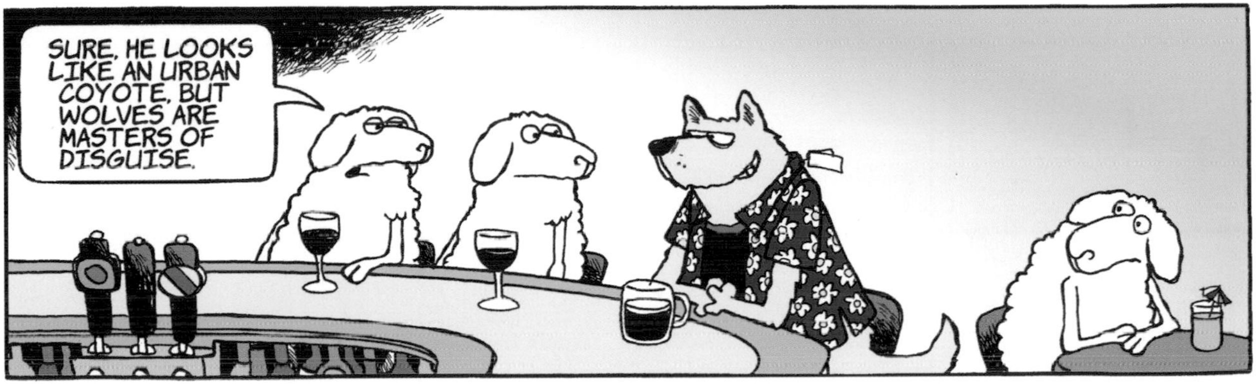
SURE, HE LOOKS LIKE AN URBAN COYOTE, BUT WOLVES ARE MASTERS OF DISGUISE.

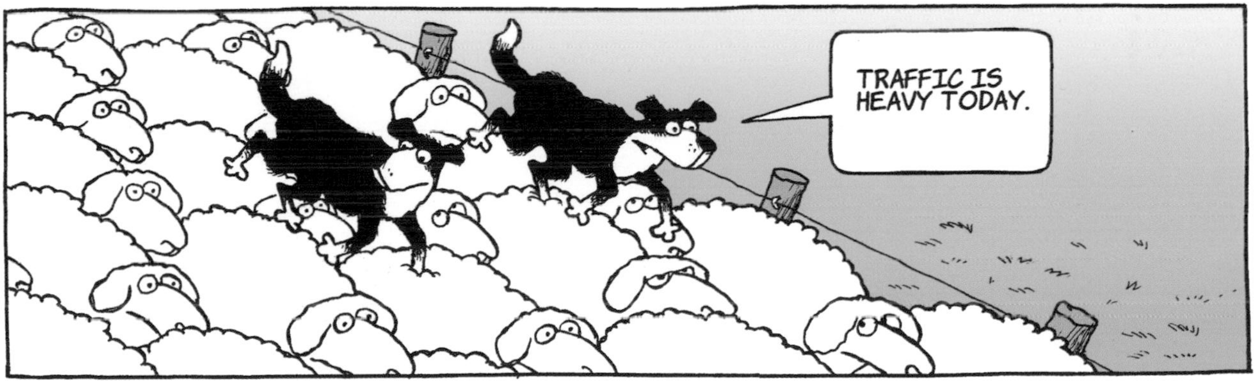
TRAFFIC IS HEAVY TODAY.

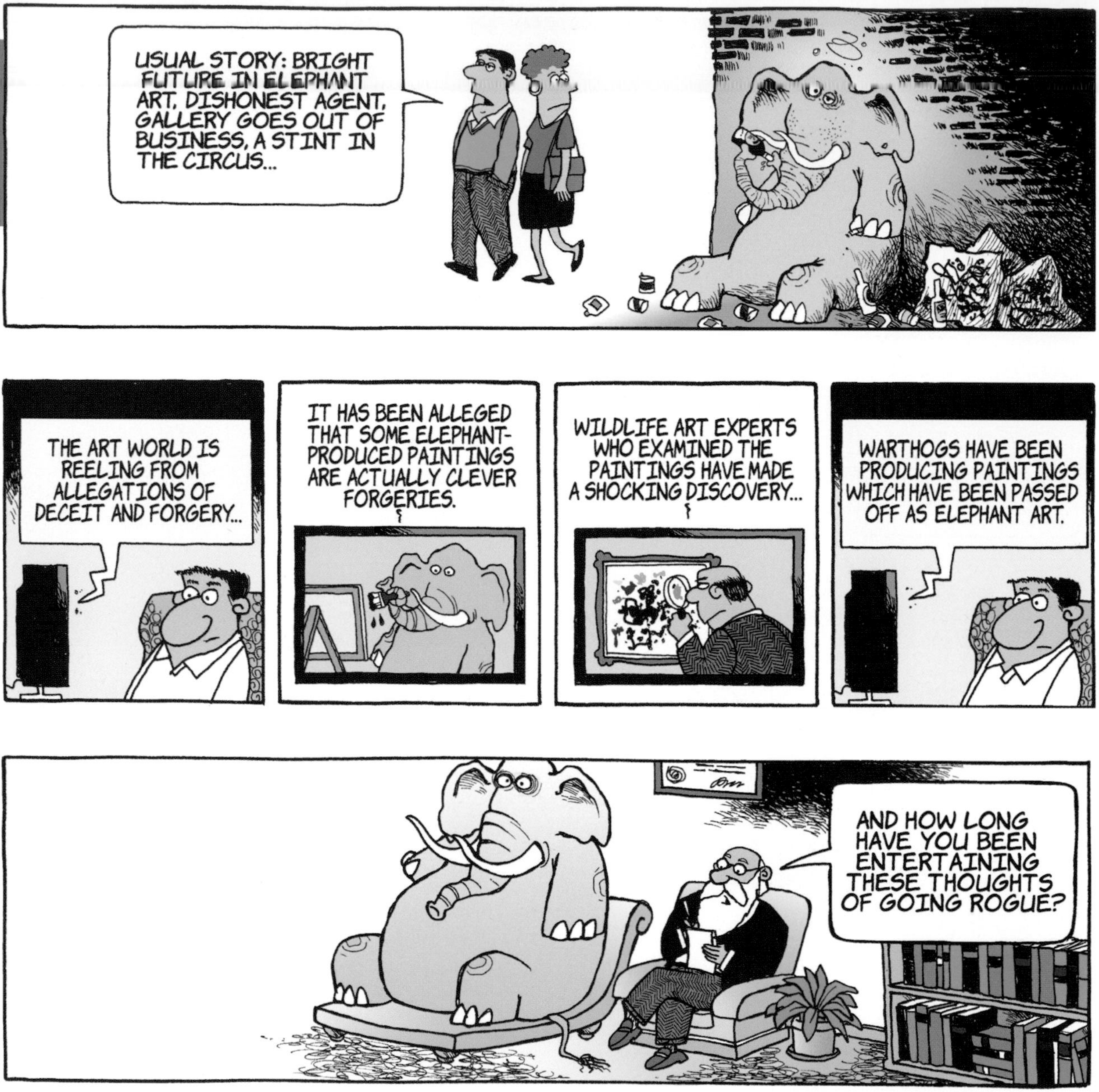
USUAL STORY: BRIGHT FUTURE IN ELEPHANT ART, DISHONEST AGENT, GALLERY GOES OUT OF BUSINESS, A STINT IN THE CIRCUS...
THE ART WORLD IS REELING FROM ALLEGATIONS OF DECEIT AND FORGERY...
IT HAS BEEN ALLEGED THAT SOME ELEPHANT-PRODUCED PAINTINGS ARE ACTUALLY CLEVER FORGERIES.
WILDLIFE ART EXPERTS WHO EXAMINED THE PAINTINGS HAVE MADE A SHOCKING DISCOVERY...
WARTHOGS HAVE BEEN PRODUCING PAINTINGS WHICH HAVE BEEN PASSED OFF AS ELEPHANT ART.
AND HOW LONG HAVE YOU BEEN ENTERTAINING THESE THOUGHTS OF GOING ROGUE?

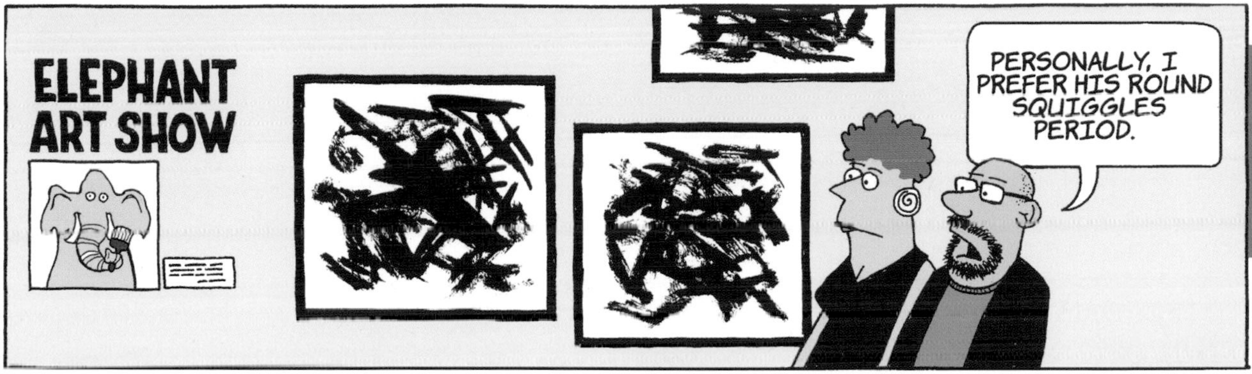
ELEPHANT ART SHOW
PERSONALLY, I PREFER HIS ROUND SQUIGGLES PERIOD.

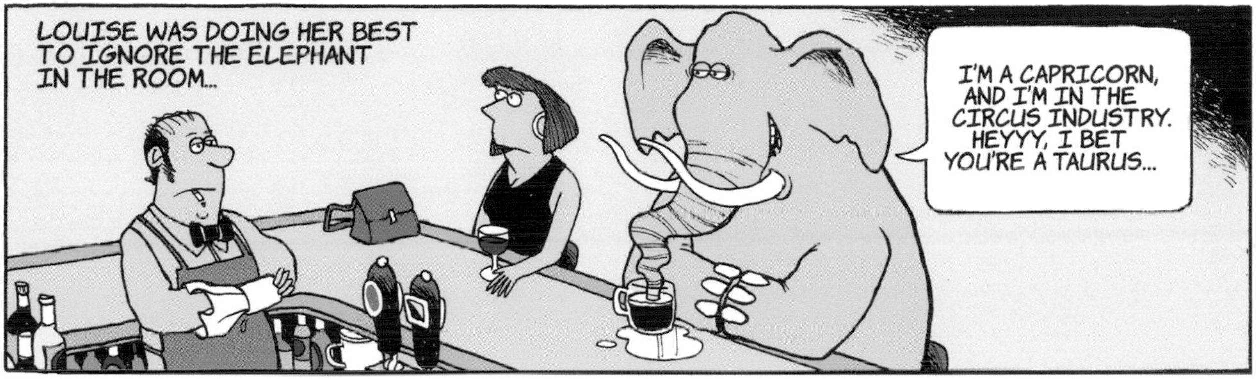
LOUISE WAS DOING HER BEST TO IGNORE THE ELEPHANT IN THE ROOM...
I'M A CAPRICORN, AND I'M IN THE CIRCUS INDUSTRY. HEYYY, I BET YOU'RE A TAURUS...

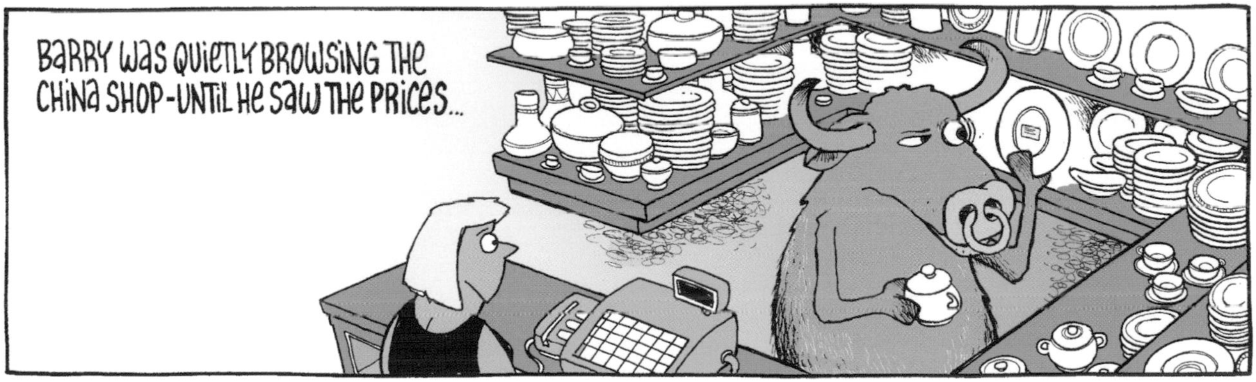
BARRY WAS QUIETLY BROWSING THE CHINA SHOP-UNTIL HE SAW THE PRICES...

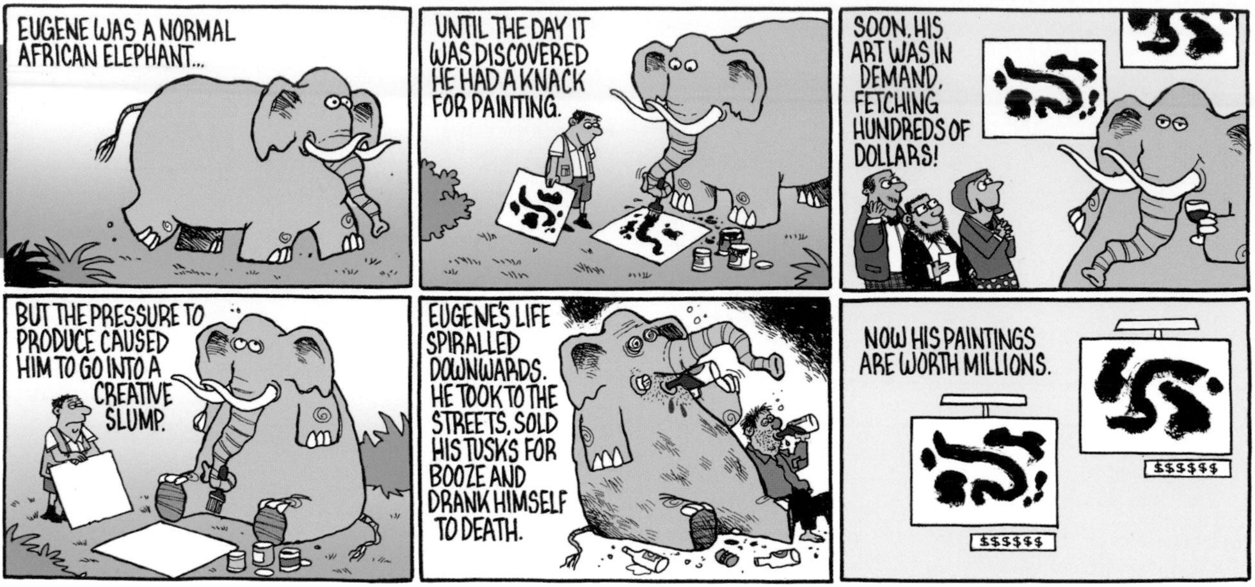
EUGENE WAS A NORMAL AFRICAN ELEPHANT...
UNTIL THE DAY IT WAS DISCOVERED HE HAD A KNACK FOR PAINTING.
SOON, HIS ART WAS IN DEMAND, FETCHING HUNDREDS OF DOLLARS!
BUT THE PRESSURE TO PRODUCE CAUSED HIM TO GO INTO A CREATIVE SLUMP.
EUGENE'S LIFE SPIRALLED DOWNWARDS. HE TOOK TO THE STREETS, SOLD HIS TUSKS FOR BOOZE AND DRANK HIMSELF TO DEATH.
NOW HIS PAINTINGS ARE WORTH MILLIONS.
$$$$$$
$$$$$$

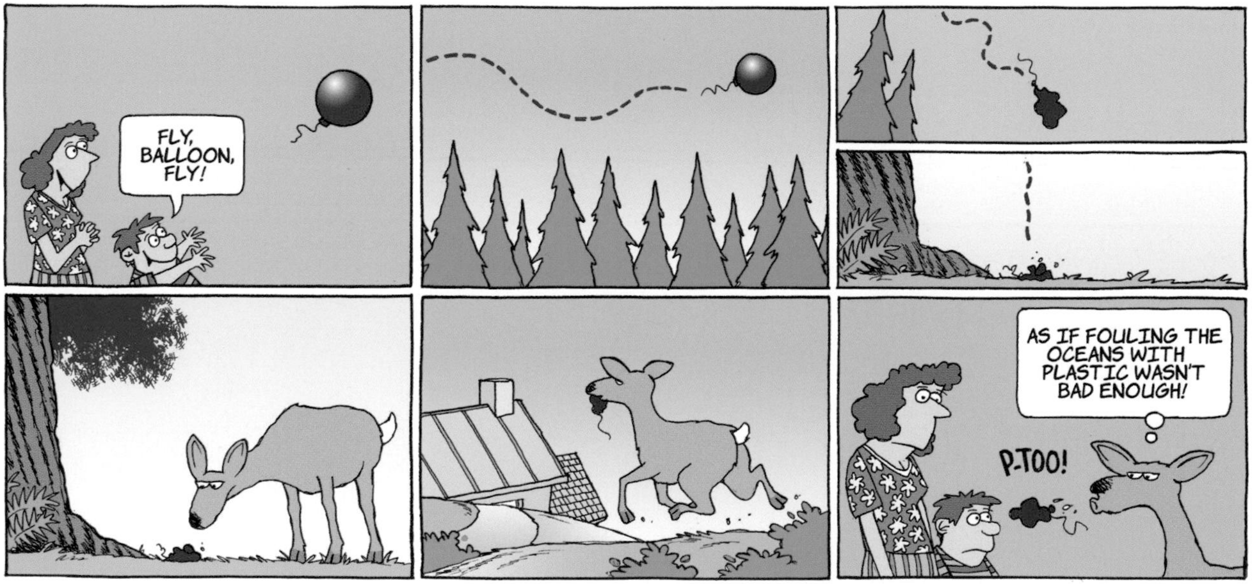
FLY, BALLOON, FLY!
P-TOO!
AS IF FOULING THE OCEANS WITH PLASTIC WASN'T BAD ENOUGH!

POLAR PERSONALITIES 11

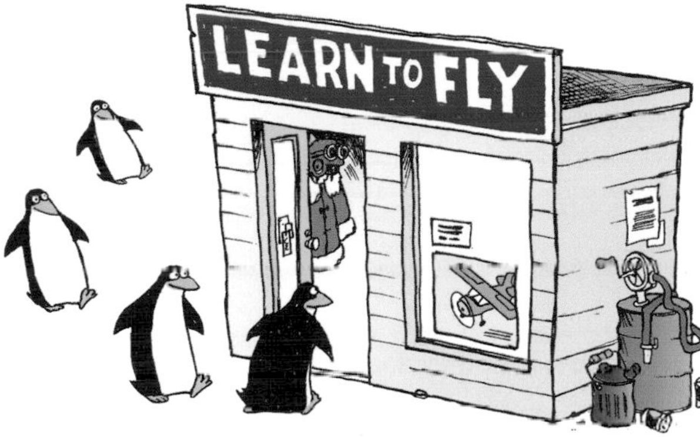

LEARN TO FLY

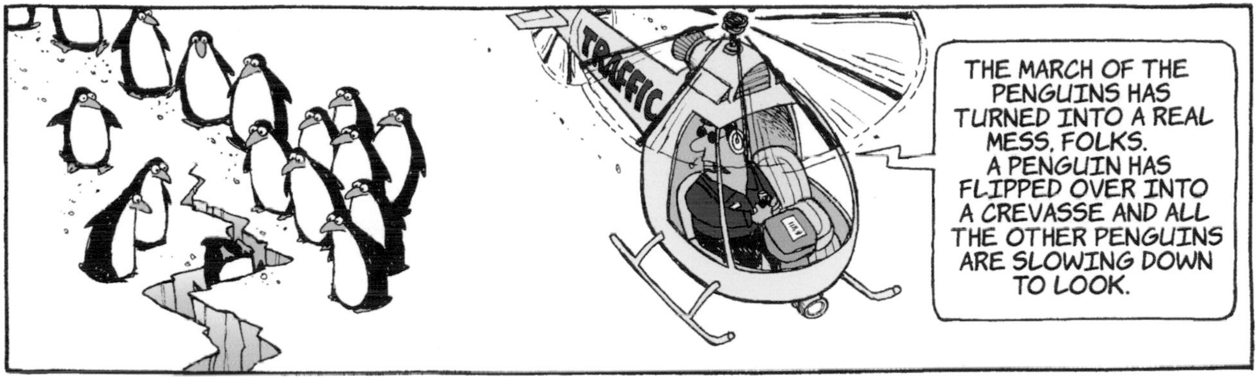

TRAFFIC
THE MARCH OF THE PENGUINS HAS TURNED INTO A REAL MESS, FOLKS. A PENGUIN HAS FLIPPED OVER INTO A CREVASSE AND ALL THE OTHER PENGUINS ARE SLOWING DOWN TO LOOK.

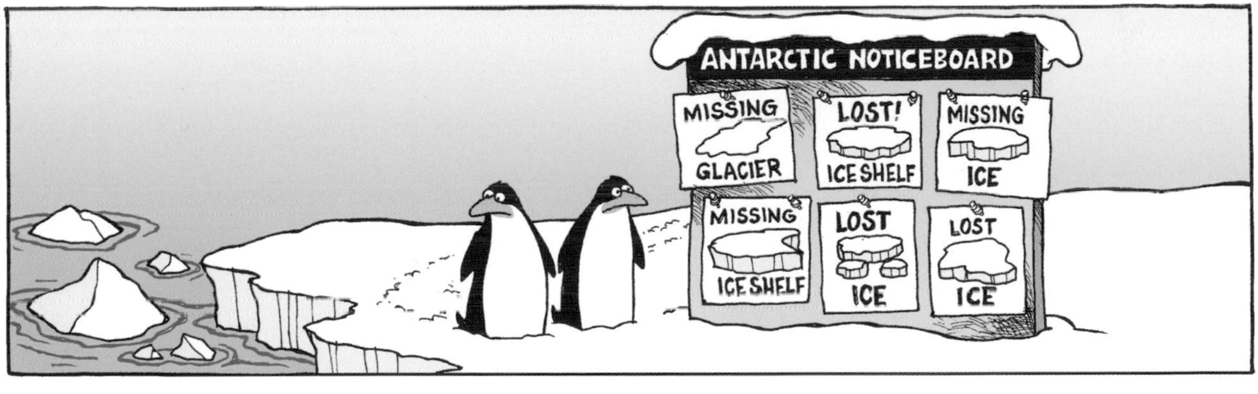

ANTARCTIC NOTICEBOARD
MISSING GLACIER
LOST! ICE SHELF
MISSING ICE
MISSING ICE SHELF
LOST ICE
LOST ICE

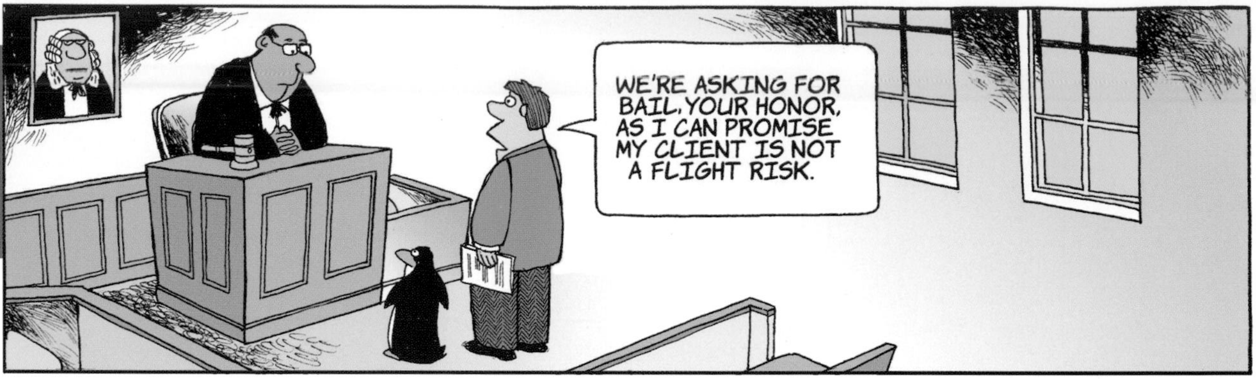
WE'RE ASKING FOR BAIL, YOUR HONOR, AS I CAN PROMISE MY CLIENT IS NOT A FLIGHT RISK.

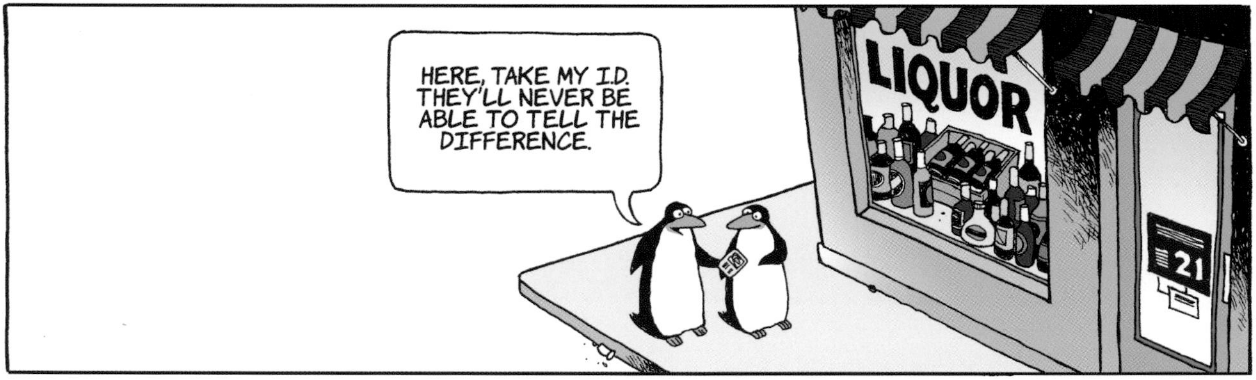
HERE, TAKE MY I.D. THEY'LL NEVER BE ABLE TO TELL THE DIFFERENCE.
LIQUOR
21

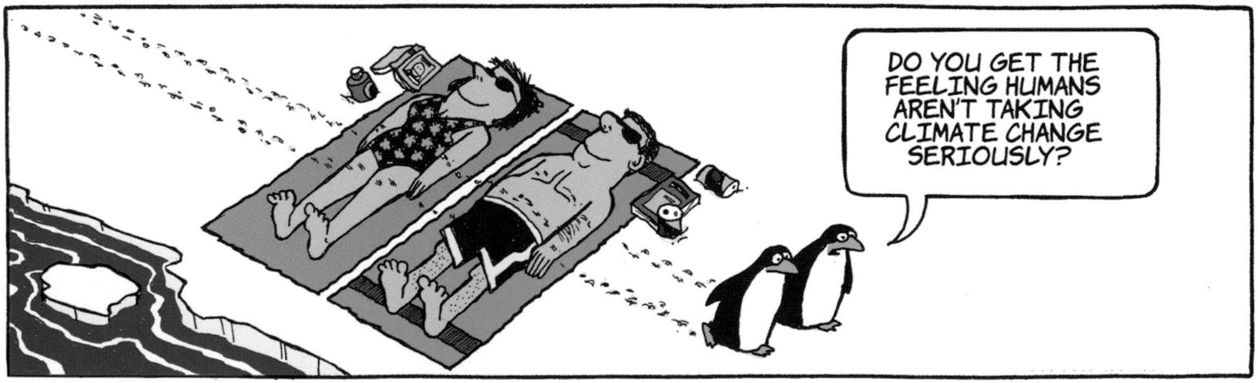
DO YOU GET THE FEELING HUMANS AREN'T TAKING CLIMATE CHANGE SERIOUSLY?

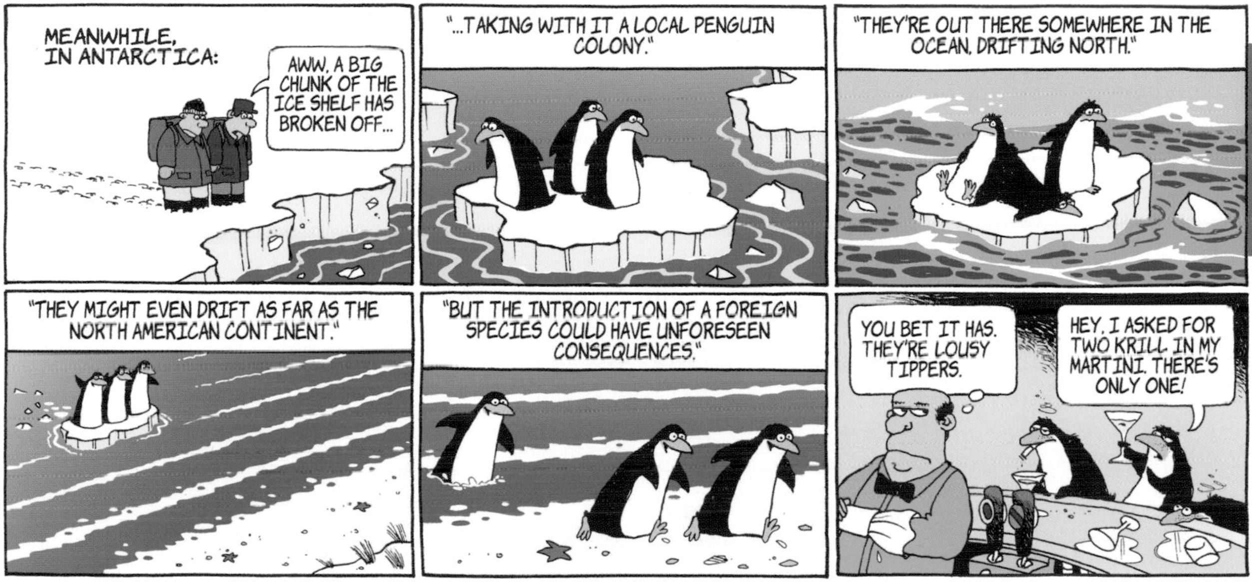
MEANWHILE, IN ANTARCTICA:
AWW, A BIG CHUNK OF THE ICE SHELF HAS BROKEN OFF...
"...TAKING WITH IT A LOCAL PENGUIN COLONY."
"THEY'RE OUT THERE SOMEWHERE IN THE OCEAN, DRIFTING NORTH."
"THEY MIGHT EVEN DRIFT AS FAR AS THE NORTH AMERICAN CONTINENT."
"BUT THE INTRODUCTION OF A FOREIGN SPECIES COULD HAVE UNFORESEEN CONSEQUENCES."
YOU BET IT HAS. THEY'RE LOUSY TIPPERS.
HEY, I ASKED FOR TWO KRILL IN MY MARTINI. THERE'S ONLY ONE!

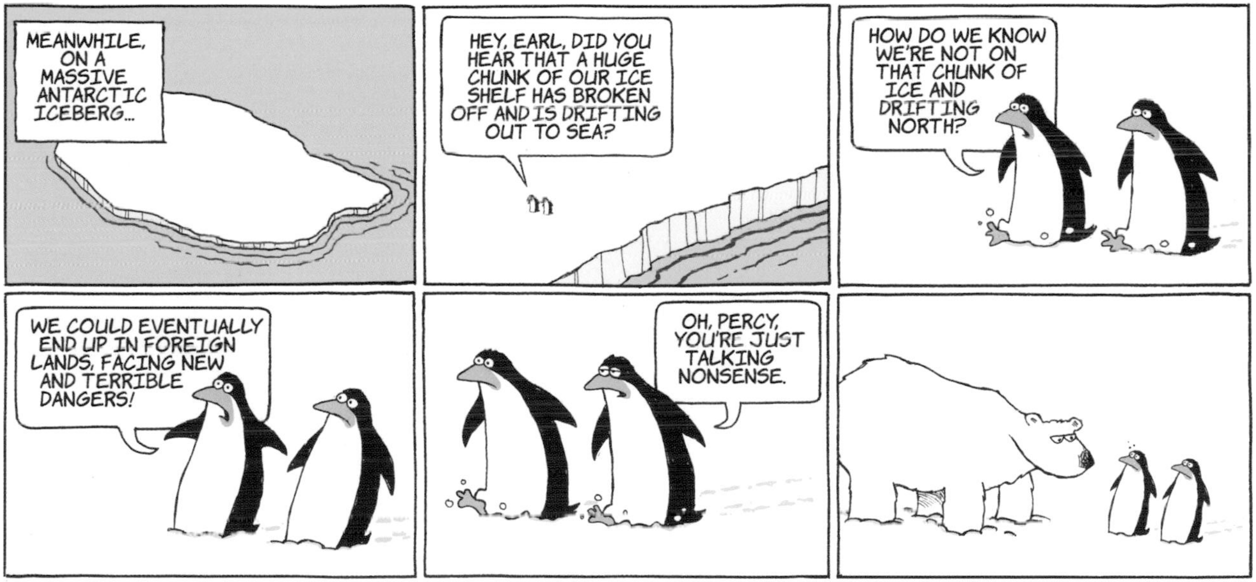
MEANWHILE, ON A MASSIVE ANTARCTIC ICEBERG...
HEY, EARL, DID YOU HEAR THAT A HUGE CHUNK OF OUR ICE SHELF HAS BROKEN OFF AND IS DRIFTING OUT TO SEA?
HOW DO WE KNOW WE'RE NOT ON THAT CHUNK OF ICE AND DRIFTING NORTH?
WE COULD EVENTUALLY END UP IN FOREIGN LANDS, FACING NEW AND TERRIBLE DANGERS!
OH, PERCY, YOU'RE JUST TALKING NONSENSE.

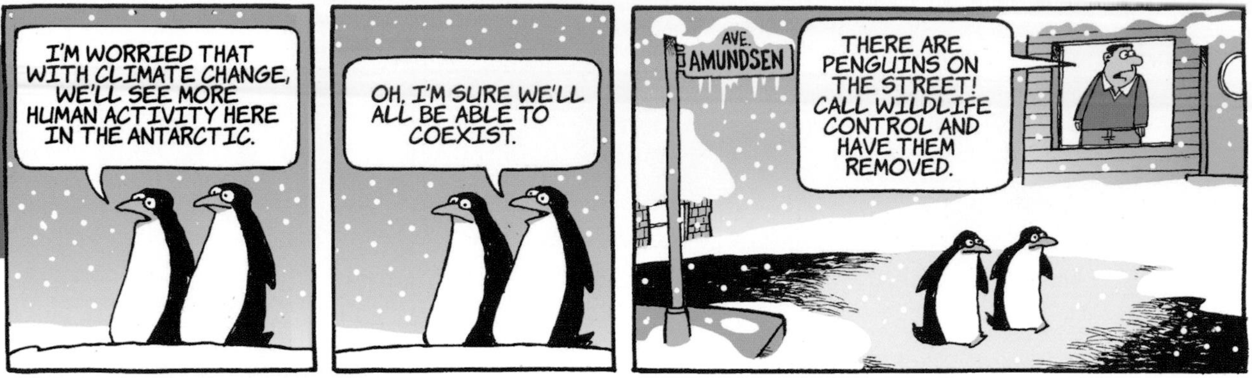
I'M WORRIED THAT WITH CLIMATE CHANGE, WE'LL SEE MORE HUMAN ACTIVITY HERE IN THE ANTARCTIC.
OH, I'M SURE WE'LL ALL BE ABLE TO COEXIST.
AVE. AMUNDSEN
THERE ARE PENGUINS ON THE STREET! CALL WILDLIFE CONTROL AND HAVE THEM REMOVED.

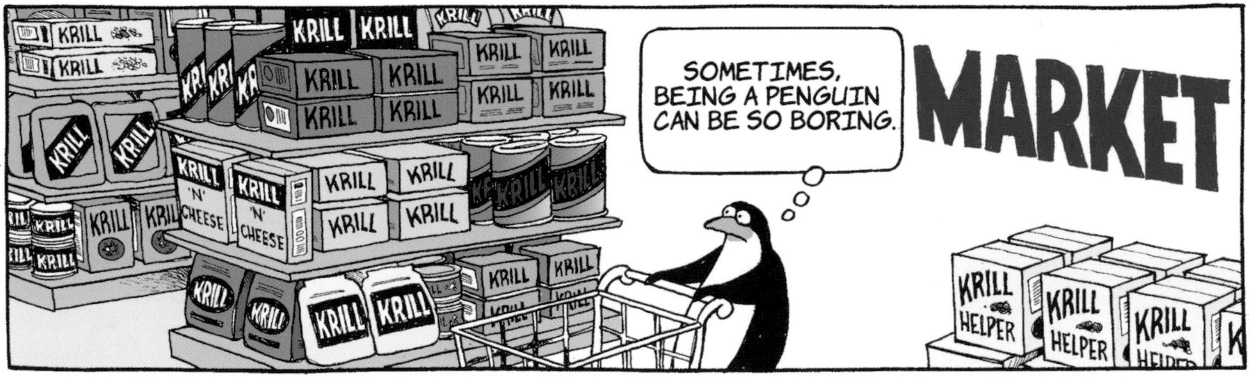
SOMETIMES, BEING A PENGUIN CAN BE SO BORING.
MARKET
KRILL 'N' CHEESE
KRILL HELPER

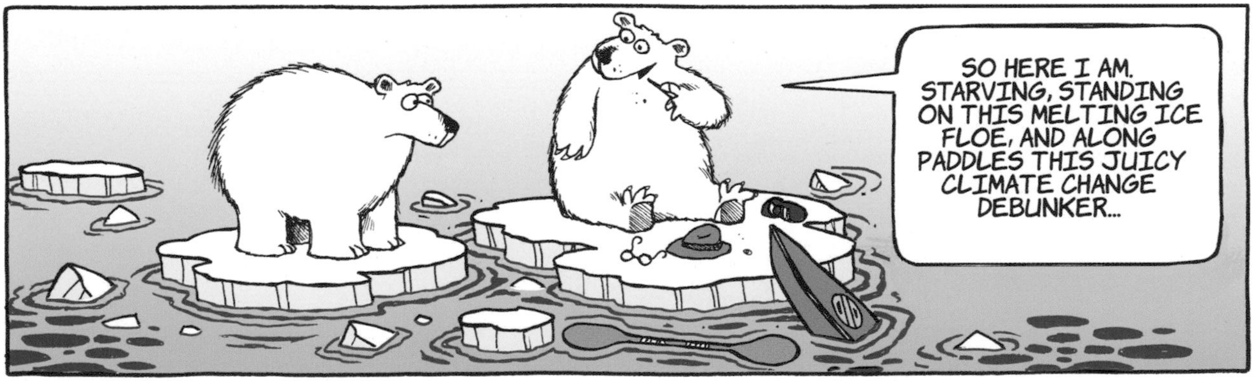
SO HERE I AM. STARVING, STANDING ON THIS MELTING ICE FLOE, AND ALONG PADDLES THIS JUICY CLIMATE CHANGE DEBUNKER...

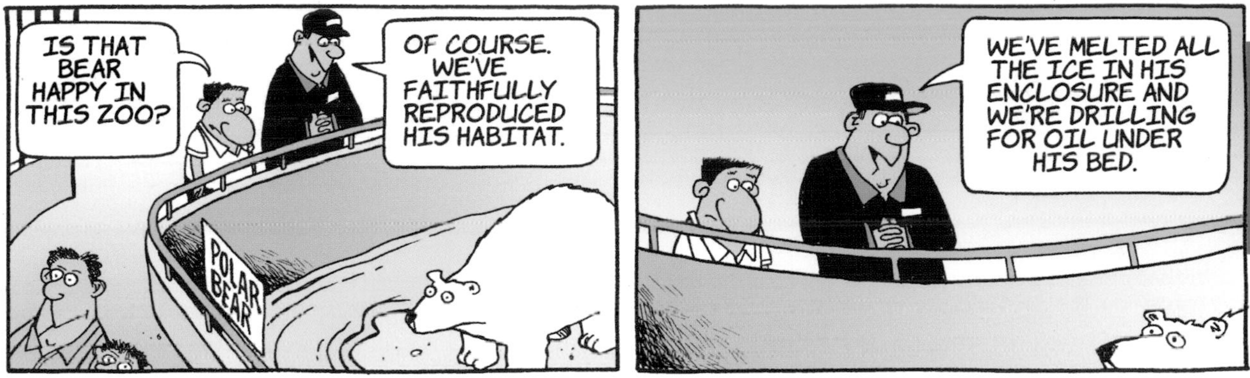
IS THAT BEAR HAPPY IN THIS ZOO?
OF COURSE. WE'VE FAITHFULLY REPRODUCED HIS HABITAT.
POLAR BEAR
WE'VE MELTED ALL THE ICE IN HIS ENCLOSURE AND WE'RE DRILLING FOR OIL UNDER HIS BED.

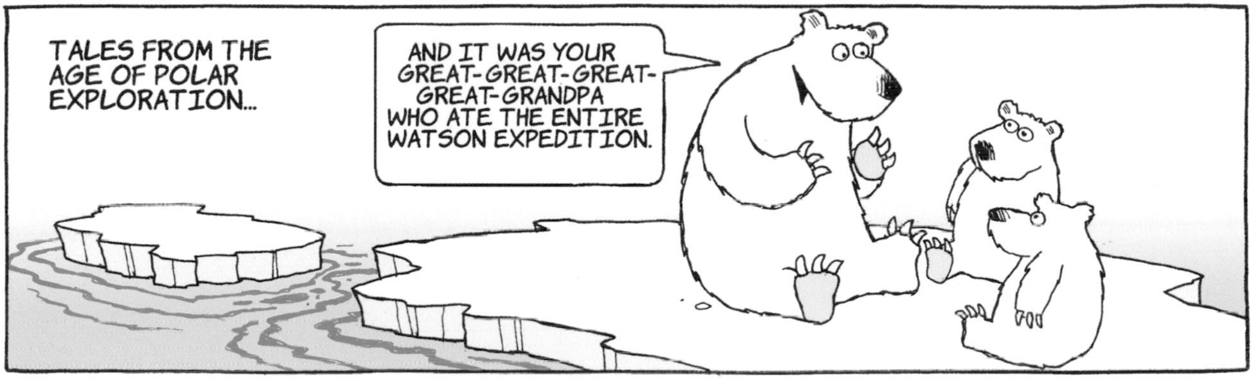
TALES FROM THE AGE OF POLAR EXPLORATION...
AND IT WAS YOUR GREAT-GREAT-GREAT-GREAT-GRANDPA WHO ATE THE ENTIRE WATSON EXPEDITION.

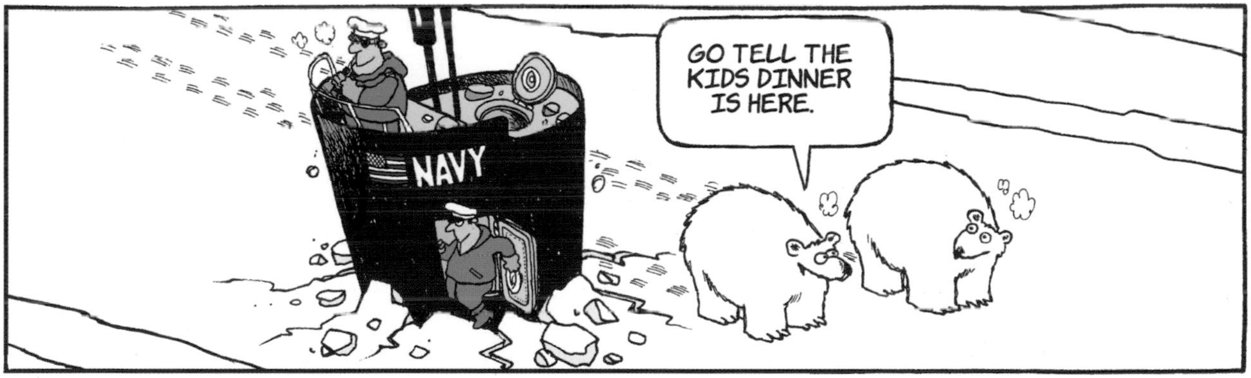
NAVY
GO TELL THE KIDS DINNER IS HERE.

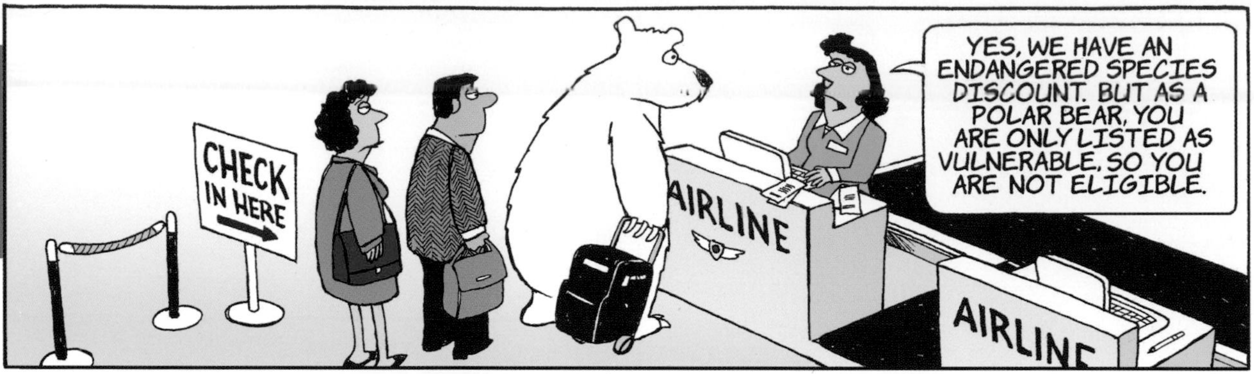
CHECK IN HERE
AIRLINE
YES, WE HAVE AN ENDANGERED SPECIES DISCOUNT. BUT AS A POLAR BEAR, YOU ARE ONLY LISTED AS VULNERABLE, SO YOU ARE NOT ELIGIBLE.
AIRLINE

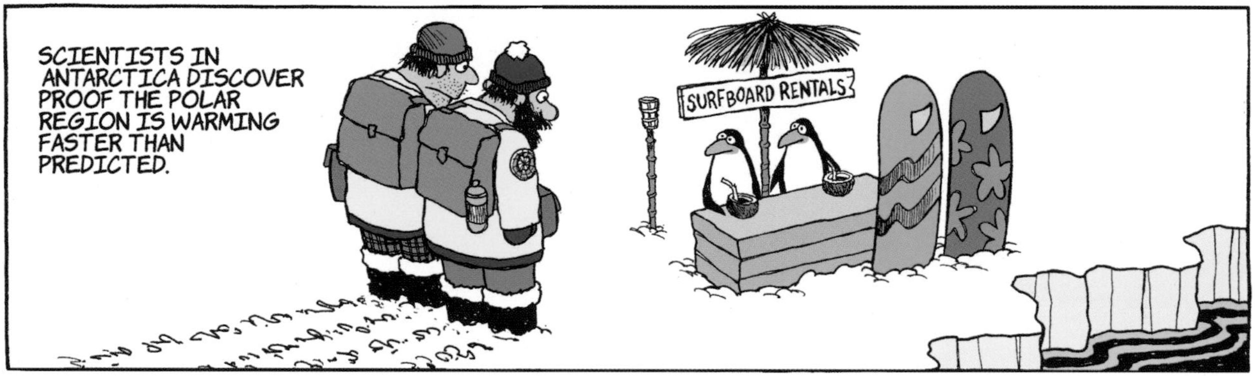
SCIENTISTS IN ANTARCTICA DISCOVER PROOF THE POLAR REGION IS WARMING FASTER THAN PREDICTED.
SURFBOARD RENTALS

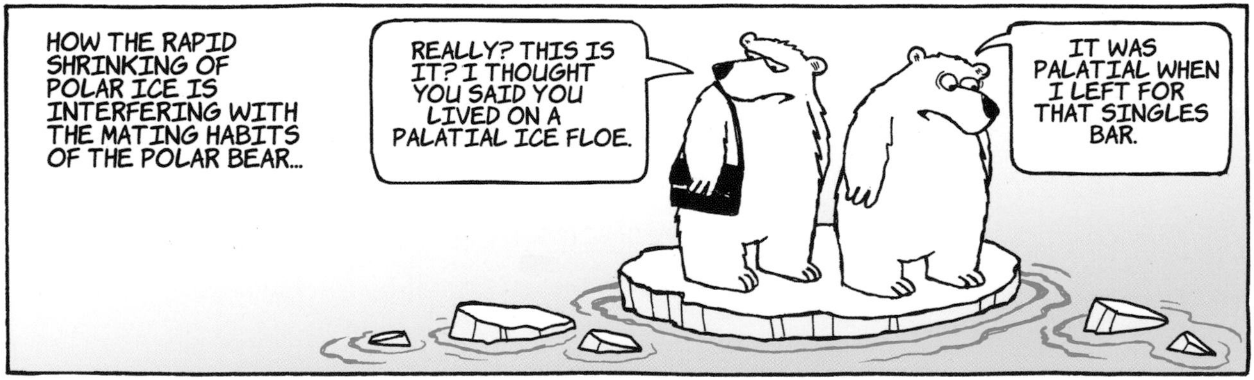
HOW THE RAPID SHRINKING OF POLAR ICE IS INTERFERING WITH THE MATING HABITS OF THE POLAR BEAR...
REALLY? THIS IS IT? I THOUGHT YOU SAID YOU LIVED ON A PALATIAL ICE FLOE.
IT WAS PALATIAL WHEN I LEFT FOR THAT SINGLES BAR.

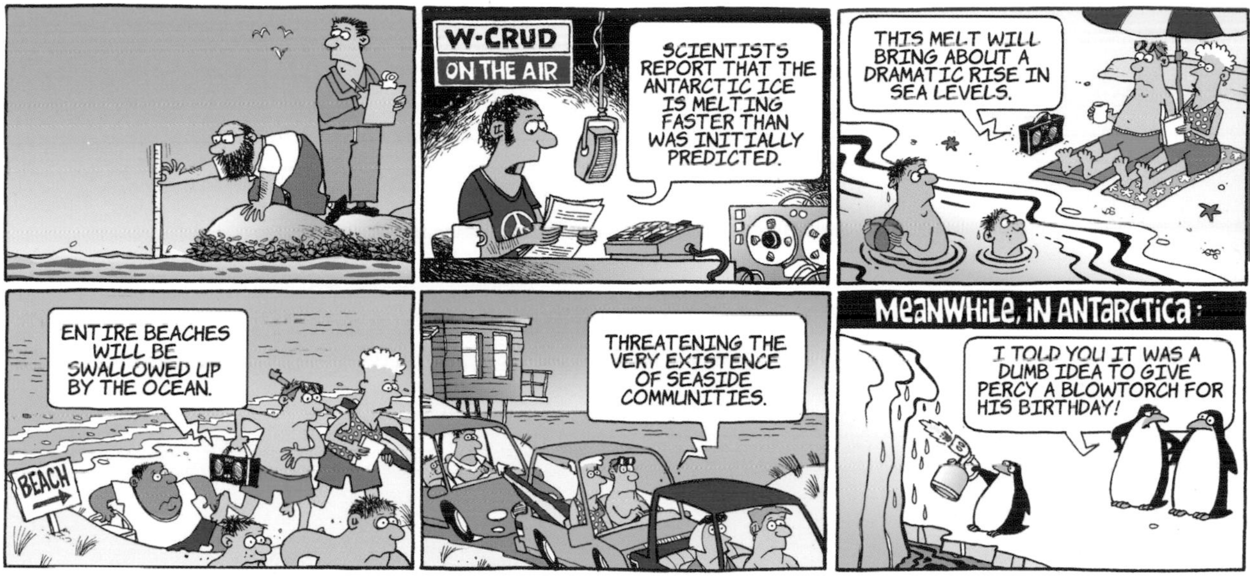
W-CRUD
ON THE AIR
SCIENTISTS REPORT THAT THE ANTARCTIC ICE IS MELTING FASTER THAN WAS INITIALLY PREDICTED.
THIS MELT WILL BRING ABOUT A DRAMATIC RISE IN SEA LEVELS.
ENTIRE BEACHES WILL BE SWALLOWED UP BY THE OCEAN.
BEACH
THREATENING THE VERY EXISTENCE OF SEASIDE COMMUNITIES.
MEANWHILE, IN ANTARCTICA:
I TOLD YOU IT WAS A DUMB IDEA TO GIVE PERCY A BLOWTORCH FOR HIS BIRTHDAY!

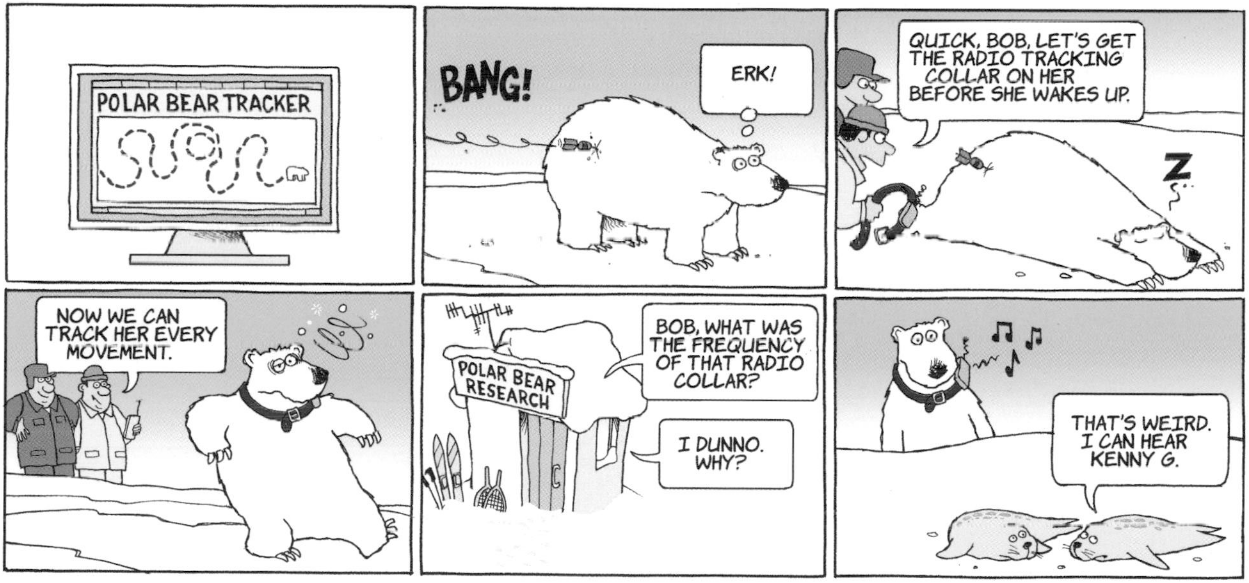
POLAR BEAR TRACKER
BANG!
ERK!
QUICK, BOB, LET'S GET THE RADIO TRACKING COLLAR ON HER BEFORE SHE WAKES UP.
Z
NOW WE CAN TRACK HER EVERY MOVEMENT.
POLAR BEAR RESEARCH
BOB, WHAT WAS THE FREQUENCY OF THAT RADIO COLLAR?
I DUNNO. WHY?
THAT'S WEIRD. I CAN HEAR KENNY G.

12 RARE SIGHTINGS

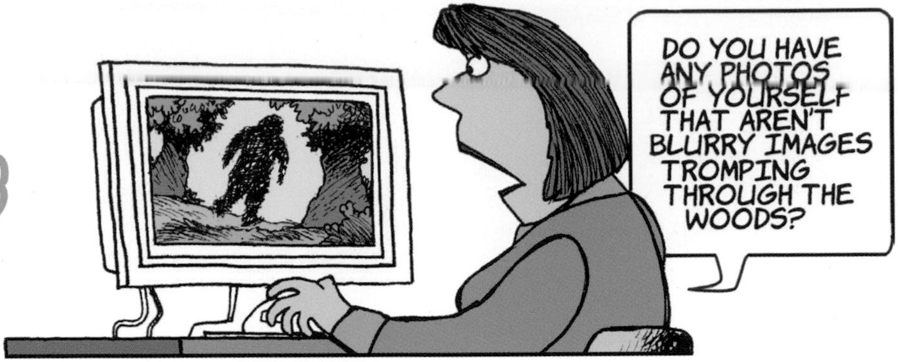
DO YOU HAVE ANY PHOTOS OF YOURSELF THAT AREN'T BLURRY IMAGES TROMPING THROUGH THE WOODS?

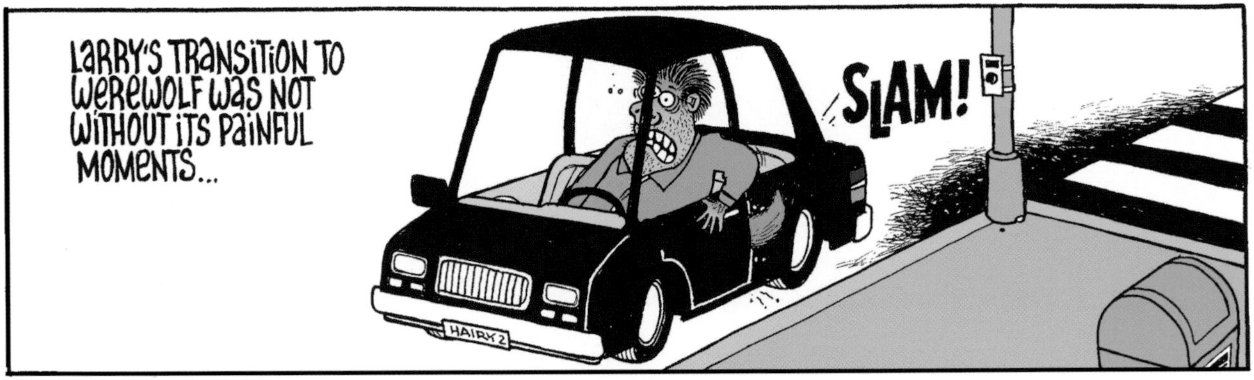
LARRY'S TRANSITION TO WEREWOLF WAS NOT WITHOUT ITS PAINFUL MOMENTS...
SLAM!
HAIRY 2

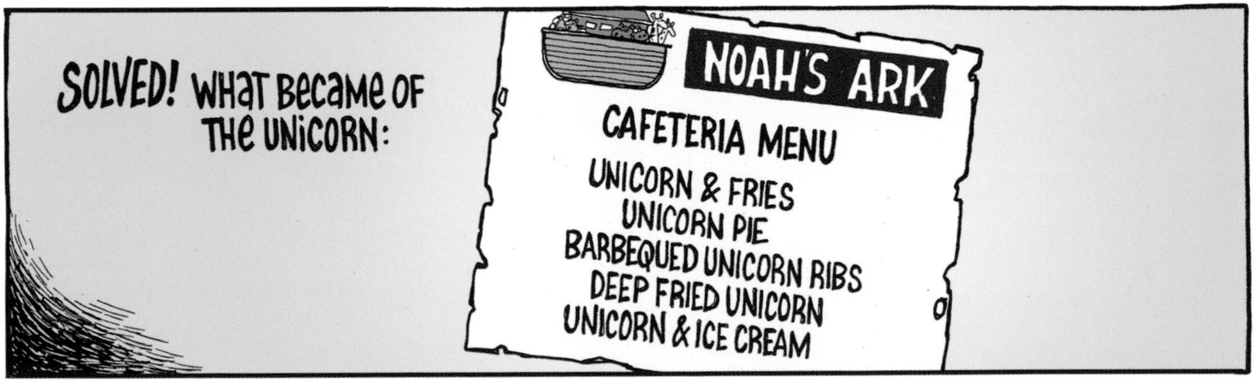
SOLVED! WHAT BECAME OF THE UNICORN:
NOAH'S ARK
CAFETERIA MENU
UNICORN & FRIES
UNICORN PIE
BARBEQUED UNICORN RIBS
DEEP FRIED UNICORN
UNICORN & ICE CREAM

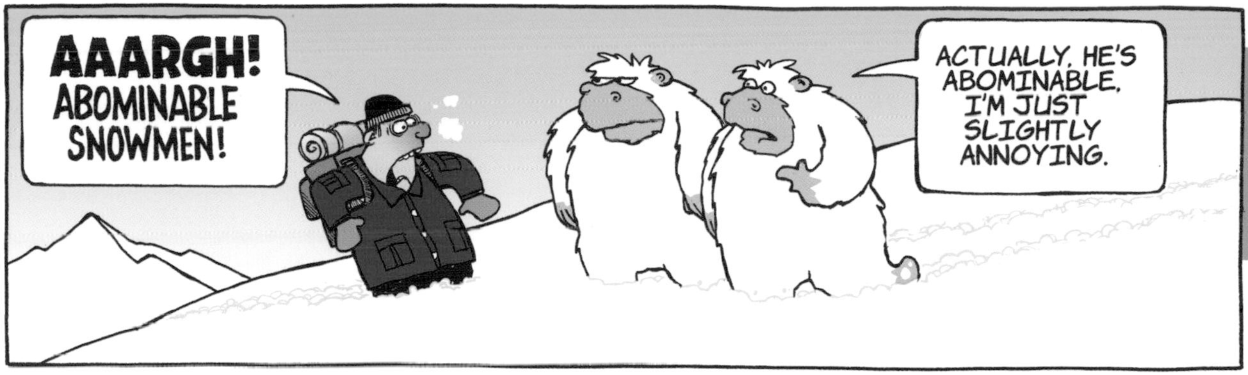
AAARGH! ABOMINABLE SNOWMEN!
ACTUALLY, HE'S ABOMINABLE. I'M JUST SLIGHTLY ANNOYING.

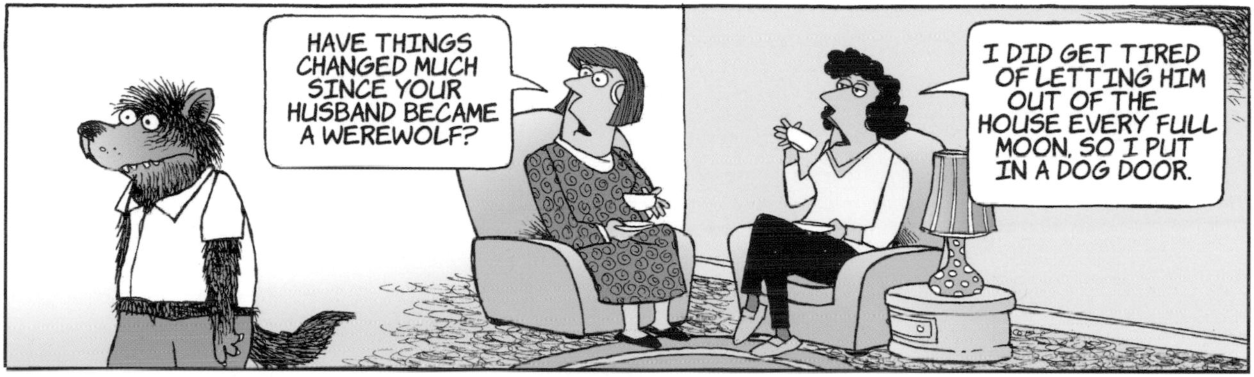
HAVE THINGS CHANGED MUCH SINCE YOUR HUSBAND BECAME A WEREWOLF?
I DID GET TIRED OF LETTING HIM OUT OF THE HOUSE EVERY FULL MOON, SO I PUT IN A DOG DOOR.

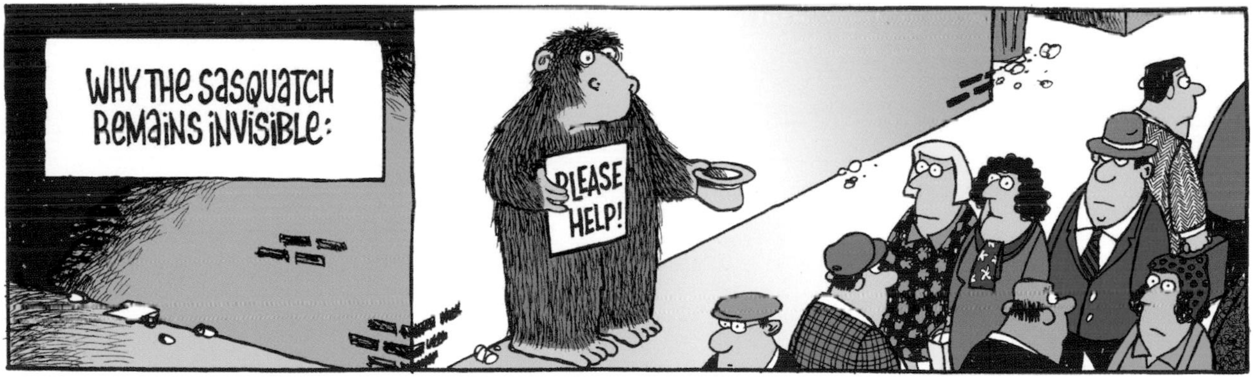
WHY THE SASQUATCH REMAINS INVISIBLE:
PLEASE HELP!

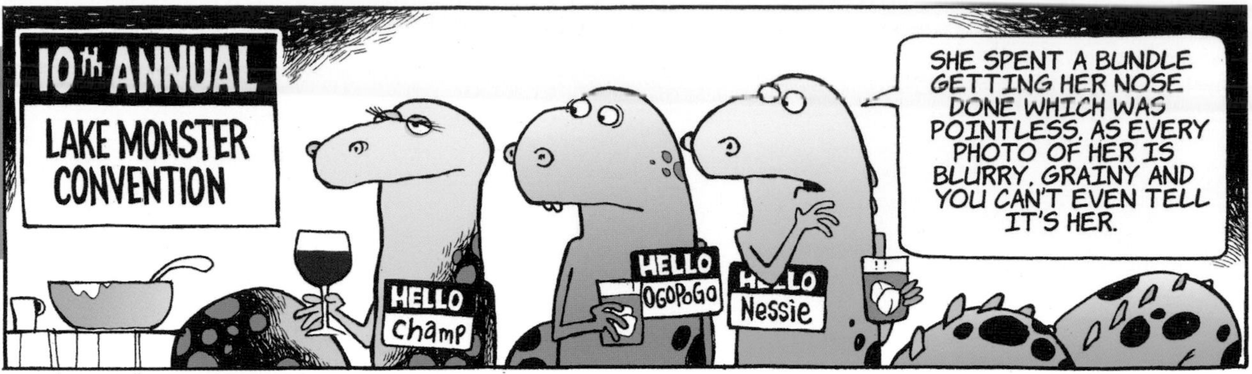
10th ANNUAL
LAKE MONSTER CONVENTION
SHE SPENT A BUNDLE GETTING HER NOSE DONE WHICH WAS POINTLESS, AS EVERY PHOTO OF HER IS BLURRY, GRAINY AND YOU CAN'T EVEN TELL IT'S HER.
HELLO Champ
HELLO OGOPOGO
HELLO Nessie

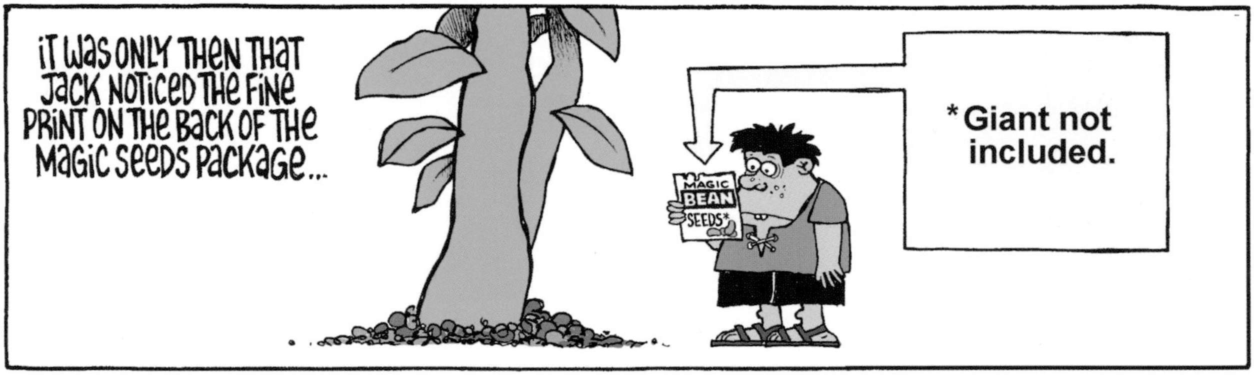
IT WAS ONLY THEN THAT JACK NOTICED THE FINE PRINT ON THE BACK OF THE MAGIC SEEDS PACKAGE...
MAGIC BEAN SEEDS*
*Giant not included.

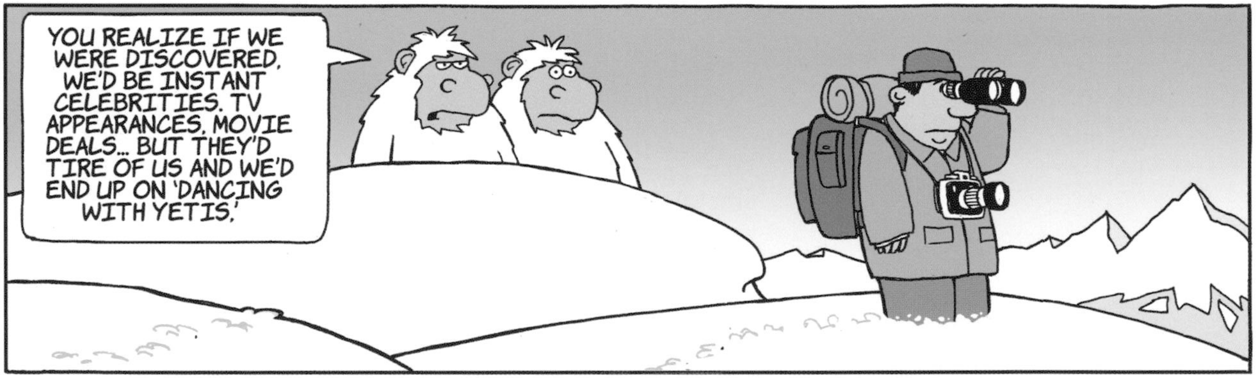
YOU REALIZE IF WE WERE DISCOVERED, WE'D BE INSTANT CELEBRITIES. TV APPEARANCES, MOVIE DEALS... BUT THEY'D TIRE OF US AND WE'D END UP ON 'DANCING WITH YETIS.'

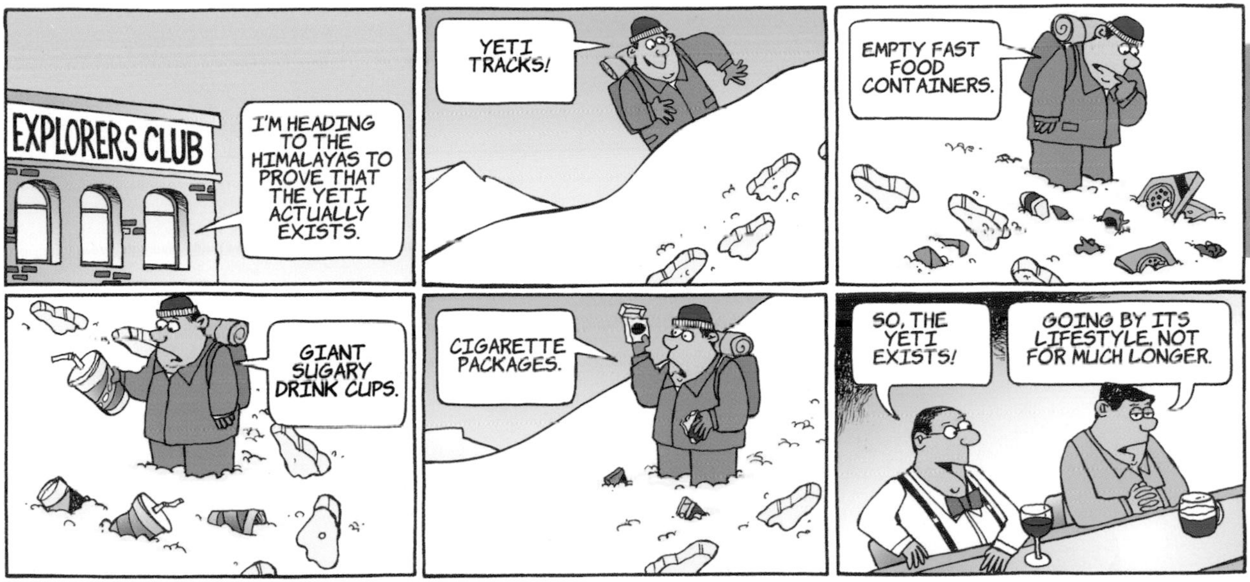
EXPLORERS CLUB
I'M HEADING TO THE HIMALAYAS TO PROVE THAT THE YETI ACTUALLY EXISTS.
YETI TRACKS!
EMPTY FAST FOOD CONTAINERS.
GIANT SUGARY DRINK CUPS.
CIGARETTE PACKAGES.
SO, THE YETI EXISTS!
GOING BY ITS LIFESTYLE, NOT FOR MUCH LONGER.

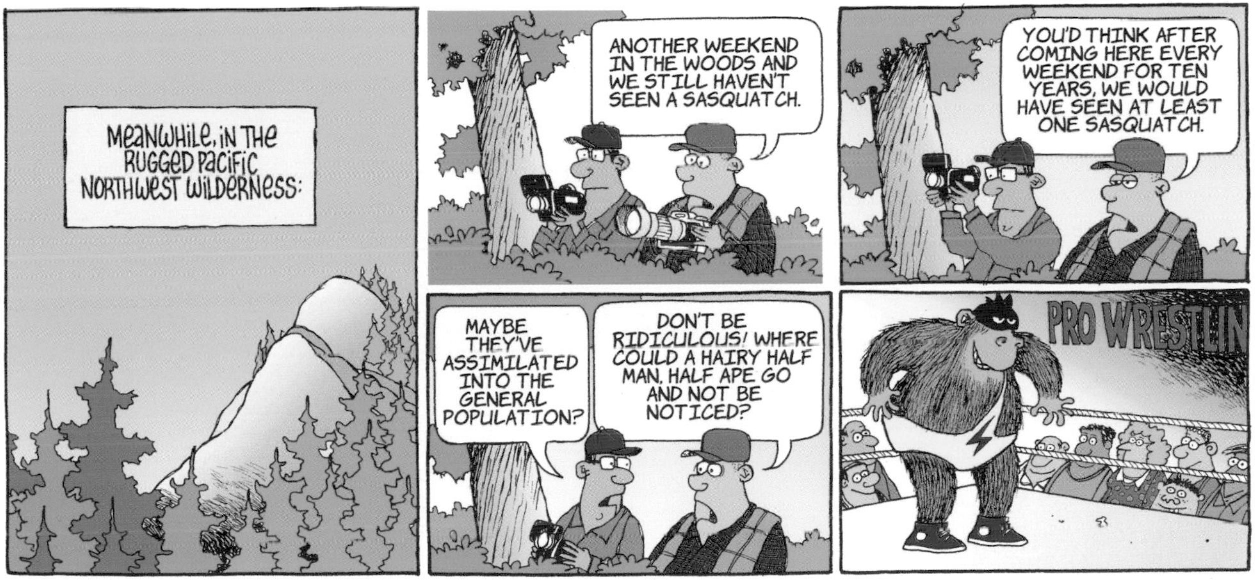
MEANWHILE, IN THE RUGGED PACIFIC NORTHWEST WILDERNESS:
ANOTHER WEEKEND IN THE WOODS AND WE STILL HAVEN'T SEEN A SASQUATCH.
YOU'D THINK AFTER COMING HERE EVERY WEEKEND FOR TEN YEARS, WE WOULD HAVE SEEN AT LEAST ONE SASQUATCH.
MAYBE THEY'VE ASSIMILATED INTO THE GENERAL POPULATION?
DON'T BE RIDICULOUS! WHERE COULD A HAIRY HALF MAN, HALF APE GO AND NOT BE NOTICED?
PRO WRESTLIN

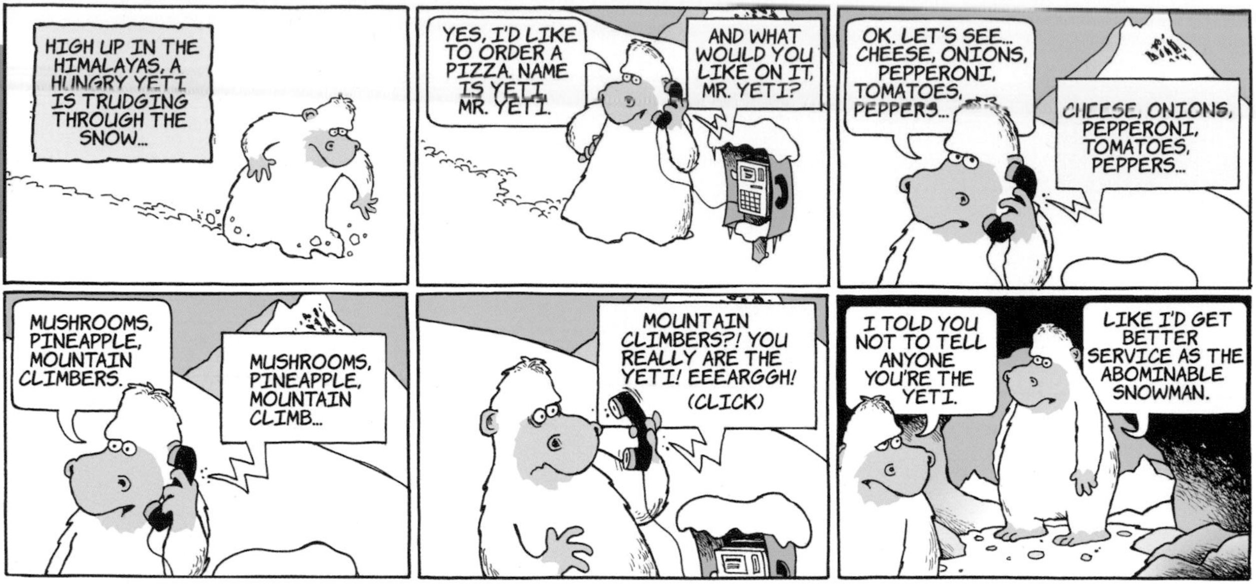
HIGH UP IN THE HIMALAYAS, A HUNGRY YETI IS TRUDGING THROUGH THE SNOW...
YES, I'D LIKE TO ORDER A PIZZA. NAME IS YETI. MR. YETI.
AND WHAT WOULD YOU LIKE ON IT, MR. YETI?
OK. LET'S SEE... CHEESE, ONIONS, PEPPERONI, TOMATOES, PEPPERS...
CHEESE, ONIONS, PEPPERONI, TOMATOES, PEPPERS...
MUSHROOMS, PINEAPPLE, MOUNTAIN CLIMBERS.
MUSHROOMS, PINEAPPLE, MOUNTAIN CLIMB...
MOUNTAIN CLIMBERS?! YOU REALLY ARE THE YETI! EEEARGGH!
(CLICK)
I TOLD YOU NOT TO TELL ANYONE YOU'RE THE YETI.
LIKE I'D GET BETTER SERVICE AS THE ABOMINABLE SNOWMAN.

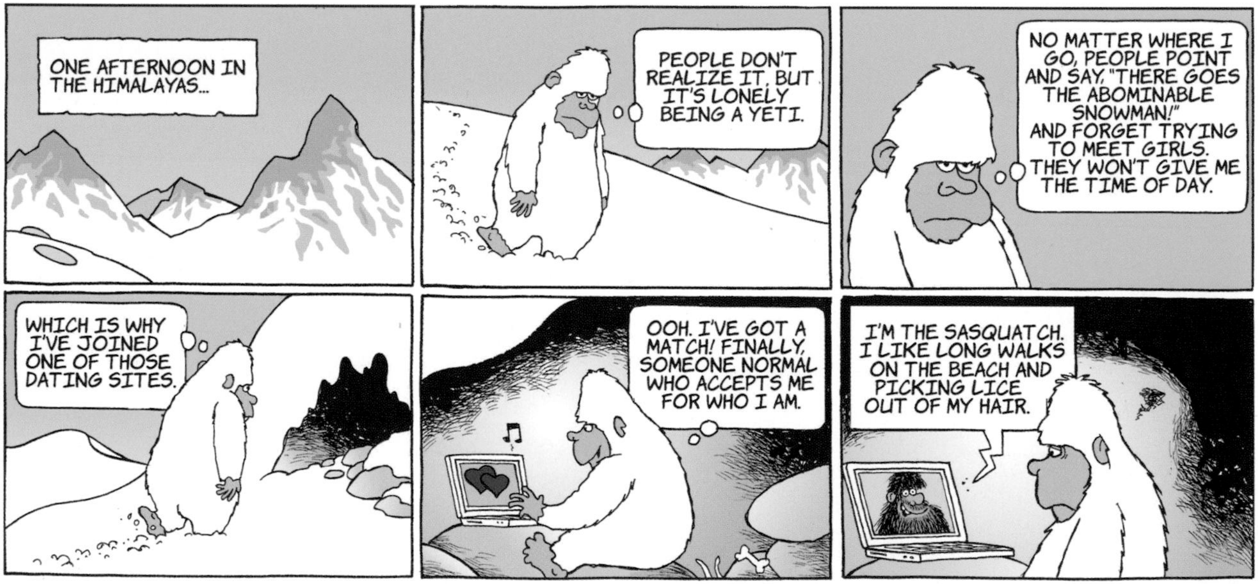
ONE AFTERNOON IN THE HIMALAYAS...
PEOPLE DON'T REALIZE IT, BUT IT'S LONELY BEING A YETI.
NO MATTER WHERE I GO, PEOPLE POINT AND SAY, "THERE GOES THE ABOMINABLE SNOWMAN!" AND FORGET TRYING TO MEET GIRLS. THEY WON'T GIVE ME THE TIME OF DAY.
WHICH IS WHY I'VE JOINED ONE OF THOSE DATING SITES.
OOH. I'VE GOT A MATCH! FINALLY, SOMEONE NORMAL WHO ACCEPTS ME FOR WHO I AM.
I'M THE SASQUATCH. I LIKE LONG WALKS ON THE BEACH AND PICKING LICE OUT OF MY HAIR.

HUMOROUS HUMANS 13

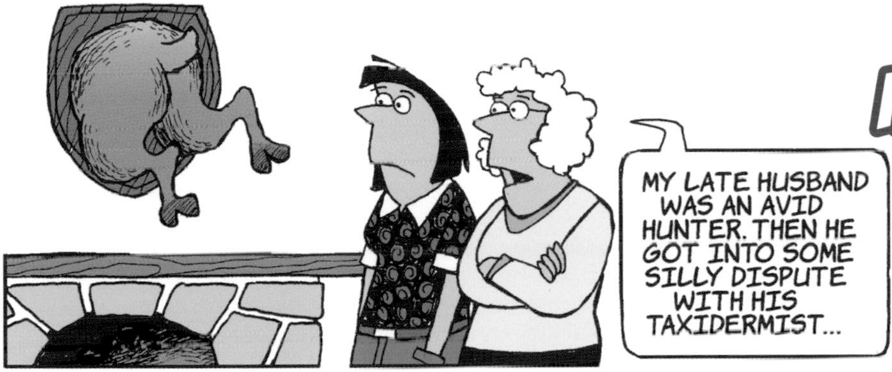
MY LATE HUSBAND WAS AN AVID HUNTER. THEN HE GOT INTO SOME SILLY DISPUTE WITH HIS TAXIDERMIST...

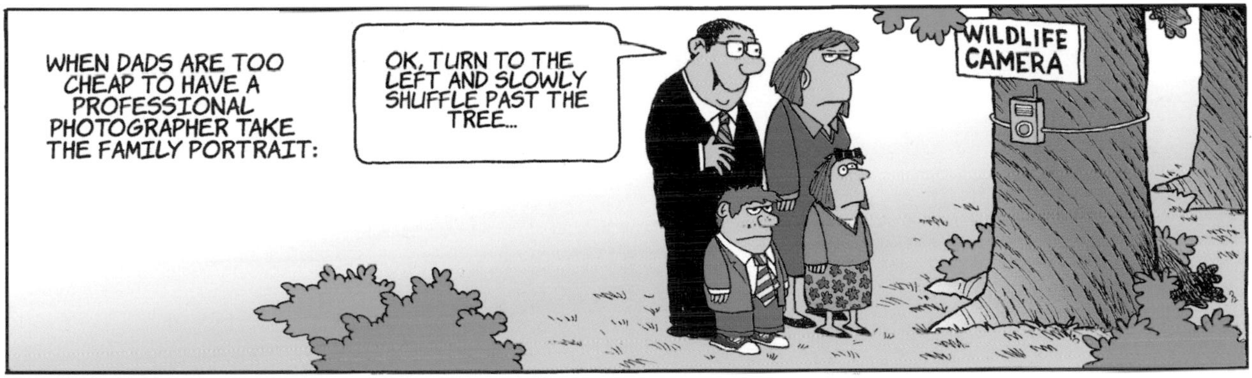
WHEN DADS ARE TOO CHEAP TO HAVE A PROFESSIONAL PHOTOGRAPHER TAKE THE FAMILY PORTRAIT:
OK, TURN TO THE LEFT AND SLOWLY SHUFFLE PAST THE TREE...
WILDLIFE CAMERA

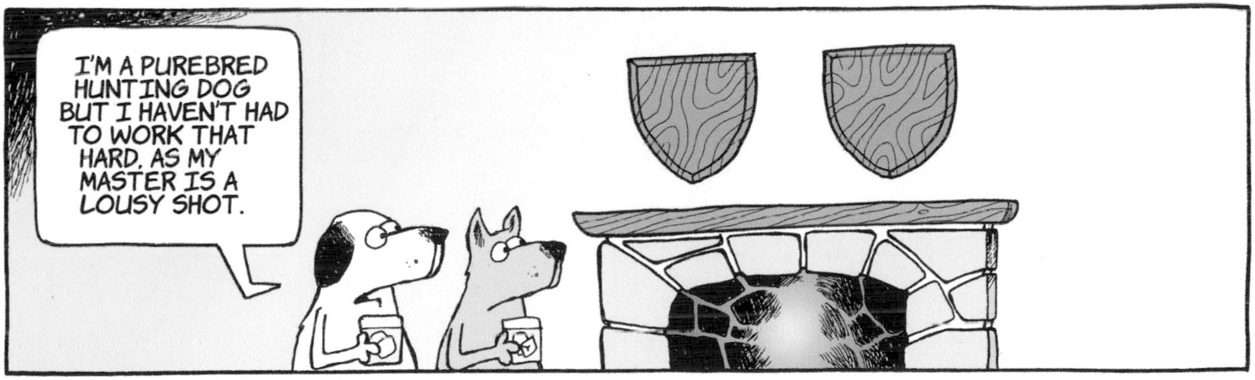
I'M A PUREBRED HUNTING DOG BUT I HAVEN'T HAD TO WORK THAT HARD, AS MY MASTER IS A LOUSY SHOT.

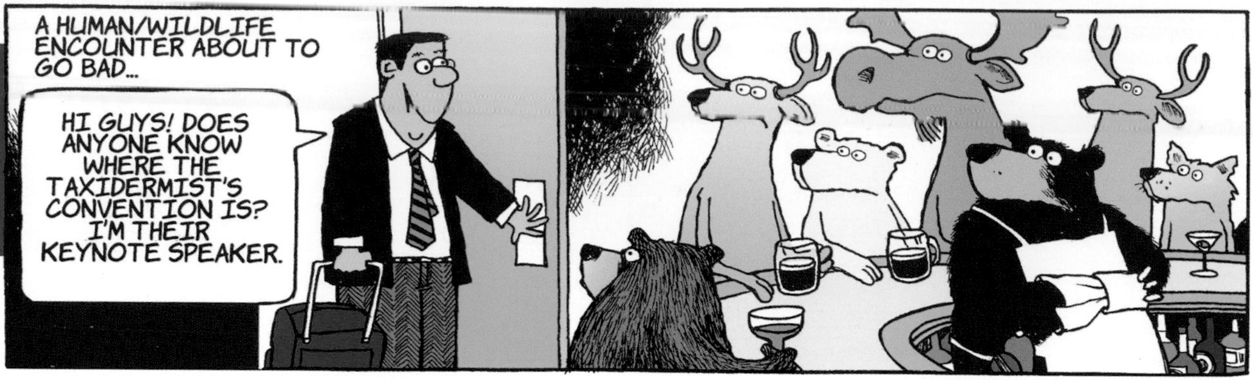
A HUMAN/WILDLIFE ENCOUNTER ABOUT TO GO BAD...
HI GUYS! DOES ANYONE KNOW WHERE THE TAXIDERMIST'S CONVENTION IS? I'M THEIR KEYNOTE SPEAKER.

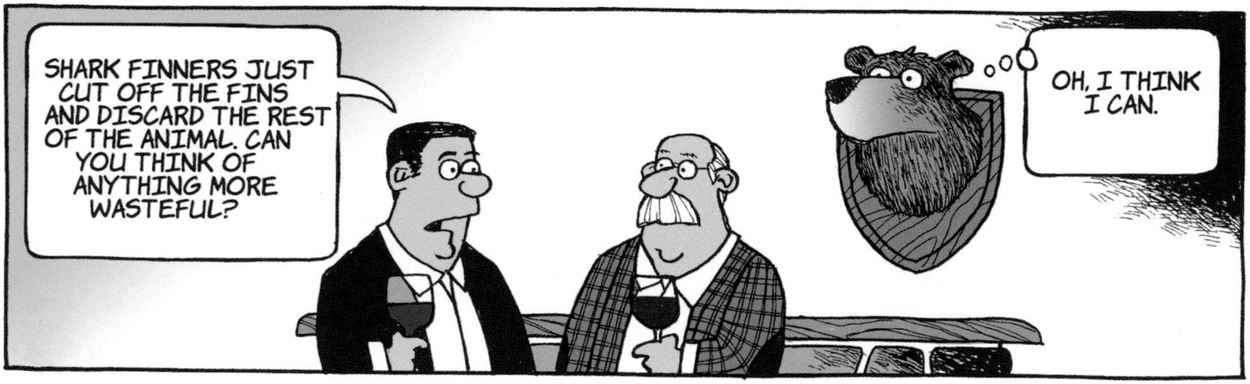
SHARK FINNERS JUST CUT OFF THE FINS AND DISCARD THE REST OF THE ANIMAL. CAN YOU THINK OF ANYTHING MORE WASTEFUL?
OH, I THINK I CAN.

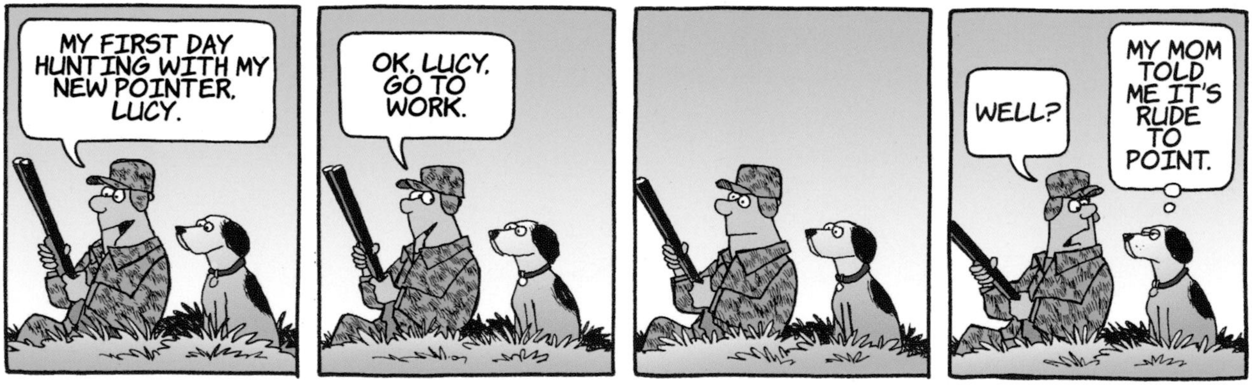
MY FIRST DAY HUNTING WITH MY NEW POINTER, LUCY.
OK, LUCY. GO TO WORK.
WELL?
MY MOM TOLD ME IT'S RUDE TO POINT.

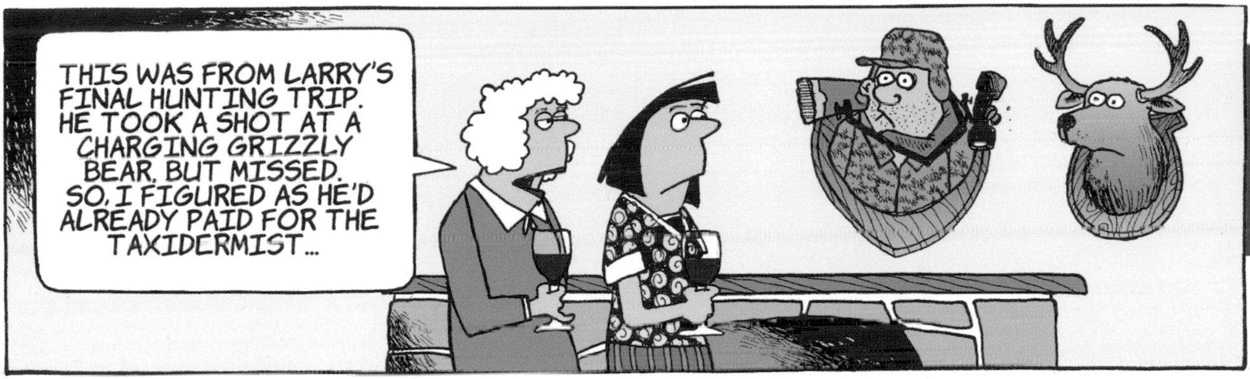
THIS WAS FROM LARRY'S FINAL HUNTING TRIP. HE TOOK A SHOT AT A CHARGING GRIZZLY BEAR, BUT MISSED. SO, I FIGURED AS HE'D ALREADY PAID FOR THE TAXIDERMIST...

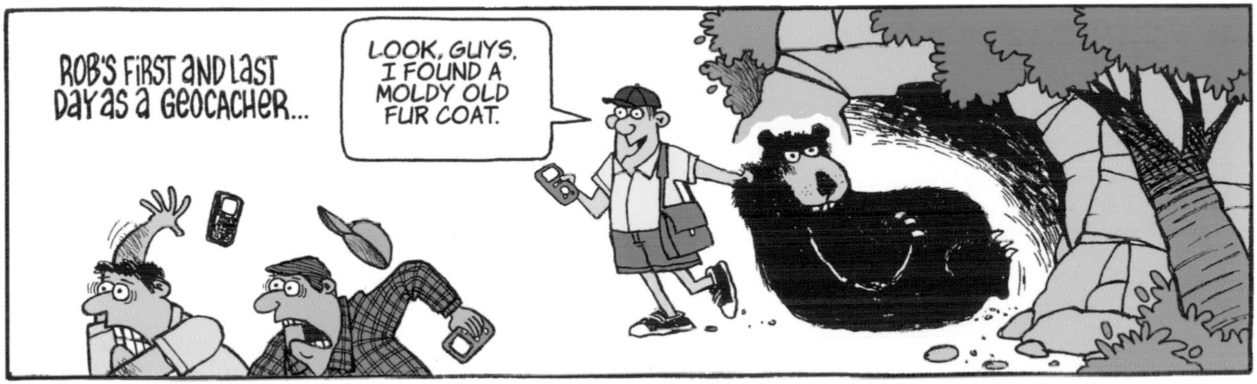
ROB'S FIRST AND LAST DAY AS A GEOCACHER...
LOOK, GUYS, I FOUND A MOLDY OLD FUR COAT.

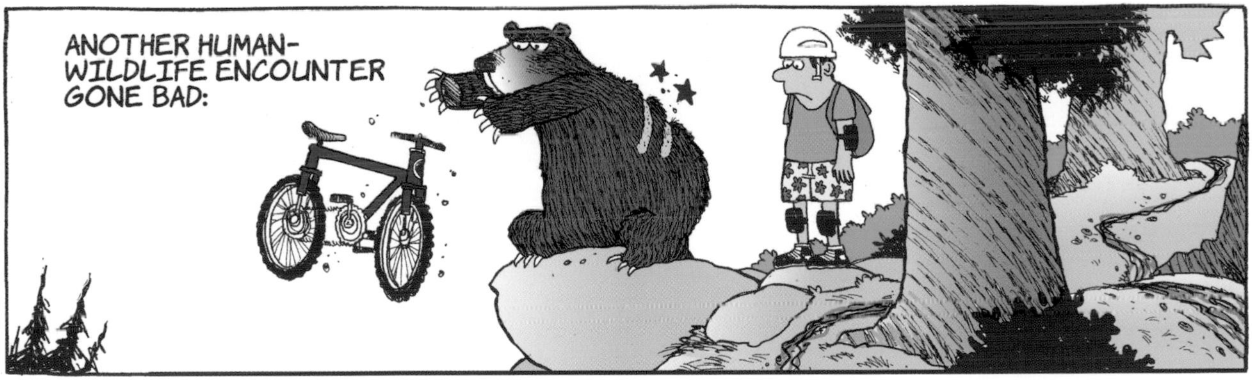
ANOTHER HUMAN-WILDLIFE ENCOUNTER GONE BAD:

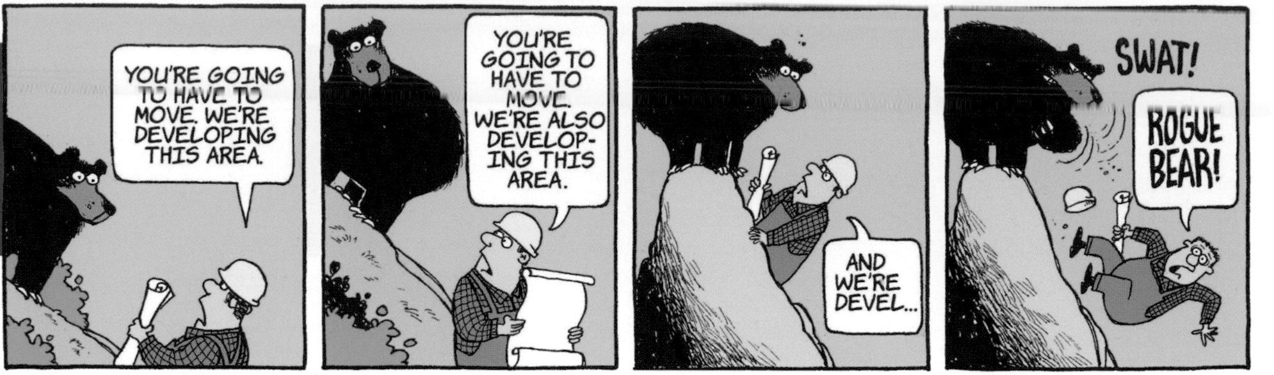
YOU'RE GOING TO HAVE TO MOVE. WE'RE DEVELOPING THIS AREA.
YOU'RE GOING TO HAVE TO MOVE. WE'RE ALSO DEVELOPING THIS AREA.
AND WE'RE DEVEL...
SWAT!
ROGUE BEAR!

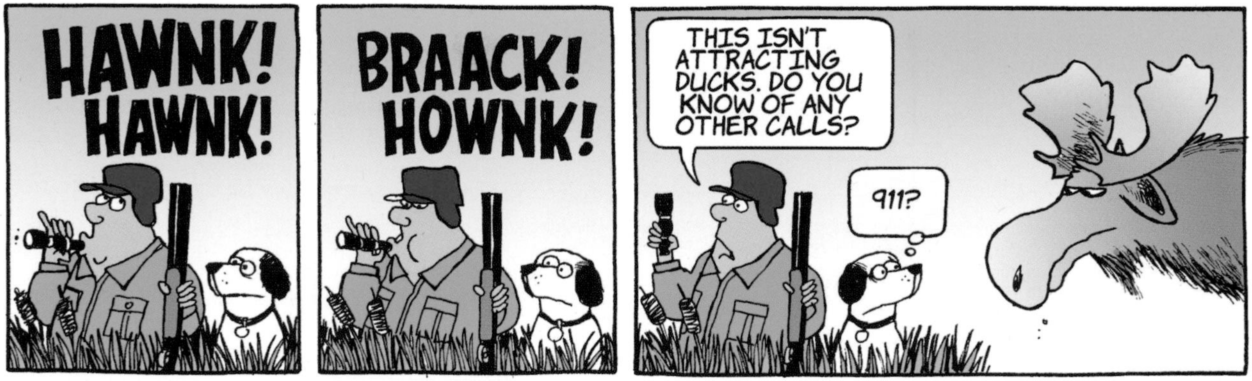
HAWNK! HAWNK!
BRAACK! HOWNK!
THIS ISN'T ATTRACTING DUCKS. DO YOU KNOW OF ANY OTHER CALLS?
911?

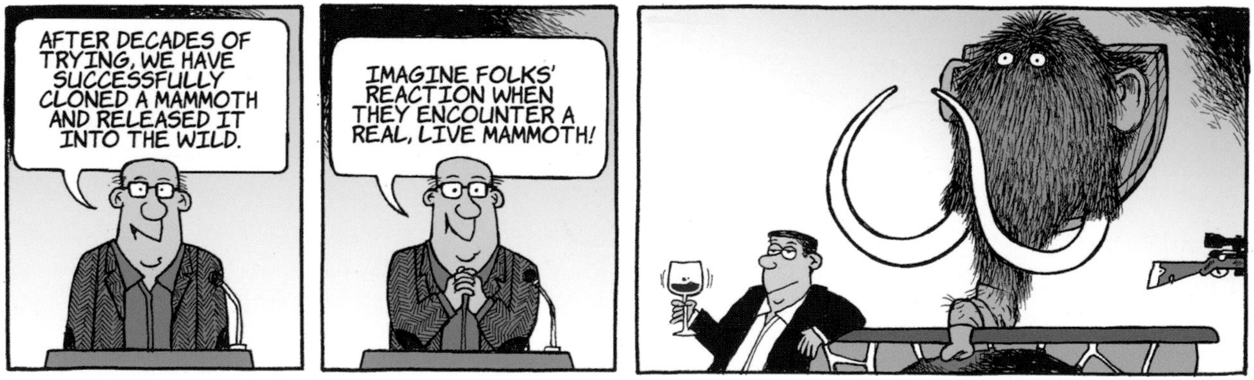
AFTER DECADES OF TRYING, WE HAVE SUCCESSFULLY CLONED A MAMMOTH AND RELEASED IT INTO THE WILD.
IMAGINE FOLKS' REACTION WHEN THEY ENCOUNTER A REAL, LIVE MAMMOTH!

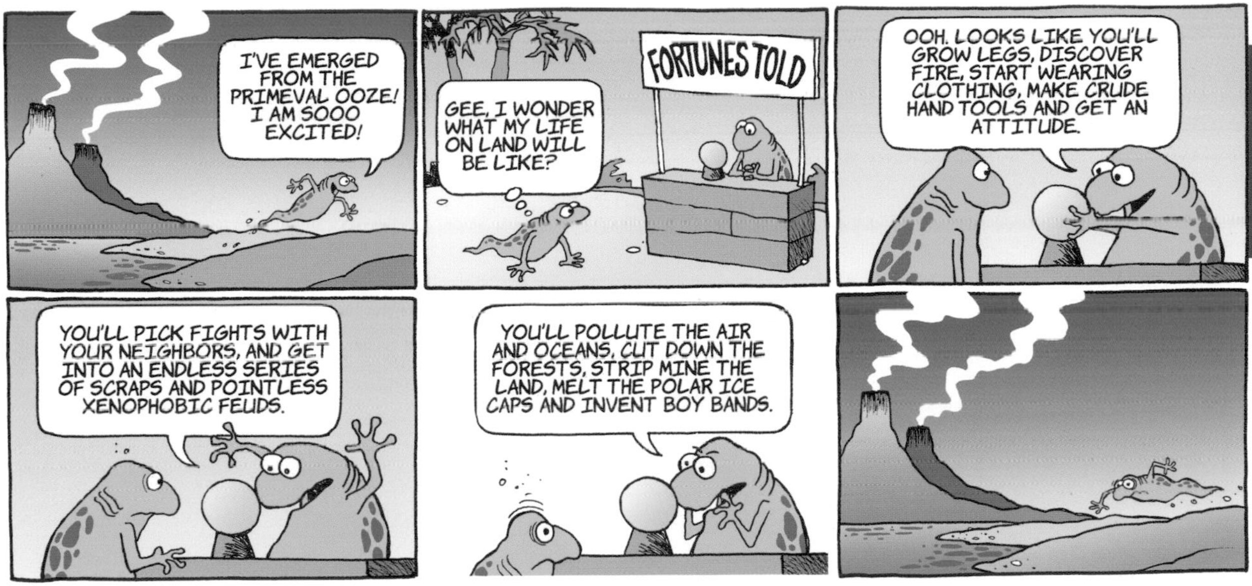
I'VE EMERGED FROM THE PRIMEVAL OOZE! I AM SOOO EXCITED!
GEE, I WONDER WHAT MY LIFE ON LAND WILL BE LIKE?
FORTUNES TOLD
OOH. LOOKS LIKE YOU'LL GROW LEGS, DISCOVER FIRE, START WEARING CLOTHING, MAKE CRUDE HAND TOOLS AND GET AN ATTITUDE.
YOU'LL PICK FIGHTS WITH YOUR NEIGHBORS, AND GET INTO AN ENDLESS SERIES OF SCRAPS AND POINTLESS XENOPHOBIC FEUDS.
YOU'LL POLLUTE THE AIR AND OCEANS, CUT DOWN THE FORESTS, STRIP MINE THE LAND, MELT THE POLAR ICE CAPS AND INVENT BOY BANDS.

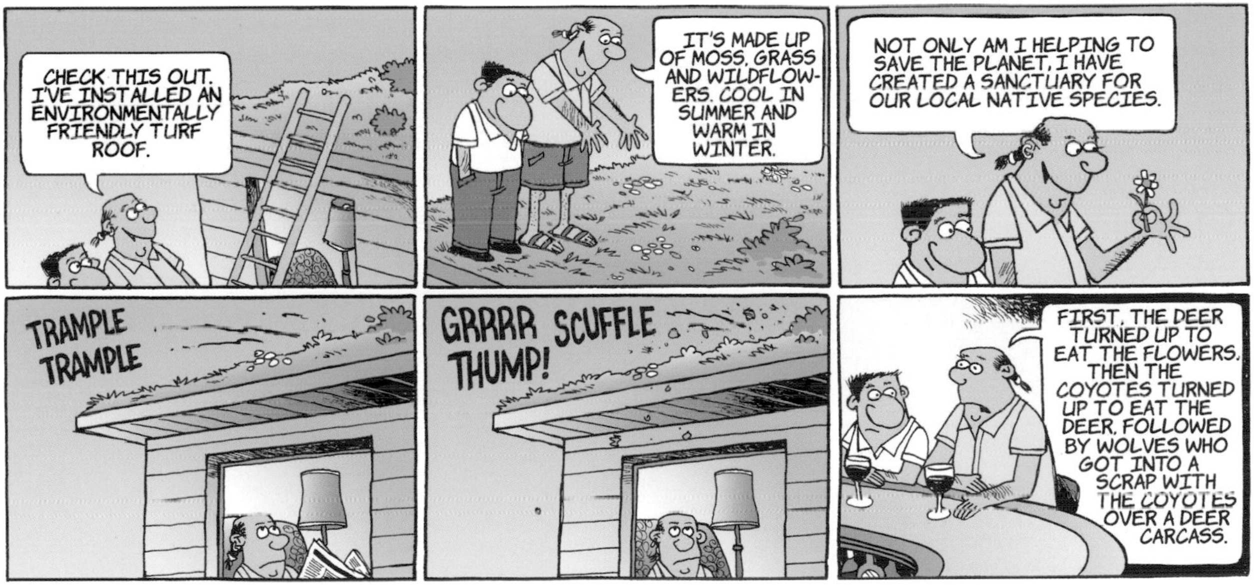
CHECK THIS OUT. I'VE INSTALLED AN ENVIRONMENTALLY FRIENDLY TURF ROOF.
IT'S MADE UP OF MOSS, GRASS AND WILDFLOWERS. COOL IN SUMMER AND WARM IN WINTER.
NOT ONLY AM I HELPING TO SAVE THE PLANET, I HAVE CREATED A SANCTUARY FOR OUR LOCAL NATIVE SPECIES.
TRAMPLE TRAMPLE
GRRRR SCUFFLE THUMP!
FIRST, THE DEER TURNED UP TO EAT THE FLOWERS. THEN THE COYOTES TURNED UP TO EAT THE DEER, FOLLOWED BY WOLVES WHO GOT INTO A SCRAP WITH THE COYOTES OVER A DEER CARCASS.

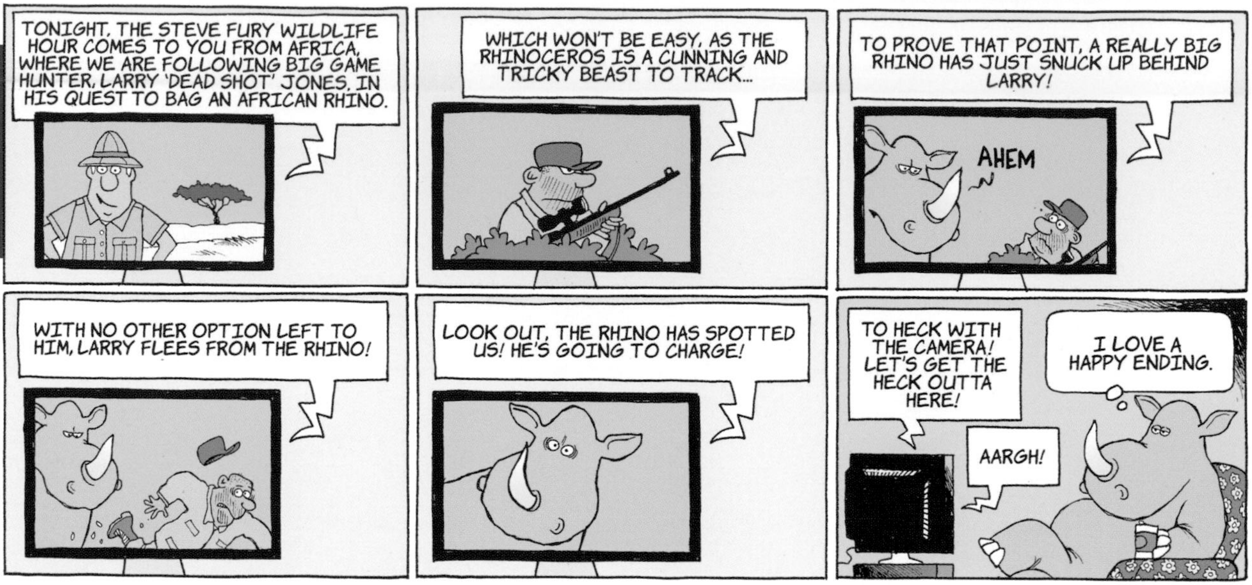
TONIGHT, THE STEVE FURY WILDLIFE HOUR COMES TO YOU FROM AFRICA, WHERE WE ARE FOLLOWING BIG GAME HUNTER, LARRY 'DEAD SHOT' JONES, IN HIS QUEST TO BAG AN AFRICAN RHINO.
WHICH WON'T BE EASY, AS THE RHINOCEROS IS A CUNNING AND TRICKY BEAST TO TRACK...
TO PROVE THAT POINT, A REALLY BIG RHINO HAS JUST SNUCK UP BEHIND LARRY!
AHEM
WITH NO OTHER OPTION LEFT TO HIM, LARRY FLEES FROM THE RHINO!
LOOK OUT, THE RHINO HAS SPOTTED US! HE'S GOING TO CHARGE!
TO HECK WITH THE CAMERA! LET'S GET THE HECK OUTTA HERE!
AARGH!
I LOVE A HAPPY ENDING.

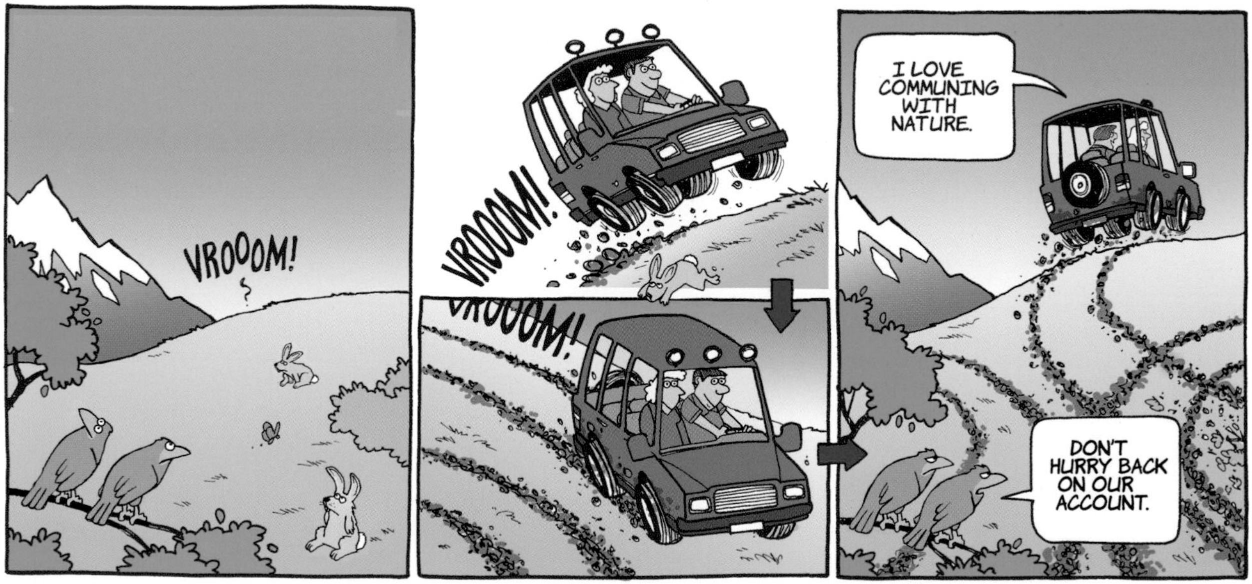
VROOOM!
VROOOM!
VROOOM!
I LOVE COMMUNING WITH NATURE.
DON'T HURRY BACK ON OUR ACCOUNT.